HIGH–TECH WARFARE

HIGH–TECH WARFARE

CRESCENT BOOKS
New York

A Salamander Book

© Salamander Books Ltd. **1991**

ISBN 0 517 06673 4

This 1991 edition published by
Crescent books, distributed by Outlet
Book Company, Inc., a Random
House Company, 225 Park Avenue
South, New York, New York 10003.

Printed and bound in Belgium.

8 7 6 5 4 3 2 1

Credits

Editor: Graham Smith
Designer: Phil Gorton
Colour art: © Salamander Books Ltd
Diagrams: TIGA
© Salamander Books Ltd
Filmset by: InterPrep Ltd.
Colour reproduction:
P&W Graphics, Singapore.
Printed in Belgium by Proost
International Book Production,
Turnhout .

Endpapers: An F-111 returns from
one of the first missions over Iraq,
still with one Rockeye cluster bomb
attached.
p1: A Patriot launcher stands guard
as night falls over Saudi Arabia.
p2/3: British infantry in a pre-war
training exercise.
p4/5: A US F-15 Eagle on combat air
patrol tops up from a KC-135 tanker.

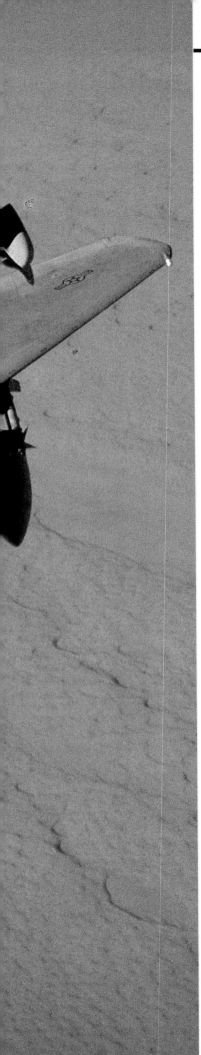

Contents

The Authors

Doug Richardson is a freelance defence journalist and author specialising in the fields of aviation, guided missiles and electronics. He has been the Editor of "Military Technology" and Editor of "Defense Materiel". He has written Salamander's "Modern Warplanes", Guide to Electronic Warfare", "The Intelligence War", "Stealth Warplanes" and "Military "Jets".

Bill Gunston was an RAF fighter pilot and instructor before becoming a freelance journalist, writer and broadcaster. One of the most respected aviation and defence authors, he has contributed to many books, including Salamander's "Rockets and Missiles", "Fighter Missions" "Advanced Technology Warfare", "Modern Air Combat" and "Passenger Airlines".

Ian Hogg is a world-renowned authority on land weapons, artillery and firearms. He has contributed to many military titiles including "Military Small-Arms of the 20th Century" (Arms & Armour Press), "Infantry Weapons of World War II" and "Artillery 2000" (Arms & Armour Press). He also produces a major international year book on infantry weapons and systems.

Introduction

On January 17th 1991, the regular ABC Television evening news was interrupted by a report from Gary Shepard, its correspondent in Baghdad. "Throughout the night sky there are flashes of light," Shepard reported from the window of his room in Baghdad's Al-Rashid hotel. "Something is definitely under way here." Within minutes, reporters from the CNN news channel were holding a microphone at the window of their room so that listeners could hear the sound of a massive barrage of anti-aircraft fire over the city, and the heavy thump of bombs exploding. At the White House, US Presidential spokesman Marlin Fitzwater told reporters in the press room that the battle to liberate Kuwait – Operation "Desert Storm" – had begun.

The crisis that led to war started on May 28th, 1990, when Iraqi President Saddam Hussein accused some oil-producing nations of waging "economic war" on Iraq by overproduction of oil. This forced the price down, he claimed, creating economic problems for Iraq.

Between 1980 and 1988, Iraq had fought a long war against Iran, and had enjoyed the financial support of many Arab states in the region. Worried lest Iran's brand of revolutionary Islamic fundamentalism spread into Arabian countries, the Gulf states had been happy to provide the massive loans that Iraq needed to pay for weaponry used against Iran.

With the ending of the war in what effectively amounted to a stalemate, Iraq faced demands that these war loans be repaid at a time when overproduction was driving down the price of oil, Iraq's main currency-earning export. Having taken heavy casualties in what it saw as an attempt to contain the Iranian Revolution, Iraq was angered by these demands for repayment, arguing that the massive war loans be waived as compensation for the damage it had suffered during the long war.

In July 1990, foreign minister Tariq Aziz claimed that Kuwait had stolen $2.5 billion worth of Iraqi oil, and had built military positions in Iraqi territory. Both nations had oil facilities along a frontier whose exact location had been a source of disagreement for many years. To Kuwait, its wells were on its own side of the frontier, but Iraq claimed that the frontier had been imposed by the British during the period following the First World War and was not valid.

On July 24th, as 30,000 Iraqi troops were moved to the Iraq/Kuwait border, Egyptian President Hosni Mubarak set out on a visit to Iraq, Kuwait and Saudi Arabia in an attempt to find a political solution to the problem. By the time that representatives of Iraq and Kuwait met in Jeddah for talks on July 31st, the force building up along the border had risen to some 100,000.

The most important issues under discussion in Jeddah were Iraq's demands for compensation for alleged oil theft and low pricing, its territorial claims to Bubiyan and Warba (two Kuwaiti islands that controlled the waters through which Iraq maintained access to the Gulf), and Iraqi insistence that Kuwait write off loans made to Iraq during the Iraq/Iran War.

Kuwait rejected Iraq's demands, and walked out of the talks on August 1st. Late that night, the Iraqi units along the border went into action. Crossing the border at 2am local time, they overran Kuwait, meeting little resistance. As the Emir of Kuwait, Sheikh Jaber Ahmed al-Sabah and his Government fled into exile in Saudi Arabia, Iraq announced that its forces had moved into the country at the request of a newly-established revolutionary government that had toppled the al-Sabah dynasty. The fiction would be short-lived; on August 8th Iraq formally annexed Kuwait as its "19th province."

World reaction to the invasion of Kuwait was almost universally hostile. On the day of the attack, the UN Security Council passed the first of what would become a series of resolutions on the crisis. This condemned the invasion, called for an immediate and unconditional withdrawal, then for negotiations between Iraq and Kuwait to settle their differences. The US Government banned all trade with Iraq, and froze all Iraqi assets; also those of Kuwait, a move intended to prevent the latter falling into Iraqi hands. France and the UK also froze all Kuwaiti assets. The US took its first overt military action by ordering an aircraft carrier in the Indian Ocean to move toward the Gulf, while the Soviet Union suspended all arms deliveries to Iraq.

On August 3rd, Iraqi units moved to the south of Kuwait, taking up positions along the border with Saudi Arabia, raising the possibility that another nation in the area might be about to fall. As the US announced the formation of a naval task force, Japan and Germany also froze Kuwaiti assets. On August 6th, a second UN resolution called for mandatory sanctions against Iraq.

AIRLIFT

Consultations between Saudi Arabia and the USA on August 6th led to a request that US troops be sent to the area. On the following day, President Bush despatched an initial force of fighter aircraft plus 4,000 troops, while some 50 US, British, French, and Soviet warships headed for the Gulf. Operation "Desert Shield" was underway. In practice, the Soviets played no role in the subsequent military build-up,

Above: General Norman H. Schwarzkopf ("Stormin' Norman"), Commander US and Allied forces in the Gulf in a typically forceful pose at a press conference.

Below: The Panavia Tornado IDS formed the backbone of the Royal Saudi Air Force and British RAF strike components. These are two Saudi examples, taken a few years before the war.

but did support further UN resolutions calling for a naval blockade and for UN members to use "all necessary means" to restore international and security in the area.

The fighter and bomber pilots may have grabbed the headlines in the war that followed, but when the Gulf War is analysed and studied at Staff colleges over the next decade, equal attention is likely to be paid to the effect on the war of the massive airlift capability of the U.S.

For pilots of an earlier generation who flew piston-engined transports such as the C-46 and C-47, the big airlifts of their day were missions over the "The Hump" flying supplies from India to southern China to support the Chinese armies fighting Japan during the Second World War, or the massive Berlin Airlift that kept that city alive when the Soviet Army had closed all land routes in an attempt to starve the city and cause an Allied withdrawal.

The Vietnam War saw another generation of US airmen committed to airlift operations, this time flying jet and turboprop aircraft over global ranges carrying payloads that dwarfed those of earlier airlifts. A new phrase was added to the vocabulary of airlift –"widebody" – but before the first Lockheed C-5A Galaxy and Boeing 747 transports could enter service, the US had begun its slow process of withdrawal from Vietnam. Widebody aircraft played a major role in the 1973 Yom Kippur war when the US rushed urgently-needed weaponry and even main battle tanks to an embattled Israel.

By the time that Saddam Hussein invaded Kuwait in 1990, many of the narrow-body aircraft that had supported the Vietnam war were obsolete. The world's airlines were extensively equipped with long-range wide-body aircraft, and at a time of trade recession, were hungry for work. The airlift that Saddam's invasion of Kuwait triggered into life would be the largest in history. It confirmed the ability of the US to deploy military forces

anywhere at short notice.

To boost the military transport fleet, 14 Air Force Reserve and Air National Guard squadrons were also recalled to active duty, initially for a 90-day period but later extended by a further 90 days. Seven flew the C-141 Starlifter, the remainder the C-5. Within the first few weeks more than a dozen airlines had become involved in the airlift. Boeing 747s were in particular demand, also DC-10s and L-1011 TriStars.

The Yom Kippur War airlift to Israel had shown how equipment being carried in USAF transports could be speeded to its destination by airborne refuelling. The same technique would now be used to reduce the need for ground refuelling at bases in Europe. Incoming flights could rendezvous over the Mediterranean with KC-135 and KC-10 tankers, then continue their flight to Saudi Arabia without the delay of refuelling stops.

In little more than a month from

Above: This Lockheed C-5 Galaxy is typical of those that formed the massive airlift to Saudi Arabia. Allied forces and support equipment were moved into the Gulf from all over the world.

the order to begin, the initial "Desert Shield" airlift moved more men and materiel into the Gulf than had gone to Southeast Asia in the first eight months of the Vietnam War. The scale of this early airlift can be judged by the fact than on one day – August 29th – Dover AFB despatched more than 1,000,000lb (453,000kg) of cargo to the Gulf. Despite the fact that unrepaired wing cracks forced most of the C-141B Starlifter fleet to fly with reduced payload – about two-thirds of the normal maximum – this restriction had no effect on the speed of the buildup. Handling capacity on the ground in Saudi Arabia proved the limiting factor, not the cargo capacity of the transport fleet. The efforts and skills of those organising distribution on the ground is one of the great unsung stories of the war.

Left: Cheerful Iraqi troops in Kuwait immediately after the invasion on 2nd August 1990. The tank is a Chinese-built T-59, one of many supplied to Iraq during the Iran-Iraq war.

Below: Before the Gulf War, the most recent action by US troops was the invasion of Panama. Many of the lessons learnt here would be put to good use in the much bigger conflict to come.

Left: Egytian commandos in training before the war started. One of the surprising facets of this conflict was the willingness of other Arab countries to provide military forces to the Coalition.

(500), Senegal (500) and Czechoslovakia (a 300-man chemical-warfare decontamination unit).

The navies of the Gulf states were small in size, but other nations joined the coalition naval forces. Largest contributor was the USA, with vessels in the Gulf, Arabian Sea, and Red Sea. The UK provided warships for the Gulf, while French warships joined the Arabian Sea and Red Sea fleets. Also in the Gulf were warships from the Soviet Union, Denmark and Canada, with Norway providing a supply ship. Argentina, Australia, Italy, the Netherlands and Spain sent warships to the Arabian Sea, with Belgium adding minesweepers and a supply ship. Greece sent a warship to the Red Sea.

International co-operation also built up a large air force. Some Kuwaiti A-4s and Mirage F1s had escaped to Saudi Arabia and were available to fight alongside the other Arab air forces. Largest was Saudi Arabia, well equipped with F-15s and Tornados (both strike and interceptor versions), but the bulk of the air power came from the USA. Most of the USAF arrivals were stationed at Saudi bases, but F-16s were also sent to Dubai and Qatar, while USN F-18s went to Bahrain.

Royal Air Force Tornado GR.l and F.3 fighters were based in Saudi Arabia, with Jaguars going to Bahrain, and several Nimrods operating from Muscat. France sent Mirage 2000s, F.lCRs and Jaguars to Saudi Arabia, while Italy's small detachment of Tornado strike aircraft were based in Abu Dhabi. Turkey acted as a base for US fighters, and its air force was also reinforced by Alpha Jets, Mirage 5s and F-104S Starfighters, plus batteries of Patriot SAMs.

By the time this build-up was complete, Saddam Hussein had stationed 590,000 troops, and 4,200 tanks in Kuwait and southeastern Iraq. Total air strength of the Iraqi air force was around 500 aircraft and 250 combat helicopters.

INTELLIGENCE

To gather information on targets in Kuwait and Iraq, the US launched a massive intelligence-gathering operation. With the recent retirement of the SR-71 Blackbird, this Mach 3 reconnaissance aircraft was not available and would be sorely missed. The Lockheed TR-l was able to use its sensors to look across the border into Iraq and Kuwait, but until the Iraqi air defenses were knocked out, is likely to have conducted few if any overflights. The TR-1 was designed to operate over friendly territory anyway, to avoid the heavy SAM threat in Europe.

The first stage of calling up civil aircraft under the Civil Reserve Air Fleet (CRAF) programme was activated on August 17th. Within 24 hours the airlines had made available the requested 17 passenger aircraft and 21 cargo aircraft. By the end of September, US commercial aircraft had already flown more than 500 missions, delivering some 66,000 personnel and 5,000,000lb (2,270,000kg) of cargo, with up to 40 airliners taking part each day. The airlift mounted by Britain's Royal Air Force was more modest in scale, with C-130 Hercules plus chartered cargo aircraft such as three Boeing 707s moving around 680,0001b (308,000kg) of freight every day.

Like the airlift, the Desert Shield and Desert Storm flight-refuelling operations were the largest ever undertaken. Tankers used to support the first US fighters to reach the area were available to fly operations from Saudi Arabia within 24 hours of arrival, and

more than 8,500 sorties had been flown by mid-February.

The funds spent a decade earlier on buying the KC-10 Extender, and the re-engining and refurbishing of the KC-135 fleet, paid off handsomely. The latter had been heavily worked during the Vietnam War, and the Gulf War would eat into the additional airframe life obtained by modifications such as wing reskinning. Such was the pace of Gulf operations that a tanker squadron could clock up more sorties during the war than most would make in a year of peacetime training operations.

By mid-January 1991, a massive military force had been deployed in the Gulf by a total of 30 nations. The coming war would pit Arab against Arab, with close to 100,000 soldiers and 900 tanks being provided by eight Middle Eastern nations and one North African state. Largest Arab forces were those of Saudi Arabia (40,000 men, 200 tanks),

Above: This Mirage F1 of the Qatar air force is identical to those used by the Iraqis - and shows the problems faced in co-ordinating the efforts of so many nations.

Syria (35,000 men, 200 tanks), and Egypt (35,000 men, 450 tanks). The Gulf Co-operation Council, consisting of Bahrain, Qatar, Oman and the United Arab Emirates, sent forces which operated alongside Kuwaiti units which had fled to Saudi Arabia in the wake of the Iraqi invasion - a combined force of 10,000 men and 50 tanks from the five members. Morocco sent a contingent of 1,200 soldiers.

The US had sent 225,000 troops and 1,900 tanks, figures which were still rising, plus 90,000 marines with their 300 tanks. The UK had sent 25,000 soldiers with 170 tanks, while France's contribution was 10,000 soldiers and 72 tanks. The remainder of the anti-Iraq coalition ground forces came from Pakistan (8,000), Bangladesh (6,000), Niger

Above: Most of the heavy equipment and vehicles had to be moved into the area by sea. This merchant vessel has been chartered by the US Military Sealift Command.

Above: Why redeploy the aircraft when you can move the airfield? The crowded hanger of this US carrier gives some idea of the air-power on board these ships.

Much of the information on potential targets was gathered by spy satellites, particularly the KH-"Keyhole" series of image-gathering spacecraft. At least two, and perhaps three KH-ll were available, along with two of the newer KH-12. The latter is a new-generation spacecraft, the first of which had been orbited in June 1989. A second launched in February 1990 may have failed, but a third was launched in June. All-weather imagery of lower resolution could be provided by a single Lacrosse synthetic-aperture radar satellite launched in 1988.

Eavesdropping on Iraqi radio communications was made possible by three types of SIGINT (signals intelligence) spacecraft - three Magnum satellites (the last of which was launched by the space shuttle Atlantis on 15th November 1990) and a single Chalet, plus at least four triple-spacecraft clusters of White Cloud satellites in orbit at lower altitudes. Aircraft used for SIGINT mis-

sions included the Lockheed TR-l, the RC-135 "Rivet Joint", and the Aerospatiale/MBB "Gabriel" ELINT version of the Transall C-160G.

Iraq obviously expected to come under air attack, but despite this was completely overwhelmed by the Allied air campaign launched on January 17th 1991. Saddam Hussein and his senior commanders seem to have underestimated the accuracy and destructiveness of the latest generation of Western warplanes and their weaponry. The Iraqis had repeatedly stressed that in their

Below: The British also moved their heavy armour by sea. This Challenger is rolling ashore from a Landing Ship Logistic (LSL) of the Royal Fleet Auxiliary .

opinion, the US would be unable to withstand the casualties of a major land campaign. The long years of near-static warfare against Iran seem to have blinded them to the effect of air power.

THE AIR WAR

When the air campaign began, some news reports of Gulf combat recalled scenes from the Vietnam War. As B-52 Stratofortress bombers left their bases to drop heavy loads of iron bombs, A-6 Intruders rose from carrier decks, laser-guided bombs downed bridges, ground crew loaded Sidewinder and Sparrow missiles onto fighters, F-4 Phantoms taxied out for takeoff and AH-l Cobra helicopter gunships went tankhunting. Two decades seemed at first sight to have done little more than swap desert sand for jungle green.

Nothing could be further from the truth. Those two decades had seen the maturation of electronics technology. When used in Vietnam, many of these weapons relied on vacuum-tube technology or first-generation solid-state electronics. Desert Storm would be the first war fought and even controlled by microelectronic technology. It's possible that the crews of some B-52s were sons of the men who flew the same aircraft into battle over Hanoi in 1972, but as the result of a massive rebuild programme more than a decade ago these elderly airframes now carried avionics as different from those of the Vietnam era as those of the original B-52s were from the B-17 Flying Fortress.

Old and familiar weapons were also deployed in updated forms. During the conflicts of the last quarter century, the AIM-9 Sidewinder has been the dominant air-to-air

missile. The semi-active radar AIM-7 Sparrow has not been so successful . Combat reports often spoke of the AIM-7 missing its target, and the attacker then engaging with an AIM-9. On at least one occasion during the Gulf War, this sequence was reversed; a pilot who had failed to down a MiG-25 Foxbat with an IR shot loosed a Sparrow and scored a kill. Desert Storm showed that the AIM-7 had finally come of age. In one engagement that pitted two USAF F-lSs against three MiG-23s and a single Mirage Fl, the US pilots f ired three AIM-7 and two AIM-9 . One AIM-7 fired at beyond visual range missed its target, one damaged a MiG-23 which then was despatched with an AIM-9, while two other two AIM-7 downed a MiG-23 and the Mirage. An AIM-9 destroyed the third MiG-23.

In drawing up the plans for Desert Storm, US commanders decided to exploit the several potential advantages offered by US technology, such as the accuracy of modern weapons and fire-control systems, the ability to fight by night, the flexibility given by advanced command, control and communications, plus the high mobility offered by helicopters.

NIGHT VISION

US superiority in night-vision systems allowed many strike missions to be flown by night without loss of accuracy. This greatly hampered the few attempts made by the Iraqi air force to defend their country. The radar carried by the MiG-29 is at best probably comparable with that of the F-16, while US pilots assessed the systems in the Mirage F1 as being little better than those in a Vietnam-era F-4 Phantom. Darkness also hampered the low-altitude anti-aircraft threat, making it hard for the crews of optically-sighted anti-aircraft guns to locate their target, and reducing the chance that the operator of a shoulder-fired SA-7 or SA-14 would be able to aim his weapon close enough to get IR lock-on.

Most important of the night vision systems was the Martin Marietta LANTIRN pod-mounted nav/attack system fitted to the F-15E and some F-16s. When the F-15Es arrived in the Gulf, they were equipped with the LANTIRN navigation pod, which carries a radar and IR sensor. Technical problems delayed deliveries of the associated targeting pod, so training on this system did not begin in the US until several months after the Iraqi invasion of Kuwait.

Teamed with the high-resolution air-to-ground modes of the APG-70 radar, LANTIRN gives F-15E crews the ability to deliver ordnance at night with pinpoint accuracy. Even without the targeting pod and its x17 magnification FLIR, crews had already demonstrated an ability to toss a bomb to within 35ft (11m) of the target from a range of several miles, or perhaps as close as 10ft (3m) – the exact figure is classified - if prepared to overfly the target.

The F-117A Stealth fighter has a built-in EO (Electro-optics) system, with turrets in the nose and belly of the aircraft, while the AH-64A Apache is fitted with the nose-mounted TADS/PNVS system that follows the pilot's gaze, superimposing on the outside view a thermal image which allows combat on the darkest nights.

Older US EO systems such as Pave Tack and Pave Spike served well in the Gulf, on the F-lll and Buccaneer respectively, while a small number of Royal Air Force Tornado GR.ls were fitted with the British-developed TIALD.

In the past, Grumman A-6 Intruders flying night attacks have flown at heights of around 500 800ft (150 - 250m), a restriction imposed by their radar, while manoeuvres to take advantage of terrain masking were limited to bank angles of no more than 45 degrees. A few weeks before the invasion of Kuwait, the Navy installed NVG (Night Vision Goggle) systems, blue-green NVG-compatible cockpit lighting, and windscreens with better IR transparency on some of its A-6s. Experience quickly showed that the NVGs gave visibility out to around seven miles under good conditions. When the crew wore NVGs, they could safely fly as low as 200ft (60m) on a clear night, and bank the aircraft more aggressively to make best use of terrain features. Confident of their ability to rely on the NVGs, they could turn the radar off, denying the enemy any signal that might warn of an incoming attack. NVGs proved less effective during attack runs, so crews learned to re-energise the radar and standard A-6E nav/attack sensors.

NAVSTAR

When the crisis started, the US had orbited only 14 of the planned constellation of 18 Navstar Global Positioning System (GPS) spacecraft. Coverage of the Gulf area, although not continuous, was good enough to ensure that no tactical problems resulted. Britain and France hastily retrofitted some of their aircraft with GPS receivers. RAF Tornado GR.1s were given receivers which used lower-accuracy C-code, which gives an accuracy of around 300ft (100m), good enough for tactical navigation. Two French Puma helicopters assigned to the search-and-rescue role used newly-installed GPS receivers as navaids when flying over the desert. As the weather over Iraq and Kuwait deteriorated during late January, Allied aircrew

Above and Below: Night vision goggles are a relatively simple way of giving aircraft a low-level night-flying capability without the need for radar emissions. This CH-53 is in darkness, yet is perfectly visible to other pilots in the same formation.

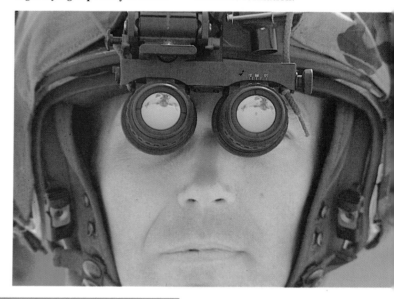

Left: Satellite communication systems are portable, easily set up and hard to intercept. They can be used by special forces operating behind enemy lines.

Below: The Navstar satellite-based Global Positioning System (GPS) enables aircraft, ships and vehicles to find their location to within a few feet.

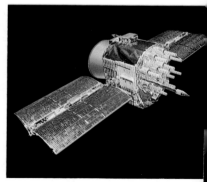

Right: Advanced semiconductor technology is necessary for modern computerised battle management systems and displays. These operators are keeping radar watch on board the USS Independence.

relied on their GPS receivers and low-drift laser-gyro INS systems to bring them within range of their targets.

The naval war was as one-sided as the air campaign. Allied aircraft, helped by surface vessels, attacked and sank 23 warships and 18 auxiliary vessels, while damaging 34 and eight more respectively. In theory at least, the large Allied fleet operating in the Gulf should have been an ideal target for Iraqi anti-ship missile units. In practice, Exocet-armed vessels and aircraft were all knocked out before coming within range of potential targets, while the only example of the larger Silkworm anti-ship missile to pose any threat to Allied warships was shot down by a Sea Dart anti-aircraft missile. Iraq's sole successes were achieved by the use of mines.

The total failure of the Iraqi Navy's warships to engage the Allied fleet will be studied by other navies of similar size. The limitations of a frigate/fast-attack craft navy when pitted against a major surface fleet operating at full combat readiness have been cruelly exposed.

SCUD v PATRIOT

Attacks by ballistic missile became commonplace in the closing stages of the Iran/Iraq war, so use of these weapons in the Gulf conflict was inevitable. Except for the short-lived battle for Khafji early in the war, strikes by Scuds and the longer-ranged Iraqi Al Hussein and Al Abbas variants of the Soviet missile were to be Iraq's sole attempt to strike at the Allies.

For the first time in war, attempts were made to deploy anti-ballistic missile (ABM) defenses by stationing Patriot SAMs around critical targets. More than 12 Patriot batteries were deployed in Saudi Arabia to protect Riyadh and other possible targets. Supplies of Patriot reached Israel in the first few days of January in the form of two batteries provided free by the United States, but this deployment was to prove "too little, too late". When the missile bombardment of Saudi Arabia and Israel began on January 18th, the Patriots

in Israel proved less effective than those defending Saudi Arabia.

Several systems were teamed to deal with the threat from mobile ballistic-missile launchers. The first problem was to locate the mobile launchers. This seems to have been done using the Lacrosse radar-imaging satellite, and FLIR-equipped reconnaissance aircraft such as the Tornado GR.1A.

First warning of an impending launch was obtained by elint (electronic intelligence) – Scud units operating in conjunction with a radar known as End Tray. Signals from this equipment would have been detectable, allowing a "Scud Alert" to be sent to all potential target areas.

Orbited to monitor Soviet and Chinese ballistic missile fields, the Defense Support Program (DSP) early-warning satellites were able to use their 12ft (4m) focal length infra-red telescopes to watch for the hot exhaust plumes from Scud, Al Abbas and Al Hussein missiles. Most recent DSP launch prior to the war was DSP 14, orbited on 12th November 1990. Although the IR energy from a Scud rocket motor was only about a third that of the Soviet ICBMs the DSP series was designed to detect, tests carried out against Scuds fired during the Iran/Iraq war showed that they were still detectable. At least two DSP satellites were repositioned to cover the entire Gulf area.

From their orbital position over the Indian Ocean, the DSP satellites were able to take an IR image of Iraq every 12 seconds. These allowed lift-off of a Scud to be detected in near real-time, and an image of the exhaust plume transmitted to the Air Force Space Command ground station at Alice Springs, Australia, then relayed to US Space

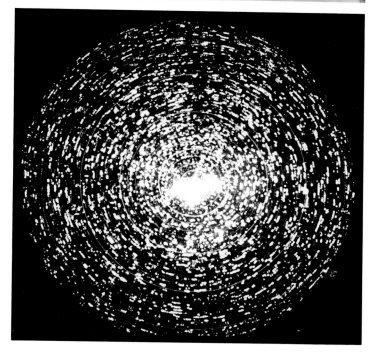

Command's Missile Warning Centre at Cheyenne Mountain, Colorado. With two satellites tracking the target from different orbital positions, DSP data was used to create a three-dimensional model of the trajectory in order to predict the likely impact area of the missile.

Flight time of a Scud was around seven minutes, so the amount of trajectory data that could be gathered in this amount of time was limited. Within two minutes of launch detection, a reliable impact prediction was available. Around three minutes were needed to flash that to military commanders in the Gulf, and for them to raise the alert. In practice, around 90 seconds of early warning would reach the defending Patriot batteries during the first Scud attacks.

Luckily for the Allies, in the last weeks before the air war began, Iraq carried out two Scud launches. Although probably intended as last-minute training exercises for the launcher crews, these also helped the Allies test their missile-warning procedure, and focussed attention on how the entire warning process could be further streamlined.

Within days of the first Scud attacks, data from the DSP satellites was being fed to the crews manning the Patriot batteries in Saudi Arabia and Israel, and warning time rose to around 5 minutes, increasing the chances of interception.

Patriot exists in two variants, both of which were used in action. The original round was designed for use against aircraft targets, but a modification known as PAC-1 updated the computer software used in the missile and the ground radar. The newer PAC-2 missile that entered production in the winter of 1989/90 has a faster fuze and an improved warhead both intended to improve lethality against tactical ballistic missiles. Deliveries of the PAC-2 were brought forward from January 1991 to September 1990. Patriot units in Saudi Arabia and Israel used a mixture of PAC-1 and PAC-2 rounds, but the latter was probably used for all Scud engagements.

Patriot's MPQ-53 phased-array radar normally detected incoming Scuds at a range of more than 60 miles (100km). Engagements took place at around 6 - 18 miles (10 30km), with a two-round salvo

Above: The Iraqis increased the range of the Soviet Scud missile with their Al Hussein and Al Abbas variants. All that were fired used a conventional HE warhead.

Below: A US Army operator at the radar screen of a Patriot missile system. On some interceptions the Patriot sites only had around 90 seconds of warning time.

Above: Tornados suffered the highest casualties of Allied aircraft during the war - largely due to them being employed against heavily defended airfields.

being fired at each target. Typical SAM flight times were 15 - 18 seconds, at combined closing speeds of around Mach 8.

A total of 49 Scuds was fired at Saudi Arabia, and 39 at Israel. Of these, 11 impacted harmlessly in Saudi Arabia, and ten in Israel. Twenty-nine of the rounds heading for Saudi targets were intercepted, although in about a quarter of these cases, debris from the incoming Scud hit the target area.

Patriot systems in Israel proved less successful, particularly in the early stages of the war. Two batteries were simply not enough to protect a city the size of Tel Aviv. Even the dozen or so in Saudi Arabia were not enough to cover the whole of Riyadh. To boost Israel's defenses, the US rushed US Army Patriot batteries and their crews to the country. The distance from launch sites in Western Iraq to Israel was longer than that between southern Iraq and Riyadh, so the velocity of the incoming missiles was higher, making the task of interception more difficult. Many incoming warheads landed in their target areas.

What became known as "Anti-Scud" operations consumed a growing number of Allied sorties in late January and early February. DSP

data gave the Allies a rough indication of the Scud launch point. This probably allowed an orbiting E-8A JSTARS aircraft to map the area by radar in an attempt to locate the transporter-erector-launchers (TELs). F-15Es could then use their LANTIRN systems to locate and attack the vehicles. Attempts were probably made to do this using AGM-65D IIR Mavericks, but a simpler form of attack using cluster bombs seems to have been the most effective way of bringing the maximum amount of firepower to bear as rapidly as possible on these small and mobile targets.

Large numbers of ISCB-1 area-denial weapons are reported to have been used to reduce the mobility of the missile TEL vehicles. Based on the Rockeye cluster bomb, the ISCB-1 scatters small fragmentation mines, and was used against roads and likely launch or missile storage areas. This tactic was particularly aimed at the Al Hussein and Al Abbas, which required the use of the locally-built Al Waleed launch vehicle. Based on a Scania 112 tractor unit, these had little off-road capability.

A final anti-Scud weapon rushed to the Gulf but not fired in anger was the AIM-120A AMRAAM Advanced Medium Range Air-to-Air Missile. Operational deployment of this missile had been repeatedly delayed through the late 1980s, and the final series of initial operational capability tests was not completed until mid-February. Although the Iraqi Air Force was no longer an effective threat, AMRAAM-equipped F-15C and -15D aircraft of the 33rd Tactical Fighter Wing were rushed to the Gulf for possible Scud defence.

Above: Patriot intercepts an incoming missile above Riyadh in Saudi Arabia. Debris from the explosion can be seen in the distance as it falls to ground.

Below: One that got through - Scud damage in Israel. Such scenes had a political and propaganda effect out of all proportion to the military damage caused.

Below: These are GBU-15 guided bombs before loading onto a Coalition aircraft. The GBU-15 was spectacularly successful in precision air strikes.

NEW WEAPONS

During the air war, the Allies used a range of specialised weaponry to knock out key Iraqi command and control centres, air-defence and GCI radars, and airfields. In some cases the rule book was rewritten, with unexpected platforms being used to attack these targets. As might be expected, the opening shots of Desert Storm were fired against the radar sites which could have warned of incoming air strikes. In theory, this was a job for the F-4G Wild Weasels, but in practice the task was assigned to a formation of AH-64A Apaches.

In the hours that followed, two novel weapons played a major part in attacking the Iraqi defenses. The first was the Lockheed F-117A stealth fighter, an aircraft whose reputation had been marred by its having apparently missed one of its targets during the 1989 invasion of Panama. In the opening hours of the air war, the two squadrons of F-117As in Saudi Arabia flew some 30 sorties against 80 targets. The F-117A made up only 3 per cent of the Allied aircraft numbers, but was tasked with attacking more than 40 per cent of the targets. Its success rate on these missions was high. Conventional doctrine claims that "Make only one pass - hold on to your ass". Invisible to radar as they flew through the night skies, the F-117As were able to ignore this maxim, orbiting over the target area until their pilots were sure that the correct target had been identified and laser-designated.

The other new weapon was the General Dynamics Tomahawk cruise missile. Tomahawk exists in several versions, the types used against Iraq being the BGM-109C and -109D. The C model is armed with a 1,000lb HE warhead originally devised for the Bullpup missile, while the D carries up to 166 BLU-97D submunitions. Both use the same guidance technology, with terrain contour mapping (TERCOM) being combined with a digital scene-matching area correlator (DSMAC). At various points along the flight path, the TERCOM system measures the profile of the ground below the missile using a radar altimeter, then compares this with geographic data stored in the guidance computer in order to determine its exact position. This is then used to update the on-board inertial-navigation system. Once close to the target, the missile activates its DSMAC sensor and compares the external scene with a digitised version carried in its electronic memory.

US Navy ships fired more than 196 BGM-109C in the opening hours of Desert Storm, and more would be launched during the six-week campaign. Newsmen largely confined to the Al-Rashid hotel in Baghdad became used to the sight of Tomahawks flying along the highway outside the hotel, a navigational landmark that had obviously been programmed into the missile's guidance systems.

Flying a few hundred feet above the ground at a speed of around 500mph (800km/hr), the cruise missiles were not invulnerable to AAA fire, and on several occasions were successfully engaged and shot down. These losses were acceptable, given that these expensive weapons

Above: A line-up of F-117A stealth fighters before deployment to the Gulf. Beneath the open weapons bays are cargo pods for spares.

Below: A Tomahawk launch from the USS Wisconsin. The effectiveness of Tomahawk was no surprise to those who built and operated it.

were being used against some of the most heavily-defended targets in Iraq, as were a shorter-ranged weapon - the US Navy's Standoff Land Attack Missile (SLAM) version of the Harpoon anti-ship missile.

GUIDED BOMBS

Once the first wave of low-level air strikes had almost grounded the Iraqi air force, knocked out key air-defence and GCI radar and communications sites, and blunted the effectiveness of the SAM defenses, the attackers switched to medium altitudes of between 8,000 - 12,000ft (2,500 - 3,500m) which would keep aircraft above the ceiling of most AAA fire. As TV reports from Baghdad showed, the AAA fire lit up the sky every night during air raids, but those massive pyrotechnics were largely at heights of up to 4,500ft (1,400m), well below the Allied aircraft.

In previous conflicts, such tactics would have reduced bombing accuracy, but high-accuracy navigation systems allowed even unguided ordnance to be delivered accurately, while "smart" weapons such as laser-guided and infra-red guided bombs displayed unprecedented accuracy. Circular Error Probable (CEP) of ordnance delivered by aircraft such as the F-15E, F-16 and F/A-18 was around 30 - 40ft (9 - 12m) - a fifth of that achieved during the Vietnam War. CEP of LGB and IR-guided bombs was in the order of a few feet. In Vietnam, LGBs had been specialised weapons used only on a few high-priority targets, but "smart" weapons were now available in sufficient numbers to allow widespread use against targets such as bridges, bunkers and hardened aircraft shelters.

One force which could not immediately join the USAF and USN at medium altitude were the RAF and Royal Saudi Air Force Tornado GR.1s. Tasked with attacking Iraqi airfields, they had to fly at heights of a few hundred feet, dictated by requirements of the JP233 airfield-attack munition. Within three days, Iraqi combat air operations had almost ceased, allowing the Tornado crews to switch weapons to LGBs and conventional 1,000lb (450kg)

Above: The Stand-off Land Attack Missile (SLAM) uses the motor and airframe of Harpoon, the sensor head of Maverick and the data-link from the Walleye glide bomb.

bombs, and move to higher altitude. An anti-runway weapon able to be delivered from medium altitude will probably be a development priority for the USAF in the early 1990s.

Iraq tried hard to repair its runways, but faced the fact that its grounded air force was being slowly destroyed night by night as the Allies attacked the hardened aircraft shelters and the aircraft sheltering within them. Even the super-hardened shelters protected by up to 10 -12ft (3 - 3.6m) of concrete were no match for US LGBs, particularly the 2,000lb (900kg) GBU-27.

During the Second World War, German U-boats had been able to

Above: AS-3OL is a French laser-guided missile used in the Gulf by French Jaguars. Its warhead is optimised for the penetration of thick concrete.

shelter between missions inside strong concrete pens. There would be no such havens in the Iraq of 1991. As the Allied ground forces prepared for battle, back in the USA engineers were rushing to complete custom-designed 3,000lb (1,360kg) LGBs able to destroy the deeply-buried command and control centres used by the Iraqi high command. By the last night of war, only two were ready for use. Released from 20,000ft (6,100m), these scored hits on what US intelligence had

Below: The bombs on the inner pylons of this F-4G are Rockeye cluster weapons, ideal for attacking dispersed or lightly protected ground targets.

Right: The French have also developed their own anti-radiation missile in the form of the Matra Armat, seen here under the fuselage of a Mirage F1.

identified as the most important remaining command and control facility in Iraq.

LGBs also proved an effective means of dealing with heavily dug in Iraqi tanks. Realising the rate of attrition it was suffering to air strikes, the Iraqi army had buried tanks even deeper in protective sand, making them harder to detect and hit. At night, the metal structure of the tank retained the daytime heat, making it a good IR target for

Right: Another F-4G totes HARM anti-radiation missiles on the outer pylons and imaging infra-red Maverick on the inner. HARM was re-programmed for Iraqi targets.

Above: The Alarm anti-radiation missile can zoom up to over 30,000ft (9,000m) where it hangs under a parachute until a target emitter is detected.

F-15Es and F-llls equipped with IR sensors and LGBs. Up to 200 tanks were destroyed each night once the Coalition switched to these new attack tactics.

SUPPRESSION

Iraq's ground-based radar network proved highly vulnerable to Allied anti-radiation missiles. The main US anti-radar weapon was the Texas Instruments AGM-88B High Speed Anti-Radiation Missile (HARM). This missile had first seen action against Libya in 1986, but the rounds now being carried by USAF F-4Gs and USN F/A-18s were the latest Block 4 version.

The seeker had been designed with Soviet targets and NATO operating conditions in mind, but the threat tables that formed part of the seeker software were reprogrammed to optimise the seeker logic for use against the missiles being used by Iraq. In Western Europe, the radar signals from a Franco/German Roland mobile SAM are "friendly", for example, but over Iraq or Kuwait, any Roland signals would be coming from the fire units supplied to Iraq during the 1980s. An older generation system such as Shrike would not have been so easy to re-programme.

The UK probably performed similar software "tweaks" on its BAe Alarm lightweight anti-radiation missile. Development of this weapon had ended in the late autumn of 1990 with the test-firing of seven production-standard missiles, allowing production rounds to be shipped to the Gulf and used successfully in combat.

THE LAND WAR

After 38 days and nights of bombing, it was the turn of the ground forces. At 8pm on Sunday February 24th, allied units rolled over the border into Iraq and Kuwait. As a young US army cadet, Norman Schwarzkopf had been fascinated by the battle of Cannae in 216BC, when an outnumbered Carthaginian force under the command of Hannibal surrounded and destroyed a massive Roman army. For the trapped legions, this encirclement and destruction produced a casualty rate to rival that of Hiroshima or Nagasaki two millennia later. For generations of military officers to the present day, Cannae represented a spectre of defeat, a warning than even the biggest and most combat-seasoned army could be dragged down to destruction. Now a General, and commander of Operation Desert

Storm, "Stormin' Norman" Schwarzkopf – known to his men as "The Bear" – was about to emulate the Carthaginian military leader he had for so long admired.

With their air force effectively knocked out in the first days of the air war, the Iraqis had almost no reconnaissance information. The only imagery they could gather was that broadcast from the three US NOA weather satellites. Flying in polar orbit, these provided low-resolution imagery of the Gulf six times a day. Taken in visible light and IR wavelengths, such images were too small in scale to show military targets, only the degree of cloud cover over Allied bases and operational areas. As a result, the Iraqi general staff probably knew little more about the Allied deployment against them than did the news reporters in TV studios around the world.

Effectively blinded, the Iraqis had to rely on crossborder raids and SIGINT when trying to build up a picture of the Allied formations moving into place along the border in mid-February. As a result, they became the target of a massive deception operation in which recorded radio traffic was transmitted from areas south of Kuwait vacated by Allied units sent to join the main force building up on the left flank.

With its air defenses stripped away, the Iraqi Army was open to round-the-clock air attack. Unable to move without exposing themselves to bombardment, Iraq's thousands of main battle tanks were destroyed in large numbers.

When the main Allied ground attack was unleashed, the tanks and APCs sliced through the defences at a speed that surprised even the most optimistic observers. Vehicle top speeds are usually "book" figures only attainable in test runs in the best conditions. However, the new generation powerplant and

suspension systems of the Western AFVs, especially that of the M1A1 Abrams tank, allowed real operational gains in speed and mobility. The fast-moving freewheeling tactics of the American, British and French armoured forces came as a profound shock to an Iraqi army used to dealing with massed infantry in frontal assaults.

The French "Daguet" 6th Light Division had been trained and equipped to fight in exactly this kind of terrain, and operating with elements of the US 82nd Airborne Division, had advanced over 60 miles (96km) into Iraq within hours to secure the western flanks of the land operation. Slightly to the east, AirLand battle tactics were epitomised by the US 101st Airborne Division - the pioneers of the "Air Cav" role. The biggest helicopter lift in history established a massive logistics and fire base some 60 miles (96km) into Iraq, from which airmobile units leapt forward again to sieze river crossings on the Euphrates, in conjunction with the US 24th Mechanised Division.

The heavy units of the US 1st Armoured, 3rd Armoured, 1st Infantry, 1st Cavalry and British 1st Armoured Divisions poured through the Iraqi border defences near the west edge of the Kuwait-Saudi Arabia border, swinging round to the east to destroy the Republican Guard and cut off the Iraqi army in Kuwait. Egyptian, Saudi and Kuwaiti forces pushed into Kuwait itself, supported by the US 1st and 2nd Marine Divisions.

What rapidly became apparent was the startling disparity in effectiveness between Iraqi and Coalition forces. Even allowing for the chaos in their command and control system, the disruption to their supplies and the morale effects of 38 days of bombing, the Iraqi army achieved remarkably little. The performance of elderly T-55 and T-62 tanks against M-1A1s and British Challengers was perhaps no surprise, but not even the modern T-72 was able to cause any tank casualties to the Allies. Artillery was an area where Iraqi equipment could be expected to equal or even outperform that of the

Coalition, but without air cover the guns and their ammunition supply system were slowly destroyed.

AFTERMATH

After 100 hours of ground fighting, and six weeks of air war, the Allies had shattered what had been the fourth largest armed forces in the world. Even Schwarzkopf seems to have been surprised by the speed with which his forces knocked out those of Iraq. Had he known how quickly it would be over, he told a press conference a few hours before ceasing hostilities, he wouldn't have waited to build up enough supplies and materiel for 60 days of full-scale combat.

Yet it is hard to see how the war could have ended in anything other than an Iraqi defeat. A high-technology military machine originally devised to counter the massive strength of the Soviet Union and its Warsaw Pact allies had been released against a Middle Eastern nation whose forces had been shaped by years of combat against Iran. Forces trained to fight a Third World War were opposed by an army whose last war had seemed more reminiscent of the First World War. The firepower of the latest generation of combat aircraft, battle tanks, guided missiles and "smart" bombs was being focussed on defences whose bunkers, trenches and barbed-wire triggered memories of Verdun, the Somme, and Passchendaele. The only question that remained as the Allied tanks and vehicles rolled north on February 24th was how many lives the fighting would cost.

In the weeks and months before Desert Storm began, there had been no shortage of pundits - particularly on the, political left - prepared to predict disaster. Against a litany of warning that the Allied coalition would fragment or collapse, the public was warned how the war could last until the autumn, involve the use of nuclear weapons, and cost thousands or even tens of thousands of Allied casualties. Some 40 to 50 per cent of world oil supplies would be lost for years, driving the price of oil to $65 a barrel, and bringing about a world recession and the collapse of the US banking system.

A few weeks after the Iraqi invasion of Kuwait, secret Pentagon computer studies of a campaign to liberate Kuwait had suggested a very different picture, predicting Allied casualties of around 100 in a ten-day war that might cost Iraq between 20,000 and 30,000 casualties. When these figures leaked to the British newspaper "The Sunday Times", their publication was greeted with a mixture of disbelief and derision. The suggestion by one of the paper's columnists that "I can envisage superior American targeting from the air might take out every Iraqi tank, lorry and grounded aircraft in a three- day turkey shoot" was dismissed by a rival newspaper as "brutalism masquerading as realism". In practice, the prediction was not too far out, with a four-day ground war costing 140 Allied dead. Some 2,200 years after Hannibal, "The Bear" had won his Cannae.

The Allies had inflicted on the Iraqis the most disastrous rout in modern warfare.

Below: The Warrior IFV was another combat vehicle that recieved its baptism of fire in the Gulf. Warrior carries 10 men and is armed with a 30mm Rarden cannon.

ANALYSIS

For the Soviet Union, the sight of its long-standing Middle East client state being shattered militarily in such a short time not only triggered memories of 1967 and the Six-Day War, but also refocussed attention on the shortcomings of its own military doctrine. If the Gulf War had effectively been a scaled-down version of the possible war on the NATO central front for which both sides had endlessly trained during the Cold War, the Soviet military had to face the fact that against the fast-moving high-technology tactics of Air/Land war, its own ideas were hopelessly outdated.

Even before the war, the challenge to current Soviet tactics and technology posed by US AirLand war plans had been recognised. Since 1987, a debate had been under way in the pages of Voyennyy Vestnik (Military Herald), the most widely-circulated Soviet tactical military journal, on

Below: T-72 tanks in Soviet service. The poor showing of Soviet equipment in Iraqi hands is forcing a rethink of tactics and procurement policy in Moscow.

the best way of coping with the new threat. One faction argued that the best solution was to modify current defensive practice, while the other claimed that new tactics would be needed.

Officers who favoured new tactics claimed that beefing up traditional defences that remained tied to adjacent units as part of a larger formation in the long- established manner was no solution. Such positions are slow to construct, and hard to conceal. A more mobile, flexible and less engineer-oriented formation is needed, they argued, one that can be quickly set up, and able to manoeuvre its firepower in any direction. Dispersed deployment of independent units are essential in dealing with AirLand warfare, it is claimed, and the new tactics must allow several such groups able to mass their firepower against enemy forces attacking from any direction.

As the guns fell silent in Kuwait and Southern Iraq, the need for a Soviet postmortem was readily admitted at the highest level. "We have weak points in the anti-aircraft system, and we need to examine them," Defence Minister Dmitry Yazov told the Soviet Parliament.

Above: US Airborne troopers run into position. They are carrying the M-16A1 rifle with the M-203 40mm grenade launcher attachment fitted under the barrel.

Left: This M1A1 main battle tank of the US Army shows off its 120mm gun. The M1A1 has a thermal imaging sight which can see through smoke and darkness.

Right: The world will need to reassess the US soldier after the Gulf war. The spectre of Vietnam has finally been laid to rest in the sands of Iraq and Kuwait.

Right: A frightening satellite photograph of black smoke covering Kuwait, after the Iraqi army set fire to the oil wells in a last act of senseless destruction.

"When we ask ourselves 'Did it work in Iraq?', we have to answer 'Mostly it did not.' And then we ask, 'Why not?'". A special conference would be held at the Defence Ministry to assess the performance of Iraq's Soviet- supplied weaponry, he told delegates.

Maj. Gen. Nikolai Kutsenko told the Soviet newspaper Izvestia that the "Iraqi arms of Soviet manufacture were designed essentially in the 1960s and 1970s, and trail by one or two generations the corresponding weapons of the multinational force.

Asked if the Soviet forces were currently equipped by high-tech weaponry equivalent to that used by the Allies, he admitted that in some cases they did not.

In the years of the Reagan Administration, the US had been willing to spend large sums of money to create a new generation of weapons that the Soviets would be unable to match. Many of those weapons helped win the Gulf War. The sight of Iraq's army marching into captivity left the Soviets with little option than to contemplate the difficulty their weakened economy would face in an all-out effort to close that technology gap. As reformers and hardliners in the Soviet Union promote their alternative ideas for that nation's future, the performance of the weapons of the Gulf War may yet set a yardstick by which success or failure will be measured.

FIRES IN KUWAIT CITY

Landsat image of morning 23 February 1991

Aerial Weapons

The Gulf War will go down in history as remarkable on many counts. Where air weapons are concerned not the least remarkable feature was the virtual non-appearance of the strong and well-equipped Iraqi air force, which could not be explained solely on the basis of attacks by Coalition aircraft (basically Tornado GR.1s of the RAF) on airfield runways and aprons. This absence of hostile airpower greatly eased the task of Coalition air commanders, and enabled them to cut down on defensive fighter missions and concentrate on attacking ground targets in an ideal textbook manner.

Many observers have contrasted the Gulf War with the previous war involving the United States, Vietnam. Leaving aside the vexed political control of that earlier conflict, the terrain, the targets and the policies between the two wars could hardly have been more different. Precision air/ground munitions of a sort have existed since the radio-controlled glider and rocket bombs of World War 2. Several early species were available to the USAF, Navy and Marines in Vietnam; but their effectiveness was greatly reduced by the lack of positive target location. Targets tended to be barefoot teenagers in forests or trucks on the Ho Chi Minh trail, moving at night and under dense natural cover.

In the Gulf the targets might well be underground, or hardened, but except for 'Scud' launchers their location was known precisely. Virtually nothing was hidden.

The whole scenario was tailor-made for precision attack from the air.

In World War 2 the targets were often airfields, giant factories or cities. Bombs were rained down by the thousand. If the CEP (circular error probable, the radius of the circle containing half the strikes) was something like 2,000ft that was fine. But what today's warfare proclaims loud and clear is that a CEP of 20ft is often too great. The degree of precision required today is of a wholly new order. Such precision can now be achieved with well-equipped aircraft, which makes it possible to continue using 'iron bombs'. One can deliver from five to ten such bombs for the price of a single smart LGB (laser-guided bomb) or air/surface missile. Yet, when it comes to the crunch, and field commanders have to take out high-value point targets, these same incredibly accurate aircraft are invariably loaded up with LGBs. If you are going to use an LGB it matters little -- give or take a quarter of a mile, depending on release height -- where you drop it from. The accuracy comes in its homing on to the 'illuminated' target. If we are going to use no more 'iron bombs', perhaps we can throw away our clever aircraft and their highly trained crews and instead hang LGBs under a simple, cheap delivery platform. We could even use small Remote Piloted Vehicles (RPVs) which would carry the LGB to the launch area, with the target illuminated by a ground designator. The pilot would not even need to leave the ground.

Head-on Visibility Comparison

Above: The MiG-21 from head-on is nearly invisible at two miles. Not so the mighty F-15 Eagle. In a dogfight, small is beautiful.

Above: An RAF Tornado F3 over Saudi Arabia fires an AIM-9L Sidewinder at a target drone. The rocket flare makes the launch obvious to other aircraft.

AIR-TO-AIR

AAMs, air-to-air missiles, played hardly any role in the Gulf War. All evidence suggests that none of the Coalition aircraft losses were caused by Iraqi aircraft, but by SAMs and Triple-A. Apart from a few early sorties on the first few days, most Iraqi aircraft appear to have been concerned to leave Iraq and fly to a safe haven in Iran. A number of AAMs were successfully used in combat however, although there is no record of the Iraqi Air Force firing any at Allied aircraft. While air-to-air missiles are mainly carried by fighter aircraft, most strike aircraft will carry one or two short-range heat-seekers for self-defence. Even after air superiority had been achieved in the Gulf, A-10s were seen carrying two Sidewinders on an outer pylon. AAMs fall into three main categories, each with their own characteristics and attack mathods.

Close Range
All close-range dogfight missiles have IR (infra red) seeker cells on to which optical (telescope type) systems focus the heat radiated by the jetpipes and other hot parts of hostile aircraft. Out to a range of 9 to 11 miles (15 to 18km) such missiles are quite effective, though their warheads may not be lethal against the largest targets. Their great advantage is that they are 'fire and forget' weapons. Once locked-on and launched, they fly to the target by themselves; the launch aircraft can turn away from the enemy or engage a fresh target. Examples are AIM-9 Sidewinder and Matra 550 Magic.

Missile Homing Methods

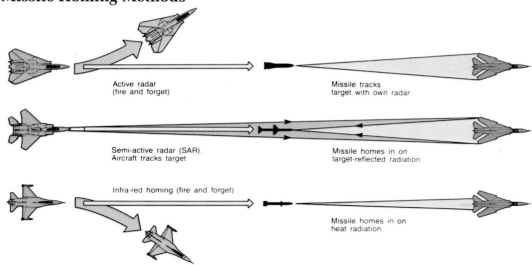

Active radar (fire and forget)

Missile tracks target with own radar

Semi-active radar (SAR). Aircraft tracks target

Missile homes in on target-reflected radiation

Infra-red homing (fire and forget)

Missile homes in on heat radiation

Above: The three types of missile homing. Top: the active radar homer is a "fire-and-forget" weapon, has long-range but tends to be heavy and costly. Centre: the semi-active radar homer needs target tracking by the launching aircraft to home. With current fighters, the launching aircraft needs to fly directly towards the target while the missile is in flight. With most aircraft, only one target can be engaged at any time. Bottom: the heat seeker is a "fire-and-forget" weapon, very accurate and relatively cheap. Recent heat seekers can engage targets from almost any angle.

The Sidewinder has been continuously developed since its introduction in the 1950s, and the current -9L and 9M versions have all-angle capability.

A recent development has seen short-range AAMs deployed on attack helicopters. The anti-tank helicopter is such a threat to ground forces that many armies are now training for helicopter-to-helicopter combat. US Cobras and Apaches have been seen with AIM-9s, but more commonly use the air-launched version of the Stinger SAM. The French use a similarly modified Mistral on their helicopters.

Medium-range

These larger missiles have radar receivers in the nose with which they can home on to radar signals reflected from the target. The drawback of most such weapons (Sparrow and Sky Flash) is that the target has to be 'illuminated' by the radar of the fighter. In turn this means the fighter has to keep flying towards the enemy until the missile strikes home, which is the last thing one wishes to do. It largely nullifies the range advantage of 30-60 miles (50-100km) of these costly weapons. This severe fault is eliminated in the AIM-120 AMRAAM (Advanced Medium-Range AAM) now carried by some F-15s, F-16s and F/A-18s. This missile has its own small active radar, and is a fire/forget missile which homes by itself from a range of 30 miles (48km). The difficulty with beyond visual range (BVR) combat lies in positively identifying the target as hostile. In Vietnam, the US rules of engagement demanded positive visual identification, by which time the target was often inside the minimum range of Sparrow. In the Gulf, E-3 AWACS aircraft enabled the Coalition to engage BVR targets safely.

Long-range

The US Navy's AIM-54 Phoenix has from the start had its own active radar, enabling it to home on enemy aircraft in the terminal phase without external help. In conjunction with the F-14 Tomcat's AWG-9 radar the Phoenix is guided to within range of its own radar system before switching to autonomous tracking. Phoenix can destroy hostile aircraft from ranges exceeding 100 miles miles (160km). Phoenix is a large and expensive missile, however, and is often not carried by Tomcats on Combat Air Patrol (CAP). Phoenix has never been fired in anger; on the occasions where US F-14s have engaged in combat they have used Sidewinders or Sparrows. There is also no record of the few serviceable Iranian F-14s being able to use Phoenix during the Iran-Iraq war.

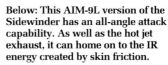

Below: The radar display from an F-14 Tomcat. Two targets are shown in the current scan area, each has a velocity vector marked. Other numeric data is also displayed.

Below: This AIM-9L version of the Sidewinder has an all-angle attack capability. As well as the hot jet exhaust, it can home on to the IR energy created by skin friction.

Above: Tooled up with four AIM-9L, four AIM-7 Sparrow and a 20mm M-61 cannon the powerful and manoeuvrable F-15 Eagle totally dominates hostile airspace.

Above: The Tornado F-3 fires a semi-active Sky Flash. This development of Sparrow has shown extremely high levels of accuracy and reliability in tests.

Right: A Mirage 2000 firing a test round of the Matra Super 530D. This French semi-active homer can hit targets at ranges of up to 25 miles (40km), and has a good "snap-up" capability.

Above: Inflatable "ballute" tails pop out of these retarded bombs. The extra drag ensures that the bombs detonate after the F-111 aircraft has passed out of range.

Below: An A-6 Intruder banks over the desert with a mixed ordnance load. Mk 82 retarded bombs hang beside a rocket pod, and a HARM missile sits under the port wing.

AIR-TO-GROUND

Free-fall unguided

By far the most common free-fall weapons are so-called 'iron bombs', or GP (general purpose) bombs. Some Middle East countries use Soviet bombs with a bluff cylindrical shape which causes high drag, especially when large numbers are carried externally. Western forces use 'slick' streamlined shapes, the most common being the Mk 82 (500 lb/250kg size), M117 (750lb/380 kg), Mk 83 (1,000lb/500kg) and Mk 84 (2,000lb/1,000kg). There are many other versions, some of which can be equipped with parachute, inflated ballute or airbrake retarder systems (one common family are the US Snakeye series). The retarded bombs enable attacking aircraft to release free-fall bombs from very low 'under the radar' altitudes. Free-fall bombs can have any kind of head, such as HE, armour-piercing, fragmentation, incendiary or (if the politics permit) napalm, nuclear, biological or chemical.

Iron bombs (or ballistic bombs) are normally dropped in a shallow dive and require accurate sighting equipment. Most strike aircraft use a gyro-stabilised sight linked to the fire-control computer, which allows for wind strength and direction, aircraft speed and altitude, air temperature and density and the configuration of the bomb itself. To allow the system to compute accurately, the pilot needs to fly steadily without violent manoeuvres during the last few seconds of the attack, thereby increasing the risk from anti-aircraft fire.

A particularly important class of free-fall munitions are the FAE (fuel/ air explosive) varieties. These are merely ballistically stable containers filled with a liquid fuel and a carefully configured explosive charge. At a chosen height above the ground (generally below 100ft/30m, and triggered by radar altimeter) the explosive charge is detonated. The entire fuel filling is blasted into a cloud of fine particles, possibly 200ft (90m) across. As soon as the cloud is fully developed, which takes a fraction of a second, it is detonated by a second explosion. The entire cloud, mixed with the oxygen of the air, explodes with enormous power over a wide area. The chief USAF FAE munitions are the BLU-72 (Pave Pat I), containing 992b (450kg) of propane, and BLU-73 filled with ethylene oxide and triggered near the ground by a long nose-probe standoff fuze. Probably the chief uses of FAEs in modern warfare are to crush HASs (hardened aircraft shelters) and detonate minefields.
One of the most effective weapons against pressure-detonated mines is the CBU-55A/B, which dispenses three BLU-73s.

Typical attack profiles

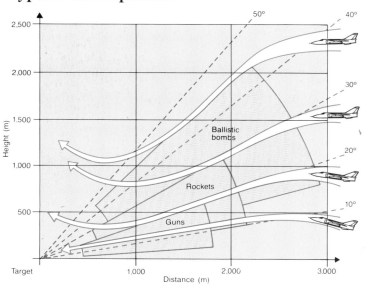

Left: Weapons characteristics dictate attack profiles. Unguided munitions require the attacking aircraft to fly a steady path for a few seconds for stable aiming and weapons release. For an aircraft travelling at 450-650mph (200-250m/sec), air defences would have about four to six seconds in which to engage.

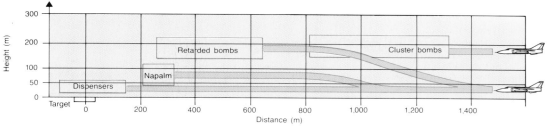

Left: Even attack weapons that can be dropped in straight and level flight require different combinations of height and distance at the release point. Notice how most of these weapons force the aircraft to climb from the optimum approach altitude, for reasons of weapons effect and aircraft safety.

Left: Low-drag or "slick" bombs are normally dropped from medium altitude in a shallow dive. This F-16 is also carrying Sidewinders on the wingtips and outer pylons.

Above: SG.357 cratering munitions dropped by a JP.233 dispenser. A shaped charge drills through the runway to allow a second charge to detonate below the surface.

Cluster Dispensers

The blast effect of an explosive weapon reduces in proportion to the square of the distance from the detonation. Therefore, placing the explosive closer to the target has much greater effect than increasing the size of the warhead. It follows that, against scattered or unprotected targets, a large bomb will destroy anything close to the impact point but have significantly less effect further away. Ground troops, especially those in desert conditions, react to this by dispersing units at wide intervals that one bomb will only affect one vehicle or trench.

Cluster bombs were first introduced during the Vietnam war as a more effective method of attacking such targets in jungle and forest terrain. They consist of a container for large numbers of munitions which are scattered, usually after the container has been dropped from the aircraft but before it hits the ground. The type of munition depends on the nature of the target, they can be anti-personnel fragmentation bomblets, anti-armour, delayed-action mines, incendiary devices or even specialised anti-runway munitions.

Ideal targets for cluster bombs include troop concentrations, armoured columns, anti-aircraft sites, transport nodes and airfields. Cluster bombs are often used where targets are imprecisely located, such as by electronic support measures (ESM) or during night attacks.

British Tornados carry up to eight Cluster Bomb No.1, better known as the Hunting Engineering BL.755. This scatters 147 bomblets each with a small shaped charge able to penetrate up to 10in (250mm) of armour and also giving a secondary anti-personnel fragmentation effect over a wide area.

France's Armée de l'Air uses Belouga, a streamlined container carried in multiple. Each strews 151 munitions which can be GP fragmentation, hollow-charge against armour, or area-interdiction for road/rail/airfield targets. The US forces have CBUs (cluster bomb units) numbered from CBU-l to CBU-87, of which at least 15 types are in wide service. Almost all CBUs can be released from any height, from any attitude and from any speed up to 700kt. In many cases the height at which the submunitions are released can be preset, to give any desired ground pattern. Most submunitions are designed for a particular effect, but the newest CBU (87/B) contains 202 BLU-97/B (BLU = bomb, live unit), which does a bit of everything. Weighing 3.4lb (1.54 kg), the 97/B comprises a downward-pointing shaped charge for piercing 4.65in (118mm) of armour, a fragmentation steel case and a Zirconium ring serving as an incendiary device. Clearly 202 of these would have far more effect than a crude GP bomb of the same aggregate weight.

While not strictly a cluster weapon, the French BAT.120 is a small bomblet carried in groups of 18 on a special dispensing pylon. Released at precisely timed intervals, each BAT has a parachute retarder and a 53lb (24kg) twin warhead which scatters lethal pre-formed fragments over a radius of over 66ft (20m).

JP.233 is a more specialised airfield attack weapon comprising two kinds of munition released in salvo from a large dispenser unit, tailored to the aircraft type. The Tornado carries two dispensers under the fuselage, each comprising two parts, which are jettisoned after the attack. The rear section carries 30 SG.357 runway-busting munitions, powerful penetrators which first pierce the

runway or apron and then detonate underneath, causing major heave damage. The forward section carries 215 HB.376 area denial mines, designed to hamper repair efforts. These fragmentation devices are fused to detonate if moved, putting repair equipment and personnel at risk. Some are also set to detonate at random time intervals, which compound the problems for repair crews.

JP.233 demands that the attacker flies straight over the target airfield at very low level, beneath the minimum altitude for SAMs but vulnerable to AAA fire.

The Tornado losses the first few days of Gulf operations were partly due to their employment on these hazardous missions. For the future, it would be relatively simple to put a rocket motor and folding wings on a modified JP.233 dispenser. The USAF and RAF must consider a stand-off airfield denial weapon to be a priority in the next decade.

Above: Rockeye II cluster bombs on an F-4G Phantom. The "windmill" fuse in the nose controls the small bursting charge which spreads out the submunitions at a preset height.

Below: A typical anti-armour bomblet as carried by cluster dispensers. The stand-off probe causes detonation of the shaped charge at the optimum distance from the target.

Precision guided

Purists sometimes cast a distinction between ASMs (air/surface missiles) and 'smart bombs' or PGMs (precision-guided munitions) and the LGB (laser-guided bombs). The borders between these groups are blurred and often non-existent, and certainly the fine distinctions would be of no interest to the recipient. Their warheads are much the same. The only groupings that make sense are into two categories: those in which the aircraft still has to approach the target and where the guidance is purely to ensure an accurate hit; and 'cruise' type missiles in which the launch aircraft does not have to go anywhere near the target, and so has to leave the missile to fend for itself. Where the target does not stand out from the background, as in the case of a troop bunker or a single house in a built-up area, assistance from the launch aircraft will probably be essential. The most difficult case is when a heavily defended target is also difficult to discern. Then one or more attacking aircraft may have to search for the target at quite close range, a most dangerous situation. Finding and pinpointing static targets can often be done by specially equipped reconnaissance aircraft (see later). Once the co-ordinates are known, it can be attacked by cruise missiles without hazarding friendly manned aircraft.

In terms of numbers the most important PGM in the Gulf War was the Paveway series of LGBs. Tens of thousands have been dropped since April 1965, in three main generations. The first were existing GP bombs to which were added a nose guidance and control unit. This starts, at the tip of the nose, with optics which receive light from an intense spot on the target illuminated by a friendly laser. The laser can be aimed by a soldier, by a friendly aircraft or by the aircraft that dropped the LGB. The laser detector sends signals to a guidance computer which in turn pivot four control fins at the back of the guidance section to steer the bomb so that it strikes the spot of light. The current Paveway III weapons have flick-out tailfins, a microprocessor and a digital autopilot which enables them to be used in poor visibility or with a very low cloudbase. The most common version used against Iraqi targets was one of the largest, the GBU-10 based on the 2,000lb (4,000kg) GP bomb.

France is well equipped with LGBs, most of them made by SAMP or Matra. Though totally unlike GBU-10 in appearance they are identical in principle, the targets being illuminated by Atlis II lasers. The US Navy and Marines deployed the AGM-123A Skipper II, essentially a Paveway III in the Mk 83 1,000lb (500kg) size but with a rocket motor added to give a range exceeding 10 miles (16km). At such a range the launch aircraft can no longer accurately designate the target. Instead a friendly laser closer to the target is needed; the LGB is merely tossed into a figurative 'basket' in the sky from which it can 'see' the bright spot on the target. When everything works, LGBs have been shown to be accurate to within feet or even inches. There are, however, pitfalls. It is not unknown for the man aiming the designating laser to aim the tiny bright spot at a place hidden from the attacking aircraft. A spot on the side of an upright H-section girder or at the top of a wall under the eaves of a house would be invisible to anyone overhead. The RAF found the occasional LGB simply failed to guide, and this was one cause of unwanted civilian casualties. In the Falklands War, LGBs were lobbed from a distance in a high-speed climb.

Above: A trials AGM-130 seen on an F-16. This missile has a rocket motor beneath a warhead and guidance system derived from the GBU-15 guided bomb.

Right: Laser-guided weapons need the target to be illuminated by a designating beam. This can be from an aircraft, or as seen here, from a ground observer.

Below: Walleye II is a somewhat elderly TV-guided bomb, originally developed for the US Navy. This is the extended range version, seen on an A-7 Corsair.

Left: The French Durandal is a specialised anti-runway bomb. A parachute retarder points the bomb downwards before a rocket motor drives it into the concrete to detonate beneath the surface.

Above: A spectacular sequence showing a French BGL laser-guided bomb impacting within inches of the designated mark on the target. Laser-guided weapons were first used in Vietnam.

Above: GBU-15 uses a TV or imaging IR tracking system which is locked on to a high-contrast area of the target. The bomb can also be manually steered via a data link.

Right: Many thousands of the laser-guided Paveway II series have been built. This well-known trials shot demonstrates the accuracy of these weapons.

Left: The AGM-65 Maverick is one of the smallest self-homing air-to-surface missiles in use. Guidance can be by television, laser or imaging IR.

Right: An F-16 with Mavericks, Sidewinders and extra fuel. The twin pods of the LANTIRN all-weather nav/attack system can also be seen under the chin inlet.

Below right: A test shot demonstrates how Maverick can hit targets such as the entrances to bunkers. Many such attacks were carried during Gulf operations.

Apart from LGBs the most important heavy attack missile was the GBU-15, also called the CWW (cruciform-wing weapon) or EOGB (electro-optical glide bomb). Weighing a hefty 2,617lb (1,187kg), this is basically a Mk 84 (2,000lb/ 1,000kg size) GP bomb with important additions. At the front is added a fuze, tubular adapter and either of two target-detecting devices, TV or IIR (imaging infra-red). At the rear are an autopilot and various other components including four large fins with powered rudders and a data-link for communication with the launch aircraft. In the Gulf War it was said the GBU-15 forced the launch aircraft to stay high enough (and thus very vulnerable) for the operator in the rear cockpit to watch the image of the target as seen from the nose of the missile and steer it by a line-of-sight radio link. This is strange, because during GBU-15 trials in 1977-82 it was normal practice to toss the weapon from low level in the direction of the target and then (in a few seconds) steer it until its seeker could be locked on the target. From then it could home by itself.

Of course a logical move would be to add a rocket motor to an LGB to give it the ability to fly to a more distant target. Such stand-off capability can make a great difference to the attrition rate when attacking heavily defended targets. The AGM-123A has been mentioned. Work on developing GBU-15 into AGM-130A was completed in 1985-86. The resulting weapon weighs about 3,000lb (6,000 kg), and after motor burnout (exhaustion of the propellant) at Mach 1 the ACM-130A can fly to targets up to 15 miles (24km) away with pinpoint accuracy.

The LGB Paveway III kit could also be attached to a special giant shaped-charge warhead to produce the GLU-109/B. This was specially designed for attacking hardened targets such as blockhouses and concrete bunkers, which are almost immune to GP bombs. GLU-109/B is claimed to penetrate 30ft (9m) of reinforced concrete.

Hardened bunkers are also fair game for most kinds of AGM-65 Maverick, though these are smaller missiles with warheads ranging from 463 to 677lb (210 to 307kg). All have a rocket motor and thus can be launched from 0.6 to 10 miles (1 to 16km) from the target at sea level, and from a greater distance at altitude. Guidance can be by TV (steered by an operator in the aircraft), IIR or laser-spot homing. The different Maverick versions are versatile, small enough to be carried in multiple, extremely accurate and ideal for taking out hard point targets such as MBTs or small bunkers. Allied weapons in this class include the RAF's TV-guided Martel and the French AS.30L with laser homing.

For the most heavily defended targets some form of cruise missile is needed. These have to have autonomous (self-contained) guidance, so that the launch aircraft can stand off at a distance beyond the reach of the target's defences. The typical cruise missile has a configuration resembling a miniature aeroplane, with propulsion by a small air-breathing turbojet or turbofan engine fed from a tank of kerosine-type fuel. An exception is the AGM-84 Harpoon, which has four small cruciform wings indexed in line with four tail fins. Various forms are used by US Navy/Marines aircraft and B-52Gs,

with ranges up to 75 miles (120km). The SLAM (Standoff Land Attack Missile) mates the Harpoon with Maverick IIR guidance and a data link to the launch aircraft for attack on land targets which do not stand out from the background. B-52Gs in the Gulf were also armed with the Israeli Have Nap, a cruise missile of roughly similar capability (68 miles, 110km range), with mid-course guidance by the GPS precision satellite method. This brings the missile dead on course for the target, so that over the crucial last stretch an IIR homing method can be activated to steer the missile exactly to the desired impact point. Because they are extremely difficult to shoot down cruise missiles do not have to fly very low, and thus can obtain a clear view of the target from a distance.

ARMs
Anti-radar missiles are designed to home automatically on to hostile radars of all kinds. Of course, for an ARM to work, it must be precisely tuned to the wavelength of the target. The enemy therefore designs his radars to hop from one frequency to another, or in some other way to

make life difficult for the ARM. If he detects an ARM attack he usually switches all his radars off, at least temporarily. The most important ARM in the West today is AGM-88 HARM (usually pronounced as the word), meaning High-speed ARM. This massive missile has a slant range of up to 10 miles (16km), though the range is much shorter at low level. It can be used in various modes, called Self-Protect, Target of Opportunity and Pre-Briefed (in which it is merely fired in the direction of known emitters in the hope that it will find something on which to home). For ARM duties, France uses the AS.37 version of Martel and the much more advanced Armat, which was also supplied to Iraq.

Probably the best and most useful of all ARMs is Britain's Alarm. This is small and light enough for a Tornado to carry nine (plus tanks, jammer and dispenser); alternatively a Tornado can be loaded up with a full attack load and then have two or four Alarms clipped on the sides of the inboard pylons. Alarm is wholly autonomous and makes no demands on the launch aircraft.

It can operate in many modes, in one of which it can zoom from a launch at 'treetop height' to 40,000ft (12,000m) and then descend slowly by parachute studying all the emitters within a large radius. Picking the most important threat, it releases the parachute and homes on the target, irrespective of whether the radar is subsequently switched off or not. The very advanced warhead has a laser proximity fuze.

Alarm has had a somewhat difficult development history, although most problems have been with the rocket motor rather than the seeker or software.

The RAF concept is for self-defence; each attacking aircraft should carry sufficient equipment and ARMs for its own protection. The US Air Force believe that this is not enough and that specialised defence suppression aircraft or "Wild Weasels" are essential to clear a path for a strike force. The venerable Phantom currently fulfils this role in F-4G guise. Equipped with the APR-38 radar homing and warning system, the F-4G detects, analyses and locates hostile emitters. These are then attacked by HARM or other munitions such as Maverick or cluster bombs.

F-4Gs have been working in "hunter-killer" teams with F-16s, the location of the target being transmitted to the F-16 by a data link. This system was not ready for use in the Gulf, and only the F-4G component was deployed.

French Mirage F-1EQ, Mirage 2000 and Jaguar aircraft use the Matra Armat missile. The successor to the AS.37 Martel, Armat has much greater range but almost identical size and weight. A sophisticated Electronique Serge Dassault seeker gives it good performance and decoy discrimination against a wide range of targets.

Anti-ship

Apart from their own surface/air weaponry, surface vessels are the 'easiest' of targets. They are relatively slow-moving, large in size, usually have an enormous RCS (radar cross section) and usually also generate many IR and radio/radar emissions. Compared with the land the sea is flat and regular, so it is simple to design a missile as a sea skimmer, held by a radar altimeter and autopilot to fly just above the wavetops. Its speed and extremely small RCS make it difficult to detect and even harder to intercept, and the wavetop height is usually an ideal height at which to penetrate an enemy hull, above any armour belt yet not so high that the missile passes harmlessly over the deck. The warhead, like the missile itself, is designed to disable a particular class of ship, from the largest aircraft carrier to small missile armed patrol boats.

Smaller vessels can be engaged by almost any kind of armed aircraft. Weapons can include guns and rockets, as described later, but the most effective munitions are dedicated anti-ship missiles. Of these the largest is AGM-84 (84A/B/C/D) Harpoon, which, as already mentioned, is not so much a sea skimmer as a cruise missile. Unlike other anti-ship weapons it is carried only by fixed-wing aircraft, typically four at a time (the sea-control B-52G can carry 12, though eight is the usual number). Harpoon is a cruise missile with turbojet propulsion and a range up to 57 miles (92km) in some versions and 75 miles (120km) in others. All the original versions were sea-skimming anti-ship missiles with radar homing guidance and a 488lb (222kg) warhead powerful enough to disable most ships at least up to frigate size.

Right: This aerobatic F/A-18 is carrying a pair of Harpoon antiship missiles, which give this multi-role aircraft a powerful maritime strike capability.

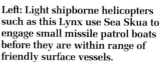

Left: Light shipborne helicopters such as this Lynx use Sea Skua to engage small missile patrol boats before they are within range of friendly surface vessels.

Above: The Saudis use the SA 365 Dauphin helicopter and AS-15TT missile in a similar role. The AS-15TT is command-guided, using signals from the helicopter's radar.

An even more powerful warhead is fitted by the British Aerospace Sea Eagle, carried by aircraft as diverse as the Sea Harrier, Buccaneer and Sea King helicopter. This weapon also has radar homing, and of a particularly advanced kind, switched on during the final phase of a trajectory of up to 68 miles (110km). Another large weapon is France's rocket-propelled AM.39 Exocet, with a range of around 30 miles (48km) and warhead of 364lb (165kg). This was also used by Iraq (for example to destroy USS Stark in 1987).

As the Royal Navy found out in the Falklands war, air-to-air refuelling allows land-based aircraft to have a dominating effect on naval warfare. Large helicopters such as the Sea King can also carry anti-ship missiles when operating from land bases or major warships. The only reliable defence for surface units is a flexible combination of carrier-based early-warning aircraft and combat air patrols to engage any firing platform before it gets within missile launch range.

The first AM-39 Exocet fired in anger caused catastrophic damage to HMS Sheffield in 1982, even though the warhead failed to detonate (the missile's fuel exploded and burned). During the Iran-Iraq war, more than 50 were fired at merchant shipping targets, over 90% of which hit. Most of these missiles were fired from Iraqi aircraft, usually the Mirage F.l. Large tankers with their multiple bulkheads proved themselves remarkably resilient to this type of attack, more so than densely packed but lightly armoured frigates such as the USS Stark.

Smaller missiles are more important in a war involving only light naval craft, such as FPBs (fast patrol boats), missile boats and small landing ships. These are ideal targets for lighter missiles carried by ship-based helicopters. Latest, and probably most effective, of this family is the Sea Skua. Despite weighing only 325lb (147kg), so that a Lynx helicopter can carry four, Sea Skua has a warhead able to cripple a destroyer. Rocket-propelled over a range up to about 10 miles (16km), it has semi-active radar homing guidance, the target being 'illuminated' by a radar in the launching helicopter and the missile homing on the reflected radiation. A rather heavier weapon is the Norwegian Penguin, carried in Mk 3 form by fighters and as the Mk 2 Mod 7 by helicopters, including the SH-60B Seahawk of the US Navy. The latter version has an extra booster rocket and larger wings to counteract the slower speed at launch. All Penguins have passive IR homing guidance which senses the heat emitted by various parts of the target. As the most prominent heat source may be the top of the funnel the warhead is quite large (250lb, 113kg). Yet a third guidance method is used in France's AS.15TT, a small 227lb (103kg) weapon with a range up to 9 miles (15km). The launch helicopter continuously compares the sightlines to the target and to the missile and a computer tries always to make the difference zero. The difference compared with semi-active homing is that the missile does not need a nose radome and scanner, only a cheap antenna at the rear. Of course, a drawback of all the radar methods is that it ought to alert the target that it is being 'illuminated', and should also indicate the direction from which the attack comes. Penguin, being passive, gives no warning.

Anti-armour

In contrast to the tricky, manually-steered missiles of the past, which needed prolonged operator training and even then often flew into the ground or went past the target, today's dedicated anti-tank missiles are invariably deadly accurate and, when they strike home, deadly. Of course armour can also be knocked out by such missiles as Maverick, and by dispensed bomblets with hollow-charge warheads. This section is concerned with missiles specifically designed to kill MBTs (main battle tanks). All are carried in multiple by helicopters.

Manufactured in larger numbers than any other missile in history, TOW (Tube-launched, Optically tracked, Wire-guided) is in service in various versions, each more powerful than the last. Two stages, boost and sustainer, of rocket propulsion accelerate TOW out of the tube and, with the four wings and four control fins, hinged open, accelerate it to close to the speed of sound. The operator has magnifying optics which are kept centred on the target, and a sensor in the sight notes the position of the missile (which has an IR flare in the tail) and keeps it centred on the LOS (line of sight) to the target. The operator does not have to 'fly' the missile, guidance to the LOS being automatic. TOW versions have ranges up to 12,300ft (3.75km) and of course, like all such missiles, a shaped-charge warhead guaranteed to pierce even the latest types of MBT frontal defences. A generally similar missile is the European HOT (High subsonic, optically guided, Tube fired), which is marginally heavier and longer-ranged.

By far the most powerful and most effective anti-tank missile is AGM114A Hellfire, specifically developed for the AH-64A Apache helicopter but now carried by several other types of helicopter. Hellfire is not tube-launched, and its rocket motor has a single high-thrust charge which, whilst producing almost no visible smoke, propels the missile at supersonic speed. Launch weight is 99lb (45kg), yet Apache can carry 16 Hellfires and 'ripple' away groups of four separated by minute fractions of a second. Behind the glass nose is a laser seeker, so that the missile homes with absolute precision on to whatever target is illuminated (designated) by a friendly compatible laser (tuned to the same wavelength and coding).

Above: For more clout, larger helicopters carry missiles which can cripple a major warship. This Super-Frelon is firing an AM-39 Exocet sea-skimmer.

Below: The decision to risk valuable reconnaissance assets, such as this Harpoon-carrying P-3 Orion, on surface strikes, must be carefully considered.

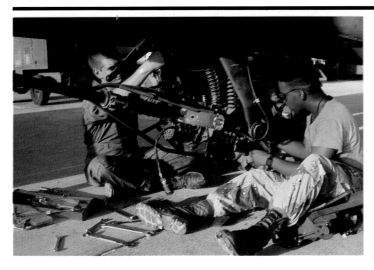

Normally the designation is done by the helicopter itself. Perhaps the first shots fired in the Gulf War were Hellfires which destroyed air-defence radars on the night of 17 January. Normally Hellfire would be used against hard targets, such as hostile armour and fortifications. Hellfire has also been developed with 'launch and leave' IIR guidance and with dual-wavelength RF (radio frequency) and IIR guidance, but this would be less effective against block-houses and similar targets which lack any hot spot which would stand out against the cool background.

Rockets

Though they will always be to some degree inaccurate 'scatter weapons', spin-stabilized but otherwise unguided rockets are relatively cheap and can be used in hundreds or thousands where 'smart' weapons might be restricted to tens. By far the heaviest weapon in this category (outside Sweden and the Soviet Union) is the American Zuni, used since 1944 by the Marine Corps. With a calibre of 5in (127mm), this powerful rocket can demolish bunkers and similar static and fairly large hardened fortifications. It also has a considerable morale effect. All other rockets are pinpricks by comparison, though their sheer numbers

Below: Loading up in a hardened shelter, this A-10 is carrying Rockeye cluster bombs, Maverick missiles and, of course, the mighty 30mm GAU-8 cannon.

Above: The AH-64 Apache has a single M-230 30mm cannon on a steerable mount. Targets can be acquired and engaged using the gunner's helmet sight.

and high velocity can have a devastating effect. Equally important, many types, such as the mass-produced American Hydra 70 series, can have any of several kinds of head: anti-tank shaped charge, HE, HE multiple submunitions, flechettes (needles), illumination, smoke and chaff dispensing.) Rocket speeds vary, the fastest being the Canadian CRV-7 at up to 4,900ft (1.5km)/sec. Range naturally varies with the height and inclination at launch as well as with speed and other factors. The longest effective range is 26,250ft (8km), claimed for the Hydra 70mm (2.75 in) series, but at extreme range the miss-distance may well be 300ft (100m) or more.

Guns

Aircraft guns vary greatly, the only thing common to all types being that they are automatic weapons. Guns of fighter and attack aircraft are always fixed to fire ahead, though the barrel axis may not be precisely parallel with the major longitudinal axis of the aircraft. Similar guns can be fixed to fire ahead from pods carried on external pylons on both fixed-wing aircraft and helicopters. Some attack helicopters have guns mounted in power-driven turrets able to cover

Above: Clouds of smoke engulf this A-10 Thunderbolt II on a live firing run. The 30mm GAU-8 cannon has a muzzle velocity of over 3,500ft (1,060m) per second.

the entire hemisphere under the air-craft, with remote sighting by a magnifying stabilized optical system (sometimes the same sight system as that used for anti-armour missiles). Most troop-carrying and assault transport helicopters have at least one machine gun on a pintle mount, aimed by hand from the doorway.

By far the most powerful gun is the GAU-8/A Avenger, which forms part of the primary armament of the A-10 Thunderbolt close-support aircraft. The gun and its drum magazine of 1,174 milkbottle-size rounds forms a package 21ft (6m) long weighing 3,800lb (1,700kg). This gun was specifically design to destroy armoured vehicles, and each projectile has a core of Staballoy depleted uranium weighing 0.78lb (354kg). Muzzle velocity is 3,500ft (1,060m)/sec, and firing rate selectable at 2,100 or 4,200 rds/min. From miles away an A-10 attack sounds like a chainsaw, and - especially as the attack can hit tanks from above or the rear - only a brief burst is needed on each target. The GAU-8/A is a seven-barrel weapon, but there is also a four-barrel version weighing only 339lb (154kg), firing at up to 3,000 rds/min. Fighters can carry this in an external pod, self-powered by ram air.

Most fighter and attack-aircraft guns have less than one-quarter of the muzzle horsepower of the GAU-8/A, and are fed with ammunition of various kinds, such as HE, HEI (high-explosive + incendiary), SAP/HE and API. One of the most powerful guns, the GAU-12/U Equaliser carried by the Marine Corps Harrier II, also offers APDS (armour-piercing discarding sabot), a kind of ammunition normally fired only by tanks and anti-tank guns and designed for ultra-high muzzle velocity. This gun fires 25mm ammunition at 3,600 or 4,200 rds/min. The corresponding gun in RAF Harrier IIs is the Aden 25mm, which has slightly lower m.v. and a much slower rate of fire of up to 1,850 rds/min. Tornados have the German MK27, firing special 27mm ammunition at 1,000 or 1,700 rds/min. French Jaguars have the 30mm DEFA 553, firing at 1,300 rds/min with m.v. of about 2,600ft (790m)/sec. The almost universal gun in American fighters is the M61 Vulcan, with six barrels firing 20mm ammunition at m.v. of 3,400ft (1,030m)/sec at selectable rates up to a remarkable 6,600 rds/min. This gun is also carried in external pods. Such high firing

Below: Like a swarm of deadly insects, a group of AH-64 Apaches lifts off from the desert sands. Each aircraft carries eight Hellfires and two rocket pods.

rates demand very large magazines and high-capacity feed systems, and put added pressure on the pilot to get on target before firing. Where firing rate is selectable by the pilot the higher rate is for air/air engagements, where time on target is likely to be brief, and the lower rate for ground attack. Of course, with the possible exception of the GAU-8/A, guns are ineffective against major fortifications and bunkers.

Above: Hellfire homes onto reflections from a laser, either transmitted from the launch helicopter, another aircraft, or a ground observer.

Below: Unguided rockets are a useful general purpose weapon for attacking vehicles and enemy positions. These are 2.75in versions on an F/A-18.

Helicopter guns include many of the above, as well as the 30mm M230 Chain Gun carried in a turret under the nose of the Apache. This gun fires quite effective ammunition at modest m.v. 2,600 ft (792m)/sec and rate (625 rds/min), these values being chosen as the optimum for the application. Many other guns are carried by helicopters, including the 20mm M197, basically half the M61 with three barrels instead of six,

and the 'fifty calibre' (12.7mm) Browning and Gecal. Machine guns include the M60 (as used by ground forces) and fast-firing 7.62mm ('thirty calibre') Minigun. All these are primarily for soft targets and to 'keep enemy heads down' during heliborne assault.

SENSORS

Virtually none of the air/ground ordnance could be delivered accurately without special avionics, and this is particularly the case at night or in bad visibility. In Europe bad visibility means rain, snow and fog, but in the desert it can mean sandstorms or the dense smoke from oilwell fires. Even when visibility is perfect an avionic aiming device is needed, for both 'iron bombs' and smart weapons.

In the USAF the most widely used of these devices is LANTIRN (Low-Altitude Navigation and Targeting IR system for Night), which is packaged into two pods carried externally by the F-15E and F-16C/D. The navigation pod contains a TFR (terrain-following radar) and wide FOV (field of view) FLIR (forward-looking IR). Together these enable attacks to be made at very low level at night. The targeting pod contains a targeting FLIR which the pilot can switch to wide FOV or to a narrow FOV with scene magnification, and a laser rangefinder and target designator. One could hardly ask for more, because such sensors allied to the precision navigation already installed in the basic aircraft enable the pilot to obtain a clear picture of a target by day or night, to cue smart weapons on to it, to illuminate the target for LGBs and also to obtain precision distance information for gunfire.

A few aircraft, including F-111Fs, carry Pave Tack, a single large pod recessed into the belly and with a sensor head which is rotated 180° to look down and ahead. This turret head contains a stabilized sight, called an optical bench, on which are mounted a FLIR and a laser rangefinder/designator. These sensors are boresighted together to give the pilot or WSO (weapon-system officer) a clear picture of the

Above: The French use Gazelles to hunt tanks. Each can carry up to four wire-guided HOT missiles, with a maximum range of over 4,300yds (4,000m).

terrain ahead by day or night, precise target range and a laser beam for designating the target for LGBs. A-10 and A-7D aircraft are fitted with the Pave Penny LST (laser spot tracker) which senses the spot of light on a target designated by another aircraft or a forward air controller on the ground. F/A-18 Hornets can carry a FLIR pod and LTD/R (laser target designator/range. RAF Buccaneers are among the aircraft which have the Pave Spike LTD pod. This can acquire, track and designate surface targets, either for the aircraft's own smart bombs or for munitions dropped by other aircraft. Buccaneers have collaborated with Tornado GR.1s, which originally had only a passive LRMTS (laser ranger and marked-target seeker), such as that fitted to RAF Jaguars. The Tornados were hurriedly retrofitted with the Ferranti TIALD (Thermal Imaging And Laser Designator) pod, which like Pave Tack combines a FLIR thermal imager and a laser, boresighted together. With this fitted Tornados can attack point targets with smart weapons by day or night. French Jaguars have the Atlis II pod carried externally; it contains a TV camera with selectable magnification and FOV, and a laser range-finder and target designator. This is compatible with the SAMP and Matra LGBs.

Most of the first generation of target designators and marked-target seekers looked ahead of the aircraft. One has only to look at the 'chisel windows' of an RAF Jaguar or Tornado to see that the maximum angle of depression is about 20° below the horizontal. This imposes constraints on how the attack is made. Obviously a sensor that could cover the whole region under the aircraft would be far more useful. Then a smart weapon could be dropped in a single fast run across the target and guided to the target after the aircraft had passed over it. Such an arrangement was a basic design feature of Pave Tack, and quickly proved its worth. In the F-117A stealth aircraft the attack sensors are so brilliantly

obvious one wonders why they have not been a standard fit for years. The aircraft navigates to the target using INS (inertial navigation system) and GPS (satellite global precision system), which should direct it to pass precisely overhead. The pilot switches on a FLIR above the nose, using the wide FOV. When he sees the target on the FLIR display he switches to narrow FOV, to get a magnified picture to correct his attacking run. He releases the LGB and then switches to a DLIR (downward-looking IR) under the nose, which the weapon computer has already locked on to the target. The DLIR watches the target as the aircraft flies overhead, and a boresighted (parallel) laser keeps the target illuminated for a direct hit. Time and again this system gave accuracies of the order of 6ft (2m).

Left: Taken from the TV targeting display of an Allied aircraft, this remarkable image shows an Iraqi target seconds before destruction by an LGB.

Above: The Ferranti TIALD thermal imaging and laser targeting pod was rushed into service in the Gulf. One of the first pods is seen here on an RAF Tornado.

Below: The two-seat F-15E is optimised for the low-altitude interdiction and strike role. It was used successfully on anti-Scud operations over Western Iraq.

Right: Pave Tack is an older IR and laser targeting pod, normally fitted to USAF F-111s. The long pod sits in the bomb bay with the steerable sensor head protruding.

COMMAND AND CONTROL

The first requirement of any field commander is up-to-date intelligence regarding the enemy. In modern warfare virtually nothing significant can happen without its nature and location very quickly becoming known to a technically capable enemy. Reconnaissance sensors can be carried in every kind of aerial vehicle from giant satellites to miniature unmanned aeroplanes not much bigger than an enthusiast's model. Almost all these systems can send back information in real time, in other words, as it happens. Sensors can operate at optical wavelengths (cameras), at IR wavelengths (linescan), at various radar wavelengths (SLAR, side-looking airborne radar) or at various radar or radio wavelengths (Elint, electronic intelligence, and Comint, communications intelligence). It is no exaggeration to say that the field commander today is deluged with a torrent of information, all of it 'hot' and immediate, all of it utterly reliable, and almost all of it directly relevant to the battle. Computers are needed to sift through the avalanche of material, received at the rate of millions of 'bits' per second, and pick out the parts that are needed.

Airborne platforms for surveillance include the E-3 Sentry family of AWACS (Airborne Warning And Control System) aircraft, the E-8A J-Stars (Joint Surveillance Tactical Attack Radar System) and the U-2R/TR-l family. The AWACS are the primary platforms for the control of all theatre airspace, warning of hostile aircraft out to a radius of over 230 miles (370 km). Using an extremely large and powerful pulse/pulse-doppler radar, AWACS can detect, track and identify many thousands of aerial and surface targets, if necessary transmitting any target's azimuth direction, altitude (elevation), range, code identification and IFF (identification friend or foe) to friendly forces. Such total surveillance enabled the Allies to dominate the airspace over Iraq.

During the Vietnam war, hardware was often rushed from development testing into combat, short circuiting much of the normal evaluation and procurement process. The same action was taken in the Gulf, with early deployment of weapons that promised to improve the effectiveness of the Allied attacks. Most important of these was the USAF/ Army E-8A JSTARS aircraft Similar in concept to the E-3 Sentry, but designed to monitor ground vehicle movements rather than air targets, the E-8A carries its radar in a canoe fairing under the fuselage.

Two prototypes were available, having made maiden flights in April 1988, and September 1989 respectively. By the winter of 1989/90 these aircraft were regularly flying test tracks off the east coast of Florida, testing the radar out to full radar range against road traffic on local highways, and military vehicle targets at Eglin AFB. No production decision was due until 1993, with the first production aircraft not expected in service in Western Europe until 1997. Early flight trials had shown a mean time between failures of around 100 hours. This level of reliability, plus the results a successful evaluation exercise in Europe during 1990 gave the USAF the confidence needed to take these prototype aircraft to war.

Both arrived in Saudi Arabia in mid-January, and within days were flying 12-hour sorties, monitoring ground movements and assessing bomb damage in terrain up to 120 miles (200km) beyond their flight path. Data from the aircraft was transmitted in real-time to a ground station in Riyadh. Once the ground war started, JSTARS was used to pass real-time targeting information to artillery units equipped with two new long-range weapons - the Multiple Launch Rocket System (MLRS) and the Army TACtical Missile System (ATACMS). Missile System (ATACMS). These could then pinpoint Iraqi formations miles behind the front line.

Different national forces have many other kinds of forward air control system, target-identification system and ground/air data link. Some use a data modem called the ATHS (Automatic Target Handoff System), which enables full data on a target to be transferred from the navigation or weapon-aiming computer of one aircraft to those of another. Several types of C-130 Hercules are used as special-role platforms. Notable versions include the EC-130H Compass Call and the US Air National Guard's EC-130E(RR) Rivet Riders. These versions look alike, with enormous blade antennas under the outer wings, ahead of the fin and on the fuselage, but their missions are different. Compass Call works with ground mobile C³CM (command, control, communications and countermeasures) stations to intercept and jam hostile C³ transmissions, Rivet Rider aircraft are relay stations for radio/TV programmes, for example to keep friendly populations informed and counter hostile propaganda. Many other aircraft, including some attack aircraft, carry Elint receivers; so do the Air National Guard EC-130E(CL) Comfy Levy platforms, which also have high-power jammers.

In theory, Iraq had an equivalent to the E-3 in the form of its indigenously-developed Adnan AEW aircraft. Based on the Il-76 Candid jet transport, this closely resembles the Soviet Mainstay AEW aircraft, but probably uses a different radar. The operational status of the Adnan is hard to determine. Development of an effective AEW aircraft is a very difficult task, as the UK's avionics industry learned to its cost in the mid-1980s, so it's hard to believe that the less-experienced Iraqi industry could have done better. In practice, the Adnan shared the fate of the rest of the Iraqi air force. One was destroyed on the ground, while the remaining two soon joined the aerial exodus of Iraqi warplanes to Iraq.

On the Iraqi side, command and control seems to have followed the Soviet model of rigid centralised control. Even the MiG-29 Fulcrum fighters were tied to GCI control in the traditional Soviet style, so were hampered by Allied attacks and jamming mounted against those radars. Eight of these modern Soviet-built fighters were shot down in air combat - three and possible four of these in a single action against USAF F-15s.

Surveillance from space can today assist a number of nations, but the USA is the only recipient of such information to have released much information. Following the loss of the Shuttle *Challenger* and failure of Titan launchers in 1986 much ground had to be made up, but by late 1990 the classified US satellite coverage was back to full capability. At least 12 types of satellite are available to support military operations. Some handle reconnaissance, of all the kinds previously listed. Some relay communications, and others handle weather surveillance. An unusual new twist is the use by news agencies of commercially available satellite imagery. Although of good news value, such pictures give little useful military information.

In December, (General Charles Donnelly Jr, former commander-in-chief of the USAFE, predicted to a House Armed Services Committee that Allied losses in the first ten days of war would be approximately 100 aircraft US planners anticipated that between 20 and 40 might be lost on the opening day of the campaign. In practice, losses were very much lower than this. By the end of hostilities, only 68 Allied aircraft had been lost in combat - nine Tornado GR.1, seven F-16, six AV-8B, five A10, five UH-60, four A-6, four AH64, four AH-1, three F-18, three UH-1, two F-15E, two F-5E, two OE1-58, two OV-10D, plus one each F-14, F 4G, A-4, B-52, EF-111A, AC-130, OV-1D, SH-60, CH-46E, and H-46.

Left: The E-3 AWACS was used both to detect any possible incursions into Saudi airspace and to monitor Allied offensive operations over Iraq and Kuwait.

Below: The radar and passive sensors on the E-3 feed data to the aircraft's computers. They then process and display this information on tactical displays.

Dassault-Breguet Mirage F1

Origin: France, first flight 1966.
Type: Single-seat multimission fighter; (E) all-weather strike, (R) recon, (B) dual trainer.
Engine: 15,873lb (7,200kg) thrust (maximum afterburner) SNECMA Atar 9K-50 augmented turbojet.
Dimensions: Span 27ft 6¾in (8.4m); length (F1.C) 49ft 2½in (14.1m); (F1.E) 50ft 11in (15.51m); height (F1.C) 14ft 9in (4.49m), (F1.E) 14ft 10½in (4.53m); wing area 269.1sqft (25.0m²).
Weights: Empty (F1.C) 16,314lb (7,400kg); (F1.E) 17,857lb (8,100kg); loaded (clean) (F1.C) 24,030lb (10,900kg); (F1.E) 25,450lb (11,540kg); (maximum) (F1.C) 32,850lb (14,900kg); (F1.E) 33,510lb (15,200kg).
Performance: Maximum speed (clean, both versions) 915mph (1,472km/h) (Mach 1.2) at sea level, 1,450mph (2,335km/h) (Mach 2.2) at altitude (with modification to cockpit transparency and airframe leading edges F1.E capable of 2.5); rate of climb (sustained to Mach 2 at 33,000ft/10,057m) (F1.C) 41,930-47,835ft (12,780-14,580m)/min, (F1.E) above 59,000ft (17,982m)/min; service ceiling (F1.C) 65,600ft (20,000m), (F1.E) 69,750ft (21,250m); range with maximum weapons (hi-lo-hi) (F1.C) 560 miles (900km), (F1.E) 621 miles (1,000km); ferry range (F1.C) 2,050 miles (3,300km), (F1.E) 2,340 miles (3,765km).
Background: By 1962 Dassault had been forced to recognise the limitations of the tailless delta. After prolonged study of variable-sweep the Armée de l'Air chose a shoulder-wing aircraft of conventional layout with the TF306 augmented turbofan in the 10t class. A contract was placed for the Mirage F2 in two-seat form in 1964, and the first flight was on 12 June 1966. But Dassault privately funded a smaller version, the F1, powered by a single Atar, the first flying on 23 December 1966. Dassault got this version selected instead of the large aircraft with the efficient turbofan engine. It is a very great improvement over the III/5 family, and it is amazing that the latter should have been preferred by so many air forces.
Design: Though the fuselage is derived from that of the III it is greatly refined and has integral fuel tankage throughout. The wing has LE sweep

of 47.5° and is less than three-quarters the size of the delta, thus giving a much better ride in the lo attack which has been reflected in pilot performance and delivery accuracy. Good high-lift systems dramatically reduce approach speed and field length needed, while slab tailplanes, large wing spoilers, ailerons and airbrakes ahead of the twin-wheel main gears all give superior agility. Compared with the III/5 series lo attack radius is doubled and hi patrol endurance trebled, while Dassault describes combat manoeuvrability as "more than 80 per cent increased".
Avionics: Dassault offers a spectrum of radars from the simple ranging set fitted to the F1.A series used for day ground attack by South Africa and Libya to the Cyrano IVM multimode monopulse set now standard in Armée de l'Air F1s. The F1.C originally used the IV-0 with no air/ground capability, and this is still used by many export customers. The IV-1 adds MTI for limited look-down capability against lo aircraft and the IV-2 has beam-sharpening for air/ground missions, but all displays are of the head-down type. The IVM is the most sophisticated radar for the F1 and the head-down display shows a B-type for interception and a PPI for attack. Other avionics include HF/VHF/UHF/Tacan, VOR/ILS, autopilot, IFF and optional SAGEM inertial nav, doppler, terrain-

avoidance radar (normally external), digital computer and laser ranger. The Thomson-CSF BF is the usual passive RWR, with four receivers giving 90° coverage each (all on the fin, conical fore/aft and flush discus type on each side). The jammer pods used by most customers are the DB 3163 and, for F1s earmarked as dedicated EW platforms, the Caiman. South African aircraft use the larger Alligator, with 6kVA ram-air generator for pulse and CW from 6 to 8GHz.
Armament: Two 30mm DEFA-553 cannon, each with 135 rounds; five pylons, rated at 4,500lb (2,000kg) on centreline, 2,800lb (1,350kg) inners and 1,100lb (500kg) outers; launch

rails on tips rated at 280lb (120kg) for air-to-air missiles; total weapon load 8,820lb (4,000kg). Overshadowed by the Mirage 2000 and Rafale, the F1 series continue to be developed for specific roles. The F1.CR-200 is the present reconnaissance version, with fixed flight-refuelling probe, IVMR Cyrano radar, Sagem inertial platform and comprehensive reconnaissance sensors including cameras and IR linescan, and a podded side-looking radar.
The F1.CT has the same radar and inertial system, plus a Martin-Baker Mk 10 seat, radar-warning receivers and upgraded air/ground ordnance. Delivery of 41 aircraft rebuilt to this standard is due in 1992-94.

Left: The Mirage F1 is an excellent aircraft which Dassault expected to succeed and ultimately replace the tailless delta Mirages. This example was one of the first F1.C fighters to enter service with the Armee de l'Air.

Weapon provisions:
A. Two 30mm DEFA each with 135 rounds.
B. Pylon 4,500lb (2,040kg).
C. Pylon 2,800lb (1,270kg).
D. Pylon 1,102lb (500kg).
E. Rail 280lb (127kg).

Key to stores:
1. Matra 550 Magic close-range AMM on tip rail.
2. Beluga cluster dispenser.
3. Wasp ASM (folded).
4. SAMP GP bomb, 551lb (250kg).
5. AS.37 anti-radar Martel ASM (carried on centreline only).
6. Durandal anti-runway weapon.
7. Matra R.530 AAM.
8. GP bomb, 1,102lb (500kg).
9. Largest-size drop tank, 374gal (1,700lit).

10. DEFA 553 gun with 30mm ammunition (60 rounds only shown).
11. Matra Super 530 advanced AMM.
12. Matra 155 rocket launcher.
13. SNEB rockets, 68mm (2.68in) calibre.
14. AS.30 attack missile (X35 warhead).
15. AS.30L missile (used with Atlis II guidance pod).
16. DB 3163 ECM jammer pod.
17. AIM-9L Sidewinder AAM.

Combat avionics:
A. Cyrano IV radar.
B. Avionics bay.
C. HF extra dorsal fin (Libya only).
D. RWR.

E. HF/UHF notch
F. VHF 1.
G. IFF.
H. VOR/Loc.
J. VHF 2.
K. UHF Tacan.

Fairchild Republic A-10 Thunderbolt II

Origin: USA, first flight 10 May 1972.
Type: Close-support attack aircraft.
Engines: Two 9,065lb (4,112kg) thrust General Electric TF34-100 turbofans.
Dimensions: Span 57ft 6in (17.52m); length 53ft 4in (16.25m); height (regular) 14ft 8in (4.47m); (NAW) 15ft 4in (4.67m); wing area 506sqft (47.02m^2).
Weights: Empty 21,519lb (9,761kg), forward airstrip weight (no fuel but four Mk 82 bombs and 750 rounds) 32,730lb (14,846kg), maximum

Left: The USAF has tried very hard to evaluate the ability of the A-10A to survive in the environment of a land battle on NATO's Central Front; these aircraft are on an exercise. The overriding need to fly very low makes such training hazardous even in peacetime; attrition has been high.

50,000lb (22,680kg), operating weight empty, 24,918lb (11,302kg) (NAW) 28,630kg (12,986kg)
Performance: Maximum speed, (max weight, A-10A) 423mph (681km/h), (NAW) 420mph (676km/h); cruising speed at sea level (both) 345mph (555km/h), stabilized speed below 8,000ft (2,440m) in 45° dive at weight 35,125lb (15,932kg) 299mph (481km/h); maximum climb at basic design weight of 31,790lb (14,420kg), 6,000ft (1,828m)/min; service ceiling, not stated; takeoff run to 50ft (15.2m) at maximum weight, 4,000ft (1,220m); operating radius in CAS mission with 1.8 hour loiter and reserves, 288 miles (463km); radius for single deep strike penetration, 620 miles (1,000km); ferry range 2,542 miles (4,091km).
Background: The AX specification of 1967 called for an aircraft to be powered by turboprop or fan engines. It was not required to have high speed but instead was to have the maximum lethality against hardened (armoured) targets, and to be able to achieve this lethality with the first round fired or the first store dropped. The primary weapon was to be a gun of greater muzzle horsepower than any previously flown. This was to be backed up by a heavy external weapon load. Avionics were hardly mentioned, the emphasis being laid on low cost, and short field length.
Design: Both the finalists in the AX competition were aircraft in the 20-ton loaded class, powered by two high-ratio turbofans. The winning design had these mounted high on the rear fuselage to minimize IR signature. It was claimed that the A-10A could fly home after an engine

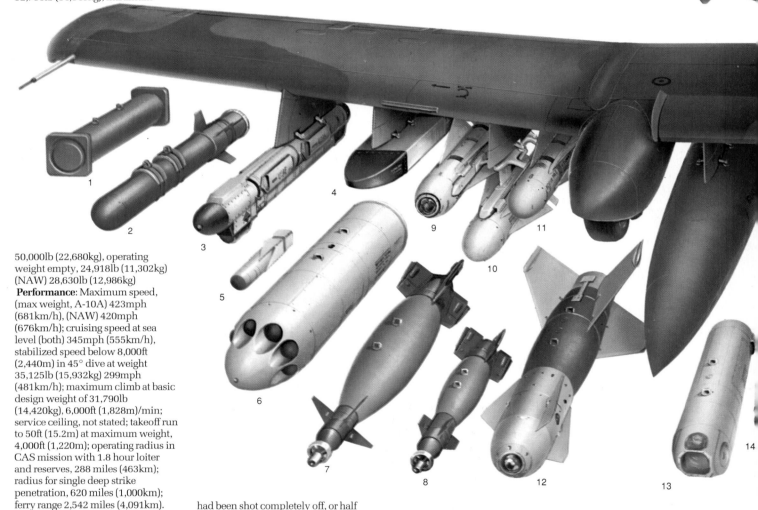

had been shot completely off, or half the twin-finned tail or many other parts. Left/right interchangeability was stressed, control and system runs are duplicated and widely separated and the main wheels project when retracted. The wing has no sweep and deep NACA 6716 profile, and the large ailerons split into top/bottom halves opening as airbrakes. The cockpit is surrounded by a "bathtub" of titanium armour proof against 23mm fire, and fuel piping is tracked inside the reticulated foam tanks.
Avionics: The original avionics suite was of officially described as "austere", despite the fact that the obvious main theatre of use has always been the Central Sector of the NATO front in Europe. Here neither offensive lethality nor survivability is possible without the highest possible standard of weapon aiming sensors and defensive electronic systems, all-weather navigation for blind at-

tack being taken for granted. Standard equipment today includes VHF/UHF/Tacan, IFF/SIF, INS, ILS, Kaiser HUD (recently updated with the ability to compute velocity vectors) and dual-reticle optical sight used in conjunction with the Pave Penny laser designation pod. The usual RHAW is the standard Itek ALR-46(V) and any of the common ECM jammer pods can be carried in lieu of a weapon. Another external option is the UTL ALQ-133 DF elint system, which measures threat bearings within about 0.5°. From 1977 Fairchild Republic worked on various augmented schemes and, built as a privately financed programme, a two-seat N/AW (Night/Adverse Weather) prototype with totally up dated avionics including Westinghouse (modified WX-50) radar, with ground MTI for mapping, terrain following/avoidance and threat detection; AAR-42 FLIR; Ferranti 105 laser ranger; new

INS and new HUD; CRT display for the added backseat crew-member; and (for comparison with FLIR) LLLTV. This was never adopted, but the USAF has added a few sparsely equipped two-seaters with no better avionic fit than the A-10A.
Armament: One 30mm GE GAU-8/A high-velocity high-energy gun with 1,174 rounds; 11 pylons for maximum load (full internal fuel) of 14,341lb (6,505kg), or (reduced fuel) 16,000lb (7,258kg). Production of the A-10A was completed at the 713th aircraft in 1984. Since then the aircraft in the inventory have been flown intensively and received minor upgrades. In 1991 it was announced that, following the USAF's policy of eliminating one-mission aircraft, there would be no successor and no significant funding for A-10 improvements. On the other hand, withdrawal is not imminent and will be phased over a period.

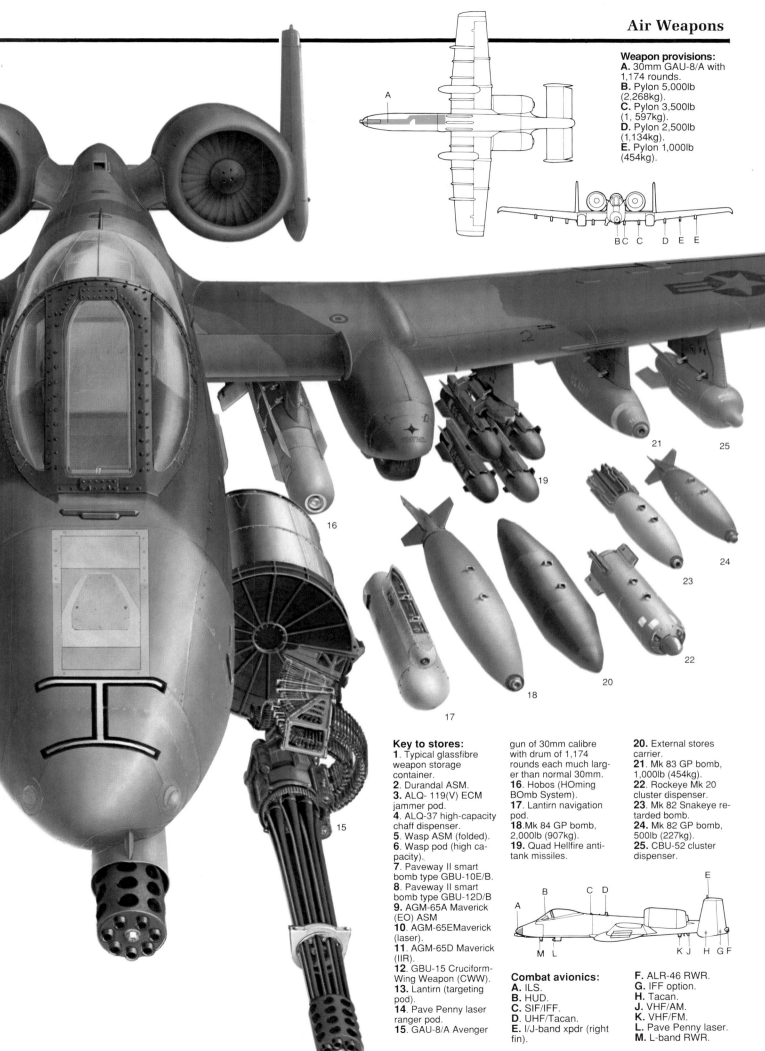

Weapon provisions:
A. 30mm GAU-8/A with 1,174 rounds.
B. Pylon 5,000lb (2,268kg).
C. Pylon 3,500lb (1, 597kg).
D. Pylon 2,500lb (1,134kg).
E. Pylon 1,000lb (454kg).

B C C   D E E

Key to stores:
1. Typical glassfibre weapon storage container.
2. Durandal ASM.
3. ALQ- 119(V) ECM jammer pod.
4. ALQ-37 high-capacity chaff dispenser.
5. Wasp ASM (folded).
6. Wasp pod (high capacity).
7. Paveway II smart bomb type GBU-10E/B.
8. Paveway II smart bomb type GBU-12D/B.
9. AGM-65A Maverick (EO) ASM
10. AGM-65EMaverick (laser).
11. AGM-65D Maverick (IIR).
12. GBU-15 Cruciform-Wing Weapon (CWW).
13. Lantirn (targeting pod).
14. Pave Penny laser ranger pod.
15. GAU-8/A Avenger

gun of 30mm calibre with drum of 1,174 rounds each much larger than normal 30mm.
16. Hobos (HOming BOmb System).
17. Lantirn navigation pod.
18. Mk 84 GP bomb, 2,000lb (907kg).
19. Quad Hellfire anti-tank missiles.

20. External stores carrier.
21. Mk 83 GP bomb, 1,000lb (454kg).
22. Rockeye Mk 20 cluster dispenser.
23. Mk 82 Snakeye retarded bomb.
24. Mk 82 GP bomb, 500lb (227kg).
25. CBU-52 cluster dispenser.

Combat avionics:
A. ILS.
B. HUD.
C. SIF/IFF.
D. UHF/Tacan.
E. I/J-band xpdr (right fin).

F. ALR-46 RWR.
G. IFF option.
H. Tacan.
J. VHF/AM.
K. VHF/FM.
L. Pave Penny laser.
M. L-band RWR.

33

General Dynamics F-16 Fighting Falcon

Origin: USA, first flight (Model 401) 2 February 1974, (F-16A) 8 December 1976.

Type: Multirole air-combat fighter with advanced ground attack capability.

Engine: (F-16A/B) one Pratt & Whitney F100-200 augmented turbofan with maximum rating of 23,830lb (10,810kg); (C/D) either F100-220 rated at 23,450lb (10,637kg) or General Electric F110-100 rated at 27,600lb (12,519kg); (C/D from 1991) either F100-229 rated at 29,100lb (13,200kg) or F110-129 rated at 29,000lb (13,154kg).

Dimensions: Span 31ft 0in (9.448m) 32ft 10in (10.2m) over missile fins); length (both versions, excl probe) 47ft 7.7in (14.52m); wing area 300.0sq ft (27.88m^2).

Weights: Empty (A) 15,137lb (6,866kg), (B) 15,778lb (7,157kg); (C, F110) 19,020lb (8,627kg); loaded (AAMs only) (A) 23,357lb (10,594kg), (C, F110) 27,185lb (12,331kg); maximum (A) 35,400lb (16,057kg), (C) 42,300lb (19,187kg).

Performance: Maximum speed (both, AAMs only) 1,350mph (2,172km/h, Mach 2.05) at 40,000ft (12,191m); maximum at SL, 915mph (1,472km/h Mach 1.2); initial climb (AAMs only) 50,000ft (15,239m)/min; service ceiling, over 50,000ft (15,239m); tactical radius (A, six Mk 82, internal fuel, hi-lo-hi) 340 miles (547km); ferry range, 2,415 miles (3,890km).

Background: An LWF (lightweight fighter), competition was won in January 1975 by the YF-16 (previously the GD Model 401). The LWF had been launched as a technology demonstrator, but by 1975 it had been recast as a slightly larger and much more capable, multirole aircraft bought for TAC, and soon afterwards sold to four European nations. Subsequent development has today led to important new versions.

Design: From the start the emphasis was on CCV technology, with FBW controls without manual reversion. The configuration chosen had a single vertical tail, mid-mounted tailerons and a mid-mounted wing, with 40° taper on the leading edge, fitted with auto-scheduled variable camber provided by leading-edge flaps and trailing-edge flaperons. Features include forebody strakes to generate strong vortices and improve handling at high AOA, an ARI (auto aileron/rudder interconnect) and YRI (yaw-rate limiter) and, in normal service aircraft, an overall limitation to within 9g and 26° AOA. Thus the pilot can fly by Hotas techniques while ignoring the possibility of losing control or damaging the aircraft (but, so quiet is the ride, he must always have broad idea of AOA, airspeed and other parameters to avoid, for example, letting speed bleed right off at low level). The cockpit has an exceptional all-round view, the only canopy frame being behind the pilot (in the single-seat models) and the only obstruction ahead being pencil-thin AOA nosewheel steering indicators.

Control inputs are by a force-sensing sidestick controller on the right console and force-sensing pedals, all ideally positioned for maximum application of force up to a point at which each control input comes up against a mechanical stop.

Avionics: The radar is the Westinghouse APG-66, an I/J-band pulse-doppler set, which was the most powerful that could be designed in 1975 without resorting to liquid cooling. Range scales are 10, 20, 40 and 80 nautical miles. The primary air-to-air mode is Downlook which gives end-on detection of fighter targets at over 30 nautical miles (56km) and shows them on a clutter-free display even when the target is at treetop height: There are 13 further modes, those vital in air combat all being controlled by thumb buttons on the throttle or stick; these include Dogfight, Radar Cursor, Designate, and Return to Search. Primary navigation system is the Singer-Kearfott SKN-2400 INS. Equipment includes UHF, VHF and Magnavox KY-58 secure voice, IFF, Tacan, ILS and Sperry air-data computer. EW includes the Dalmo Victor ALR-69 radar warning system with AEL aerials (antennae). Standard ECM pod is the ALQ-131 in various forms but other pods are used and Belgian F-16s have Loral Rapport III internal ECM housed in the extended tail compartment used to contain a drag chute in Norwegian F-16s.

Armament: One 20mm M61 A-1 gun with 500 (tight pack, 515) rounds; maximum external load 12,000lb (5,443kg).

No other aircraft of recent years has been developed in so many variants. The F-16/AFTI (Advanced Fighter Technology Integration) remained a research prototype, but many of its features, including canard foreplanes, are included in Japan's Mitsubishi FS-X version. Another model that did not go into production was the F-16XL with stretched fuselage and huge cranked-arrow wing, without a horizontal tail. The standard F-16C and two-seat F-16D have been developed through numerous upgrades in avionics, engines and other features, and many new additions are planned for production from 1993 and a further group from 1995. The F-16's versatility is saving it from the 'instant termination' of all one-mission USAF aircraft. The NF-16D is a variable-stability research aircraft. The F-16ADF replaces the F-4 and F-106 as the air-defence fighter of the Air National Guard; these are 270 remanufactured and upgraded F-16A/B. The A-16 is the USAF's close air support and battlefield air interdiction aircraft; these 146 aircraft have the 30mm GPU-5/A pod under the fuselage, night capability and an automatic target handoff system. The F-16N is a GE-engined supersonic adversary aircraft for the US Navy (single and two-seat), with no gun and various

Above: Two early production Fighting Falcons of the USAF, with the original small tailplanes.

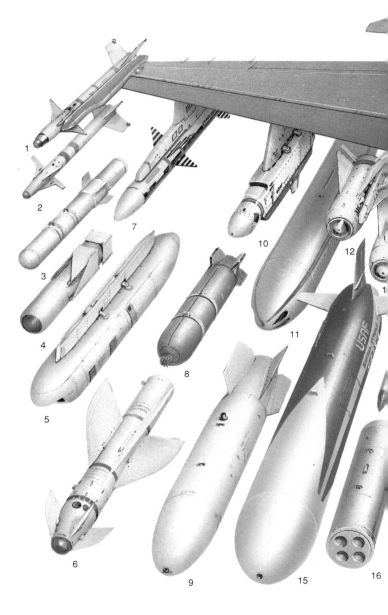

other changes including wings modified for incessant high-g loads. The RF-16 is to replace the RF-4C in the reconnaissance role, with seven cameras and advanced IR and EO sensors and real-time data links. The next generation is planned to be the Agile Falcon, with larger all-composite wings, refined aerodynamics, an uprated engine (PW or GE) and completely upgraded avionics.

Key to stores:
1. AIM-9L Sidewinder AAM.
2. AIM-9J Sidewinder AAM.
3. Durandal ASM.
4. Wasp ASM (folded).
5. Oldelft Orpheus re-connaissance pod.
6. Penguin Mk 3 ASM (Norway only).
7. AIM-1 20A Amraam.
8. CBU-528 dispenser.
9. B43 nuclear weapon.
10. ALQ-131 ECM jammer pod.
11. Gepod 30mm gun pod.

12. AGM-65A Maverick EO ASM.
13. AGM-65E Maverick laser ASM.
14. AGM-65D Maverick IIR ASM.
15. AGM-109H MRASM (not developed).
16. SUU-25E flare pod.
17. LAU-3/A rocket pod.
18. SUU-20 practice dispenser.
19. EO-FLIR.
20. LST pod.
21. Atlis II pod.
22. Paveway I smart bomb KMU-351 A/B.
23. M61 gun (internal).

Weapon provisions:
A. 20mm M61 gun with 515 rounds.
B. Pylon 2,200lb (9,985kg).
C. Pylon 4,500lb (2,041 kg).
D. Pylon 3,500lb (1,587kg) .
E. Pylon 700lb (318kg).
F. 425lb (193kg).

24. Ammunition, 20mm, for (23).
25. Mk 82 bombs (one with stand-off fuze fitted).
26. Hobos (HOming BOmb System).
27. Mk 84 GP bomb, 2,000lb (907kg).
28. Mk 82 Snakeye.
29. AGM-78 Standard ARM (proposed Wild Weasel).
30. External carry pod.
31. Mk 83 GP bomb, 1,000lb (454kg).
32. Non-slick GP bomb, 750lb (340kg).
33. AGM-45 Shrike ASM (proposed Wild Weasel).
34. AGM-88A Harm ASM (proposed Wild Weasel).
35. Data link pod.

Combat avionics:
A. APG-66 radar.
B. HUD.
C. Tacan.
D. UHF/IFF.
E. RWR.
F. Rapport III ECM (FAN only) .
G. Pave Penny or other sensor.
H. UHF/IFF.
J . Forward RWR.

General Dynamics F-111

Origin: USA, first flight 21 December 1964.

Type: A,D,E,F, all-weather attack; FB, strategic attack, EF, tactical ECM jammer.

Engines: Two Pratt & Whitney TF30 afterburning turbofans, as follows, (A,EF) 18,500lb (8,390kg) TF30-3, (D,E) 19,600lb (8,891kg) TF30-9, (FB) 20,350lb (9,231kg) TF30-7, (F) 25,100lb (11,385kg) TF30-100.

Dimensions: Span (fully spread) (A,D,E,F,EF) 63ft 0in (19.2m), (FB) 70ft 0in (21.33m), (fully swept) (A,D,E,F,EF) 31ft 11^{1}/2in (9.74m) (FB) 33ft 11in (10.33m); length (except EF) 73ft 6in (22.4m), (EF) 77ft 1.6in (23.51m), wing area (A,D,E,F,EF, gross, 16°) 525sq ft (48.79m^2) .

Weights: Empty (A) 46,172lb (20,943kg), (D) 49,090lb (22,267kg) (E) about 47,000lb (21,319kg), (EF) 53,418lb (24,230kg), (F) 47,481lb (21,537kg), (FB) close to 50,000lb (22,680kg); loaded (A) 91,500lb (41,500kg), (D,E) 92,500lb (41,954kg), (F) 100,000lb (45,360kg), (FB) 114,3oolb (51,846kg), (EF) 87,478lb (39,680kg).

Performance: Maximum speed at 36,000ft (10,972m), clean and with max afterburner, (A,D,E) Mach 2.2, 1,450mph (2,335km/h), (FB) Mach 2,1,320mph (2,124km/h), (F) Mach 2.5, 1,653mph (2,660km/h), (EF) Mach 1.75; 1,160mph (1,865km/h); cruising speed, penetration, 571mph (919km/h); initial climb (EF) 3,592ft (1,094m)/min; service ceiling at combat weight, max afterburner, (A) 51,000ft (15,544m), (F) 60,000ft (18,290m), (EF) 54,700ft (16,670m); range with max internal fuel (A,D) 3,165 miles (5,093km), (F) 2,925 miles (4,707km), (EF) 2,484 miles (3,998km); takeoff run (A) 4,000ft (1,219m), (F) under 3,000ft (914m), (FB) 4,700ft (1,433m), (EF) 3,250ft (991m).

Background: The 1960 USAF specification for a new tactical fighter (TFX) reflected such new technology as titanium structure, variable-sweep "swing wings", high-lift airfoils, augmented turbofan engines, terrain-following radar and advanced AAM armament to permit standoff interception without the need for dogfighting. The result was intended to be a gigantic programme to replace existing fighters and attack aircraft of the USAF, Navy and Marine Corps and most friendly air forces. The first of 18 F-111A (USAF) prototypes flew on 21 December 1964, and the first of five F-111 B (Navy) fighters followed on 18 May 1965. The B programme collapsed but the A eventually overcame severe difficulties and entered USAF service as an attack bomber. Subsequent production totalled 537, subdivided into six versions, of which 42 of the earliest are being rebuilt as EW jamming platforms.

Design: Having accepted the configuration of a high-mounted swing-wing, slab tailerons for pitch and roll (plus wing spoilers augmenting roll at low speeds), twin engines in a wide fuselage housing the retracted main gears, and side-by-side crew seats, GD then concentrated on the difficult attack and ferry missions and provided large internal fuel capacity, large multimode nose radar plus terrain-following radar linked through the autopilot to the flight controls, a very small weapon bay plus large external weapon pylon capacity (despite the entire underside of the fuselage being sterilized by the landing gears and air brake) and full-span vari-camber slats and double-slotted flaps on the outer wings to hold down field length despite the growing MTO weight. Problems with drag and engine mismatch led to further increases in fuel capacity and MTO weight, until the latter had climbed from the target 60,000lb (27,215kg) to more than 90,000lb (40,823kg). Successive versions introduced engine inlets of higher efficiency, engines of greater thrust, a new and very complex avionic fit and, finally, a better version of the same engine and a third state of avionics. SAC and the RAAF bought versions with long-span wings and strengthened landing gear.

Avionics: The colossal nose is filled with avionics, in standard racking for easy module replacement. The forward-looking radar was the first in a major GE family with designation APQ-1 13. A large liquid-cooled set operating in J-band (16-16.4GHz), it is used by the F-111A, C and E navigator (right-hand seat) for navigation, air/ground ranging and weapon delivery and (in theory) in the air/air mode using the 20mm gun (seldom fitted) or Sidewinders. In the "Mk II" avionic fit of the F-111 D the main radar is the APQ-130, with MTI, doppler beam sharpening, illumination for radar-guided AAMs and many other advanced features. For the FB-111A bomber the radar is the APQ-114, derived from the -113 with added beacon mode, photo recording and a north-oriented display. The F-111F has the GE APQ-144 with a new 2.5 mile (4km) display ring made possible by a 0.2s pulse-width capability; digital MTI was tested but not built into production 144 sets. Under the main radars are TFRs, usually the TI APQ-110, which gave all tactical versions the unique ability of automatic terrain-following flight at a selected low height, in any weather. Other items include Litton INS, GPL doppler, Sanders ALQ-94 noise deception jammer, Dalmo-Victor ALR-62 RWR, Cincinnati Electronics AAR-44 IRWR, Textron RHAWS and Avco ECM receiver. Today the ALQ-94 is being replaced by the Sanders ALQ-137, though active jammer pods are carried under the rear fuselage, the usual pod being the ALQ-119 (V) or ALQ-131. It is planned eventually to fit the ALQ-165 ASPJ. The most useful add-on to the F-111 Fs of the 48th TFW is Ford's AVQ-26 Pave Tack which combines a laser with a FLIR both boresighted in a powered turret giving all-weather magnified clear pictures of targets integrated with the cockpit avionic displays and weapon-aiming systems. Not yet operational is the Grumman/Norden Pave Mover battlefield surveillance radar which was flown in a tailormade belly pod in 1982 and could be used to direct Assault Breaker type guided-submunition bus vehicles.

Armament: Internal weapon bay for two 750lb (340kg) or two (various) nuclear bombs or other loads, or one 20mm M61A-1 gun with 2,084 rounds. Four pivoting wing pylons for 24 bombs of 750lb (340kg), 500gal (2,273lit) tanks or other loads (see main illustration). Provision for four fixed pylons under outer wings, the inboard pair very occasionally being fitted (same ratings).In 1990 it was intended to transfer the FB-111A force from SAC to USAF Europe, with modifications resulting in the designation F-111G.

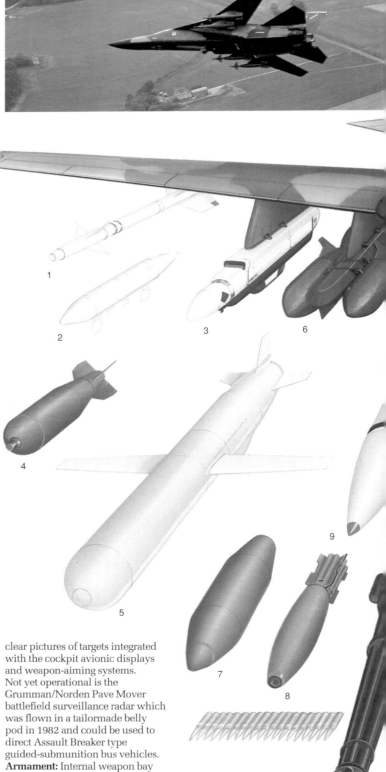

In 1991, in a sweeping elimination of all one-mission aircraft, this plan was abandoned, together with various other active or planned upgrade proposals. Thus, despite an enormous and recent expenditure on a major avionics upgrade, the F-111 force is progressively to be phased out. One reason given is that these aircraft had "become expensive to operate" before 1985.

Left: The stores and missions of F-111s depend to a considerable extent on the sub-type concerned. This example is an F-111F, the first type to be qualified to use the Pave Tack sensor pod. It is carrying four Paveway II type smart bombs.

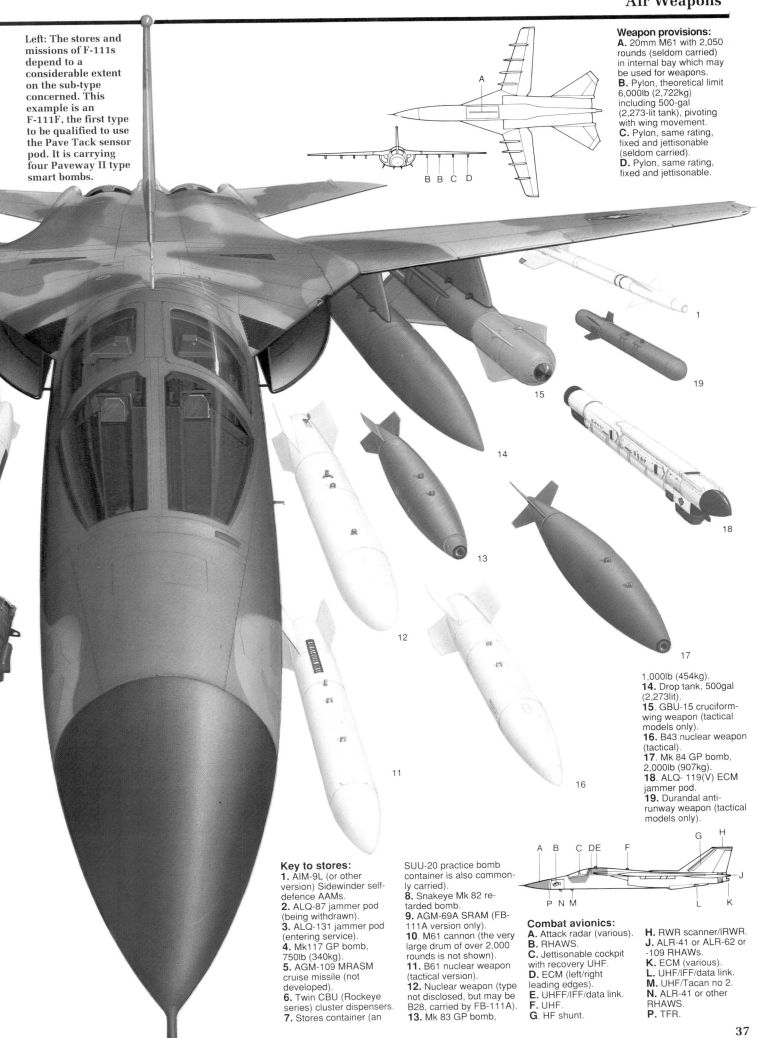

Weapon provisions:
A. 20mm M61 with 2,050 rounds (seldom carried) in internal bay which may be used for weapons.
B. Pylon, theoretical limit 6,000lb (2,722kg) including 500-gal (2,273-lit tank), pivoting with wing movement.
C. Pylon, same rating, fixed and jettisonable (seldom carried).
D. Pylon, same rating, fixed and jettisonable.

1,000lb (454kg).
14. Drop tank, 500gal (2,273lit).
15. GBU-15 cruciform-wing weapon (tactical models only).
16. B43 nuclear weapon (tactical).
17. Mk 84 GP bomb, 2,000lb (907kg).
18. ALQ- 119(V) ECM jammer pod.
19. Durandal anti-runway weapon (tactical models only).

Key to stores:
1. AIM-9L (or other version) Sidewinder self-defence AAMs.
2. ALQ-87 jammer pod (being withdrawn).
3. ALQ-131 jammer pod (entering service).
4. Mk117 GP bomb, 750lb (340kg).
5. AGM-109 MRASM cruise missile (not developed).
6. Twin CBU (Rockeye series) cluster dispensers.
7. Stores container (an

SUU-20 practice bomb container is also commonly carried).
8. Snakeye Mk 82 retarded bomb.
9. AGM-69A SRAM (FB-111A version only).
10. M61 cannon (the very large drum of over 2,000 rounds is not shown).
11. B61 nuclear weapon (tactical version).
12. Nuclear weapon (type not disclosed, but may be B28, carried by FB-111A).
13. Mk 83 GP bomb,

Combat avionics:
A. Attack radar (various).
B. RHAWS.
C. Jettisonable cockpit with recovery UHF.
D. ECM (left/right leading edges).
E. UHFF/IFF/data link.
F. UHF.
G. HF shunt.

H. RWR scanner/IRWR.
J. ALR-41 or ALR-62 or -109 RHAWs.
K. ECM (various).
L. UHF/IFF/data link.
M. UHF/Tacan no 2.
N. ALR-41 or other RHAWS.
P. TFR.

Grumman A-6 Intruder

Origin: USA, first flight 19 April 1960.

Type: Two-seat carrier-based all-weather attack.

Engines: Two 9,300lb (4,218kg) thrust Pratt & Whitney J52-8B turbojets; (E, post-1991) 12,000lb (5,443kg) J52-409 turbojets.

Dimensions: Span 53ft (16.15m); length (except EA-6B) 54ft 7in (16.63m); height (A-6A, A-6C) 15ft 7in (4.74m); (A-6E, EA-6A) 16ft 3in (4.95m); wing area 528.9sq ft (49.15m²).

Weights: Empty (A-6A) 25,684lb (11,650kg); (EA-6A) 27,769lb (12,557kg); (A-6E) 26,746lb (12,132kg); maximum loaded (A-6A and E) 60,400lb (27,397kg).

Performance: Maximum speed (clean A-6A) 685mph (1,102km/h) at sea level or 625mph (1,006km/h, Mach 0.94) at height; (EA-6A) over 630mph (1,014km/h); (A-6E) 648mph (1,043km/h) at sea level; initial climb (A-6E, clean) 7,600ft (2,221 m)/min; service ceiling (A-6A) 41,660ft (12,679m); (A-6E) 44,600ft (13,595m); range with full combat load (A-6E) 1,077 miles (1,733km); ferry range with external fuel (all) about 3,100 miles (4,989km).

Background: Despite the subsequent success of the A-4, experience in the Korean War had repeatedly demonstrated to the US Navy and Marine Corps the urgent need for a larger jet attack aircraft with all-weather avionics able to make blind first-pass bombing runs on point targets. A requirement was issued in 1956, and in December 1957 the Grumman G-128 proposal was accepted from 11 designs submitted by eight companies. The prototype flew as the YA2F-1 on 19 April 1960, and led not only to the mass-produced A-6A and updated A-6E attack versions but also to the Navy/Marines dedicated tanker aircraft (KA-6D rebuilds) and EW platforms (EA-6B Prowler, all new-builds).

Design: Though area-ruled, the A-6 has no pretensions at speed but concentrates on the much more important capabilities of flying low and flying accurately in bad weather or by night. The wing has surprisingly high aspect ratio and full-span leading- and trailing-edge flaps, roll control being by spoilers. Pure jet engines are on the flanks of the fuselage under the wing roots, the massive main gears retracting forwards into compartments in the lee of the inlets under the wing roots. Pilot and navigator sit almost side-by-side in Martin-Baker GRU.7 seats under a clamshell canopy, there is room for no less than 1,986 gal (9,028 litres) of internal fuel, and the entire nose is formed by a giant radome over a large search radar and small tracking radar, feeding an early digital computer and displays. Later this entire system was superseded, as outlined in the next section.

Avionics: The A-6A gave the Navy/Marines their first real all-weather capability against surface targets other than ships. This was done at the cost of severe

Left: Grumman built a straight run of 482 of the original A-6A model, followed by conversions to A-6B, A-6C and KA-6D standard. This is one of today's A-6Es, the definitive attack version, of which about 350 are to be delivered. Some 230 of these will be rebuilds of earlier models. All current aircraft are being delivered with the TRAM chin turret and capability to launch Harpoon anti-ship missiles.

time" (unserviceability) and many other difficulties, most of which could be swept away by new solid-state microelectronics. Today's A-6E has a totally different Norden APQ-148 multi-mode radar replacing the two previous sets and vastly outperforming either except possibly in the mission against small vehicles and other moving targets against a land background, and AMTI (airborne moving target indication) was added in 1981-83 for this purpose. There is no HUD but instead an HDD of remarkable character, the Kaiser AVA-1, which was the first display ever to use a CRT to show the pilot basic flight data such as aircraft attitude, nav information and weapon-delivery cues. The bright display includes synthetic terrain/sea and sky and can incorporate radar pictures and other data for use in basic all-weather flight, navigation, all forms of weapon delivery (including terrain following or terrain avoidance) and approach and landing. Basic navigation is by an INS updated by Litton's ASN-92 CAINS (carrier-aircraft INS). A-6Es have been fitted with TRAM (Target Recognition and Attack Multisensor). This adds an under-nose turret containing a FLIR and a laser. The navigator flies on the main radar and AVA-1 VDI (vertical display indicator) on which he acquires targets. He switches to the FLIR, using optical zoom to give an enhanced and magnified image. He then uses the laser to mark the target for "smart" weapons; alternatively the laser can detect a target marked by other lasers.

Armament: All attack versions, including EA-6A, five stores locations each rated at 3,600lb (1,6333kg) with maximum total load of 15,000lb (6,804kg); typical load thirty 500lb (227kg) bombs;

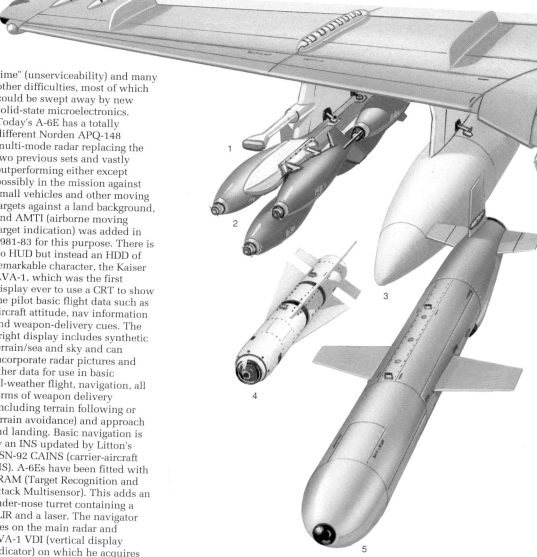

(EA-6B, KA-6D) none.

With the cancellation of the A-12A (planned as the A-6's replacement) the A-6 will have to soldier on much longer than had been intended. What has made the position doubly difficult is that the planned A-6F Intruder II programme, which among other things involved new composite-structure wings made by Boeing Military Airplanes, was cancelled to save money in 1989. It was

replaced by a plan to upgrade 167 (later reduced to 113) A-6Es to A-6G standard, with the Intruder II's digital avionics, but this too was abandoned. Instead the final 21 A-6Es have composite wings, and about 342 A-6Es are being upgraded with a new radar, new HUD, digital displays and controls, extra pylons and chaff/flare dispensers, and provision for HARM, Harpoon, Maverick and Amraam missiles.

Weapon provisions:
A. TRAM turret (IR, laser).
B. Pylon 3,600lb (1,633kg).
C. Pylon 3,600lb (1,633kg) or 250-gal (1,135-lit) tank.

Key to stores:
1. Forward emitting aerials of ALQ-41/ALQ-100 deception jamming system (not always carried).
2. Tandem triple low-drag GP bombs of 250 or 500lb (113 or 227kg) size.
3. 250gal (1,136lit) long-range tank.
4. AGM-65A standard Maverick; several other versions are compatible, and the Marine Corps uses the AGM-65E laser model.
5. AGM-1091 dual-role version of MRASM with DSMAC II (digital scene matching area correlation) and IIR guidance and large unitary warhead for anti-ship or land attack missions.
6. AGM-84A Harpoon long-range anti-ship missile
7. CBU Rockeye Mk 20 Mod 1 anti-armour cluster dispenser.
8. Mk 82 GP bomb of 500lb (227kg) with stand-off probe fuze.
9. Snakeye (Mk 92 GP bomb) fitted with tail retarder.
10. Mk 83 GP bomb, 500lb (227kg).

Combat avionics:
A. APQ-148 radar.
B. AVA-1 display.
C. ARA-48 UHF/ADF.
D. ARN-84 Tacan.
E. L-band UHF,
F. APN-153 doppler.
G. Jammer option ALQ-41 or -100.
H. L-band UHF.
J. FLIR and laser.

Grumman F-14 Tomcat

Origin: USA, first flight 21 December 1970.

Type: Two-seat carrier-based multi-role fighter.

Engines: (F-14A) two 20,900lb (9,480kg) thrust Pratt & Whitney TF30-414A afterburning turbofans. (A-Plus and D) two General Electric F110-400 afterburning turbofans each rated at 27,000lb (12,247kg).

Dimensions: Span (68° sweep) 38ft 2in (11.63m), (20° sweep) 64ft 1$\frac{1}{2}$in (19.54m); length 62ft 8in (19.1m); height 16ft (4.87m); wing area (spread) 565sqft (52.50m^2).

Weights: (A) Empty 40,104lb (18,191kg); internal fuel 16,200lb (7,348kg); loaded (clean) 58,715lb (26,632kg): maximum 74,349lb (33,724kg).

Performance: Maximum speed, 1,564mph (2,517km/h, Mach 2.34) at height, 910mph (1,464km/h, Mach 1.2) at sea level; initial climb at normal gross weight, over 30,000ft (9,144m)/min; service ceiling-over 56,000ft (17,067m); range (fighter with external fuel) about 2,000 miles (3,200km).

Background: Grumman was teamed with General Dynamics on the F-111B. When in 1968 it became evident that this programme might collapse work was urgently started on a possible replacement, starting from almost a clean sheet of paper. Items transferred bodily from the F-111B were the TF30 engine, Hughes AWG-9 radar and Hughes AIM-54 Phoenix long-range AAM. The F-14 itself was totally new and uncompromised, and was announced winner of the hastily contrived VFX competition on 15 January 1969. The first of six R&D prototypes flew on 21 December 1970. Unlike the F-111 no attempt was made to achieve commonality with any other aircraft, and the needs of the fighter sweep/escort, CAP (combat air patrol) and DLI (deck-launched intercept) missions were given priority.

Design: It is ironic that, though the F-14 has a swing wing able to take up any angle automatically between 20° and 68° according to the varying demands of the mission, its actual usage has been almost totally in the fighter/interceptor role. The main advantages of the swing wing for the F-14 are to reduce takeoff and landing speeds, facilitating cat (accelerated) launches at high gross weights, and to reduce fuel consumption in subsonic loiter and enable higher altitudes to be reached at low subsonic speeds. Though the two aircraft could hardly be more different in other ways, the F-14 and A-6 share a similar inlet duct, wing and main

landing gear geometry, the latter folding forwards alongside the duct into compartments faired under the wing roots. Unlike the A-6 the long fully augmented engines extend far downstream to variable nozzles at the extreme rear of the aircraft, widely separated throughout by fuselage tankage and with a canted vertical tail above each engine and with the airbrakes above and below in the wide gap between the nozzles. Pilot and naval flight officer sit well separated in a capacious tandem cockpit with a long one unit upward-hinged canopy. Aerodynamics are complex, with large fixed wing gloves carrying the outer-wing pivots 17ft 10in (5.43m) apart and incorporating retractable canards (called glove vanes) which are fully extended at maximum 68° sweep. Prolonged and dangerous problems with the original engine led to the decision to fit a different engine to a version called F-14A(Plus). This replaced the F-14A in production from November 1987; in addition 32 F-14As are being re-engined. The F110 engine is also fitted to the F-14D, which introduces an almost completely suite of digital avionics, including the APG-71 radar and a new IR search/track unit (see Avionics, below).

Avionics: The F-14 is believed to have been the world's first production aircraft with a lookdown shoot-down capability. This capability against low-flying aircraft was the last major gap that had to be closed in air defence, and it is claimed the F-14 has almost total capability against not only hostile aircraft but also sea-skimming anti-ship missiles. The AWG-9 radar is a hefty (1,293lb/586.5kg; 28cu ft/0.79m^3) liquid-cooled package with the vital coherent pulse-doppler mode for lookdown capability. It was also the first fighter radar with TWS (track while scan), enabling it at unprecedented ranges of well over 100 miles (161km) to detect, select and track more than 20 air targets, pick out the six most threatening and launch six Phoenix AAMs against these, each missile being code-keyed to its own target. The severe problem of long-range recognition is greatly assisted by the Northrop TCS, (TV camera set). With it fitted the only crippling shortcoming is the need to keep flying towards the enemy whilst providing target illumination for the AIM-7 medium-range AAMs. Kaiser provides the AVA-12 vertical situation display and electronically separate but mechanically integrated HUD, the latter having no combiner glass but simply using the inside face of the windscreen. Other kit includes

Above left: An F-14A serving with VF-84 "Jolly Rogers" as part of Carrier Air Group 8 aboard USS *Nimitz*.

Above: Two F-14As with wings fully swept. ECM gear is largely internal.

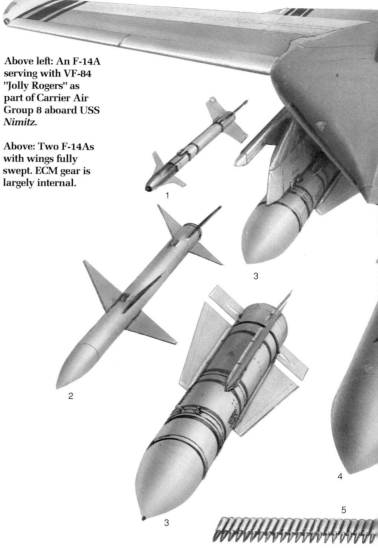

an expanded-memory digital computer, laser-gyro INS (being retrofitted when funds permit, and, after long delays, the definitive Westinghouse/ITT ASPJ (airborne self-protection jammer) and Hughes-ITT JTIDS combined with the Itek ALR-67 threat-warning system. Since 1982 Hughes has been retrofitting a completely new backseat all-digital display and control system, with programmable signal processor. Pending development of a dedicated recon aircraft 49 F-14s have been fitted to carry the TARPS (Tac Air Recon Pod System) with cameras and IR linescan.

Armament: One 20mm M61A-1 gun; fuselage pallets for four AIM-54 Phoenix AAMs or recesses for four AIM-7 Sparrow or (F-14D) AIM-120 Amraam; wing pylons for two Phoenix or Sparrow or AIM-120 plus

two AIM-9 Sidewinders or four Sidewinders. Attack weapons can replace AAMs to limit of 14,500lb (6,577kg). Plans to build 127 F-14Ds were cancelled in 1989, but it is still the intention that Grumman should remanufacture approximately 400 F-14A and A (Plus) aircraft to F-14D standard. In order to preserve its aircraft design and manufacturing capability Grumman has offered the Navy a new-generation Tomcat-21, with major advances in all areas. This is claimed to offer "90 per cent of the capability of the Navy ATF for 60 per cent of the cost". The Tomcat-21 is also one of the few possible replacements for the cancelled A12A stealth attack aircraft, especially in the reconnaissance role.

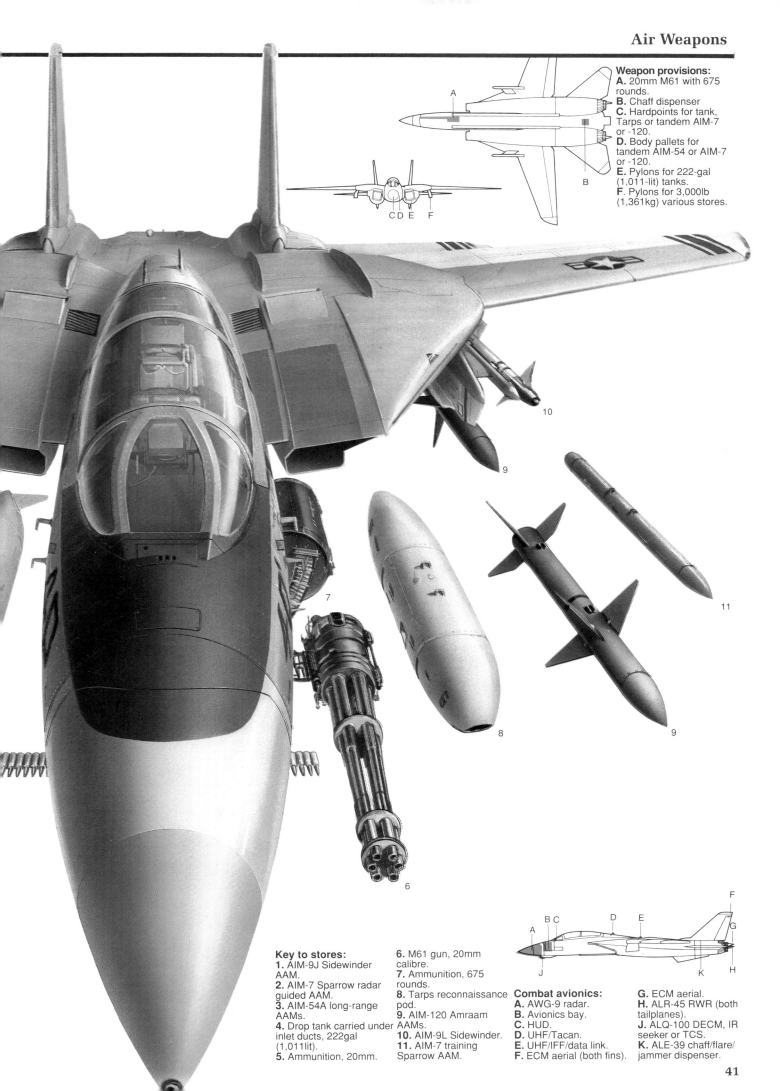

Weapon provisions:
A. 20mm M61 with 675 rounds.
B. Chaff dispenser
C. Hardpoints for tank, Tarps or tandem AIM-7 or -120.
D. Body pallets for tandem AIM-54 or AIM-7 or -120.
E. Pylons for 222-gal (1,011-lit) tanks.
F. Pylons for 3,000lb (1,361kg) various stores.

Key to stores:
1. AIM-9J Sidewinder AAM.
2. AIM-7 Sparrow radar guided AAM.
3. AIM-54A long-range AAMs.
4. Drop tank carried under inlet ducts, 222gal (1,011lit).
5. Ammunition, 20mm.
6. M61 gun, 20mm calibre.
7. Ammunition, 675 rounds.
8. Tarps reconnaissance pod.
9. AIM-120 Amraam AAMs.
10. AIM-9L Sidewinder.
11. AIM-7 training Sparrow AAM.

Combat avionics:
A. AWG-9 radar.
B. Avionics bay.
C. HUD.
D. UHF/Tacan.
E. UHF/IFF/data link.
F. ECM aerial (both fins).
G. ECM aerial.
H. ALR-45 RWR (both tailplanes).
J. ALQ-100 DECM, IR seeker or TCS.
K. ALE-39 chaff/flare/jammer dispenser.

Lockheed F-117A "Senior Trend"

Origin: USA,

Type: Single seat attack fighter

Engines: Two non-afterburning General Electric F404 F1D2 turbofans, rating, c.12,000lb (5,440kg)

Dimensions: Span 43ft 4in (13.2m); length 65ft 11in (20.1m); height 12ft 5in (3.78m)

Weights:: Empty: 29,500lb (13,380kg); loaded: c.48,000lb (21,800kg): max: 52,500lb (23,800kg)

Performance: Max speed, high subsonic; tactical radius; 800-1,200nm (1,500-2,200km)

Background: As a result of the successful flight testing of the XST technology demonstrators starting in 1977, President Carter was able to authorise the development of a production stealth fighter in the following year. The project was codenamed "Senior Trend". Although probably based on the general configuration of the XST, the F-117A was scaled up in size. This would give a militarily useful range, and allow the carriage of operational sensors and stores. The XST had been powered by a pair of General Electric J85 turbojets, and was probably short of thrust. The new fighter's increased size and weight required a more powerful engine, so GE was given a contract to develop a non-afterburning F1D2 version of the F404 turbofan, the engine that powers the F/A-18 Hornet. The aircraft that project head Ben Rich and his "Skunk Works" team created was of very different shape to the widely- projected "F-19" seen in mid1980s books and magazines. To keep radar cross-section (RCS) to a minimum, extensive use was made of faceting, a technique that confines radar echoes from the airframe to a small number of narrow beams which an enemy radar will have difficulty in detecting. Straight lines and flat surfaces rather than curves dominate the aircraft's configuration. Its angular lines make one half-seriously wonder whether Ben Rich had impounded every set of French curves owned by "Skunk Works" personnel. The sawtooth edges on features such as the canopy also form part of the faceting scheme. The F-117A was developed too soon to take large-scale advantage of radar-absorbent structural (RAS) materials. Its structure is made from aluminium, on top of which the radar-absorbent material (RAM) is applied. This takes the form of RAM tiles, plus a coating of ferrite-based "iron-ball" paint. Other probable RCS- reduction measures include keeping the use of metal fasteners to a minimum, and careful electrical bonding of all structural elements to eliminate small gaps which might re-radiate RF energy. Conventional inlets are prominent radar targets and to keep radar energy out of the F-117A inlets, both are fitted with a screen consisting of 22 vertical slats and 35 horizontal. These are impervious to the 10cm signals from search radars, and greatly attenuate 3cm signals from tracking and airborne intecept radars. Total area is well above the three square feet or so of the inlets on the F/A-18 Hornet, but despite this, auxiliary blow-in doors on the upper side of each inlet are used on takeoff. Part of this extra airflow is diverted to flow around the engines, mixing with and cooling the exhaust gases.

Below: An F-117A approaching the boom of a KC-10 Extender to refuel before deploying to the Gulf. The nose FLIR is clearly seen through its mesh cover.

Right: A fine Lockheed publicity shot, released as the F-117A first came out of the shadows to start daylight training missions. The slot outlets at the rear mix hot engine gasses with cool by-pass air and eject this mixture in a diffuse stream.

The twin F404 engines are located about halfway down the length of the fuselage, access for servicing being via bellymounted engine bay doors. After being mixed with inlet air, the engine efflux is ducted to the 6ft (1.8m) wide 6in (15cm) high slot outlets on the rear fuselage. These release the gases in wide flat "beavertail" plumes, increasing the rate at which the gases cool. Approaching F-117As emit a distinctive high-pitched whine, while rearward noise is a muffled rumble. The lower lip of each outlet is extended, and slightly upturned. Probably made from heat-resistant ceramic tiles, it hides the slot from

the IR seekers of ground-based weapons such as SA-7 Grail. If fitted with conventional flying controls, the F-117A would be near-impossible to fly, given its odd shape and tiny tail surfaces. To get around the problem, it is fitted with a quadruplex digital fly-by-wire flight control system based on that of the F-16. F-117A crews are reported to have dubbed the aircraft the "Wobblin' Goblin". Two FLIR (forward-looking infrared) systems are carried -one with an optical turret located in a cavity just below the front panel of the canopy, the other in a similar cavity on the belly of the aircraft just to the port side of the front portion of the nose gear door. Both are thought to

incorporate laser designators, allowing the aircraft to designate its own targets for laser-guided bomb (LGB) attack. Like the intakes, these cavities are screened to keep radar signals out, in this case, by a fine mesh similar in pitch to that used on antiglare screens fitted to personal computers. Mesh screens are also fitted to various vents on the top surfaces of the fuselage. First flight of an F-117A took place in June 1981, and the type was ready for operational service by the fall of 1983. First operator was the 4450th Tactical Group, which became operational in October 1983. This consisted of three squadrons - the 4450th, 4451st, and 4452nd TS. The designation "stealth fighter" is partly a misnomer; the aircraft is essentially a strike aircraft designed to fly close to a target at slow speed, launch a guided missile or 'smart' bomb, then turn away. In terms of speed or agility it is no match for a traditional fighter. Distinctly subsonic, it could be a vulnerable target if caught by an enemy fighter. To avoid this, it normally operates at night, conditions under which it is virtually undetectable. Initial flight operations were conducted under cover of darkness. When the shape of the aircraft was declassified late in 1988, the USAF was finally able to operate the aircraft by day. The 4450th Tactical Group, was reclassified as the 37th TFW, its three squadrons becoming the 415th TFS "Nightstalkers", 416th TFS "Ghostriders", and 417th TFS "Bandits". As its combat record in the Gulf has shown, the F-117A is probably the most effective manned penetrator in the world for tactical strike missions. In terms of radar penetration, the aircraft has met its specifications, but at a price of restricted speed and manoeuvrability. Its successors such as the Advanced Tactical Fighter will combine stealth with improved speed, altitude and manoeuvrability.

Above: This artwork reveals what must be one of the strangest shapes to fly since the 1930s. Flat panels on the fuselage and wings reflect radar energy in a few carefully controlled directions, away from the transmitting radar. The metal skin is covered in "iron ball" absorptive paint with RAM applied to many areas. The small protrusion along the fuselage side is a radar reflector so that the F-117A shows up on air traffic control radars during peacetime training missions.

McDonnell Douglas A-4 Skyhawk

Origin: USA, first flight 22 June 1954.

Type: Single-seat attack bomber; OA, two-seat FAC; TA, dual-control trainer.

Engine: (E, J) 8,500lb (3,856kg) Pratt & Whitney J52-6 turbojet; (F, G, H, K) 9,300lb (4,218kg) J52-8A; (M, N, Y) 11,200lb (5,080kg) J52-408A.

Dimensions: Span 27ft 6in (8.38m); length (E,F,G,H,K,L,P,Q,S) 40ft 1½in (12.22m), (M, N, Y) 40ft 3¼in (12.27m), (OA, and TA, excluding probe) 42ft 7¼in (12.98m); height 15ft (4.57m), (TA series 15ft 3in, 4.64m).

Weights: Empty (E) 9,284lb (4,211kg), (typical single-seat, eg Y) 10,465lb (4,747kg), (TA-4F) 10,602 (4,809kg); maximum loaded (shipboard) 24,500lb (11,113kg); (land-based) 27,420lb (12,437kg)

Performance: Maximum speed (clean) (E) 685mph (1,102km/h), (Y) 670mph (1,078km/h), (TA-4F) 675mph (1,086km/h); maximum speed (4,000lb 1,814kg bomb load) (Y) 645mph (1,038km/h); initial climb (Y) 8,440ft (2,572m)/min; service ceiling (all, clean) about 49,000ft (14,935m); range (clean, or with 4,000lb weapons and max fuel, all late versions) about 920 miles (1,480km); maximum range (Y) 2,055 miles (3,307km).

Background: Douglas Aircraft's El Segundo plant was awarded the prototype contract for a new tactical attack jet for the US Navy and Marine Corps in 1952 after chief engineer Ed Heinemann had convinced the Bureau of Aeronautics his design would meet the challenging specification and yet weigh just half the suggested 30,000lb (13,607kg). The prototype flew in June 1954 and not only fully met the requirements but set a world speed record and proved such a good basis for improvement that the A-4 remained in production 26 years.

Design: The requirements were based on Korean experience and called for the maximum payload/range and equipment for carrier operation, but not for all-weather avionics. The A-4 bristled with novel features intended to reduce weight and complexity. The main gears, tall enough for large underwing clearance, fold forwards to lie under the main wing box

without cutting into it. The wing is a curved-tip delta so small it does not need to fold, the entire box being an integral tank and the leading edges having full-span slats. The cockpit was put high above the nose for good view, and in the final versions the canopy was enlarged. There are large airbrakes on the rear fuselage, flight controls are powered, and the unique rudder hastily redesigned to eliminate "buzz" by having a single skin on the centreline with ribs on the outside remained in production to the 2,960th and last aircraft in 1980!

Avionics: The basic design was tailored to the attack mission exclusively, and concentration on saving weight and complexity resulted in an austere avionic fit in early versions, augmented later by simple nose radar offering mapping, ranging and terrain-avoidance, and later with Labs (for toss-bombing), improved auto flight control and heading references, doppler, tacan and radar altimeter. Many items of nav/com avionics had to be packaged in the added "camel hump" above the fuselage. The most important model, developed for the US Marines only, is the A-4M of 1970 with numerous improvements throughout the aircraft including the Hughes ARBS (Angle/Rate Bombing System), comprehensive radar warning, internal ECM jammers and payload dispensers and a modern HUD. The extra quipment called for an uprated engine-driven generator and a back-up windmill generator extended below the forward fuselage. Probably the most effective Skyhawks of all are the A-4Ns of Israel's air force, and the earlier Israeli aircraft which have been brought up to almost the same standard using Israeli avionics and airframe modifications. About 100 (of 267 single-seat and 27 two-seat) remain in Heyl Ha'Avir service. Their most obvious distinguishing feature is an extended jetpipe to reduce vulnerability to IR-homing missiles. Locally installed manoeuvre flaps are fitted under the wings.

Armament: Standard on most versions, two 20mm Mk 12 cannon, each with 200 rounds; (H, N, and optional on other export versions) two 30mm DEFA 553, each with 150 rounds. Pylons under fuselage and

wings for total ordnance load of (E, F, G, H, K, L, P, Q, S) 8,200lb (3,720kg); (M, N, Y) 9,155lb (4,153kg). McDonnell Douglas have maintained a profitable business modifying or refurbishing A-4s for export, but this is a diminishing activity and the last US model, the conversion of TA-4F trainers into OA-4M FAC (Forward Air Control) models was handled in house by the US Navy. No funding exists for further updating of US Marine Corps aircraft, but substantial stocks of airworthy ex-US Navy and Marines aircraft exist and should they find customers they are almost certain to be updated. The A-4 did

well in the Falklands campaign, flown on purely visual attacks against easily visible ships with free-fall bombs dropped from such low level they often failed to explode. The aircraft were refurbished A-4Bs and Cs with simple avionics, but with the important addition of Ferranti ISIS weapon-delivery sights. Israel Bedek Division continues to market major Skyhawk upgrades, with the jetpipe extension mentioned previously plus avionics improvements, chaff/flare dispensers, wing spoilers, extra pylons, a brake chute, 30mm guns and many other changes.

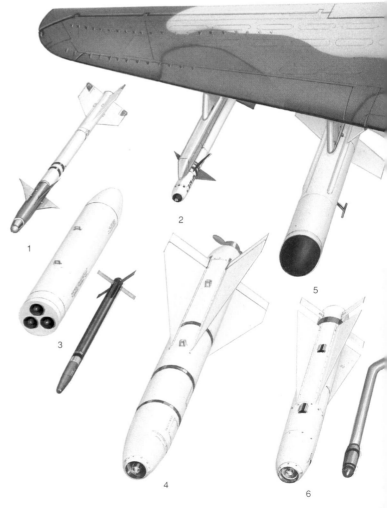

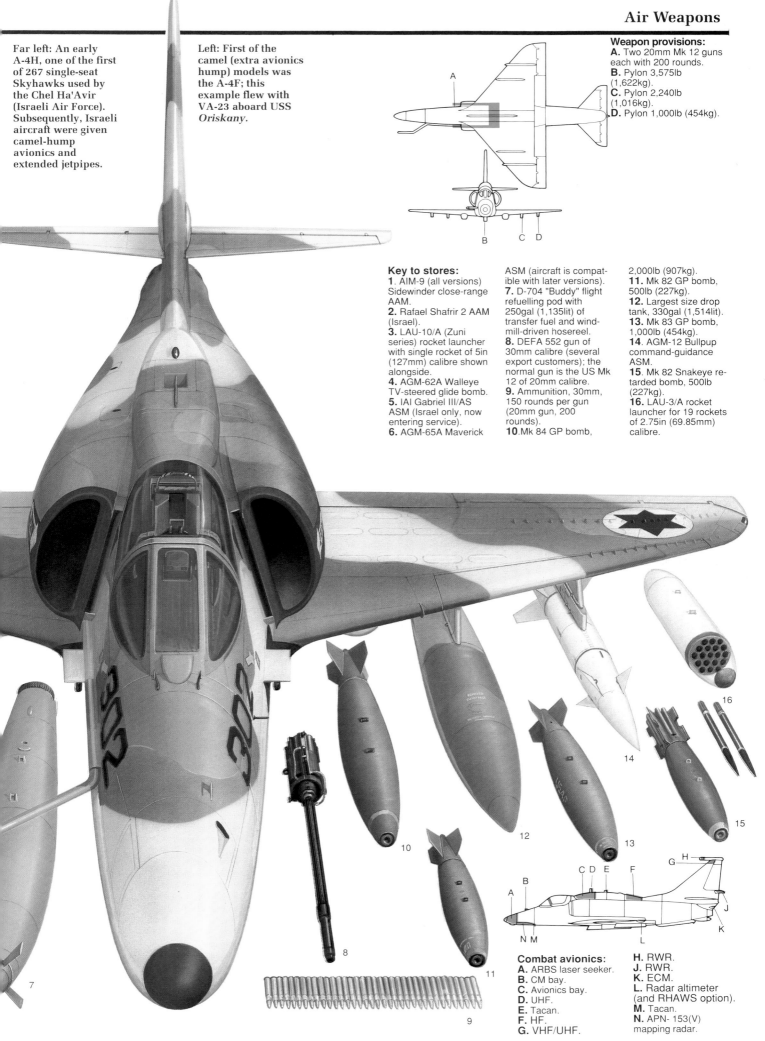

Far left: An early A-4H, one of the first of 267 single-seat Skyhawks used by the Chel Ha'Avir (Israeli Air Force). Subsequently, Israeli aircraft were given camel-hump avionics and extended jetpipes.

Left: First of the camel (extra avionics hump) models was the A-4F; this example flew with VA-23 aboard USS *Oriskany*.

Weapon provisions:
A. Two 20mm Mk 12 guns each with 200 rounds.
B. Pylon 3,575lb (1,622kg).
C. Pylon 2,240lb (1,016kg).
D. Pylon 1,000lb (454kg).

Key to stores:
1. AIM-9 (all versions) Sidewinder close-range AAM.
2. Rafael Shafrir 2 AAM (Israel).
3. LAU-10/A (Zuni series) rocket launcher with single rocket of 5in (127mm) calibre shown alongside.
4. AGM-62A Walleye TV-steered glide bomb.
5. IAI Gabriel III/AS ASM (Israel only, now entering service).
6. AGM-65A Maverick ASM (aircraft is compatible with later versions).
7. D-704 "Buddy" flight refuelling pod with 250gal (1,135lit) of transfer fuel and windmill-driven hosereel.
8. DEFA 552 gun of 30mm calibre (several export customers); the normal gun is the US Mk 12 of 20mm calibre.
9. Ammunition, 30mm, 150 rounds per gun (20mm gun, 200 rounds).
10. Mk 84 GP bomb, 2,000lb (907kg).
11. Mk 82 GP bomb, 500lb (227kg).
12. Largest size drop tank, 330gal (1,514lit).
13. Mk 83 GP bomb, 1,000lb (454kg).
14. AGM-12 Bullpup command-guidance ASM.
15. Mk 82 Snakeye retarded bomb, 500lb (227kg).
16. LAU-3/A rocket launcher for 19 rockets of 2.75in (69.85mm) calibre.

Combat avionics:
A. ARBS laser seeker.
B. CM bay.
C. Avionics bay.
D. UHF.
E. Tacan.
F. HF.
G. VHF/UHF.
H. RWR.
J. RWR.
K. ECM.
L. Radar altimeter (and RHAWS option).
M. Tacan.
N. APN-153(V) mapping radar.

McDonnell Douglas/BAe AV-8B Harrier II

Origin: USA with UK principal subcontractor, first flight 5 November 1981.

Type: STOVL multi-role attack (probably also reconnaissance).

Engine: One Rolls-Royce Pegasus vectored-thrust turbofan, (RAF) 21,750lb (9,866kg) Pegasus 105, (USMC) 23,800lb (10,796kg) F402-408.

Dimensions: Span 30ft 4in (9.25m); length 46ft 4in (14.12m); height 11ft 8in (3.56m); wing area 230sqft (21.37m^2).

Weights: Empty 12,750lb (5,783kg); maximum (VTO) 19,550 (8,867kg), (STO) 31,000lb (14,061kg).

Performance: Maximum Mach number in level flight 0.93 (at sea level, 673mph, 1,083km/h); combat radius (STO, seven Mk82 bombs plus tanks, lo profile, no loiter) 748 miles (1,204km); ferry range 2,418 miles 3,891km).

Background: One of the modern world's most significant warplanes, the AV-8B Harrier was developed at St Louis by McDonnell Douglas from the original British Harrier to meet the specific needs of the US Marine Corps. Until 1975 it had seemed obvious that further development of the Harrier would be either British or a 50/50 partnership with the USA, but unfortunately in that year the then British government said there was "not enough common ground" for collaboration. The inevitable result is that the Harrier II is a US programme, but because of its purchase for the RAF the UK industry does have a share (40 per cent in US/UK aircraft, 25 per cent in sales to other countries).

Design: The needs of the Marines revolved entirely around close support of friendly ground troops in amphibious landings. In contrast the RAF was extremely interested in air combat and reconnaissance and these were allowed to exert a small influence on the design, in particular in increasing instantaneous rate of turn. Almost every part of the original British design has been refined to improve vertical lift or reduce weight or the need for maintenance. Principal new item is the wing, a one-piece structure mainly of graphite-epoxy composite and with a deep supercritical section, increased span and area and reduced sweep. It gives better lift at all speeds, provides more pylon space and increases internal fuel capacity by 50 per cent. British Aerospace research added the curved LERX (leading-edge root extension) which increases rate of turn. McDonnell Douglas contributed the very large slotted flaps which are lowered for vertical lift, the rearranged geometry of the wing and extended zero-scarf (square-cut) nozzles giving a STOL lift gain of over 6,700lb (3,039kg). Other features include improved engine inlets, improved LIDs (lift-improved devices) under the belly, raised cockpit giving more interior space and better pilot view,

and a generally strengthened structure. Despite this the equipped empty weight is almost the same as the original Harrier's.

Avionics: The chief weapon-delivery system in both the AV-8B (USMC) and Harrier GR.5 (RAF) is the Hughes ARBS (angle/rate bombing system) in the nose, which comprises a dual TV/laser target seeker and tracker linked to the advanced Smiths HUD via a computer. Other new features are an advanced autopilot with two-axis stabilization computer which was used in December 1982 for an automatic vertical landing, Ferranti INS, Garrett digital air-data computer, Conrac fibre-optics CNI (com/nav/IFF) data converter, radar altimeter, Bendix APX-100 IFF, forward/rear RWR installation and Goodyear ALE-39 chaff/flare dispenser in the underside of the rear fuselage. In the greatly improved cockpit is a CRT multifunction display and (GR.5) moving-map nav display. The GR.5 has the usual nose-mounted camera and a British RWR and, it is expected, internal ECM.

GR.5 has a Zeus comprehensive internal ECM system, incorporating a multimode jammer linked with the warning system. In the tailboom is

Above: An AV-8B Harrier II operating from NAS Patuxent River on ordnance release tests.

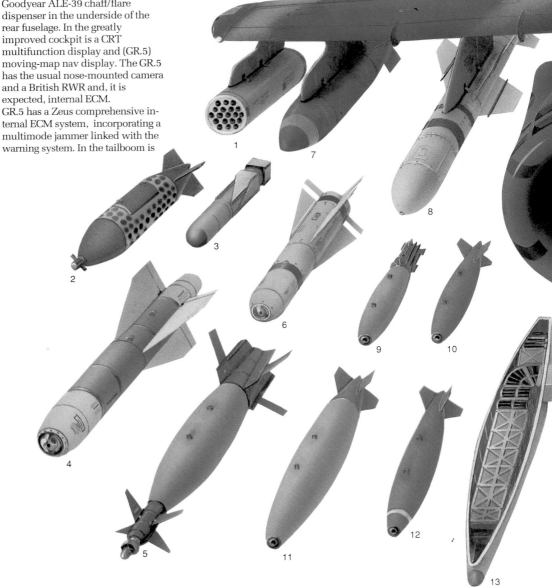

an MAW (missile approach warning) receiver. The GR.7 night attack version has a new HUD/HDD, digital colour map display, Flir and cockpit compatible with night-vision goggles. The Night Attack AV-8B has almost exactly the same features, the FLIR causing a bump above the nose in both aircraft. The GR.7 in addition has two EW antenna blisters under

the extreme nose. The TAV-8B is a dual-pilot trainer with a substantially modified airframe with only two underwing pylons. The Harrier T.10 is the corresponding RAF aircraft.

Armament: The AV-8B has a single General Electric GAU-12/U Equaliser 25mm five-barrel gun with 300 rounds. A single weapon attach-

ment rated at 1,000lb (454kg) is on the centreline, and there are three pylons under each wing. Maximum external stores load is 9,200lb (4,173kg). The RAF GR.5 and GR.7 have two Royal Ordnance 25mm guns each with 100 rounds. Weapon attachments are the same as for the AV-8B with the addition of an additional pylon for a self-defence Sidewinder.

Key to stores:
1. LAU-3/19 rocket pod.
2. Beluga.
3. Wasp ASM (folded).
4. AGM-72 Walleye ASM
5. GBU-10E/B Paveway II smart bomb.
6. Laser Maverick ASM.
7. UK GP bomb, 1,000lb (454kg).
8. AGM-84A Harpoon anti-ship missile.
9. Mk 82 Snakeye.
10. Mk 82 GP bomb.
11. Mk 84 2,000lb (907kg) GP bomb.

Weapon provisions:
A. GAU-12/U gun.
B. Fairing for 25mm ammunition .
C. Fuselage pylon, 1,000lb (454kg).
D. Inboard wing pylon, 2,000lb (907kg).
E. Centre wing pylon, 1,000lb (454kg).
F. Outboard wing pylon, 630lb (286kg).

12. Mk 83 GP bomb.
13. Gun magazine, 300 rounds (right pod)
14. GAU-12/U 25mm gun (left pod) (RAF Harrier GR.5 replaces items 13, 14 by 30mm Aden guns).
15. AGM-12 Bullpup ASM.
16. Combat tank, 100-gal (4551it).

17. 30mm Gepod gun pod.
18. BAe Dynamics Sea Eagle anti-ship missile.
19. BL.755 cluster bomb.
20. AIM-9L Sidewinder AAM.
21. Durandal anti-runway weapon.
22. GBU-15CWW (cruciform wing weapon).

Combat avionics:
A. ARBS.
B. IFF.
C. RWR.
D. VHF/UHF CNI.

E. Radar altimeter (chaff dispenser is adjacent).
F. Tacan.
G. ILS.

McDonnell Douglas F-4 Phantom II

Origin: USA, first flight 27 May 1958.

Type: Originally carrier-based all-weather interceptor; now all-weather multi-role fighter for ship or land operation; (F-4G) EW defence suppression; (RF) all-weather reconnaissance.

Engines: (C, D, RF) two 17,000lb (7,711kg) General Electric J79-15 turbojets with afterburner; (E, F, G) 17,900lb (8,120kg) J79-17; J, N, S) 17,900lb J79-10; (K, M) 20,515lb (9,305kg) Rolls-Royce Spey 202/203 augmented turbofans.

Dimensions: Span 38ft 5in (11.7m); length (C, D, J, N, S) 58ft 3in (17.76m), (E, G, F and all RF versions) 62ft 11in or 63ft (19.2m), (K, M) 57ft 7in (17.55m); height (all) 16ft 3in (4.96m); wing area 530sqft (49.2m²).

Weights: Empty (C, D, J, N) 28,000lb (l12,700kg), (E, F and RF) 29,000lb (13,150kg), (G, K, M) 31,00lb (14,060kg); maximum loaded (C, D, J, K, M, N, RF) 58,000lb (26,308kg), (E, G, F) 60,630lb (27,502kg).

Performance: Maximum speed with Sparrow missiles only (low) 910mph (1,464km/h, Mach 1.19) with J79 engines, 920mph (1,480km/h) with Spey, (high) 1,500mph (2,414km/h, Mach 2.27) with J79, 1,386mph (2,230km/h) with Spey; initial climb, typically 28,000ft (8,534m)/min with J79, 32,000ft (,753m)/min with Spey; service ceiling, over 60,000ft (18,287m) with J79, 60,000ft with Spey; range on internal fuel (no weapons) about 1,750 miles (2,816km); ferry range with external fuel, typically 2,300 miles (3,700km), (E and variants), 2,600 miles (4,184km).

Background: Company studies in the mid-1950s centred on the AH-1 attack aircraft with two of the new J79 engines and armed with cannon and a heavy ordnance load on 11 pylons. But in April 1955 the Navy had the project completely changed into the F4H fleet defence fighter with only a single pylon (for a large drop tank) and no guns, but equipped with a powerful radar, two seats and with belly recesses for four AAMs. In this form the prototype flew in May 1958, but the tremendous capability and performance cried out to be fully used and gradually the pylons were put back and, as late as 1967, an internal gun. Production totalled 5,211 airframes.

Design: Fundamental to the F-4 was the tremendous propulsion system of two afterburning J79s with optimized variable ramp inlets and fully controllable nozzles surrounding the variable primary afterburner nozzles. The disturbance caused by the installation of the much more powerful Spey engine in British Phantoms actually resulted in these versions being slower. The wing is so acutely tapered it is almost a delta, but divided into a flat centre section and sharply dihedralled outer panels with extended-chord leading edges and large dogtooth discontinuities.

The F-4E and related versions have powerful slats, and all have blown flaps and powered ailerons inboard of the hinge axis, the outer panels having fixed trailing edges. The fuselage is broad (even broader in British aircraft because of the greater airflow) with six or seven fuel cells filling the space between and above the engines (other tanks fill the wing between the front and main spars as far out as the hinge). The tail has a low aspect-ratio vertical surface, side area being augmented by the acute anhedral of the slab tailplanes. US Navy/Marines F-4J, N, S and variants, and RAF F-4K and M Phantoms have inflight-refuelling probes; USAF F-4E and G Phantoms, but not export versions or Japanese EJs, have a dorsal boom-receptacle.

Avionics: All Phantoms have nose radar, varying from giant liquid-cooled Westinghouse sets with 32in (813mm) dishes in Navy and RAF models, through the solid-state Hughes APQ-120 in the slimmer nose of the F-4E variants to the small APQ-99 in most RF recon models. Some have a sensitive IR detector in a pod under the nose, while other equipment includes autopilot, various nav systems, CNI package, radar altimeter, air-data computer, INS (RAF FGR.2) and such extra sensors as Northrop Tiseo and a succession of Pave-series laser designators culminating for the USAF in 180 F-4Es and 60 RF-4Cs being converted to carry the comprehensive Pave Tack with Flir for target acquisition and a laser for designation and ranging.

Armament: (All versions except RF models which have no armament) four AIM-7 Sparrow or Sky Flash (later Amraam) air-to-air missiles recessed under fuselage; inner wing pylons can carry two more AIM-7 or four AIM-9 Sidewinder missiles; in addition E versions except RF have internal 20mm M61 multi-barrel gun, and virtually all versions can carry the same gun in external centreline pod; all except RF have centreline and four wing pylons for tanks, bombs or other stores to total weight of 16,000lb (7,257kg). Today all F-4s, especially those based on the E, remain useful multirole aircraft with air-combat patrol endurance exceeding 3h, good stand-off kill capability, fair avionics and excellent capability to carry advanced sensors and weapons. The F-4G is the standard USAF Wild Weasel tactical defence-suppression aircraft with the APR-38 EW system for detecting, analysing and locating hostile emitters and with weapons such as HARM and Maverick for their suppression. It is probable that other air forces may use available F-4 airframes as the basis for their own future EW aircraft. In the surface-attack role the F-4 is still effective and lacks only modern cockpit display systems and, in the case of almost all existing aircraft, adequate sensors and aiming systems which, with minor difficulties, can be added. It is only in the air-combat role that the basic outdated nature of the aircraft and engine is giving rise to problems. The F-4 has never been able to turn with a MiG-21 and the characteristics of most F-4 radars and AIM-7 missiles (which demand target illumination until impact) are no longer fully competitive. Possibilities long under discussion include retrofitting RAF aircraft with Foxhunter radar and Luftwaffe F-4Fs with APG-65 or APG-66, the latter with a small L-band illuminator matched to the future AMRAAM missile.

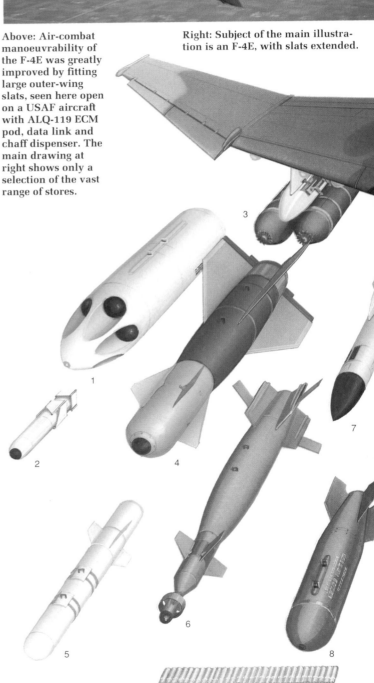

Above: Air-combat manoeuvrability of the F-4E was greatly improved by fitting large outer-wing slats, seen here open on a USAF aircraft with ALQ-119 ECM pod, data link and chaff dispenser. The main drawing at right shows only a selection of the vast range of stores.

Right: Subject of the main illustration is an F-4E, with slats extended.

Key to stores:
1. Wasp tandem launch pod.
2. Wasp missile (folded).
3. British BL.755 cluster dispensers.
4. GBU-14 Cruciform-Wing Weapon.

ammunition drum.
11. 20mm ammunition, typically about 639 rounds.
12. ALQ-119 jammer pod.
13. BAe Sky Flash AAM.
14. AGM-65D Maverick.

Weapon provisions:
A. 20mm M61 gun with 639 rounds.
B. Pylon 3,500lb (1,588kg).
C. Recess for AIM-7 or -120.
D. Pylon 3,500lb 91,588kg0.
E. Pylon 2,240lb (1,016kg)

5. Durandal anti-airfield weapon.
6. GBU-16B/B (1,000lb) Paveway II smart bomb.
7. AGM-78 ARM anti-radar missile.
8. TAL cluster bomb, 551lb (250kg) (Israel).
9. AIM-9L Sidewinder.
10. M61 20mm gun with

15. AIM-7 Sparrow medium-range AAM.
16. Mk 82 Snakeye retarded bomb.
17. AGM-88A Harm (Wild Weasel F-4G only).
18. AGM-12 Bullpup ASM.
19. GE 30mm Gepod (gun installation).

20. Mk 82 GP bomb of 500lb (227kg).
21. Mk 83 GP bomb of 1,000lb (454kg).
22. Mk 84 GP bomb of 2,000lb (907kg).
23. AGM-45 Shrike (F-4G only).
24. AIM-1 20A Amraam advanced AAM.

Combat avionics:
A. PQW-120 radar.
B. IFF.
C. Tacan.
D. VHF.
E. RWR.
F. Forward RWR.
G. Ranging aerial (right wing).
H. Avionics bays.
J. VHF/UHF.

McDonnell Douglas F-15 Eagle

Origin: USA, first flight 27 July 1972.

Type: Air-superiority fighter with secondary attack role.

Engines: A/B Two 23,930lb (10,855kg) thrust Pratt & Whitney F100-100 afterburning turbofans; (C/D) 23,450lb (10,637kg) F100-220; (E) F100-220 or 29,000lb (13,154kg) General Electric F110-129.

Dimensions: Span 42ft 9³/₄in (13.05m); length (all) 63ft 9in (19.43m), height 18ft 7¹/₂in (5.68m); wing area 608sqft (56.5m²)

Weights: Empty (basic equipped) 28,000lb (12,700kg); loaded (interception mission, max internal fuel plus four AIM-7, F-15A) 41,500lb (18,824kg), (C) 44,500lb (20,185kg); maximum with max external load (A) 56,500lb (25,628kg), (C) 68,000lb (30,845kg).

Performance: Maximum speed (over 36,000ft/10,973m with no external load except four AIM-7), 1,653mph (2,660km/h, Mach 2.5), with max external load or at low level, not published; initial climb (clean) over 50,000ft (15,239m) /min, (max wt) 29,000ft (8.8km)/min; service ceiling 65,000ft (19,811m); takeoff run (clean) 900ft (274m); landing run (clean, without brake chute) 2,500ft (762m); ferry range with three external tanks, over 2,878 miles (4,631km), (with FAST packs also) over 3,450 miles (5,562km).

Background: USAF funding for a new fighter was sought in 1965. McDonnell Douglas was selected on 23 December 1969, by which time the MiG-25 had thrown a scare into the Pentagon. Unlike the Soviet aircraft the F-15 was designed for unrivalled capability in close combat. Until 1976 there was hardly any attempt to explore missions other than air-to-air.

Design: Basic features include two new augmented turbofan engines in a wide body rear fuselage, a shoulder-high wing of 5.9/3 per cent thickness with sharp taper on the leading edge and conical camber outboard, a plain fixed leading edge, plain flaps and ailerons, structural beams projecting aft of the engine nozzles to carry the widely spaced vertical tails with fixed fins and low tailplanes with large inboard dogteeth (the latter become rolling stabilators at hi-AOA), and neat main gears with single high-pressure tyres. The two-dimensional external-compression inlets have automatically scheduled variable throats and spill doors, and at high AOA the entire inlet rotates nose-down about a hinge at the top. After landing the nose is held high with the large dorsal airbrake open; there is no braking parachute or any thrust-reverse. Some 26.5 per cent of the structure weight is titanium, including most of the rear fuselage whose engine bays are uncluttered and designed for easy maintenance and rapid engine changes. Even the original F-15A has no less than 11,635lb (5,277kg) internal fuel; the 600 US-gal drop tank was a new design, and the FAST (Fuel And Sensor, Tactical)

packs shown in the main illustration are large containers which conform to the sides of the fuselage and add a further 9,750lb (4,423kg) of usable fuel as well as providing space for extra sensors and EW equipment. FAST packs were introduced with the F-15C which replaced the F-15A in June 1979 and apart from avionic improvements has 13,455lb (6,103kg) of internal fuel. The corresponding two-seaters, with unchanged internal fuel are the F-15B and D. Between 1987 and June 1993 the USAF is receiving 200 F-15E dual-role (fighter/ attack) Eagles. These are two- seaters, the backseater being a weapon-system officer. Features include a strengthened structure, almost completely new avionics and a very wide range of external weapon loads.

Avionics: The Hughes APG-63 was designed for the F-15 as a multi-mode PD (pulse-doppler) radar optimised for A/A operation, and with all controls conforming to the concept of Hotas (hands on throttle and stick) which the F-15 pioneered. The main HDD is a VSD (vertical situation display), with a 4 x 4 graticule on which can be set various range scales and alphanumerical information together with digitally processed symbology showing targets and nothing else (unless the pilot calls up other pictorial information). The information is to a large extent repeated on the HUD which again can operate in various modes and in current aircraft serve vital functions in air/ground weapon delivery. Radar mode is selected by the AR (air refuelling disconnect) button, which in the forward position gives a boresight mode and when pulled aft gives Supersearch which scans the HUD field of view and locks on to the first detected target, which is likely to be the most threatening. Long-range search is the chief surveillance mode with distances to 160nm (296km) and interleaved high and medium PRFs. Pulse is a low-PRF non-doppler mode for shoot-up (anti-MiG-25) engagements. The outstanding CC (central computer) set a new standard in presenting processed information on the HUD and the F-15A was a revelation when it entered service in 1974 in enabling the pilot to fly Hotas and select any radar or HUD mode and any weapon (gun, SRMs or MRMs) without taking his eyes off the target. Today's F-15C has a programmable radar processor and larger radar memory (from 26K to 96K). All USAF F-15s have the Loral ALR-56 RWR system mounted internally, Northrop ALQ-135 internal counter-measures set and Hazeltine APX-76 IFF.

Armament: One 20mm M61A-1 gun with 940 rounds; fuselage flank ejectors for four AIM-7 Sparrows or AIM-120 Amraam; centreline pylon for 4,500lb (2,041 kg) or 500gal (2,273lit) tank; other pylons rated as with 3-view,

Above: This F-15 was modified by McDD as the F-15E Enhanced Tactical Fighter.

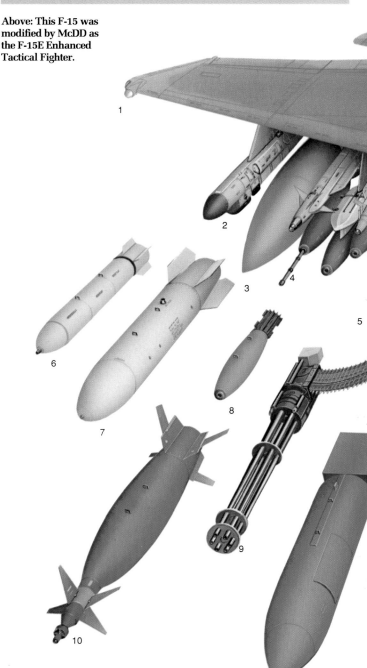

inboards having provision for paired AIM-9 Sidewinders and being plumbed for 500gal tanks. Total weapon load (excluding gun) 16,000lb (7,258kg). Enhanced Eagle F-15E has expanded capability and greater diversity of stores (see main illustration) to maximum of 24,500lb (11,113kg).

First flown in September 1988 the F-15S/MTD (Stol and Manoeuvring Technology Demonstrator) has large powered

canard foreplanes, rectangular two-dimensional vectoring engine nozzles, new structural materials, an 8,000lb/sq in hydraulic system and completely different avionics including a digital fly-by-wire flight control system. The objective is to manoeuvre better while carrying heavier payloads and, especially, to operate by night and in adverse weather from runways not much more than 1,500ft (457m) long.

Weapon provisions:
A. 20mm M61 gun with 950 round drum.
B. Pylon 4,500lb (2,041kg) or 500-gal (2,273-lit) tank.
C. Corner ejector/launcher for AIM-7 or -120 missiles (tandem).
D. Attachment for FAST (fuel and sensor, tactical) pallets.
E. Pylon 5,100lb (2,313kg).
F. Pylon 1,000lb (454kg).

Key to stores:
1. ECM aerial.
2. Westinghouse ALQ-119(V) jammer pod.
3. 500gal (600 US gal, 2,273lit) tank.
4. Multiple ejector rack carrying three Mk 82 bombs (one with stand-off contact fuze), one AIM-9P and one AIM-9M AAMs.
5. FAST pack.
6. MER-200 dispenser for Mk 20 Rockeye cluster bomblets.
7. Tactical special (nuclear) weapon.
8. Mk 82 Snakeye.
9. M61 gun with 940 rounds of 20mm.
10. GBU-10E/B (Mk 84 2,000lb) Paveway II smart bomb.
11. AVQ-26 Pave Tack sensor pod.
12. GBU-12 (Mk 82 500lb) Paveway II bomb.
13. CBU-52B/B cluster bomb dispenser.
14. AIM-7 Sparrow AAM.
15. AGM-84A Harpoon anti-ship missile.
16. SUU-20 practice dispenser.
17. Mk 84 2,000lb GP bomb.
18. GBU-15(V)-4-B Cruciform-Wing Weapon.
19. AGM-88A Harm anti-radar missile.
20. AGM-65 IIR (imaging infra-red) Maverick precision missile.
21. Two AGM-65A (TV) or AGM-65C (laser) Mavericks, all three on multiple ejector rack.
22. General Electric Gepod housing 30mm multibarrel gun and complete ammunition and drive system (this would not be mounted on an outboard pylon).
23. AIM-120 Amraam advanced medium-range AAM.

Combat avionics:
A. APG-63 radar.
B. HUD.
C. TEWS suite.
D. UHF.
E. RWR front/rear (L fin), ALR-56 ECM (R fin).
F. ECM (both fins).
G. ECM (both tailplanes).
H. ALR-56 ECM (both tips).
J. Tacan.
K. Avionics bay, plus ADF and ILS.
L. UHF.

51

McDonnell Douglas/Northrop F/A-18 Hornet

Origin: USA, first flight
18 November 1978.

Type: (F/A) single-seat carrier-based multi-role fighter, (TF) dual trainer, (CF) single-seat land-based attack fighter.

Engines: Two 16,000lb (7,257kg) thrust General Electric F404-400 augmented turbofans.

Dimensions: Span (with missiles) 40ft 4³/₄in (12.31m), (without missiles) 37ft 6in (11.42m); length 56ft (17.07m); height 15ft 3¹/₂in (4.66m); wing area 400sq ft (37.16m²).

Weights: empty 23,050lb (10,455kg); loaded (clean) 36,710lb (16,651kg); loaded (attack mission) 49,224lb (22,328kg); maximum loaded (catapult limit) 50,064lb (22,710kg):

Performance: Maximum speed (clean, at altitude) 1,190mph (1,915km/h, Mach 1.8), (maximum weight, sea level) subsonic; sustained combat manoeuvre ceiling, over 49,000ft (14,935m); combat radius (air-to-air mission, high, no external fuel) 461 miles (741km); ferry range, more than 2,300 miles (3,700km).

Background: Concerned at what then appeared to be the high cost of the F-14, the US Navy obtained DoD approval in spring 1974 for a VFAX lightweight multimission fighter. Six companies submitted bids, one being the McDonnell 263. In August 1974 Congress terminated VFAX, directing the Navy to look instead at the USAF YF-16 and YF-17 . Neither was suitable, but Northrop entered discussison with an experienced builder of carrier aircraft, McDonnell Douglas, with a view to incorporating as much Model 263 as possible in the YF-17 to meet the NACF (Navy Air Combat Fighter) specification. The result was a total redesign with a wider fuselage, doubled internal fuel capacity, larger wing, strengthened structure and totally new avionics. After substantial further changes during prototype development the decision was taken to build a single basic single-seat model to fly both fighter and attack missions.

Design: The YF-17 of 1974 established the basic shape, with a 5/3 per cent thick wing with most taper on the leading edge, fully variable profile with powered leading and trailing edges, very large wing-root extensions and wingtip AAM rails, two slim engines with plain fixed inlets under the wing roots, large outward-canted vertical tails (fixed, with small inset rudders) mounted midway between the wing and the mid-mounted stabiliators (tailerons), and main gears retracting rearward to lie under the inlet ducts with the wheels turned through 90° to the horizontal position. Poor roll rate (Mach 0.9/ 10,000ft (3,047m) max 100°/s compared with 180° required) led to many changes including increasing inner and outer wing torsional stiffness, removing dogtooth snags from LE of both wings and tailplanes, increasing differential authority of tailplane for roll and extending ailerons 20in (508mm) out

to wingtips. These and other changes give 220°/s. Rudder toe-in reduces nosewheel liftoff speed by 35kt on takeoff, 45° aileron droop reduces approach speed 10kt, and drag is reduced by eliminating the axial slots along the wing roots. The tandem-seat F/A-18B has 6 per cent less internal fuel (11,000lb/4,990kg in single-seater).

Avionics: Major challenges were optimizing design to equal capability in both fighter and attack missions with crew of one. Demand for radar-guide MRM capability (AIM-7F, later Amraam) met by Hughes APG-65 water-cooled PD multimode radar able to track 10 targets and display 8, has RAM (raid-assessment mode) and DBS (doppler beam sharpening) for good air/ground clarity. Cockpit claimed to be most advanced known, with three Kaiser CRT displays all used simultaneously in different modes plus advanced HUD to give exceptional info display power (though pilots take a long time to become proficient in system management). Large UFD (up-front display) keyboard serves as main man/machine interface, and one or more HDD can present radar, Flir, laser/EO (if fitted) and weapon-seeker images, while others show systems/engine health, RWR data and BITE information. Flight info also appears in cockpit, but pilot flies mainly on HUD symbology, with Hotas throughout a normal mission. Central HSI display is a moving map with superimposed symbology for nav, target data (including sensor FOVs) and location of defence threats. Three master avionic modes are Nav, A/A and A/G. In A/A main radar progresses through 80nm (148km) range-while-search mode, 40nm track-while-scan matched to MRMs, 30nm (55.59km) RAM (raid-assessment mode) and down to 20nm (37.06km) mode for AIM-9s and 5nm (9.26km) mode with pulse-to-pulse frequency agility for 20mm fire. In A/G the radar has exceptional ability to search for and define targets, lock-on and provide for multiple passes. Standard extra A/G sensors are Flir on left side of engine inlets and Laser Spot Tracker and strike camera on right side. After build-

ing 410 F/A-18A/B, 138 Canadian CF-18A/B, 75 Australian AF/ATF-18A and 72 C.15/EC.15 for Spain, McDonnell Douglas switched to building 390 F/A-18C and two-seat F/A-18D with upgraded avionics.

Armament: One 20mm M61A-1 gun with 570 rounds; nine external weapon stations rated as shown with 3-view, with theoretical maximum load of 17,000lb (7,711kg), but in practice loads are much lower, eg maximum of 10 Mk 82 bombs, 9 Mk 83 or four Mk 84. Centreline

and inboard wing hardpoints plumbed for 262gal (1,192lit) tanks. A reconnaissance Hornet was tested in 1982 but not adopted. In 1991 a different version, the F/A-18D(CR), was being developed for the Marine Corps. This can fly reconnaissance or, after overnight conversion, fighter/attack missions. It has a synthetic-aperture radar, IR and optical systems, and a real-time data link. Hornets are in production with the 17,700lb (8,029kg) F404-402 engine for Switzerland, Kuwait and South Korea.

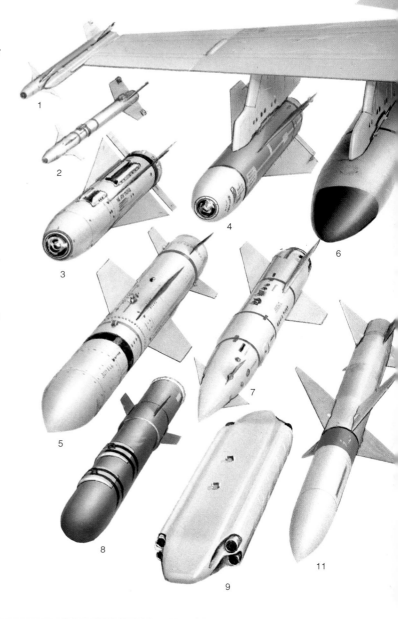

Below: One of the development prototypes during carrier qualification aboard USS *America* in November 1979.

Key to stores:
1. AIM-9L Sidewinder AAM.
2. AIM-9J Sidewinder AAM.
3. Maverick ASM (various models).
4. AGM-62 Walleye ASM.
5. AGM-109 Harpoon anti-ship missile (up to four).
6. Drop tank, 262gal (1,192lit) .
7. AGM-12 Bullpup (no longer used by front-line units).
8. Durandal anti-runway weapon.

Weapon provisions:
A. 20mm M61 gun with 570 rounds.
B. Pylon (two Mk 82 or CBU-59, one tank or other conventional stores to 1,000lb).
C. Pylon (Sparrow AAM or FLIR or laser tracker/strike camera).
D. Pylon (bombs to 2,000lb, Maverick or Harm).
E. Pylon (bombs to 2,0001b including B57 or B61 nuclear).
F. Pylon (AIM-9).

AS missile.
13. Gun port.
14. M61 gun with 570 rounds of 20mm.
15. GBU-10E/B (Mk 84, 2,000lb, 907kg) LGB Paveway II series.
16. FLIR pod.
17. Mk 84 GP bomb, 2,000lb (907kg).
18. Triple Mk 82 GP bombs, 500lb (227kg).
19. Mk 82 Snakeye retarded bomb.
20. M117GP bomb, 750lb (340kg).
21. Stores carrier.
22. Data-link container

(flight test and Walleye).
23. Rockeye II CBU-59.
24. Twin Mk83 GP

9. SUU-20 practice bomb/rocket dispenser.
10. ASQ-173 LST.
11. AIM-7 Sparrow medium-range AAM.
12. AGM-88A Hamm

bombs, 1,000lb (454kg).
25. LAU-61 A/A and 68B/A rocket pods.

Combat avionics:
A. APG-65 radar.
B. HUD.
C. Tacan.
D. UHF/IFF.
E. Front hemisphere

ECM.
F. VHF.
G. RWR.
H. Main avionics bays.
J. UHF.
K. IR sensor.

Mikoyan/Gurevich MiG-21

Origin: Soviet Union, first flight (Ye-6 prototype) early 1957.

Type: (Most) fighter, (some) fighter/bomber or reconnaissance.

Engine: (21) one 11,243lb (5,509kg) Tumanskii R-11 afterburning turbojet, (21F) 12,677lb (5,750kg) R-11F, (21PF) 13,120lb (5,951kg) R-11F2, (21FL, PFS, PFM, US) 13,668lb (6,199kg) R-11-300, (PFMA, M, R) R-11F2S-300, same rating, (MF, RF, SMT, UM, early 21bis) 14,550lb (6,599kg) R-13-300, (21bis)16,535lb (7,500kg) R-25-300.

Dimensions: Span 23ft 5½in (7.15m); length (almost all versions, including instrumentation boom) 51ft 8½in (15.76m), (excluding boom and inlet centrebody) 44ft 11in (13.46m); wing area 247.57sqft (23m²).

Weights: Empty (F) 12,440lb (5,643kg), (MF) about 12,882lb (5,843kg), (bis) 12,600lb (5,715kg); loaded (typical, half internal fuel and two K-13A) 15,000lb (6,800kg), (full internal fuel and four K-13A) 18,078lb (8,200kg), maximum (bis, two K-13A and three drop tanks) 20,725lb (9,400kg) .

Performance: Maximum speed (typical of all, SL) 800mph (1,290km/h, Mach 1.05), (36,000ft/10,972m, clean) 1,385mph (2,230km/h, Mach 2.1), initial climb (F) about 30,000ft (9,144m)/min (bis) 58,000ft (17.677m)/min, service ceiling (bis, max) 59,055ft (17,999m); practical ceiling (all), rarely above 50,000ft (15,239m); range with internal fuel (F) 395 miles (635km), (bis) 683 miles (1,100km); max range with three tanks (bis) 1,800 miles (2,898km).

Background: Soviet air staff and OKB leaders in 1954 studied Korean experience and TsAGI produced two optimised shapes for future fighters, similar except that one had swept wing (62°LE) and the other a delta (57°LE). MiG OKB evaluated prototypes of both from June 1956 and eventually chose Ye-5 delta which developed through refined Ye-6 variants into production MiG-21 of 1958. Original aircraft outstandingly light

and agile, but extremely limited in weapons and load.

Design: Throughout 25 years of development basic wing never varied from 57° delta with 5/4.2 per cent thickness and plain "hard" LE with neither dogtooth nor camber. Flaps originally area-increasing slotted, from 1961 plain with SPS flap-blowing. Conventional ailerons sole roll control, slab tailplanes used for pitch only. Area of vertical tail progressively increased, along with engine thrust and fuel/weapons capacity. Forward view restricted in A/G mode by wide nose ducting engine airflow past centrebody with radar; rearwards view poor due to sidehinged canopy being followed by dorsal spine of same height and cross-section. Overall result was extremely high-performance and agile aircraft with enjoyable flying qualities but even in latest versions deficient in mission endurance, all-weather avionics, navigation (and in export versions ECM/IFF), weapon load and modern cockpit displays, but extremely good in reliability and availability (typically six sorties per day for several days) and, except in fuel burn, low cost of operation.

Avionics: All current single-seat models have simple search/track radar for A/A interception, but with very limited value in A/G role. From about 1961 to 1966 usual set was R1L or R2L "Spin Scan": I-band, 100kW, PRFs 925/950pps for search and 1,750/1,850pps for track, range in good weather 31 miles (50km), provides target illumination for AA-2-2 Advanced Atoll. Until 1979 no HUD radar symbology, but good HDD with three modes visible in bright sunlight. So far as known, no MiG-21 has had Hotas cockpit controls, radar having pushbuttons and rotary knobs around periphery of display. Sole radar input to HUD sight is target range. Since 1966 standard radar has been so-called Jay Bird: J-band, 100+kW,12.88/ 13.2GHz, PRFs various bands up to 2,724pps, max range again about 31 miles (50km), provides target

illumination for AA-2-2. Still no advanced cockpit displays but post-1970 aircraft have improved radar with limited downlook and navigation capability, though not normally used in A/G role. Thus, so far as known, no MiG-21 has any all-weather capability except against aerial targets and with close ground control to vector close astern (in bad weather within 19 miles, 30km). All current single seaters have VOR/ILS/ADF and standard SR0-2 IFF and Sirena III 360° RWR. Basic nav by twin-gyro platform, with doppler in most late versions, radar altimeter, MRP-56P beacon receiver, ARL-S data-link and provision for front/rear ECM jammers in removable wingtip pods (seldom seen in Soviet photos but supplied with many exported aircraft). Soviet ECM jammer pods, are routinely carried by FA regiments using these aircraft. The only Western pod in full scale service with MiG-21s appears to be the Italian Selenia ALQ-234, used by several Arab air forces including Egypt and Syria.

Armament: Varies greatly with model, but nearly all current tactical versions have one GP-9 comprising one 23mm GSh-23L v gun with 200 rounds; centreline pylon for reconnaissance pod or 108gal (490lit) tank; four wing pylons normally rated at 1,102lb (500kg) each, but aircraft has no effective radius with all at max load. Normal loads include FAB-500 (1,102lb) bombs or 108gal tanks on outer pylons and K-13A or twin AA-8 missiles on inners, or alternatively four FAB-250 (551lb) bombs.

With some 2,500 in the Soviet inventory, of which an estimated 1,300 are in front-line regiments, the MiG-21 remained a threat because of its sheer numbers, and surviving single-seaters are being subjected to routine update programmes. AA-8 Aphid AAMs have been carried since before 1980, and there are major avionic update programmes on MiG-21s of the FA. Indian production of the bis-N until late 1984 introduced no major variation. Chinese production

of the much older MiG-21F, with local designation J-7, was resumed in about 1980 after a gap of 14 years, with only minor changes. Some were being supplied to Egypt as operational trainers, where front-line MiG-21s - despite progressive replacement by the F-16 - are being retrofitted with Soviet-compatible Teledyne IFF and doppler, and often a Smiths HUD and Ferranti INS. Egypt and India are expected to replace AA-2 and AA-2-2 AAMs by AIM-9s or other types.

Left: Like the French delta-wing Mirages, the MiG-21 is fundamentally extremely limited in almost all parts of its mission capability except speed and basic agility. Like the Mirage, it has proved a worldwide best-seller. This example is an obsolecent MiG-21PF used by Romania.

Key to stores:
1. AA-2-2 Advanced Atoll AAM (radar guided version compatible with Jay Bird radar).
2. UV-16-57 rocket launcher (several other patterns are in use).
3. Rockets, 2.24in (57mm).
4. "Non-slick" GP bomb, 1,102lb (500kg) size (48 basic types of free-fall bomb, including nuclear, chemical, napalm and fuel/air explosives, are qualified on the MiG-21, but few have been identified in the West).
5. Drop tank, 108gal

Weapon provisions:
A. GSh-23 with 200 rounds.
B. Pylon 500kg (1,102lb).
C. Pylon 250kg (551lb).
D. Pylon 108-gal (490-lit) tank.

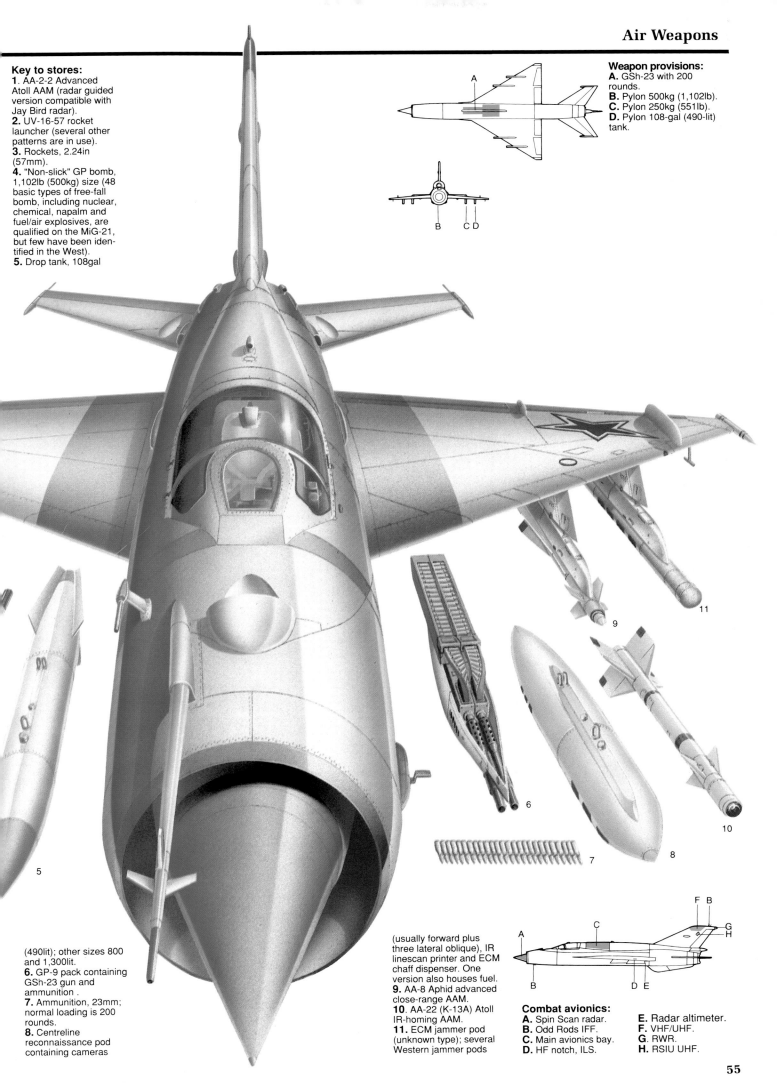

(490lit); other sizes 800 and 1,300lit.
6. GP-9 pack containing GSh-23 gun and ammunition .
7. Ammunition, 23mm; normal loading is 200 rounds.
8. Centreline reconnaissance pod containing cameras

(usually forward plus three lateral oblique), IR linescan printer and ECM chaff dispenser. One version also houses fuel.
9. AA-8 Aphid advanced close-range AAM.
10. AA-22 (K-13A) Atoll IR-homing AAM.
11. ECM jammer pod (unknown type); several Western jammer pods

Combat avionics:
A. Spin Scan radar.
B. Odd Rods IFF.
C. Main avionics bay.
D. HF notch, ILS.
E. Radar altimeter.
F. VHF/UHF.
G. RWR.
H. RSIU UHF.

Mikoyan/Gurevich MiG-23

Origin: Soviet Union, first flight (Ye-231 prototype) probably 1966.
Type: Multi-role fighter, attack and trainer.
Engine: (Early and most export fighters and all trainers) one Tumanskii R-27 afterburning (7/10.2t) thrust; (all current Soviet operational versions) one Tumanskii R-29B afterburning turbofan rated at 27,500lb (12,475kg) with max augmentation turbojet rated at 15,430/22,485lb (7/10.2t); (most) Tumanskii R-29BN turbojet rated at 17,635/27,500lb (8/12.475t); (ML, MLD) Tumanskii R-35F-300 turbojet rated at 18,520/ 28,660lb (8.4/13t).
Dimensions: Span (16°) 45ft 10in (13.965m), (72°) 25ft 6in (7.78m); wing area (spread, gross) 401.5sq ft (37.3m²).
Weights: (ML) Empty 22,485lb (10.2t); maximum takeoff 39,250lb (17.8t).
Performance: Maximum speed (with AAMs) 1,553mph (2,500km/h), Mach 2.35, at height, 875mph (1,410km/h, Mach 1.15, at SL; rate of climb 47,250ft (1.4km)/min; service ceiling 59,055ft (18km); takeoff run 1,640ft (500m); landing run 2,460ft (750m); combat radius (six AAMs) 715 miles (1,150km).
Background: Bearing not the slightest resemblance to the MiG-21, the next-generation MiG tactical fighter was designed around the TsAGI 1962 variable geometry shape for unfettered new designs (also used for the Su-24), with outboard pivots on a minimal fixed glove (inboard portion of wing). Ye-231 prototype flown with Lyul'ka engine 1966 and substantial development batch included many MiG-23S (possibly 50) used in FA regiments to gain service experience. Aircraft largely redesigned with shorter and lighter Tumanskii engine and subsequently built in extremely large numbers in many single- and MiG-23M two-seat forms with interceptor or attack nose and fixed-

or variable- geometry engine installation, the latter being designated separately as MiG-27. (All versions of -23 and -27 have the NATO name Flogger.)
Design: The wing is mounted in shoulder position, level with the top of the lateral inlet ducts to the single augmented turbofan engine but with a substantial fuselage spine passing above the upper surface. Wing and slab tailerons have no dihedral, and the fin area is the greatest that could be provided, even including a large ventral which is extended automatically by retracting the landing gear. Swing wings adjustable to 16°, 45° or 72°, sweep beyond 16° revealing the two largest leading-edge dogtooth vortex inducers on any aircraft. Leading-edge droop flaps automatically lowered with extension of three-section slotted flaps with wing at 16°. Uppersurface spoiler/dumpers can operate differentially as primary roll control together with differential tailerons. Four petal airbrakes around rear fuselage. Soft-surface landing gear with steerable twin-wheel nose unit with mudguard retracting to rear and main legs horizontal on ground carrying single wheels on long-stroke levered suspension. Fully variable Phantom-type inlets with large perforated splitter panels, and fully variable nozzle. Small framed canopy hinged up from opaque fuselage downstream with top level with top of fuselage, giving limited rear view either direct or via two mirrors facing pilot and one in blister above. Aircraft generally easy to fly, popular and said to be extremely reliable in adverse conditions.
Avionics: Usual radar in MiG23MF called High Lark by NATO and said to have range of 53 miles (85km) for search and 34 miles (54km) in lock-on tracking mode. Can be used for ground mapping, surface search, terrain avoidance (not TFR) and all forms of interception against aerial targets including lookdown/

Above: One of the best air-to-air photographs of any modern Soviet-built combat type, showing a Libyan-operated MiG-23 variant known to NATO as Flogger-E. The picture was taken by a US Navy aircraft over the Gulf of Sirte in August 1981.

shootdown against aircraft at very low level. Popular published account implies usage against targets simulating Western cruise missiles. Laser ranger (possibly also used as marked surface-target seeker) under nose, doppler flush aerial further aft, and radar altimeter. Sirena 3 RWR aerials facing forward from leading edge of left and right gloves, just outboard of pylon, and astern from top of fin. Odd Rods SRO-3A IFF ahead of windscreen between additional pitots and yaw sensors, with AOA sensor on left side and Swift Rod ILS aerial on underside. CW illumination for radar-guided AAMs in all Soviet fighter versions, and many aircraft have small avionics blister on each side under nose ahead of nose gear (not the same as on the Flogger-H version of MiG-27). There are several small variations in avionic fit, and most recent aircraft have a blade (possibly VOR) aerial under the left taileron (which like its partner has a kinked trailing edge with reduced chord outboard). The following are major variants: MiG-23M, initial production model with R-27 engine; MiG-23MF, R-29B engine, new J-band radar, IRST, doppler and Sirena-3 warning system;

MiG-23UM, dual trainer, R-27; MiG-23MS, R27, small radar, no doppler or IRST, for export; MiG-23B, fighter/bomber with engine installation and gun of 23MF in airframe of MiG-27; MiG-23ML, lightened version, R-35F engine, repackaged radar, modified nose gear, smaller dorsal fin, no aft tank; MiG-23BN, as 23B with two radar warning receivers on lower sides of forward fuselage; and MiG-23MLD, dogtooth notches at wing glove roots, dorsal fin as ML, smaller folding ventral fin, pivoting outer-wing pylons, new IFF, AA-11 missiles.
Armament: One GP-9 centreline installation of GSh-23L gun with 200 rounds; five pylons (centreline, under inlet ducts and under wing gloves) rated as shown by 3-view, centreline only plumbed for 176gal (800lit) tank. All have option of twin, triple or tandem twin stores ejector racks, eg for twin AA-8. With some 2,700 aircraft delivered to Soviet units (including MiG-27 versions) these aircraft are the most numerous in service with any air force, and will probably remain important until the end of the century.

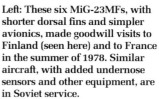

Left: These six MiG-23MFs, with shorter dorsal fins and simpler avionics, made goodwill visits to Finland (seen here) and to France in the summer of 1978. Similar aircraft, with added undernose sensors and other equipment, are in Soviet service.

Weapon provisions:
A. GSh-23 with 200 rounds.
B. Pylon 176-gal (800-lit) tank.
C. Pylon 750 (possibly 1,000) kg.
D. Pylon 1,000kg (2,205lb) .

Key to stores:
1. These drawings merely suggest possible appearance of Soviet tactical ASMs, including the elusive AS-7 Kerry (which is believed not to be the missile seen on an Su-22 in a released Soviet photograph).
2. Twin paired installation of AA-8 Aphid close range AAMs.

3. GP-9 installation of GSh-23 gun and 23mm ammunition .
4. 176gal (800lit) tank normally carried on centreline pylon.
5. AA-2 Atoll IR-homing AAM (AA-2-2 Advanced Atoll can also be carried).

Combat avionics:
A. High Lark radar.
B. Main avionic compartments.
C. EO tracker (left wing), RHAWS (right).
D. VHF.
E. HF notch.
F. VHF/UHF.
G. ILS.
H. VOR.
J. Unknown.
K. LRMTS.
L. ILS.

Mikoyan/Gurevich MiG-25

Origin: Soviet Union, first flight (Ye-26 prototype) 1964 or early 1965.

Type: (25) high-altitude interceptor, (R) strategic reconnaissance, (U) trainer.

Engines: Two Tumanskii afterburning turbojets; (25) R-31-300, with maximum ratings of 20,500lb (9,300kg) dry and 27,000lb (12,250kg) with afterburner; (25M) R-31F-300, uprated to 31,025lb (14,075kg); (25R) R-15B-300, with afterburning rating of 24,700lb (11,200kg).

Dimensions: Span 45ft 9in (13.94m), (25R) 44ft 0in (13.49m); length (all known variants), (overall), 78ft 1$\frac{3}{4}$in (23.82m), (fuselage only) 63ft 7$\frac{3}{4}$in (19.39m); height 20ft 0$\frac{1}{4}$in (6.10m); wing area. gross, 612sqft (58.63m^2). (25R) slightly less.

Weights: (typical) empty equipped (25) just over 44,090lb (19,999kg): (25R) 43,200lb (19,595kg); maximum loaded (25) 79,800lb (36,197kg), (25R) 90,385lb (41,000kg).

Performance: Maximum speed (low level) about 650mph (1,050km/h, Mach 0.85), (36,000ft/10,972m and above, MiG-25 clean), 2,115mph (3,400km/h, Mach 3.2), (36,089ft, 11,000m and above, 4 AAMs) 1,850mph (2,978km/h, Mach 2.8); maximum rate of climb 40,950ft 2,480km)/min; time to 36,090ft (10,999m) with sustained afterburner, 2.5min; service ceiling (25) 80,000ft (24,382m), (both 25R versions) 88,580ft (26,997m); combat radius (25) 700 miles (1,125km). (25R, max) 900 miles (1,448km); takeoff run (25, max w eight) 4,525ft (1,380m); landing (25) touchdown 168mph (270km/h). run 7,150ft (2,180m).

Background: When the USAF planned its WS-110A strategic bomber in 1956-57 the Soviet Union studied possible defences against this vehicle with a high-altitude cruise speed of Mach 3. When the American XB-70 was contracted for in December 1957 Soviet contracts were immediately placed for a new super-long-range SAM system and a new super-fast interceptor. Mach 3 was attempted but in the event the MiG OKB settled for 2.8 in a combat mission, though 3.2 can be achieved in the clean configuration. Cancellation of the B-70 in 1961 did not halt the Ye-266 prototype programme, which led to a series of impressive world speed, height and climb records from April 1965. The definitive aircraft went into production as the MiG-25 interceptor and two forms of MiG-25R reconnaissance aircraft as well as a dual trainer without combat equipment. In 1975 production switched to the MiG-25M with more powerful engines, a new 'look down, shoot down' radar and an IRST (infra-red search track) pod. The related Ye-266M development aircraft set climb records and still holds the

absolute altitude record at 123,524ft (37.65km). In the early 1980s a further variant entered production (NATO name 'Foxbat-F') dedicated to suppressing hostile air defences. It has special radar receivers and signature analysers, and carries AS-ll Kilter anti-radar missiles. The MiG-31 is a new-generation aircraft, generally similar in layout but totally different in detail.

Design: The MiG-25 was designed as a single-mission aircraft to operate only from long paved runways and to fly at great speeds and altitudes. No attempt was made to operate at low levels or engage in any form of close combat, so while the propulsion system has fully variable inlets and nozzles, linked by a simple turbojet of low pressure-ratio, the wing has fixed geometry apart from plain ailerons and flaps. Design owed much to A-5 Vigilante and F-108, both by same company which built the B-70 (North American Aviation), with high-mounted wing with taper rather than sweep, twin canted vertical tails (but with fixed fins and separate rudders), a broad box-like fuselage flanked by large lateral air ducts, a slim nose for the pilot and radar, and main gears folding into the fuselage. Many items including engines, radar, hydraulic /fuel/ environmental/ WM-injection and electrics, missiles and reconnaissance systems, were specially designed for this aircraft, whose very high cost was considered worthwhile because of its ability to operate with virtually no chance of enemy fighter interception. In recent years new versions have brought lookdown/shootdown capability, much better manoeuvrability (with stronger structure, leading-edge root strakes and tailerons used as primary roll controls) and even greater engine thrust.

Avionics: For the necessarystand-off kill capability the main radar had to be large and powerful, and when it was designed in 1958-9 the Fox Fire was the most powerful for regular AI use with average electrical load of 600kW. Operating in I-band at frequencies near 9GHz, it is a typical thermionic-valve (vacuum-tube) set of this era, with Freon cooling and five operating modes which include ground mapping but offer no capability against low-flying aircraft. By modern standards it is bulky and lacking in sophistication, though of course it provides CW guidance for AAMs. Search range typically 75 miles (120km), with tracking of single targets reliably achieved at 43 miles (70km) in most weather conditions. The main computer is large and capable for a 1959 analog device, with automatic vectoring under guidance from the widespread Markham electronic environment and data-link (formerly operated by the IA-PVO) with reception by a blade aerial

under the nose. Sirena 3 RWR with additional IR warning has 270° coverage from side-looking aerials in the wingtip antiflutter pods and rear of right fin tip, giving quadrantal cover for pulse/ CW/TWS emitters. Active ECM jammer in each tip pod with horn emitter at front and rear. HF in left fin tip, VHF blade above fuselage and UHF below. IFF in right fin tip and ahead of windshield. ATC/SIF in right fin tip, and nose aerials for ILS, two beacons, doppler, radio compass and (usually removed)

radar altimeter.

Armament: Normally all armament is carried on four underwing pylons. Five types of AAM can be carried: AA-6 Acrid, AA-7 Apex or AA-9 Amos (all large semi-active radar guided weapons, though with the option of passive IR homing at close ranges), and AA-8 Aphid or AA-ll Archer IR homing missiles can be carried in pairs.

The defence-suppression aircraft carries four large AS-ll Kilter anti-radar weapons.

Below: Libyan MiG-25 seen in August 1981. It has two giant AA-6 Acrid missiles, the right one being radar homing.

Weapon provisions:
A. Inboard wing missile pylons (various AAMs, but usually M-6 of IR homing type).
B. Outboard wing missile pylons (various AAMs, but usually AA-6 of SARH type).
C. Unconfirmed report of internal gun in some aircraft.

Key to stores:
1. AA-6 Acrid AAM SARH (semi-active radar homing) version.
2. AA-6 Acrid AAM IR (infra-red) homing version.
3. AA-7 Apex medium range AAMs. Note: early examples of MiG-25 frequently carried older AAMs, notably including AA-5 Ash (normally seen only on the Tu-128 Fiddler), and these are still in service.

Combat avionics:
A. Instrumentation pitot probe .
A. Main Fox Fire radar.
B. SLAR (MiG-25R versions only).
C. Odd Rods IFF.
D. Rear avionics bays.
E. VHF Tacan.
F. IFF and Sirena 3 RWR.
G. ATC/SIF and Sirena 3 RWR .
H. Sirena 3 RWR (dispensers added in MiG-25R).
J. UHF and marker beacon receiver.
K. Flush ILS.

Panavia Tornado F.3

Origin: Germany/ltaly/UK, with UK responsibility for assembly and test, first flight 27 October 1979.

Type: Two-seat long-range interceptor.

Engine: Two Turbo-Union RB.199 Mk 104 each rated at 16,520lb (7.500kg) thrust with maximum afterburner.

Dimensions: Span (25°) 45ft 7¼in (13.9m), (65°) 28ft 2½in (8.6m); length 59ft 3in (18.06m); height 18ft 8½in (5.7m); wing area not published.

Weights: Empty, equipped, about 31,970lb (14,500kg); takeoff weight (clean, max internal fuel) 47,500lb (21,546kg); maximum 61,700lb (27,986kg).

Performance: Maximum speed (clean, at height) about 1,500mph (2,414km/h, Mach 2.27); combat mission with max AAM load, 2h 20min on station at distance of 375 miles (602km) from base with allowance for combat.

Background: The UK bears a heavy responsibility in policing a block of airspace extending from the Arctic to Gibraltar and from Iceland to the Baltic. This calls for interceptors with long range and endurance. and exceptional avionic capabilities. From early in the Tornado programme it was evident that with minor modifications the basic aircraft could serve as the basis for an outstanding new interceptor to cover the UK Air Defence Region and replace first the Lightning and later the Phantom. Full-scale development on a one-nation basis was authorized on March 4,1976. Though wholly a Panavia manufacturing programme the R&D was paid for by Britain, although there will be no problems in sorting out the financial side when several expected export orders materialise.

Design: Though in avionics and weapons the interceptor or ADV (Air Defence Variant) Tornado is a totally different aircraft, its basic airframe, propulsion and systems are those of the IDS version, and commonality is put at 80 per cent. The most significant change was the need to accommodate tandem pairs of Sky Flash (or Sparrow or later Amraam) AAMs recessed under the fuselage, and this demanded an increase in midfuselage length of 21.25in (539mm). This provides room for 200gal (909lit) more fuel and for extra avionics in the side compartments. As in the RAF Tornado GR.1 the fin serves as an integral tank. Instead of a demountable FR probe housed in a bolt-on external box on the right side of the nose, a permanently installed FR probe is housed internally on the left side of the nose, with hydraulic extension on demand. The main nose radome is longer and more pointed, and the radar itself slightly longer, giving an overall increase in length of 53.5in (1.35m), which improves supersonic acceleration and reduces supersonic drag. To bring

the centre of lift forward to match the forward migration of CG the fixed wing nibs are extended forwards at 68° sweep, the Kruger flaps being deleted; this again happens to give a small bonus in reduced drag. Other upgrades include AWS (automatic wing sweep) to 23°, 45°, 58° or 67°, and an AMDS (automatic manoeuvre device system). The Mk 104 engines are basically similar to the Mk 103 but have jetpipes extended by 14in (35cm) to give slightly increased thrust in the reheat regime, especially in supersonic flight. The first 18 production aircraft retained the original rear fuselage and Mk 103 engines, and were designated F.2.

To demonstrate CAP mission performance the A.01 prototype took off from the BAe base at Warton in early 1982 with two 330-gal (1,500-lit) subsonic tanks, four Sky Flash and two Sidewinders, transited to a patrol area 374 miles (603km) distant, flew CAP for 2h 20min, and on return loitered at Warton for 15min before landing after 4¼h with over 5 per cent internal fuel and less than one-eighth Lox consumed. Some of the 165 RAF interceptors are dual-pilot trainers.

Avionics: The main Marconi/ Ferranti Foxhunter radar is a pulse-doppler FMICW (FM interrupted CW) set operating in I-band at 3cm. It has extremely advanced features and of course TWS (track while scan) for multiple (between 12 and 20) targets at ranges greater than 120 miles (193km), depending on cross-section, at any flight level. Special ECCM is provided to match any expected hostile ECM to the year 2000, and though an ECM-resistant data-link is provided the aircraft is designed for autonomous operation. Foxhunter continues to scan normally while storing hostile tracks in its computer, and after computer evaluation presents a TED (threat evaluation display) to the backseater. Interceptions are normally made on the HUD, and all displays may be recorded for subsequent replay. Advanced IFF is integrated with the radar, and a particular feature is the way the entire tactical situation can be presented, if necessary in different ways, to both pilot and navigator. An extremely advanced RHWR is fitted, with its own processor. Since the start of the programme provision has been made for an EO VAS (visual augmentation system) for positive visual identifications at long range, but none has yet been fitted.

Armament: One 27mm IWKA Mauser gun. Fuselage recesses for four Sky Flash, Sparrow or AIM-120 Amraam missiles. Four auto-swivelling wing pylons, the inners normally carrying two 330gal (1,500lit) tanks (each about 2,900lb filled) plus two or four Sidewinder or Asraam missiles. Outers often not fitted but can carry wide range of stores including electronic warfare pods. If used in a multi-role capability the maximum

weapon load is 18,740lb (8,500kg). By the end of 1991 all 165 ADV Tornados for the RAF and a further 24 for the Royal Saudi AF had been delivered. The first 18, designated Tornado F.2, were to a lower avionic standard and retained Mk 103 engines. These were placed in storage, but by 1991 were being upgraded to F.3 standard (except for the engines, the Mk 104 requiring different rear-fuselage

structure) and are being redelivered as F.2As. Modification kits are being supplied to all ADV aircraft to bring the radar fully up to standard with a new data processor. Nothing has been said about adding an IRST (infra-red search/track) sensor, visual augmentation system, laser gun ranger or helmet sight, as standard on Soviet aircraft since 1982.

Left: Since this photograph was taken the RB.199 engines have been fitted with extended afterburners which both increase maximum thrust and reduce drag of the projecting nozzles. Drag is further reduced by the longer radome and body with recessed AAM installations.

Key to stores:
Note: In this illustration two air/ground stores are included as a reminder that this interceptor retains considerable attack capability
1. AR1.23246 (Sky Shadow, Ajax) ECM jammer pods.
2. Triple installation of Asraam (advanced short-range AAMs) now in advanced development by BAe Dynamics and BGT (West Germany).

Weapon provisions:
A. 27mm mauser gun (ammunition capacity not stated).
B. Flush ejectors for tandem pairs of AIM-7 or -120 or Sky Flash.
C. Pivoting pylon for weapons or 330-gal (1,500-lit) tank (about 2,800lb, 1,270kg).
D. Option: pivoting pylon.

3. 330gal (1,500lit) long-range tank on pivoting pylon.
4. AIM-9L Sidewinder AAMs (at present on single launcher on inner side of pylon).
5. GP bomb (1,000lb, 454kg, shown).
6. ASM (Kormoran anti-ship missile shown).
7. Four AIM-120 Amraam advanced medium-range AAMs.

8. Four Sky Flash AAMs (note: items 7 and 8 are carried on powered launchers which thrust the body of the missile about 12in (305mm) from the belly of the aircraft prior to release and motor ignition).
9. IKWA Mauser 27mm gun (right side).
10. 27mm ammunition (magazine capacity classified).

Combat avionics:
A. Foxhunter radar.
B. IFF.
C. HUD.
D. UHF/ADF.
E. HF.
F. MSDS RHAWS.
G. VHF/UHF/Tacan.
H. VOR.
J. RHAWS (both tips).
K. Avionics.

Panavia Tornado GR.1.

Origin: Germany/Italy, UK, first flight 14 August 1974.

Type: Two-seat multi-role combat aircraft optimised for strike, (T) dual trainer.

Engines: Two Turbo-Union RB.199 Mk 103 augmented turbofans each rated at 16,075lb (7,292kg) with full afterburner.

Dimensions: Span (25°) 45ft 7¼in (13.90m), (65°) 28ft 2½in (8.60m); length 54ft 9½in (16.7m), height 18ft 8½in (5.7m); wing area not published.

Weights: Empty, equipped, 31,065lb (14,091kg); loaded (clean) about 45,000lb (20,41lkg); maximum loaded, over 63,000lb (28,577kg).

Performance: Maximum speed (clean), at sea level, over 920mph (1,480km/h, Mach 1.2), at height, over 1,452mph (2,337km/h, Mach 2.2); service ceiling over 50,000ft (15,240m); combat radius (8,000lb/ 3,629kg bombs, hi-lo-hi) 863 miles (1,390km); ferry range 2,420 miles (3,895km).

Background: This extremely advanced blind first-pass attack IDS (interdiction strike) aircraft was designed jointly by the member-companies of Panavia (BAe, MBB and Aeritalia) to meet the specified demands of the Federal German Luftwaffe and Marineflieger, the RAF and the Aeronautica Militare Italiano. All agreed on a tandem two-seat aircraft, which with no significant changes except minor parts of the avionic fit serves with all four customers, and also serves in a dual-pilot version with small cockpit changes. The RAF also required a new long-range interceptor, and this variant is dealt with separately. The first IDS prototype flew in 1974, the first production aircraft in July 1979, and the first deliveries were to a tri-national training unit in July 1980. By early 1991 over 700 had been delivered.

Design: Despite having to carry weapons of more different types than any other tactical aircraft in history, the Tornado is also amazingly compact; and at sea level in clean condition it is the fastest combat aircraft ever built. The wing probably has the highest lift coefficient of any fitted to a supersonic aircraft, for at minimum sweep of 25° it can extend full-span double-slotted trailing-edge flaps and full-span slats, plus Krugers on the 60° fixed glove portions. Tailerons are used for roll control, augmented at low sweep angles by large wing spoilers which also serve as lift dumpers. Some 10,720lb (4,862kg) of fuel is housed in fuselage cells and the integral-tank wings, the latter also carrying four autopivoting pylons which are plumbed for 330 gal (1,500-litre) tanks. RAF aircraft have 970lb (440kg) in the fin. There is provision for a detachable package along the right of the cockpit housing a retractable inflight-refuelling probe. Engine inlets are fully variable, and the engines incorporate full augmentation, reversers and

variable nozzles. A large airbrake is fitted on each side of the vertical tail. The landing gear is designed for soft semi-prepared strips, and an arrester hook is standard.

Avionics: No aircraft of this size has ever been more richly equipped for all-weather penetration of hostile airspace. TI provides (with European licensees) the main forward radar, which comprises a GMR (ground- mapping radar) and TFR, both operating in Ku band. The GMR is the primary attack sensor but can also operate in an air/air mode, and provides various modes for high-resolution nav update, target identification and fire control. The TFR can fly the aircraft automatically, at heights known to go below 200ft (61m), or the pilot can fly manually via the HUD, selecting any level of ride comfort. Primary nav mode is by digital INS plus doppler with Kalman filtering of both outputs. The triplex fly-by-wire flight-control system and, with the autopilot/ flight director, provides for any combination of attitude, barometric-height or heading hold, radar height lock, Mach/airspeed

with autothrottle, track acquisition and auto-approach and blind ILS. RWR is always internal and jamming is always (at present) pod mounted. RAF Tornado GR.1 aircraft have a modular RWR supplied by MSDS and the ARI.23246 modular jammer pod. German and Italian aircraft use the EL/73 deception jammer by Elettronica and AEG-Telefunken.

Armament: Two 27mm IWKA Mauser guns. Centreline pylon (Germany/Italy) equipped for recon pod or MW-1 dispenser, (UK) many alternatives; two tandem fuselage pylons each rated at 2,205lb (1,000kg) fore and the same aft, so that with twin carriers eight 1,000lb (454kg) bombs can be carried under the fuselage; alternate fuselage load (UK) is two JP233 dispensers of double-length type. Four auto-swivelling wing pylons, unknown rating but inners can carry 330gal (1,500lit) tanks weighing about

Left: The basic Tornado has the highest ratio of weapon load to empty weight of any combat aircraft with supersonic performance, apart from the F-16. The main illustration shows only a selection of the more than 90 types of external store carried. Here an RAF Tornado takes off with JP.233 dispensers, tanks and jammer pods.

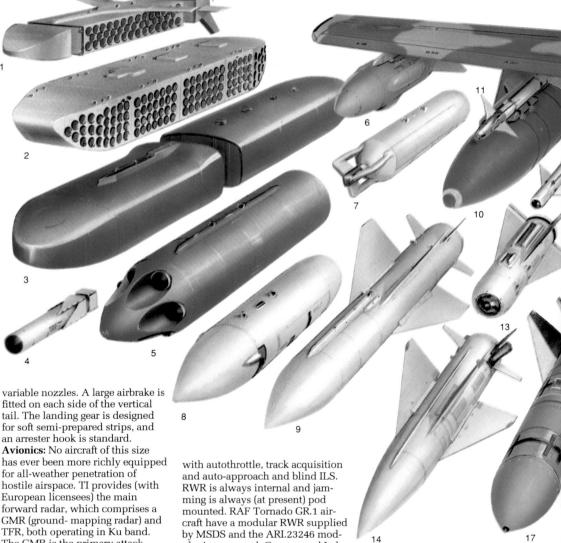

2,900lb each. Maximum weapon load exceeds 19,840lb (9,000kg). During the Gulf TIALD (thermal imaging airborne laser designator) pods were rushed into service on GR.1s to enable them to find and designate targets for LGBs at night. For the immediate future all IDS operators are planning MLU (mid-life update) programmes, which involve digital avionics based on a MIL-1553B data bus, improved radar warning and active ECM equipment and integration of new weapons.

Key to stores:
1. MBB CWS (Container Weapon System), with front and rear modules shown detached.
2. MBB MW-1 lateral dispenser.
3. Hunting JP.233 dispenser (large tandem model).
4. Wasp ASM (folded).
5. Wasp pod (12 rounds).
6. ARI.23246 Sky Shadow ECM jammer.
7. ALQ-234 (now superseded by Zeus) jammer.
8. MBB reconnaissance pod.

14. AS.30 (AS.30L can also be carried) ASM.
15. Low-drag cluster dispenser.
16. BAe Alarm anti-radar missile.
17. BAe Sea Eagle anti-ship missile.
18. Pave Spike laser pod or TIALD IR/laser pod.
19. IKWA-Mauser gun with 27mm ammunition (180 rounds each).
20. CBLS 200-series carrier for (21-24).
21. Practice bomb, 28lb (12.7kg).
22. Practice bomb, 4lb (1.8kg).

Weapon provisions:
A. Two 27mm Mauser guns (ammunition capacity not stated)
B. Pylon 2,000lb (907kg) or recon pod.
C. Four tandem twin pylons each 2,000lb (907kg).
D. Pivoting pylons, 3,000lb (1,361kg) or 330gal (1,500-lit) tank.
E. Pivoting pylon, 1,000lb (454kg)

9. Kommoran anti-ship missile.
10. Tank (various to 330gal, 1,500lit).
11. AIM-9L Sidewinder AAM.
12. AIM-9B Sidewinder MM.
13. AGM-65A Maverick ASM.

23. Pactice bomb, 20lb (9kg).
24. Practice bomb, 5lb (2 27kg).
25. LGB smart bomb, 1,102lb (500kg).
26. Paveway II Mk 13/18 British, 1,000lb (454kg).
27. Napalm dispenser.
28. GBU-15 CWW

(Cruciform-Wing Weapon).
29. Store carrier.
30. GP bomb, 1,000lb (454kg).
31. Special-weapon twin carrier.
32. Beluga dispenser.
33. BL.755 dispenser.
34. Lepus flare.
35. LR.25 rocket pod.

Combat avionics:
A. TI main radar.
B. IFF.
C. HUD.
D. UHF/ADF.
E. HF.
F. RHAWS (various).
G. VHF/UHF/Tacan.
H. RHAWS (both tips).
J. LRMTS.
K. Dopplecr.
L. Other sensor options and radar altimeter
M. TFR.

SEPECAT Jaguar

Origin: Jointly UK/France, first flight 8 September 1968.

Type: (GR. 1, A and International (I.)) single-seat all-weather attack; (T.2 and E) dual operational trainer.

Engines: Two Rolls Royce/Turbomeca Adour two-shaft augmented turbofans: (except (I.) 7,305lb (3,313kg) Adour 102; (I.) 8,400lb (3,810kg) Adour 804.

Dimensions: Span 28ft 6in (8.69m); length, excluding probe (except T.2, E) 50ft 11in (15.52m); (T.2, E) 53ft 11in (16.42m); height 16ft 1½ in (4.92m); wing area 260sq ft (24.18m²).

Weights: Empty, 15,432lb (7t); "normal take-off" (ie, internal fuel and some external ordnance) 24,149lb (10,954kg); maximum loaded 34,612lb (15,700kg).

Performance: Maximum speed (lo. some external stores) 824mph (1,350km/h, Mach 1.1), (hi, some external stores) 1,055mph (1,700km/h, Mach 1.6); attack radius, no external fuel, hi-lo-hi with bombs, 530 miles (852km); ferry range 2,614 miles (4,210km).

Background: In 1963 both the RAF and Armée de l'Air had studied their requirements for a supersonic advanced trainer, the latter also considering the same basic design as a light attack aircraft, to replace the T-33, Mystere 4A, Gnat and Hunter. For political reasons the British government pushed a joint programme in 1965, as a result of which British Aircraft Corporation developed the Breguet 121 to have new Anglo-French augmented fan engines of much greater power, resulting in a multirole tactical aircraft far more capable than the small and simple machine originally envisaged. Thus it did not serve as a trainer.

Design: The Br 121 design featured a high-mounted swept wing of near-delta shape but with blunt tips, twin engines mounted low in the fuselage fed by plain lateral inlets, an anhedralled slab horizontal tail and tall twin-wheel landing gears to give good clearance for operations from rough ground with external stores. As developed into the Jaguar, all flight controls are powered, roll control being by spoilers backed up at low speeds by differential taileron movement (the reverse of the arrangement on Tornado). The outboard leading edges have slats which even when closed give extended chord with a dogtooth aligned with a shallow fence. The trailing edge is occupied by fullspan double-slotted flaps which give extremely good field length at weights more than double the 7.5 tons originally planned. Additions during flight development included an area-rule bulge above the trailing edge housing the main heat exchanger, and, on RAF aircraft, a fore/aft fin installation of the RWR.

Avionics: At the start of the programme aircraft were divided into British and French single-seaters (called Jaguar S and A respectively) and British and

French two-seaters (B and E). Even then totally different avionic fits were chosen by the two original customers. The Armee de l'Air settled for a simple twin-gyro platform backed up by doppler, while the RAF required a digital inertial nav/attack system and HUD which in the late 1960s was the most advanced in use anywhere. Further items in the RAF aircraft include a laser ranger and marked-target seeker in a chisel nose, radar altimeter and projected map display. Both customers required passive RWR, but only the French Jaguar As have been seen regularly with jammer pods and dispensers. E:xport Jaguar Internationals have varying fits, mainly based on the British suite but in the case of Indian-built aircraft featuring a Hudwas similar to that in the Sea Harrier, the Ferranti Comed (combined map and electronic display) and a Sagem INS. Almost half the French aircraft have a panoramic undernose camera, while the final 30 As have provision to carry the Martin Marietta/Thomson-CSF Atlis II laser pod on the centreline pylon for use in conjunction with AS 30L laser missiles or any of the range of French Paveway-type LGBs. It is usual for one Atlis aircraft to illuminate the target, the laser being slaved (boresighted) to a TV giving a bright cockpit display to assist aiming, while other friendly aircraft make attack runs with smart missiles or LGBs.

Armament: Two 30mm guns (UK Aden, France DEFA) each with 150 rounds; centreline and inboard underwing pylons each rated at 2,500lb (1,134kg) and all plumbed for 264gal (1,200lit) tanks; outboard underwing pylons rated at 1,250lb (567kg). Centreline can carry (RAF) recon pod or (France) AN52 nuclear store. In addition Jaguar International has provision for overwing pylons for Magic, Sidewinder or other AAMs. Total attack weapon load 10,500lb (4,763kg). All frontline RAF aircraft have been retrofitted with the Ferranti FIN 1064 digital inertial nav/weapon aiming system which was first flown in July 1981; later an advanced VOR/ILS will be installed. There is still plenty of development left, though RAF funding is unlikely and has delayed the introduction of a new wing of larger area and with fullspan leading-edge droops, flaperons and tip AAM rails. Several stages of uprating of the engine were introduced. For research purposes BAe has built an all CFRP (carbon-fibre reinforced plastics) wing to the original aerodynamic design. BAe also completed a major flight programme with a digital quad FBW flight-control system, without manual reversion, on Jaguar XX765 which has been fitted with destabilizing rear-fuselage ballast and large leading edge strakes to convert it into the first fully CCV version of a production aircraft.

Above: This was the first test firing of a Matra Magic AAM from the overwing pylons added on the Jaguar International export versions and later fitted to RAF aircraft.

Key to stores:
1. AIM-9B Sidewinder AAM.
2. Matra 550 Magic AAM.
3. Matra Phimat chaff/flare dispenser.
4. AJ168 TV Martel ASM.
5. Harpoon anti-ship missile.
6. AS.30, AS.30L (the latter guided by item 23) ASM.
7. Durandal anti-runway weapon.
8. Kormoran anti-ship missile.
9. 264gal (1,200lit) drop tank.
10. AM.39 Exocet anti-ship missile.
11. BAe Dynamics Alarm anti-radar missile.
12. SB practice bomb.
13. 28lb (12.7kg) practice bomb.
14. 20lb (9kg) practice bomb.
15. CBLS (Container, Bomb, Light Store).
16. 4lb (2kg) practice bomb.
17. Aden 30mm gun and ammunition (two, RAF aircraft).
18. DEFA 30mm gun and ammunition (two).
19. Mk 13/18 (UK) Paveway II smart bomb.
20. JP.233 dispenser (short).

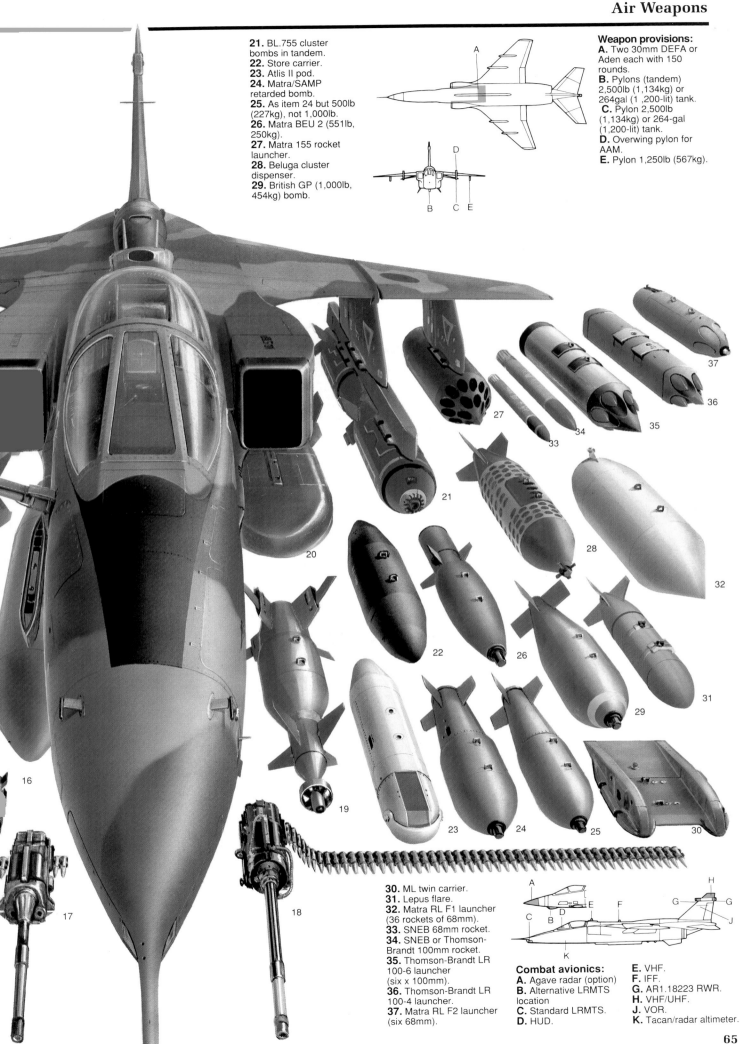

21. BL.755 cluster bombs in tandem.
22. Store carrier.
23. Atlis II pod.
24. Matra/SAMP retarded bomb.
25. As item 24 but 500lb (227kg), not 1,000lb.
26. Matra BEU 2 (551lb, 250kg).
27. Matra 155 rocket launcher.
28. Beluga cluster dispenser.
29. British GP (1,000lb, 454kg) bomb.

Weapon provisions:
A. Two 30mm DEFA or Aden each with 150 rounds.
B. Pylons (tandem) 2,500lb (1,134kg) or 264gal (1,200-lit) tank.
C. Pylon 2,500lb (1,134kg) or 264-gal (1,200-lit) tank.
D. Overwing pylon for AAM.
E. Pylon 1,250lb (567kg).

30. ML twin carrier.
31. Lepus flare.
32. Matra RL F1 launcher (36 rockets of 68mm).
33. SNEB 68mm rocket.
34. SNEB or Thomson-Brandt 100mm rocket.
35. Thomson-Brandt LR 100-6 launcher (six x 100mm).
36. Thomson-Brandt LR 100-4 launcher.
37. Matra RL F2 launcher (six 68mm).

Combat avionics:
A. Agave radar (option)
B. Alternative LRMTS location
C. Standard LRMTS.
D. HUD.
E. VHF.
F. IFF.
G. AR1.18223 RWR.
H. VHF/UHF.
J. VOR.
K. Tacan/radar altimeter.

Sukhoi Su-24

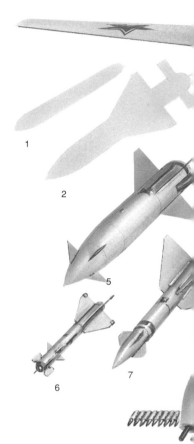

Origin: Soviet Union, first flight 1967.

Type: All-weather attack and maritime reconnaissance.

Engine: Two Lyulka AL-21F-3A afterburning turbojets each with maximum rating of 24,700lb (11,200kg).

Dimensions: Span (16°) 57ft 10in (17.63m), (68°) 34ft 0in (10.36m); length 80ft 6in (24.53m); wing area (68°) 452sq ft (42m²).

Weights: (24MK) Empty 39,900lb (18.1t); internal fuel 29,983lb (13.6t); maximum loaded 90,388lb (41t).

Performance: Maximum speed (clean, 36,000ft/11km) 1,590mph (2,560km/h, Mach 2.4), (clean, SL) about 870mph (1,400km/h, Mach 1.14); (max external load, hi) about 1,000mph (1,600km/h, Mach 1.5); (max external load, SL) about 620mph (1,000mph (1,600km/h, Mach 1.5), (max external load, SL) about 620mph (1,000km/h, Mach 0.815); service ceiling (with weapons) 57,400ft 917,5km); combat radius (lo-lo-lo, 8t bombload) 200 miles (322km), (hi-lo-hi, 2.5t bombload) 2,237miles (3,600km); ferry range (six tanks) about 4,000 miles (6,440km).

Background: Though it uses the same TsAGI-developed aerodynamics as the much smaller MiG-23, this long-range interdiction aircraft is one of the Soviet Union's rare examples of a totally new design owing no direct relationship to any existing type from the same OKB. Indeed, it owes more to the American F-111 than to any other single type, even to the almost certainly mistaken use of side-by-side seats. The mission was to carry a far greater load of more types of attack weapons and deliver them with pinpoint (180ft, 55m) accuracy over ranges never previously approached by any FA aircraft. The Su-24, even in its initial

production form, can deliver heavy bombloads from WP airbases to Scotland or Brittany on a round trip with a substantial part flown at treetop height.

Design: General design closely follows that of the F-111 except in the important respects of air inlets and landing gear. The former were brought well forward ahead of the wing to give enough length to avoid grossly distorted airflow into the engines (which caused such prolonged trouble on the US aircraft). The main landing gears fold into the fuselage and offer ample track for stability on rough ground, but are so arranged that heavy weapon loads can be carried on four fuselage pylons. The swinging outer wings are particularly efficient and of high aspect ratio, with almost zero sweep in the low-speed regime (max is 68°), with full-span slats and powerful flaps, roll control being by a combination of spoilers and tailerons (for the first time on a Soviet aircraft). The wing is at the same level as the tail, and at maximum sweep lies closer to the tailplane than in the MiG-23, though not as near as in the F-111. A single vertical tail is used, backed up by ventral fins at the corners of the very wide and flat underside, without the need for a folding ventral surface. All units of the landing gear have twin wheels, probably sized to permit operation away from runways, though this is not certain. The steerable nose unit has a mudguard and retracts to the rear. The extremely large inlets are fully variable and their inboard ramp plates stand well away from the large vertical-walled fuselage. There are probably two conventional ejection seats, behind an extremely strong multi-panel curved windscreen and with a large

one-piece clamshell canopy. There appears to be plenty of room for internal fuel, possibly including the fin, and the glove pylons can carry the largest drop tanks seen on any Soviet aircraft (about 650gal, 3,000lit) .

Avionics: There is no doubt that the main radar is a completely new type, and it almost certainly has more operating modes than any previous Soviet set. Below it are probably dual TFRs. There is likewise no doubt that the Su-24 is packed from nose to tail with avionics, and there is abundant evidence that the entire fit was designed in parallel with the aircraft so that little has to be hung externally. During the past several years each new and improved photograph that has become available has revealed more and more comprehensive avionics, invariably with flush aerials. Especially at the tail early Su-24s showed an amazing absence of RWRs, IRWRs, drag chute containers and active jammers, yet all these are carried and more evidence keeps appearing. So far more than 20 flush aerials have been seen, but trying to identify their function would be guesswork. It is highly likely that the entire suite of ECM active jammers and payload dispensers is internal. Almost the only excrescences are around the nose: air-data sensors, AOA probe, ice probe, pitots, CW blister and laser. Everything else appears to be flush, though a good view from above has not yet emerged in the West.

Armament: Two prominent blisters under the fuselage have given rise to controversy. Some observers, including the author, at one time inclined to the view that these covered two guns of different calibre. That on the left is certainly

a gun, generally regarded as a six-barrel 23mm type also carried by the MiG-27 on the centreline. The other installations probably a multisensor weapon-delivery system resembling the American Pave Tack. Weapons are carried on eight pylons, each rated at not less than 2,205lb (1,000kg), giving a total weapon load of 17,635lb (7,999kg). By 1991 total deliveries of Su-24s had reached nearly 600, in five main versions. The most important are the M, MK and MR. The Su-24M of 1980 introduced upgraded avionics giving enhanced ability to penetrate hostile airspace. The MK integrated new missiles, two of which are carried on giant inboard fairings. Visible changes in the MK include a longer nose and extended (kinked) leading edge along the lower three-quarters of the fin. A retractable flight-refuelling probe is another addition. The MR maritime reconnaissance version serving with the Baltic Fleet (replacing Tu-16s) has extensive avionics systems and can carry anti-ship missiles. From 1988 development proceeded on dedicated reconnaissance, ELINT and EW jamming versions. All began to replace the Yak-28 versions in late 1990.

Weapon provisions:
A. Multi-barrel gun ?
B. FLIR/EC sensor ?
C. Pylons (8) each 1,000kg (2,205lb).

Key to stores:

1. Note: It is possible to illustrate only a selection of stores whose appearance has become known; the very important AS-7 Kerry missile and several theatre (FA) nuclear weapons cannot be included.
1. ECM jammer pod, type unknown.
2. ASM, NATO reporting designation uncertain.
3. AA-2 Atoll AAM.
4. AA-2-2 Advanced Atoll.
5. Tactical ASM (believed not to be AS-7 Kerry) seen on Su-22.
6. AA-8 Aphid advanced snapshoot dogfight AAM.

7. AA-7 Apex medium-range AAM.
8. Giant drop tanks (about 650gal, 3,000lit, size).
9. 23mm twin-barrel gun pod (not positively identified on Su-24).
10. Unknown installation, believed to be dual-sensor weapon aiming system similar to Pave Spike or Pave Tack.
11. Multi-barrel gun of 23 or 30mm calibre.
12. Ammunition for (11), probably over 1,000 rounds.
13. GP bomb, 2,205lb (1,000kg) .
14. Standard UV-16-57 launchers with 57mm rockets.

15. GP bomb, 1,102lb (500kg).
16. Alternative 500kg bomb.

17. Concrete-destroying bomb, believed of BETAB-250 (551lb) type.

Combat avionics:
A. Pulse dopper radar.
B. HUD.
C. CW illuminator ?
D. HF ?
E. RWR ?
F. VHF/UHF.
G. IRWS.
H. RHAWS.
J. ECM ?
K. Unknown.
L. Doppler ?
M. AOA sensor.
N. Air-data.
P. LRMTS.

Vought A-7 Corsair II

Origin: USA, first flight 27 September 1965.

Type: (except K) attack, (K) combat trainer.

Engine: (D, H, K) one 14,250lb (6,465kg) thrust Allison TF41-1 turbofan; (E) one 15,000lb (6,804kg) TF41-2; (P) one 12,200lb (5,543kg) Pratt & Whitney TF30-408 turbofan.

Dimensions: Span 38ft 9in (11.8m); length (D) 46ft 1¹⁄₂in (14.06m), (K) 48ft 11¹⁄₂in (14.92m); wing area 375sq ft (34.83m²).

Weights: Empty (D) 19,781lb (8,972kg), loaded (D) 42,000lb (19,050kg).

Performance: Maximum speed (D, clean, SL) 690mph (1,110km/h); (5,000ft/1,525m, with 12 Mk 82 bombs) 646mph 91,040km/h); tactical radius (with unspecified weapon load at unspecified height), 715 miles (1,151km); ferry range (internal fuel) 2,281 miles (3,671km), (max with external tanks) 2,861 miles (4,604km).

Background: In the quickest development programme for a new combat aircraft since 1945, Vought (then LTV) were contracted in February 1964 to build a new carrier-based attack aircraft for the US Navy to replace the A-4, carrying more bombs over greater ranges. The design was based on the F-8 supersonic fighter, but with major changes to fit it to subsonic attack missions. Within three years of the initial contract large numbers were in operational service.

Design: The F-8 had a unique pivoted variable-incidence wing, but the A-7 wing is conventional and attached slightly below the high position, though leaving ample room for deep loaded pylons. The wing folds in line with the leading-edge dogtooth, with powered ailerons outboard and slotted flaps inboard preceded by symmetric-only spoilers; the entire leading edge droops. The slab tailplanes have slight dihedral and are below mid-position, and a large door airbrake is fitted under the fuselage. The fuselage is shorter than the F-8 but has a large cross-section giving ample volume for fuel, avionics and systems, the short landing gears and the nonaugmented turbofan engine. There are comprehensive armour and damage-resistant systems, as well as an exceptionally advanced autopilot and flight system for allweather operation including automatic carrier landing. In Navy versions there is a retractable flight refuelling probe on the right side of the forward fuselage; USAF A-7Ds have a refuelling boom receptacle above the left wing root (the A-7K has a universal fitting on the centreline). Emergency systems power is provided by a ram-air turbine.

Avionics: The original A-7A and B variants had basic 1960s-style equipment including doppler, multimode radar, nav computer, attitude reference system, roller-map display, Tacan and a weapon-aiming computer and optical sight. In 1968 Vought flew the A-7D for the USAF and the Navy's A-7E, both with a totally new nav/attack system. The ASN-91 computer is an advanced and versatile processor providing all nav information, guidance for the target run and weapon-release cues. It integrates inputs from an ASN-90 INS, ASN-190 doppler, APQ-126 radar with ten operating modes including TFR, an air-data computer, radar altimeter and a very wide range of basic navigation and communications equipment. Cockpit displays include the AVQ-7(V) HUD and ASU-99 projected-map display, while the ASCU (armament station control unit) provides complete management of all weapons. ECM includes the ALR-45/50 internal RHAW, ALQ-126 active ECM, chaff/flare dispensers of different kinds for the two US services, and provision for a range of jammer pods compatible with the internal ECM/EW systems. Since 1978 Navy A-7Es have been progressively equipped to carry a 720lb (327kg) FLIR pod under the right wing with a TI gimballed sensor feeding pictorial information to a new Marconi Avionics raster HUD to give greatly enhanced attack capability by night. Only 91 pods can be afforded, aircraft thus equipped acting as "mission leaders", though it has not been explained how their presence will increase attack accuracy of the other A-7Es.

Armament: The original A and B models had two Mk 12 cannon of 20mm calibre in the sides of the air inlet in the nose, each with 250 rounds. In the D and E and derived export models these are replaced by a single M61A-1 20mm gun with a tank of 1,032 rounds, though 500 rounds is the normal loading. All versions have four outboard wing pylons, each with 3,500lb (1,587kg) capacity, all plumbed for tanks. The innermost wing pylons are not plumbed, and are rated at 2,500lb (1,134kg). Fuselage side pylons each rated at 500lb (227kg) are normally used for Sidewinder self-defence AAMs. All pylons cannot simultaneously be loaded to their limit; with max internal fuel the weapon load is limited to 9,500lb (4,309kg) which brings gross weight to the limit of 42,000lb (19,051kg) at a permitted manoeuvre load factor of 4.9g. With much reduced internal fuel the external stores load can reach just over 15,000lb (6,804kg). Production of two-seat A-7Ks for the ANG and conversion of Navy aircraft to two-seat TA-7C standard was completed in 1983, the total of all versions being 1,545. Since then LTV has upgraded many aircraft. The chief programme has been to fit 75 A-7Ds and eight A-7Ks of the Air National Guard with terrain- following, a FLIR, a mission computer and a wide-angle HUD derived from that fitted to the F-16C/D to give day/night all-weather capability. Other upgrades include a strengthened birdproof one-piece windshield, AIM-9L self-defence capability and other enhanced avionics including a ring-laser gyro.

Left: Shallow dive attack by a USAF A-7D with Snakeye retarded bombs. At the time of its introduction the A-7D and very similar A-7E set new standards of bombing accuracy.

Weapon provisions:
A. 20mm M61 with 500 rounds .
B. Body pylon, 500lb (227kg).
C. Pylon 2,500lb (1,134kg).
D. Pylon 3,500lb (1,588kg) .

7. Wasp anti-tank missile.
8. Paveway II GBU-10 E/B (laser-homing 2,000lb, 907kg bomb).
9. AIM-9L Sidewinder AAMs.
10. 20mm M61 gun and short length of ammunition.
11. FLIR pod (A-7E only, under right wing).
12. AGM-62 Walleye ASM.
13. Triple 250lb (113kg) GP bombs.
14. Triple Snakeye retarded bombs.
15. AGM-88 Harpoon.
16. GBU-15 CWW (Cruciform-Wing Weapon) for stand-off attack.
17. Matra RL 100 (six 100mm rockets).

Combat avionics:
A. APQ-126 radar.
B. HUD.
C. Tacan.
D. HF shunt.
E. UHF/IFF.
F. RWR.
G. VOR.
H. Chaff/flare dispenser.
J. Strike camera.
K. ASN-190 doppler.
L. Pave Penny laser.
M. ILS.

Support Aircraft

BOEING E-3A, B AND C SENTRY

Origin: USA
Type: AEW aircraft.
Engines: Four Pratt & Whitney TF33-PW-100/100A turbofans, rated at 21,000lb (9,525kg) dry thrust
Dimensions: Span 145ft 9in (44.42m); length 152ft 11in (46.61m); height 41ft 9in (12.73m)
Weights: Max takeoff 325,000lb (147.417kg)
Performance: Max. speed 460kts (853km/hr); tactical radius 6hr at 870nm (1,610km) from base
Background: Deliveries of this long-range AEW aircraft to the USAF started in March 1977, and the type became operational in April of the following year. The first 24 production aircraft were E-3As, often referred to as the "core" version of the aircraft. These were equipped with the CC-1 computer and nine display consoles. From the twenty-first aircraft onwards, the APY-1 radar was replaced by the improved APY-2. The remaining 10 USAF aircraft were the "standard" version, with an

APY-2 radar able to track maritime targets, also a faster CC-2 central computer with expanded memory, and improved communications. This was the version of the aircraft adopted by NATO. 1982 saw first deliveries to the NATO alliance. A fleet of 18 "standard" E-3As fly in NATO markings, and are officially registered as belonging to Luxembourg. Deliveries of five examples of a CFM-56 powered variant to Saudi Arabia started in 1986. Following the failure of a UK plan to create an AEW version of the BAe Nimrod, the Royal Air Force ordered six CFM-56 powered E-3A aircraft in February 1987, with deliveries starting in 1991. Soon afterwards, France ordered three. Deliveries of the E-3B started in July 1984. Created by modifying existing

E-3A "core" aircraft, these have the CC-2 computer, five more operator consoles, better communications, including JTIDS, plus mounts for chaff/flare dispensers. Earlier APY-1 radars on the first 20 aircraft built are upgraded to the -2 version. The ten E-3A "standard" aircraft are being converted to the E-3C standard, receiving five more operator consoles, colour monitors, more radios, and improved secure communications systems. Due to be flight tested in 1992-3, the Radar System Improvement Programme (RSIP) replaces the digital Doppler processor and radar data correlator with a new radar computer. This will improve performance against low radar cross-section targets and increase resistance to ECM. Range against most targets will be doubled.

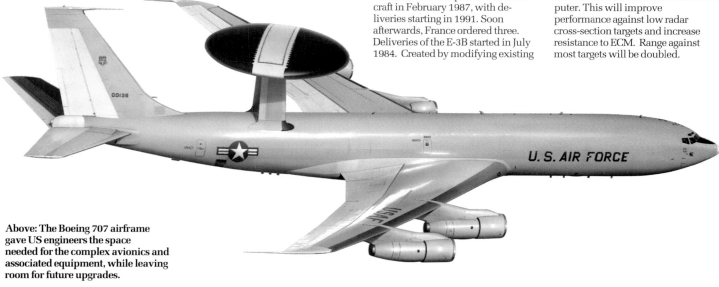

Above: The Boeing 707 airframe gave US engineers the space needed for the complex avionics and associated equipment, while leaving room for future upgrades.

BOEING RC-135

Origin: USA
Type: Strategic reconnaissance aircraft.
Engines: Four Pratt & Whitney TF33-P-9 turbofans, rated at 18,000lb (8,185kg) dry thrust
Dimensions: Span 130ft 10in (39.88m); length 134ft 6in (40.99m); height 41ft 8in (12.69m)
Weights: Empty 100,000lb (45,360kg); max. takeoff 275,000lb (124,740kg).
Performance: Max. speed 500kts (933km/hr); ceiling 36,000ft (10,900m)
Background: Ten TF33-P-9-powered KC-135 aircraft delivered to the USAF in 1964-5 were fitted out by Martin Aircraft of Baltimore to act as RC-135B reconnaissance platforms.

Since then, this large converted tanker has formed the basis for the USAF's main strategic electronic reconnaissance platform, seeing operations all around the globe. Many different versions have been created, often in small batches or even as individuals, although exact details of equipment fitted are difficult to come by. Variants include the RC-135D, incorporating large SLAR antennae in "cheek" positions on the fuselage, and the RC-135M, similar but with teardrop fairings mounted on the aft fuselage rather than a SLAR. Some have been rebuilt as RC-135Ws. The RC-135S (modified from C-135B) has these fairings along with smaller teardrop fairings at the base of the vertical fin, and dipole antennae arranged around the front fuselage. A 1972

rebuild introduced three windows on the right side of the fuselage and a black anti-reflective finish on the upper surface of the right wing and on the wing pods and pylons. Four KC-135R (unusually retaining the KC- designation rather than RC-) rebuilt to this standard were not done as a batch, but individually in 1963, 1970, then two in 1971. Features include a thimble nose radome, a towel-rail dorsal antenna on the forward fuselage, and -135M style teardrop fairings. A 1971 rebuild of

three RC-135Cs created today's RC-135U fleet. These are highly modified, having gained a chin-mounted radome, dipole antennae on the forward fuselage, large SLAR cheeks, a small ventral radome, reworked wingtips housing antennae, two wire antennae, an ovoid fairing at the top of the rudder, and an extended tailcone. Seven RC-135Cs were given similar rebuilds between 1973 and 1977 to create the -135V, while another was made by modifying a single -135U.

Left: One of the 55 Strategic Reconnaissance Wing's eight RC-135Vs. The new RC-135W model is similar in appearance, and a single RC-135X has recently been reported.

GRUMMAN E-2C HAWKEYE

Above: The Hawkeye has to keep the radome near-horizontal for effective operation; so flat, skidding turns are used.

Origin: USA
Type: AEW aircraft.
Engine: Two Allison T56-A-425 turboprops, rated 4,910shp (3,661kW)
Dimensions: Span 80ft 7in (24.56m); length 57ft 6.75in (17.54m); height 18ft 3.75in (5.58m)
Weights: Empty 38,0631b (17,265kg); Max. takeoff 51,933lb (23,556kg);
Performance: Max. speed 323kts

(598km/hr); ceiling 30,800ft (9,390m); tactical radius 3-4hr on station at 175nm (320km) from base
Background: In 1959 Grumman was given a contract to develop the E-2 AEW aircraft, while General Electric was ordered to develop the aircraft's APS-96 radar. The prototype which flew in October 1960 carried no radar, but was fitted with the 24ft (7.3m) rotodome. The APS-96 radar used a then-new technique known

as pulse compression, giving more than double the detection range of earlier systems, locating targets out to 200nm (362km). EA-2A deliveries started in April 1964, and the aircraft became operational in the following year. The APS-96 quickly gave way to the APS-111 (using moving target indication), then the more powerful APS-120 in the E-2C, along with the Litton ALR-73 passive ESM system. Radar improvements continued,

with the E-2C receiving the APS-125, followed by the APS-138 in the early 1980s, and most recently the APS-139. 1990 should see the service debut of the APS-145, to overcome problems with overland clutter. From 1988 onwards, new E-2Cs were fitted with the uprated T56-A-427 engine. Hawkeye has found a significant export role and has now been adopted by the air arms of Egypt, Israel, Japan, and Singapore.

GRUMMAN EA-6 PROWLER

Origin: USA
Type: Electronic warfare platform
Engines: Two 11,200lb (5,080kg) Pratt & Whitney J52-P-408 torbojets
Dimensions: Span 53ft (16.15m); length 59ft 10in (18.24m); height 16ft 3in (4.95m)
Weights: Max take-off 65,000lb (29,484kg)
Performance: Max speed 533kts (987km/h); service ceiling 41,000ft (12,500m)
Background: When the US Navy stated its requirement for a carrier-based electronic warfare aircraft to provide escort and stand-off jamming for strike

forces, a modified A-6 Intruder seemed the obvious place to start. The initial EA-6A packed jamming and support equipment into an A-6 fuselage, but the lack of space and only two crew members limited the capability of this modification. By stretching the basic A-6 by 54in (137cm), Grumman was able to accommodate an extra two seats for EW operators, and to pack within the fuselage and on underwing pylons the complex avionics of the ALQ-99 jamming suite. Production deliveries of the EA-6B started in 1971 and well over 100 are now in service. The airframe and construction are similar to the standard A-6, although key areas are stressed for higher landing

Below: This EA-6B is in the low visibility markings currently sported by US Navy aircraft.

weights. This extra weight and increased drag has created performance penalties for the Prowler, especially in top speed an increased stalling speed. The reason for the Prowler's existence is the ALQ-99, however, and this complex system is packaged into five external pods, the fuselage equipment bay and in the fin-top fairing. The system can operate in automatic mode, with the operators in a monitoring role, or in a fully manual model. Each transmitter (there are 10) has an output of around 2kW and can generate spot, dual-spot, sweep or noise jamming signals. The jamming system has had to be continuously improved in the light of advances in radar technology (especially Soviet) and a number of upgrades have entered service. EXCAP (EXpanded CAPability) models were first delivered in 1973 and could handle up to six threat bands. ICAP

(Improved CAPability) aircraft were standard production from 1975 and introduced new displays, reduced response time and two extra bands. The latest standard is ADVCAP (ADVanced CAPability), with a new receiver processor group, enhanced jamming capability, new navaids, displays, an additional stores station and chaff/flare dispensers. There are modification programmes planned to improve the aerodynamic performance, by redesigning the leading edge slat and flap system and recontouring the trailing edge flaps. In 1987, Pratt & Whitney were contracted to develop an engine which would give more thrust and improve safety margins for carrier operations. The J52-P-409 is rated at over 12,000lb (5,440kg) (an increase of 800lb/360kg), and accelerates to full power 20% faster than the current engine.

Support Aircraft

GRUMMAN EF-111A RAVEN

Origin: USA
Type: Electronic warfare aircraft
Engines: Two Pratt & Whitney TF30-P-3 turbofans, rated 18,500lb (8,390kg) with A/B
Dimensions: Span 31ft 11in (9.74m) swept, 63ft 0in (19.2m) unswept; length 76ft 0in (23.16m); height 20ft 0 in (6.10m)
Weights: Empty 55,275lb (25,072 kg); loaded 70,000lb (31,700kg); Max. takeoff 88,948lb (40,356kg)
Performance: Max. speed 1,227kts (2,272km/hr); ceiling 45,000ft (13,700m); tactical radius 807nm (1,495km) in the escort role
Background: Developed to replace the Douglas EB-66 electronic-warfare aircraft, the EF-111A combines the airframe and engines of the General Dynamics F-111A with the Eaton AIL ALQ-99EW suite of the US Navy's Grumman EA-6B Prowler. Work on converting two F-111As as proto-

Right: Obvious differences from the standard F-111A are the canoe fairing under the fuselage and the fin-top antenna fairing. Most of the changes are under the skin.

types for the EF-111A Tactical Jamming System (TJS) aircraft started in January 1975, leading to a first flight on 10 March 1977. The task was given not to GD but to Grumman. The Long Island company was familiar with the F-111, having developed the unsuccessful FB-111B fighter variant in the 1960s. Being the earliest version of the aircraft to enter service, the F-111A was coming to the end of its life as a combat aircraft, but enough airframes were available to make a rebuild for the new role feasible. The EW suite needed drastic modification, however. The EA-6B carries a crew of four - a pilot plus three system operators - but the GD warplane had only a two-place cockpit. Automation would have to take the place of two of the three system operators. Flight testing on the revised ALQ-99E system uncovered some problems, but tests went smoothly enough to allow the USAF to agree in November 1979 to a programme which would rebuild a

total of 42 ex-USAF F-111A aircraft as EW platforms. Between 1980 and 1985, Grumman stripped these aircraft down, rebuilding them to a build standard with an estimated fatigue life of around 8,000 hours. This added a new avionics bay in the lower fuselage, a large ventral canoe fairing, plus a Prowler-style fintop fairing. These changes created the internal volume needed to house the electronics and antennas of the ALQ-99E and the Sanders ALQ-137 CW deception jammer for self-protection. The USAF took delivery of its first EF-111A in 1981, and deployment to Western Europe came in 1984. More than a year before the final example was handed over in December 1985, Eaton AIL and General Dynamics were given a $61 million contract to upgrade the

ALQ-99E, although cost overruns and a badly slipping schedule caused cancellation in June 1988. The only upgrading currently being applied to the aircraft is the Avionics Modernisation Programme. This will improve the cockpit, upgrade the radar, fit a laser-gyro inertial navigation system, and a GPS satnav receiver. Given that the aircraft could remain in service until around the year 2010, some further modernisation is needed. Possible upgrades include the installation of the new receiver/processor developed for the USN's EA-6B, a new low-band radar and communications jammer, or AGM-88 HARM anti-radiation missiles. The ALQ-137 deception jammer could be upgraded to the improved -189 form or replaced by a unit from another manufacturer.

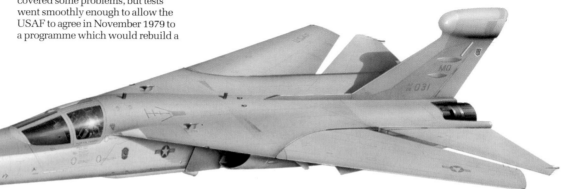

LOCKHEED EP-3E ORION

Origin: USA
Type: Elint aircraft
Engines: Four Allison T56-A-14 turboprops, rated 4,910shp (3,661kW).
Dimensions: Span 99ft 8in (30.37m); length 116ft 10in (35.61m); height 33ft 8.5in (10.27m)
Weights: Max takeoff 142,000lb (64,400kg)
Performance: Max. speed 411kts (76km/hr); ceiling 28,300ft (8,625m); tactical radius 1,346nm (2,494km) with 3hr on station
Background: In the 1950s and 1960s the US Navy relied on the piston-engined EC-121M (formerly designated WV-2Q) for the ELINT mission, but by the 1960s a replacement was needed for these

modified Lockheed Constellations. Two P-3B were converted into EP-3B ELINT aircraft and delivered to Fleet Air Reconnaissance Squadron VQ-1 in 1969. Along with ten P-3A, they were rebuilt to the definitive EP-3E standard in the early 1970s. Obvious external changes are the deletion of the MAD "sting" and the installation of dielectric equipment fairings above and below the rear fuselage, a dorsal radome mounted just ahead of the wing leading edge, plus an array of wire and blade antennas. The aircraft carries a crew of 15 - a flight crew, relief flight crew, and systems operators. The latter operate an extensive suite of ELINT sensors. The exact nature of this suite may well vary from aircraft to aircraft. Main systems identified as being carried by the EP-3E are the United

Technologies ALQ-110 Aries/Big Look SIGINT system, the GTE ALR-60 Deep Well communications intercept system, an E-Systems ALD-8 DF system, the Loral ALQ-78 ESM receiver (now being replaced by the newer ALR-77), an Argo Systems ALR-52 broadband-frequency measuring receiver, thought to cover from 0.5 to 18GHz, and the Hughes AAR-37 IR receiver. Some sources claim that the Magnavox ARR-81 airborne SIGINT system has also been carried by the EP-3. This equipment can be fitted with any two of three receivers designed to cover 1KHz-32MHz, 20-500MHz, and 500MHz-2GHz respectively. Another system thought to have served on some EP-3 aircraft is IBM's ASQ-171 automatic ELINT collection system. This covers the spectrum from A-band to J-band, but has the capability of being extended to cover K-band.

Such is the small size of the USN's ELINT fleet that some of these systems were built in only small quantities. Production run of the ALR-60 Deep Well is reported to have been only seven systems. Two other Orion variants have been built for surveillance and survey duties. Under the US Naval Oceanographic Office's Project Magnet, a single RP-3D in service with VXN-8 was used in the 1970s to map the earth's magnetic field. Four specialised WP-3As were built in 1975-6 for weather reconnaissance. These replaced the earlier WC-121N version of the Constellation, and carry a dorsal radome similar to that sported by the EP-3E. Two civil-registered WP-3Bs were used by the United States National Oceanic and Atmospheric Administration for environmental research, pollution monitoring and weather research.

Above: US Navy equivalent of the RC-135 is the little-known EP-3E Orion. Only 12 were built and their role is thought to be tracking Soviet naval formations.

LOCKHEED U-2R AND TR-1

Origin: USA
Type: High-altitude reconnaissance
Engines: One Pratt & Whitney J75-P-13B turbojet, rated 17,000lb (7,710kg) dry thrust
Dimensions: Span 103ft 0in (31.39m); length 63ft 0in (19.20m); height 16ft 0in (4.88m)
Weights: Max. takeoff 40,000lb (18,140kg)
Performance: Max. speed 373kts (692km/hr); max. range 2,600nm (4,800km); ceiling 90,000ft (27,400m)
Background: Developed to meet a 1953 USAF/CIA requirement for an aircraft able to operate beyond the ceiling of mid-1950s interceptors and SAM systems, Lockheed's U-2 operated with impunity over Soviet territory between July 1956 and April 1960. The aircraft is still in service, having been returned to production twice - once in the late 1960s to create

Below: The TR-1 variant of the U-2 has outlived the Mach-3 SR-71 and looks set to serve well past the year 2,000. An engine replacement programme is likely.

the U-2R, and again in the late 1970s as the TR-1. The original versions were the U-2A; the up-engined U-2B; the U-2C with extended nose, dorsal equipment fairing, increased fuel capacity and the J75-P-13B engine; the U-2D with modifications to carry specialised sensors or a second crew member; the U-2E with advanced ECM systems; the U-2F with facilities for in-flight refuelling, and the carrier-compatible U-2G and J models. These variants account for a production total of around 55 aircraft and all have now been retired. In 1968 the aircraft was returned to production. The U-2R has an extended-span wing, longer fuselage, and underwing equipment pods which supplement the volume of the fuselage bays. Twelve were built. The maximum altitude is reported to be 75,000ft (22,860m), slightly below that of the earlier models. The final version of the U-2 family is the TR-1. Changes from the U-2R standard are largely internal. The aircraft is heavier than the U-2R, and features an interchangeable nose plus a different pattern of dorsal UHF antenna. It carries an improved ECM system, also an advanced synthetic-aperture radar system (ASARS) based on the UPD-X sideways looking radar. Some aircraft were due to carry the Precision Emitter Location Strike System (PLSS), but plans to deploy this equipment have been cancelled.

MCDONNELL DOUGLAS RF-4C

Origin: USA
Type: Reconnaissance fighter
Engines: Two General Electric J79-GE-17 turbojets, rated 11,870lb (5,384kg) dry thrust, 17,900lb (8,119kg) with A/B
Dimensions: Span 38ft 5in (11.70m); length 62ft 11in (19.17m); height 16ft 3in (4.96m)
Weights: Empty 29,535lb (13.397 kg)
Performance: Max. speed Mach 2.2; ceiling 56,120ft (17,100m); tactical radius 700nm (1,295km) with external fuel; max. range 2,000nm (3,700km)
Background: The first Phantom variant to sport a camera-packed nose was not the US Marine Corp's RF-4B but the USAF's RF-4C. The original YRF-4C prototypes were

Right: On the RF-4C, all reconnaissance sensors are internally mounted, with the external hard points left free for fuel tanks and jamming pods.

F-4Bs converted to the new role while still on the production line. A first flight on 8 August 1963 lead to the first of 503 production aircraft entering service in September 1964. Two patterns of camera nose have been used on the RF-4C. The first was more angular, with a near flat underside to the camera fairing. The second has a rounded lower surface. Mounted in a small nose radome is the Goodyear APG-99 radar, allowing the aircraft to fly in terrain-following mode. The lower part of the nose, including the chin fairing, houses optical cameras located on three stations. Film can be processed while the aircraft is in flight, and if necessary ejected in a cartridge which can be picked up by front-line personnel. A Goodyear APQ-102A sideways looking radar records a broad strip of terrain on either side of the flight path on a film which can be processed after landing, backed up by an AAS-118 infra-red detecting set. The ALR-17 ESM set allows hostile radars to be identified and classified on the photo imagery, while the ALQ-161 normally carried on the centre pylon handles the ELINT task. The USAF has spent more than $110 million in upgrading the APQ-99 radars of 312 RF-4s, and has installed the Litton Amecon ALQ-125 Tactical Electronic Reconnaissance (TEREC) and Ford Aerospace AVQ-26 Pave Tack Laser designator/fire control system aboard selected aircraft. A more drastic rework was planned to replace cameras with electro-optical sensors able to transmit real-time imagery via a digital data link. The scheme was shelved in the spring of 1988. The first of 46 RF-4Bs built for the USMC flew for the first time on 12 March 1965. These were generally similar to the RF-4C, combining the systems of the USAF aircraft with the airframe of the Navy's F-4B fighter. In an effort to extend RF-4B service life by a further eight years, a batch of 30 was reworked in 1978. Equipment added included the APD-10 SLAR, AAD-5 infra-red reconnaissance set and a data link. The RF-4E is an export model operated by Germany, Greece, Iran, Israel, Japan and Turkey; approximately 150 were built. Spain is the sole export RF-4C operator. Many of the USAF sensors were highly classified, so could not be cleared for export, and customers ordering the RF-4E have in some cases had to accept an alternative equipment. Many are now updating their fleet.

Ground Weapons

Above: US Marines training in the desert. Their elderly M-60A3 main battle tank has been upgraded by adding Explosive Reactive Armour tiles to vulnerable surfaces.

Below: Technology in land warfare has bestowed the infantry with the ability to kill main battle tanks at long distances with missiles such as this improved TOW 2.

Left: The M-109 was the standard Allied self-propelled artillery piece in the Gulf. Continuously improved over nearly 30 years of service, the M-109 remains an effective and reliable weapon.

For all that technology promises to introduce new dimensions to ground operations, the fundamental sequence of those operations remains the same: the artillery must prepare the way by destroying enemy defences, the armour must force a way through and around the defences, and finally the infantry must consolidate the gains and occupy the ground taken.

ARTILLERY

During the darker days of the Second World War, Winston Churchill is reputed to have said "Renown awaits the commander who restores artillery to its rightful place on the battlefield", and events in the Gulf have proven the truth of this. Only in the past decade or so has any of the modern technology, poured into missiles and aircraft, been allowed to flow into the artillery field. Much of it, almost all of it, was untested before the Gulf conflict, actual combat has revealed a quantum leap in the effectiveness of the artillery arm.

Conventional artillery is an area in which Iraq was quantitatively superior, starting the conflict with some 3000 towed guns, 500 self-propelled (SP) guns, some 200 field rocket systems and about 50 surface-to surface missile launchers; this total was, of course, considerably eroded – by at least one-third – by the air attacks of the first phase of the campaign. But even though the number of weapons remaining were still far greater than those available to the Allies, the figure is misleading, since much of this artillery was worthless. Iraq acquired artillery from many sources, and even though many weapons have the same calibre, the ammunition they fire is not interchangeable. This leads to an enormous administrative and logistic problem which would not have been of any great consequence against an unsophisticated enemy but which proved to be a weak spot in the face of air superiority. A battery which cannot obtain the special ammunition it needs is no longer any sort of threat.

The Allies, on the other hand, reaped the benefit of NATO standardisation. The greater part of their artillery strength was 155mm calibre and as the guns of any NATO army are capable of firing the ammunition of another, there was practically no logistic problem of compatability.

The other major calibre in Allied use was 203mm and, since all the 203mm guns in existence, irrespective of their owners, are of American design, no ammunition supply problem arose.

Nevertheless, some of the artillery in Iraqi hands was of extremely high quality and modern specification, equal to, and in some respects better than, the weapons in use by the Allies. In recent years Iraq purchased the 155mm GHN-45 howitzer from Austria, the 155mm G5 gun-howitzer from South Africa and the Chinese version of the GHN-45, a total of some 500 pieces of very modern ordnance. These all stem from the design originally put

Below: Towed artillery, such as these US M-198s, still has a place in modern warfare, although only under conditions of air supremacy and no counter-battery threat.

forward by Dr. Gerald Bull, and they can fire an advanced projectile to a range of 19 miles (30km) and a "base bleed" shell to 24 miles (39km).

The advanced projectile is known as the Extended Range Full Bore (ERFB) shell, and is based on a design developed in Germany in 1943. The object is to shape the shell for the optimum performance in flight, then make the necessary adjustments to make it fit the gun barrel; the traditional technique was first to make it fit the gun barrel and then do what was possible to improve the flight. This meant that the shell had to have a long, parallel-sided section so that it was longitudinally stable as it travelled up the

barrel, but had a relatively short tapering section at the front and rear to give it some aerodynamic shape. The ERFB design has the shell gently tapering from the nose to a point quite close to the base, giving it the best possible aerodynamic shape, but then has aerofoil stub wings added to the shoulder of the shell. These are of bore diameter but wider than the rifling grooves, so that they rest on top of the rifling and give the necessary longitudinal stability. The aerodynamic section also allows these stub wings to add lift to the shell during flight, so that the ERFB shell will gain some 15 to 20 percent extra range over a conventional shell, with little or no reduction in accuracy.

The base bleed shell, like the ERFB (and, indeed, most of the Bull designs), is another old idea which has been finally realised due to advances in technology. One of the factors restricting the range of heavy artillery is the drag set up by the shell as it passes through the air: put simply, the shell cleaves through the air and takes with it a vacuum behind its base into which the disrupted air must swirl; this swirling placing a drag on the shell. A base

Below: First built in 1978, the French GCT 155mm howitzer is in service with France, Iraq and Saudi Arabia. This example has its loading hatches open, showing ammunition storage.

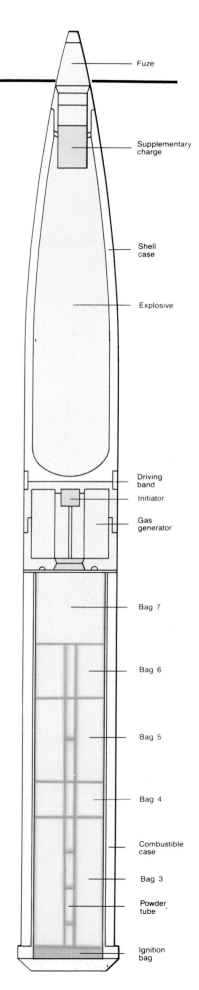

Fuze

Supplementary charge

Shell case

Explosive

Driving band

Initiator

Gas generator

Bag 7

Bag 6

Bag 5

Bag 4

Combustible case

Bag 3

Powder tube

Ignition bag

Above: This M-198 crew shows clearly the work in loading heavy shells and charges into a gun. It is even harder within the confines of a self-propelled weapon.

Above: These M-110A2s carry a long -barrelled 203mm howitzer fitted with a muzzle brake. The M-110 has no protection whatsoever for its crew and all ammunition is carried by a separate vehicle.

Right: A typical base-bleed shell is the GIAT 155mm H2. A small gas generator expels gas at low pressure to reduce drag caused by the vacuum at the base of the projectile, thus reducing drag.

range was more than compensated for in the superior methods of fire control.

The standard Allied 155mm projectiles were of the type known as "hemispherical base" shells. The rear end of the shell is hollowed out into a hemisphere and most of the vacuum is contained inside this area, so that the airflow, as it meets behind the shell, is far less disturbed and develops less drag. This, together with good shaping (though not so good as the ERFB shell) allows 155mm howitzers to reach to 16 miles (25km). The British FH-70 howitzer can also fire a base bleed projectile reaching 20 miles (32km) which is quite sufficient for the tasks in view. The American 155mm M109 howitzer has only 12 miles (18km) range with its conventional shell, an elderly design, but it can extend this to 15 miles (24km) by firing a rocket-boosted shell. This is, in some ways, like the base-bleed, carrying a charge of smokeless propellant in its base, but in this case the charge is larger and develops additional thrust to extend the trajectory.

bleed shell has a compartment in its base filled with smokeless powder; this is ignited by the flash of the propelling charge and burns at a preset rate during flight, pouring gas into the vacuum behind the shell and thus filling it. The air flowing past the shell now continues to flow smoothly past this filled space and meets some distance behind the shell, no longer causing any drag. Base bleed has the aerodynamic effect of a smooth "boat-tail" on the shell but with the simpler structure of a conventional flat end. Although it sounds simple, it has taken many years of experiments to perfect the system, but it is capable of increasing the maximum range by as much as 25 percent in some cases. Adding base bleed to an ERFB shell (which then becomes an ERFBB) gave these Iraqi howitzers a maximum range close to 25 miles (40km), although this was little used in the war.

Above: Typical of those fired by most artillery, these 155mm shells have good aerodynamic taper with a parallel section long enough to securely grip the gun barrel.

The Allied projectiles have not adopted these systems, largely because these shells were developed before the ERFB design appeared, and also because the Allied artillery placed less emphasis on sheer range. It is no use sending a shell to an enormous range if you have no means of identifying the presence of a target or of making sure the shells land upon it. It is in this area which the Allied artillery was far superior, and any shortcomings in maximum

Below: Copperhead is a 155mm artillery projectile which will guide onto a target illuminated by laser. Individual tanks can be hit with unnerving accuracy, as shown in this test shot.

What is far more significant is the availability to the Allies of "Improved Conventional Munitions" or ICMs. These are conventional insofar as they are shells without base bleed or rocket assistance, but improved by virtue of their payload. Instead of simply being filled with high explosive, they contain a number of anti-personnel or anti-tank "bomblets". The shell is fired so as to burst in the air over the target area and scatter these bomblets beneath. They detonate on impact and either shower the immediate area with fragments or develop a powerful

shaped explosive blast which will penetrate the upper surfaces of any armoured vehicle and destroy whatever it meets inside. These shells allow artillery to attack armour at ranges far in excess of what has previously been possible; until the advent of the ICM, armour had to be fought at short range with direct fire - the gunner and his target were in view of each other. This was simply because the chance of dropping a shell down on to such a tiny target as a tank at several miles range was barely worth considering. But by bursting an ICM over a known tank harbour, the odds are multiplied immensely by the sheer quantity of bomblets released.

Carrying the ICM to it's logical conclusion is the guided shell. The only system currently deployed is the American "Copperhead". An observer designates an individual target with a laser beam which Copperhead homes onto. Packing a laser seeker, guidance electronics, folding steering fins and a power pack into a 155mm shell in such a way as to survive the shock of firing was a remarkable technical achievement. Copperhead is expensive and is only worthwhile in a few special situations, but gives artillery a devastating long-range anti-armour capability when necessary.

Fire control is, today, almost entirely computerised; given the location of the gun and the location of the target, a computer can calculate the range and azimuth angle and then correct for wind, air temperature, charge temperature and many other variables with an accuracy not possible before the microchip era. This means that the first round fired will invariably land in the target area and that surprise is complete. Moreover, it also means that it is no longer so vital to have the target under actual observation; in years gone by this was necessary because the first round would probably land some distance away from the target and have to be visually

Above: The Multi-Launch Rocket System (MLRS) may look like a supply vehicle, but with twelve rockets it can devastate targets at ranges of over 20 miles (32km).

spotted and corrections made to bring the impact and target together. Today the use of "predicted" fire, where the computer determination of the gun data takes all possible variables into account, renders observation less vital: nice if you can get it, not disastrous if you can't.

Detection of targets has also benefited from technology. Remote Piloted Vehicles—"drones" or pilotless aircraft—fitted with TV and film cameras, can fly over the lines, spot targets, produce a picture in real time for the artillery commander's inspection, and so allow targets out of sight to the front line to be engaged. Laser rangefinders permit accurate determination of target

Above: A gas turbine engine, special composite armour, 120mm gun and computerised fire control give the US M1A1 main battle tank a unique combination of mobility, protection and firepower.

Below: This MLRS is letting rip with the first of a salvo of 12 rockets. Each rocket carries 644 dual purpose M-77 fragmentation/shaped charge bomblets to give a total of 7728 for the salvo.

positions when they can be seen, and at night the use of infra-red observing instruments and other night vision aids allows observation to be carried on almost as easily as by day.

ARMOUR

Tanks are much the same sort of vehicle, whichever country makes them; an armoured body, an engine and transmission, tracked suspension, a turret and gun. But how these items are developed and how they are put together is what distinguishes one tank from another, and one of the most important elements of the modern tank is its fire control system.

There are two schools of thought on tank guns; either they should be rifled or they should be smooth-bored. The Americans and Russians tend to use smoothbores, the British and French use rifled guns, and there are valid arguments on both sides. Smooth-bored guns allow very high velocities to be reached, since there is no frictional drag on the projectile due to rifling in the bore. This is important in connection with the highly specialised projectiles used for attacking tanks. The present-day standard in this area is the Armour Piercing, Fin-Stabilised, Discarding Sabot (APFSDS) shot. This consists of a long dart with fins, made of an extremely hard and dense material

Above: The older M-60A3 is still in extensive service, especially with the US Marine Corps. This M-60 is fitted with a laser system to simulate hits in exercises.

such as tungsten carbide or depleted uranium. It is no more than two inches or so in diameter, far smaller than the bore of the gun (120mm in the American Ml Abrams tank, 125mm in the Iraqi T72 tank) and so it is enclosed in a light alloy "sabot" or sleeve which is of the correct size to fit the gun barrel. This sabot is weakened in certain spots, and these shear under the shock of firing. The sabot is now in three or four pieces but is still securely locked to the dart (or "penetrator")

so long as it is travelling up the bore. As soon as the projectile leaves the gun muzzle, air resistance on the pieces of the sabot cause them to peel away from the penetrator and fly off harmlessly, to fall to the ground some distance in front of the gun. The narrow penetrator flies on towards the target.

The object behind all this complication is simply to obtain the greatest possible velocity in the penetrator. It is necessary to make it of a hard and dense material so that it will punch a hole in the armour; but made to full size it would be far too heavy to reach any decent velocity. So by using this long dart shape and making it up to full bore size with

Above: The British Challenger main battle tank has been developed from a design originally specified for the Shah of Iran. Unlike the M-1, the Challenger uses a conventional diesel propulsion system, although it can still manage a reasonable turn of speed.

Left: Criticised earlier for a poor showing in NATO gunnery competitions, the Challenger and its crews have since proved themselves in the only gunnery contest that counts - actual combat. This view shows the box for the thermal imaging sight on the side of the turret.

Above: The M-551 Sheridan was designed to provide armoured fire support to airborne units. It uses an unusual 152mm combined gun/ missile launcher system.

light alloy, you have a lightweight projectile which can be accelerated up the gun vary rapidly indeed, which then discards all the extraneous material, to leave the perfectly streamlined dart moving at something in the order of 3500 metres per second – 8400 miles per hour.

When this strikes the target, something has to give way; and it won't be the penetrator. The small diameter of the hard and dense material means that a considerable momentum

M1 Abrams Fire Control System

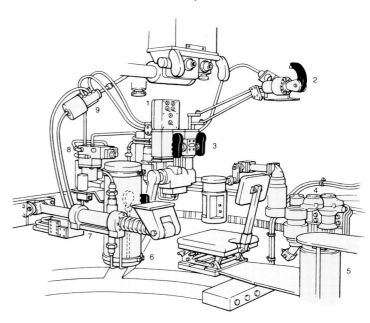

Above: The block diagram for the US Army's M-1 fire control system. The system is fully automatic and accepts atmospheric, ballistic and orientation inputs from sensors, keyboard and computer systems. It then computes pointing data for the main gun and outputs the data by controlling gun/sight servos. Such systems are rapidly becoming the most expensive single elements on modern MBTs.

Right: The Cadillac Gage power control system for the M-1, showing the gunner's position and the commander's control unit. This electrohydraulic system uses constant pressure power controls.

1 Gunner's control box
2 Commander's control
3 Gunner's control
4 Traverse mechanism
5 Power supply
6 Main accumulator
7 Elevation mechanism
8 Recoil exerciser valve
9 Superelevating actuator

M1 Abrams power control system

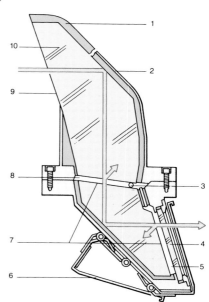

Right: A relatively new requirement for tank periscopes is protection from eye damage which could be caused by lasers in fire control and ranging systems.

Helio tank periscope

1 Polyurethane encapsulation or alloy cover for external installation
2 Shatter alloy, DMC or armour steel case for internal glass mounting
3 Dessicating valve
4 Polycarbonate anti-spall protection
5 Gas-filled desicated air gap
6 Folding blind
7 Coating or glass filter for laser protection
8 Gas-filled balistic air gap
9 Non-reflecting front face
10 Stabilised or crown glass

APFSDS ammunition effect

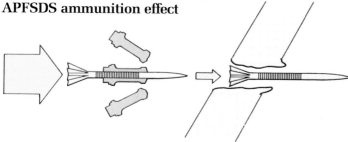

Above: The Armour Piercing Fin-Stabilised Discarding Sabot (APFSDS) round throws off its sabot as it leaves the muzzle of the gun. The penetrator rod then

travels at high velocity to the target where it punches its way through the armour plate and ricochets around the interior of the tank, causing severe damage.

Above: The French AMX-30 is also in service Qatar, Saudi Arabia, and the United Arab Emirates. Its 105mm gun is backed up by a 20mm cannon on a coaxial mount.

several thousand foot-tons of energy - is concentrated into a very small area, and since the dart is harder than armour steel, it punches a hole through the armour and then shatters as it breaks into the tank, flinging high-velocity white-hot fragments in all directions. Add to this the fragments broken from the tank's armour, and you will see why

APFSDS is considered the deadliest tank-killer available.

So how do the British and French get on with their rifled guns, and why do they prefer them? They also use APFSDS, but arrange that the 'driving band' – that portion of the projectile which bites into the rifling so as to spin the projectile and seal

the propelling gas – is designed so that it is free to rotate independently of the sabot, so that the complete shot picks up relatively little spin as it goes up the bore. It discards its sabot rather more cleanly, since the small amount of spin causes a centrifugal effect which helps the sabot sections to fly clear, and the fins on the penetrator soon damp out what spin has been picked up.

In addition, the British tanks use APDS shot-this is the original form of discarding sabot shot, developed in 1943-44, and is designed to work with rifled guns. The penetrator spins, instead of relying on fins to keep it pointed at the target, but due to this, is a good deal shorter and therefore has rather less energy on striking. Even so, when fired from the British 120mm gun it has more than enough energy to defeat any current tank.

The reason for retaining rifled guns is simply that it gives the gun a better choice of ammunition. Fin stabilising a pointed dart is simple enough, but trying to fin stabilise other types of ammunition can cause problems. The only type which has been successfully fin-stabilised is an alternative method of armour attack called the "shaped charge", which is just as well since this only works well when it isn't spinning. The shaped charge (or HEAT for High Explosive Anti-Tank) shell is a cylindrical, full calibre, shell with a tail boom carrying fins. The shell contains a charge of several pounds of high explosive, and the front end of this charge is hollowed out into a cone, lined with copper or some other dense material. In front of this goes an extended nose carrying a piezo-electric crystal in its tip.

Great velocity is not required for this projectile, merely sufficient to get it to the target before the target has moved very much. On striking, the piezo-electric crystal is crushed, which generates a pulse of electri-

cal power. This is passed down to a detonator in the rear end of the explosive charge. The charge detonates and as the detonation wave passes around the cone, so it collapses it and, by what might be considered as a "focusing" action, converts the material of the cone into a fast-moving jet of molten material and high explosive gas – and by fast-moving we mean something in the order of 7000 metres a second, say 16,000 mph. The temperature of the jet is high, and the mass, due to the use of the dense copper lining material, is also high, and the combined result of heat, mass and velocity simply punches through armour like a hot wire through cheese. A great deal of the explosive energy is left to flow through the resulting hole, leading to high temperatures and blast over-pressures inside the tank. And if the jet of hot gas and metal hits an ammunition storage area or a fuel tank, the results can be catastrophic.

A third method of attack is peculiar to the British, and is one of their reasons for keeping to the rifled gun. This is the High Explosive Squash Head (HESH) shell, another Second World War invention which has been constantly perfected in the last forty years. This works best with a rifled gun, and, like the HEAT shell, does not demand high velocity. The shell is blunt-nosed, is filled with plastic explosive, and has a fuze in its base. On striking, the shell body squashes allowing the explosive to be pressed against the target in tight

Right: The older style of "battle taxi" is epitomised by the M-113 APC. Basically an aluminium box on tracks it has seen service with many armies around the world.

HEAT ammunition

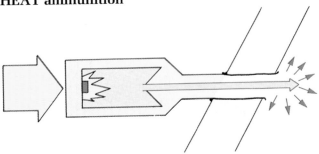

Above: HEAT rounds use the Monroe effect, involving detonation of the explosive at a critical distance from the target. The conical hollow charge focusses the

explosion into a high speed jet which slices through the armour and into the interior of the tank, causing catastrophic damage to crew and equipment.

HESH ammunition

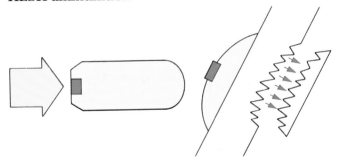

Above: A High Explosive Squash Head (HESH) round consists of a large amount of HE with a base fuse in a thin steel case. On hitting the target, the explosive spreads to form a cake and is then detonated. The shock generated is enough to

knock a scab of the interior of the plate; the scab ricochets around inside tank at high speed. The external explosion is sufficiently powerful for HESH to be used as an HE shell against unarmoured targets.

contact with the armour. The base fuze then detonates the explosive and this drives a massive disruptive shock wave into the armour. This wave reflects off the inner surface of the plate and causes it to fail, breaking off a 'scab' of steel and driving it around the inside of the tank at high velocity. This scab can be as much as a foot across and weigh 20 or 30 pounds (9 to 14kg), making it a formidable and highly destructive missile in the confined space inside the tank.

To every ill there is a remedy, or so the ordnance engineers claim; the remedy for these formidable anti-armour projectiles is either "composite armour" or "reactive armour". Composite armour is just what the name implies; an armour made of layers of different substances, each of which has some specific protective property against some specific type of attack. Precisely what this armour consists of is a closely-guarded secret, but some basic principles can be propounded. For example, two thicknesses of plate can be separated by a layer of a chemical which will absorb all the heat from a shaped charge jet, preventing piercing the inner skin. A slab of steel armour can be reinforced with a network of titanium rods; a dense penetrator coming through the steel and striking one of these rods will find something harder than itself for once, and this will deflect the nose of the penetrator. Now, a penetrator is strong under compressive stress, but far less strong under sideways 'shear' stress, and this sudden deflection will break off the major portion of the penetrator outside the armour; without the weight of that portion the penetration will fail. A layer of rubber between two slabs or armour would absorb the shock wave of a HESH detonation. So by combining this sort of approach it becomes possible to make a "sandwich" which will put up a considerable resistance to any form of attack.

Explosive Reactive Armour (ERA) is another method of protection. It takes the form of a layer of explosive sandwiched between two layers of thick steel, attached to the existing vehicle armour but spaced away from it. Reactive armour looks like a pattern of flat tiles or sometimes rectangular boxes over numerable areas of the vehicle. On being struck, particularly by a shaped charge, the explosive layer detonates, flinging the steel plates apart. The steel plates absorb much of the shaped charge jet before it hits the vehicle armour and the force of the explosion also disrupts the formation of a perfect jet. Similarly, striking with a hard penetrator will set off the reactive charge and this should be sufficient to break up the penetrator.

Bottom Right: Reactive armour was first deployed by Israel in the 1980s. Each box on the hull and turret of this M-60 tank contains an explosive element sandwiched between two steel plates.

Above: Most tanks still have to load ammunition through the turret roof hatches - and this row of APDS shells for an M-1 illustrates the magnitude of the task.

Below: Later generation reactive armour tends to be thin tiles, like those fitted to the side of this M-3 Cavalry Fighting Vehicle variant of the M-2 Bradley IFV.

Above: The Warrior IFV is the British contemporary of the M-2. Its lack of infantry firing ports and ATGW reflects a different concept of operations.

Below: Night fighting abililty was a strength of the Allied forces. Even with plentiful night vision equipment, skills need sharpening by constant practice.

Left: The US M-2 Bradley IFV carries 7 infantrymen and a crew of 3. A 25mm, turret-mounted cannon provides fire support, with anti-tank protection given by a TOW ATGW twin launcher.

Above: The poor showing of the BMP in earlier Middle East wars - as exemplified by this captured Syrian example - had led to doubts about the effectiveness of IFVs in a major land war.

INFANTRY

In the vastness of the desert the image of the infantry as "the feet" has to be abandoned; today's infantry must be capable of keeping up with the tanks which are breaking a hole in the defensive line, and this means the use of tracked vehicles to carry them. In the past this has meant the APC (Armoured Personnel Carrier) which was a lightly armoured vehicle intended to deliver the infantry close to their destined firefight, there to release them to fight on their feet in the traditional manner.

The past decade has modified this view; the infantry are no longer satisfied with a "battle taxi", they require a vehicle with better protection and, above all, with some offensive capability. This demand has led to the Infantry Fighting Vehicle (IFV), exemplified by the British Warrior and the American Bradley on the one hand and the Soviet BMP-1 and BMP-2 on the other. All four are designed to give good protection to an infantry squad (7 men in the Bradley and Warrior, 8 in the BMP), provide them with adequate support firepower (25mm cannon in Bradley, 30mm cannon in Warrior and BMP-2, 73mm low-pressure gun in BMP-1), and also allow them to carry air defence and anti-tank missiles ready for use.

The Bradley and BMP also carry anti-tank missiles as standard weapons to give every infantry section a long range tank defence. These vehicles also carry firing ports in the hull to allow the infantry section inside to fire automatic weapons in an assault. The Warrior reflects the British view that such fire is wasteful and, therefore, no firing ports are provided.

There was a certain element of the unknown in the employment of IFVs, particularly with British and American forces, since they had never been used in combat by them. The general opinion is that with well trained and well disciplined troops, they are highly effective; in less efficient hands they carry the seeds of their own destruction, since there is a terrible temptation for the commander to "play at tanks" and go hunting for an enemy to destroy, rather than attending strictly to his proper task, which is simply to shoot and move until he is in position to deploy his troops, then act as a covering vehicle for them. Like other armoured vehicles, they operate best in company, where they can cover each other; an IFV moving about on its own is simply a very attractive target.

The anti-armour weapons provided to the infantry are legion; the British used Milan, a guided missile, LAW-80, a shoulder-fired rocket, and the 84mm Carl Gustav recoilless gun. The Americans also had Carl Gustav, plus the Swedish AT-4 shoulder-fired rocket, the TOW missile and the Dragon missile. The Iraqi forces operated Soviet Sagger and Spigot missiles, the Milan missile, the French HOT missile and possibly some elderly French SS-11 missiles. All infantry anti-tank systems use HEAT warheads to give a heavy punch. Of these, Milan and TOW are superior, insofar as the weapons in the hands of the Allies were the very latest versions with superior warheads and guidance system. The arrival of composite and reactive armour led to the development of improved warheads for these two weapons, and they were quite capable of dealing with any Iraqi armour; the earlier generations of TOW, in Israeli hands, had proved the efficiency of this weapon already. Sagger and Spigot were less effective, being older technology, and Dragon, whilst good, did not have the range of the other missiles, though it was a good deal more easily portable than any of the other medium wire-guided weapons.

The shoulder-fired weapons, with the possible exception of LAW-80, will be of less use against heavy tanks but they have an undoubted ability to deal with IFVs and lighter armour, though they are not a great deal of use at ranges over about 300 metres. The Iraqi forces relied a great deal upon the Soviet shoulder-fired RPG-7, which they had in profusion, but the truth is that this weapon is obsolete against other than APCs.

The infantryman's basic weapon, the rifle, will be the focus of attention for soldiers all over the world. For the past twenty years the 5.56mm bullet has taken over the major armies, based upon its proven efficiency in close-quarter fighting. Unfortunately, the desert is not the best arena for this type of shooting, and the longer-ranging, harder-hitting 7.62mm cartridge has a role to play in this environment. It is notable that a proportion of both British and US troops were armed with 7.62mm FN-FAL or M14 rifles, and perhaps some comparative figures will eventually appear to prove the point once and for all. The Iraqi forces may have had the same question on their minds; the greater part of their army was armed with the Soviet AKM 7.62mm rifle, firing a less powerful cartridge than the NATO round of the same calibre. But in the past few years the Iraq national armoury has been making a version of the AKM in 5.56mm cali-

bre, using the old American M193 cartridge, slightly less powerful than the current NATO-standard round.

FIELD ENGINEERING

Field engineering is best defined as 'removing the obstacles to the advance' and this really means dealing with anything from buried mines to blown-out bridges. Mines are a cheap and effective method of denying ground to an attacker, and the desert is the ideal place for employing them. As a result mines were used in quantity, requiring some method of destroying them in quantity, since digging them up

individually would have been far too slow. To cut a path through any minefield the Giant Viper is the quickest method. This is simply a rocket motor attached to several hundred feet of hose which is filled with a high explosive. The hose is carefully coiled in a special trailer, together with a simple fixed launcher for the rocket. The trailer is positioned at the edge of the minefield and the rocket is fired on a trajectory which is just sufficient to drag the hosepipe to its full length and drop it on the ground. As soon as it has landed, the explosive is detonated, and the resulting blast will detonate any mine beneath the hose

Above: The final arbiter of war, the infantryman and his personal weapon. This US trooper is aiming his M-249 Squad Automatic Weapon, a version of the Belgian Minimi light machine gun.

or within a few yards on either side, leaving a path wide enough to permit tanks or wheeled vehicles to pass safely. Firing two Giant Vipers in parallel will produce a patch amply wide enough for an advance.

Sand berms, ditches and similar obstacles can be dealt with by specially-equipped tanks with bulldozer blades.

FFV 028 anti-tank mine performance

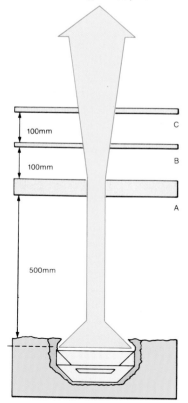

A: 50nm armour plate;
exit hole diameter approximately 65mm

B: 10mm commerical iron plate;
exit hole diameter approximately 80mm

C: 10mm commerical iron plate;
exit hole diameter approximately 140mm

C

100mm

B

100mm

A

500mm

Left: The diagram shows the operation of a typical anti-tank mine. Once triggered, the shallow shaped charge of the mine sends a massive explosive jet through the belly of the tank - here represented by a 50mm target plate. The two witness plates indicate the effect of the jet on the vehicle's interior.

Below: The Milan ATGW in its launch tube. The gas generator drives the piston to kick the missile out of the tube before ignition of the boost motor.

Euromissile Milan

Below: Command and control of land forces has been transformed by communications systems such the British Ptarmigan. Trunk nodes form a survivable and flexible grid which users link into.

Ptarmigan

▰▰▰	Corps
▰▰	Division
▰	Brigade
▼	Trunk node
▬	Headquarters/Access node
●	Single-channel radio access
◆	Brigade HQ
➤	Mobile radio subscriber

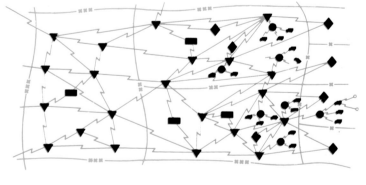

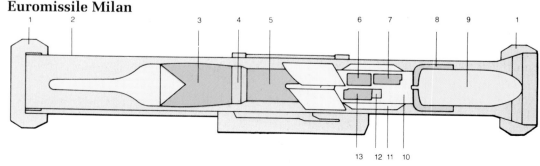

1   2   3   4   5   6   7   8   9   1

13 12 11 10

M1 and M60

M1 ABRAMS

Origin: USA
Crew: 4
Armament: One 105mm gun; one 7.62mm machine gun coaxial with main armament; one 7.62mm machine gun at loader's station; one 12.7mm machine gun at commander's station; six smoke dischargers each side of turret
Armour: Classified
Dimensions: Length including main armament 32ft 0in (9.766m); hull length 26ft 0in (7.918m); width 12ft 0in (3.653m); height 9ft 6in (2.885m)
Combat weight: 120,250lb (54,545kg)
Ground pressure: 13.7psi (0.96kg/cm^2)
Engine: Avco Lycoming AGT-1500 gas turbine developing 1,500hp (1,118kW) at 3,000rpm
Performance: Road speed 45mph (72.421km/h); range 310 miles (498km); vertical obstacle 4ft 1in (1.244m); trench 9ft 0in (2.743m); gradient 60 per cent
History: Developed from early 1970s with first production vehicles being completed in 1980; in service only with United States Army, for which 7,467 M1/M1A1s are to be built by the early 1990s
Background: Following the demise of the MBT-70, a joint development between West Germany and the United States, and the austre version

for the US Army called the XM803, it was decided to build a new tank from scratch and competitive contracts were awarded to both Chrysler and General Motors for a new MBT under the designation XM1. After trials with both vehicles the Chrysler XM1 was selected for further development and was later placed in production as the M1 Abrams at two plants, one in Lima, Ohio, and the other in Detroit, Michigan. The M1 Abrams was a revolutionary design, incorporating new composite armour and powered by a gas turbine engine which gives it a high power-to-weight ratio and good speed both on roads and across country. The main armament is the 105mm M68 installed in the older M60 but it has a new computerised fire control system incorporating a laser rangefinder which enables the tank to hit stationary and moving targets while itself moving at speed. The composite armour gives a high degree of protection against both chemical and kinetic energy attack; for enhanced survivability an explosion and fire suppression system is installed, and ammunition in the turret bustle is separated from the crew compartment by special sliding doors. The original M1 has been replaced in production by the M1A1 which has many improvements, the most significant being the 120mm smoothbore gun which is also installed in

the West German Leopard 2 and improved armour protection. Further improvements in the area of fire control are already under way. The introduction of the turbine powered M1 has not been without problems and many still believe that turbines have no place on the battlefield, but the fact is that the M1 is more reliable than the diesel engined M60 which has been in service with the US Army for some 25 years, and its speed and mobility has forced the US Army to develop new tactics.

M60

Origin: USA
Crew: 4
Armament: One 105mm gun; one 7.62mm machine gun coaxial with main armament; one 12.7mm anti-aircraft machine gun; six smoke dischargers each side of turret
Armour: Classified
Dimensions: Length including main armament 30ft 6in (9.309m); hull length 22ft 9in (6.946m); width 11ft 11in (3.631m); height 10ft 6in (3.213m)
Combat weight: 109,600lb (49,714kg)
Ground pressure: 11.37lb/sq in (0.80kg/cm2)
Engine: Teledyne Continental AVDS-1790-2A 12-cylinder air-cooled diesel developing 750bhp (560kW) at 2,400rpm

Performance: Road speed 30mph (48.28km/h); range 310 miles (500km); vertical obstacle 3ft 0in (0.914m); trench 8ft 6in (2.59m); gradient 60 per cent
History: Entered production at Detroit Arsenal Tank Plant in 1960 and still in production for export market; in service with Austria, Bahrain, Egypt, Iran, Israel, Italy also built under licence by OTO Melara), Jordan, Oman, Saudi Arabia, Singapore (AVLB and CEV only), Spain (AVLB only), Sudan, Tunisia, United States (Army and Marines) and North Yemen
Background: The M60 series is a further development of the earlier M48 MBT but has the diesel engine fitted in late production M48s and a British-designed 105mm rifled tank

Below The M1 is the latest MBT to enter service with the US Army. Its ammunition load includes smoke grenades (1), APFSDS-T (2) APDS-T (3), HESH (4), HEAT (5), HEP (6), APERS-T (7) and Canister (8) rounds plus belts of 7.62mm (9) and 12.7mm (10) machine gun ammunition. The actual mix of ammunition for the main gun depends on the tactical situation and types of target to he engaged but the main tank-killing round is the APFSDS-T.

gun. The first model, the M60, was followed by the M60A1 with a new and improved turret; the M60A2 had a 152mm gun/missile launcher but has been phased out of service; and the current production model is the M60A3, whose many improvements include a computerised fire control system, a laser rangefinder and thermal night vision equipment. Further developments include reactive armour which will defeat anti-tank guided weapons with their HEAT warheads. Turret traverse and weapon elevation is hydraulic, a feature which did not prove very popular with Israeli tank crews in the last Middle East conflict. A total of 63 rounds of 105mm, 5,950 rounds of 7.62mm and 900 rounds of 12.7mm ammunition are carried. Variants include a scissors type armoured vehicle launched bridge, the M728 Combat Engineer Vehicle armed with a 165mm demolition gun and fitted with dozer blade and A frame, and a Robotic Breaching Assault Tank which has been designed to breach enemy minefields. M60 series tanks have been used in combat by the Israeli Army, but they did not prove as survivable as the British supplied Centurion MBTs. All Israeli M60s have now been fitted with the Blazer reactive armour first revealed during the invasion of the Lebanon.

Above: A US M60A3 on excercise in Egypt uses a main armament firing simulator mounted on the barrel to add realism to the proceedings. The device produces a combination of smoke, noise and flash similar to that of the 105mm gun firing.

Above: Although the M1 and M1A1 are entering service in increasing numbers, the M60A1 and M60A3 will remain in service with the US well into the next decade and a number of improvement programmes have already been started with still more to come. The 105mm gun of the M60 series is identical to that of the original M1 and fires the same ammunition, including APFSDS-T (1), APDS-T (2), APERS-T (3), HEAT (4) and smoke (5) rounds. The smoke grenades (6) are fired from the dischargers each side of the turret while the 7.62mm (7) and 12.7mm (8) machine gun ammunition comes in belts.

Chieftain and Challenger I

CHIEFTAIN

Origin: United Kingdom
Crew: 4
Armament: One 120mm gun; one 7.62mm machine gun coaxial with main armament; one 7.62mm machine gun on commander's cupola; six smoke dischargers each side of turret
Armour: Classified
Dimensions: Length including main armament 35ft 5in (10.795m); hull length 24ft 8in (7.518m); width 11ft 6in (3.504m); height 9ft 6in (2.895m)
Combat weight: 121,253lb (55,000kg)
Engine: Leyland L60 two-stroke, compression ignition, 6-cylinder (12 opposed pistons) multi-fuel developing 750bhp (559kW) at 2,100rpm
Ground pressure: 12.8lb/sq in (0.9kg/cm^2)
Performance: Road speed 30mph (48km/h); range 250-310 miles (400-500km); vertical obstacle 3ft 0in (0.914m); trench 10ft 4in (3.149m); gradient 60 per cent
History: Developed in late 1950s

with first prototype being completed in 1961 and production (now complete) being undertaken by Royal Ordnance Leeds and Vickers at Elswick from mid-1960s; in service with Iran, Iraq, Jordan (ARV only), Kuwait, Oman and United Kingdom
Background: Between 1945 and 1962 more than 4,400 Centurion tanks were built for the home and export markets, the type being the standard tank of the British Army in the postwar period, and large numbers remain in service with Denmark, Israel, Jordan, South Africa, Sweden and Switzerland.
When requirements for Centurion's replacement were drawn up emphasis was placed first on armour protection, second on firepower and third on mobility. The end result was the Chieftain which entered service with the British Army in the mid1960s and has been continuously modified to meet changing operational requirements. Compared with the French AMX-30 and West German Leopard 1 the Chieftain has much greater armour protection and a heavier main armament; on the

other hand it is slower and more restricted in operating range. Main armament consists of a rifled 120mm gun which fires separately loaded ammunition (projectile and charge), with a 7.62mm machine gun being mounted coaxially with the main armament and a similar weapon being mounted on the commander's cupola. When the Chieftain was first introduced the 120mm gun was aimed using a ranging machine gun, but this was subsequently replaced by a laser rangefinder and then a computerised fire control system was added. Even in the early 1990s Chieftain forms a large part of the Royal Armoured Corps, though the Challenger is being introduced in increasing numbers. More recent improvements include the installation of a Thermal Observation and Gunnery System (TOGS) and appliqué armour to the turret front and sides. Variants of the Chieftain include an armoured vehicle launched bridge, an armoured recovery vehicle and, more recently, a specialised engineer vehicle designed to handle Challenger powerpacks.

CHALLENGER I

Origin: United Kingdom
Crew: 4
Armament: One 120mm gun; one 7.62mm machine gun coaxial with main armament; one 7.62mm machine gun on commander's cupola; one bank of six smoke dischargers each side of turret
Armour: Classified
Dimensions: Length including main armament 37ft 11in (11.56m); hull length 27ft 4in (8.327m); width 11ft 6in (3.518m); height 9ft 8in (2.95m)
Combat weight: 136,685lb (62,000kg)
Ground pressure: 13.79lb/sq in (0.97kg/cm^2)
Engine: Rolls-Royce Condor CV-12 12-cylinder diesel developing 1,200bhp (895kW) at 2,300rpm
Performance: Road speed 35mph (56km/h); range (estimate) 373 miles (600km); vertical obstacle 3ft 0in (0.9m); trench 9ft 2in (2.8m); gradient 60 per cent
History: Following the cancellation of the MBT-80 project, further development of the Shir 2, originally developed for Iran, was carried out;

Left: In terms of numbers, Chieftain is still an important tank in the British Army and it is now being improved with additional armour protection and the Thermal Observation and Gunnery System (TOGS). In the future the current L11 series gun will be replaced by a new high pressure gun firing new ammunition.

Below: Chieftain and Challenger ammunition includes 7.62mm (1) belts, APFSDS (2), APDS (3), APDS Practice (4) and HESH (5) rounds, charges (6,7,8 and 9), HESH practice (10), and Smoke (11) rounds, plus electric vent tube to ignite main charge (12), 66mm smoke grenades (13) and projectiles (14) for the smoke screening system. All charges are stowed below the turret in special containers to enhance the tanks' survivability.

Above: The Challenger I is the latest MBT to enter service with the British Army and by the end of the 1980s half the tank regiments in BAOR were equipped with the tank. Its fire control system and gun are virtually identical to those of the Chieftain, but a new high pressure gun is to be installed.

the end result was the Challenger, which was accepted for service by the British Army in 1982 with first production vehicles being handed over by Royal Ordnance Leeds (now owned by Vickers Defence Systems) in 1983. By the late 1980s about half the armoured regiments in British Army of the Rhine were equipped with the Challenger MBT

Background: Main overseas customer for the Chieftain was Iran, which ordered more than 700 vehicles, and further development resulted in the Shir 1, essentially a Chieftain with a new powerpack consisting of a 1,200bhp (895kW) engine and new transmission. The Iranian revolution occurred before these tanks could be delivered, though production was already underway, and in the end Jordan took delivery of 274 slightly modified Shir 1s under the name Khalid from 1981. The Shir 2, subsequently renamed Challenger, has the same powerpack, armament and fire control system as the Shir 1 but with a hull and turret of Chobham armour which gives a very

high degree of protection against both kinetic and chemical attack over the frontal arc. The tank also has a hydropneumatic suspension system which gives an improved ride across country as well as a more stable firing platform. Main armament of the Challenger is identical to that of the Chieftain, consisting of a 120mm rifled gun firing separate loading ammunition, and all the propellent charges are stowed below the turret for increased survivability. A total of 64 projectiles and charges are carried, along with 4,000 rounds of 7.62mm machine gun ammunition. The computerised fire control system includes a laser rangefinder for the gunner, and TOGS is being installed in current production vehicles.

An improved high-pressure gun was fitted to the Challenger tanks, commencing in 1989, and this, together with improved APFSDS ammunition, has greatly increased the fighting range and penetration power of the main armament. The same gun will eventually be retro-fitted to all Chieftain tanks. An armoured recovery and repair version of the Challenger has begun entering service, though the full order of 80 vehicles is not expected to be completed until 1995. Equipment on this vehicle includes winches, a crane and a front-mounted bulldozer blade.

Above: The Challenger I is seen here with the VIRSS (visual infra-red screening system) boxes on the turret, although these were not selected for British Army Service.

T-54/55, T-62 and T-72

T-54/55

Origin: USSR
Armament: One 100mm gun; one 7.62mm machine gun coaxial with main armament; one 7.62mm bow machine gun; one 12.7mm anti-aircraft machine gun
Armour: 6.7in (170mm) maximum
Dimensions: Length including armament 29ft 6in (9m); hull length 21ft 2in (6.45m); width 10ft 9in (3.27m); height 7ft 10in (2.4m)
Combat weight: 79,366lbs (36,000kg)
Ground Pressure: 11.52lb/in² (0.81kg/cm²)
Engine: Model V-54 12-cylinder air-cooled diesel developing 520hp at 2,000rpm.
Performance: Maximum road speed 30mph (48km/h); range 249 miles (400km); vertical obstacle 2ft 8in (0.8m); trench 8ft 10in (2.7m); gradient 60 per cent
History: Entered service with the Soviet Army in 1950. Exported widely, users include all Warsaw Pact countries, China, Egypt, India, Iraq, Israel, Libya, Morocco, Pakistan, Somalia, Sudan, Syria, and others. Licensed production in many countries.
Background: Over 70,000 of all models of this series have been produced since the first prototype was completed in 1947. The T-54/55 has a compact silhouette and had a good gun and armour for its day. Cramped crew conditions hamper the tank's combat effectiveness, however, and armour and firepower have been outclassed by 1960's tanks such as the Leopard I and M-60. The small size, low cost and lack of complexity have made this series popular with many operators, and the T-55 has seen action all over the World. Many users have carried out upgrade programmes, including improved fire control, propulsion and suspension. The Chinese have built thousands of their T-59 variant, and hundreds of these were supplied to the Iraqi Army and saw service in the Iran/Iraq war.

T-62

Origin: USSR
Crew: 4
Armament: One 115mm gun; one 7.62mm machine gun coaxial with main armament; one 12.7mm anti-aircraft machine gun.
Armour: 0.79 - 6.80in (20mm - 170mm)
Dimensions: Length overall 32ft (9.77m); hull length 22ft (6.71m); width 11ft (3.35m); height 7ft 10in (2.4m)
Combat weight: 80,468lbs (36,500kg)
Ground pressure: 10.24lb/in² (0.72kg/cm²)
Engine: Model V-2-62 12-cylinder water-cooled diesel engine developing 700hp at 2,200rpm
Performance: Road speed 31mph (50km/h); range 310 miles (500km); vertical obstacle 2ft 8in (0.8m); trench 9ft 2in (2.8m); gradient 60 per cent.
History: Entered service with the Soviet Army in 1963. In service with Afghanistan, Bulgaria, Czechoslovakia, East Germany, Hungary, India, Iraq, Israel, Libya, Poland, Romania, Soviet Union and Syria.
Background: Developed as the successor to the T-54/55 series, the T-62 entered service in the late 1950s. Similar in appearance, it has a longer and wider hull and a new turret. The U-5TS 115mm main gun is a smooth bore weapon firing APFSDS ammunition and has been found to be extremely accurate and effective at medium ranges (approx 1,100yds/ 1,000m). Manual loading in the cramped turret causes a slow rate of fire, and the empty shell cases have to be automatically ejected through a hatch on the turret rear. Like the T-55, the T-62 can inject diesel oil into the engine exhaust to create a thick smoke screen, although this is of limited effectiveness against the latest western tanks with thermal imagers. Extra range can be given by fitting external fuel drums above the engine compartment, these being jettisoned as the tank goes into action. The original T-62 had rudimentary night-fighting equipment, limited to an IR searchlight and driving lights. The Soviets have upgraded and improved their T-62s, the latest T-62E has side skirts, extra armour on the front of the turret, improved night-vision equipment, and a laser-ranging system. The T-62 has not seen such widespread service as the T-54/55 series, and its combat record against western tanks has not been distinguished. It would appear that the extra complexity and poorer reliability is not offset by sufficiently improved combat capability. It may be that the last upgraded T-55 will still be in service long after the last T-62 has been scrapped.

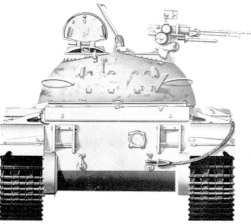

Above: These artworks show a T-54 in Egyptian service. This is an early version as the gun barrel does not have the smoke extractor normally seen at the muzzle end. Most models of the T-54 look almost identical to the T-55, the differences being details such as turret ventilator type, hatch configuration etc. For most purposes this series is referred to as the T-54/55.

Below: This view shows the low silhouette and good ballistic shape of the T-62. Its ancestry in the T-54/55 is also apparent. The two searchlights on the turret are an IR night light and a conventional white lamp. When the T-62 was designed, the Soviet Army still used infantry *desant* from tanks as an operational tactic, hence the handrails on the turret.

Above: A T-62 in Syrian service. The main recognition feature from this angle is the fume extractor halfway down the gun barrel.

T-72

Origin: USSR
Crew: 3
Armament: One 125mm gun; one 7.62mm machine gun coaxial with main armament; one 12.7mm anti-aircraft machine gun
Armour: Classified
Dimensions: Length including main armament 30ft 4in (9.24m) hull length 22ft 10in (5.80m); width 11ft 10in (6.95m); height 7ft 9in (2.37m)
Combat weight: 90,388lb (41,000kg)
Ground pressure: 11 80lb/sq in (0.83kg/cm)
Engine: Model W-46 V-12 diesel developing 780hp (581kW) at 2,000rpm
Performance: Road speed 37.2mph (60km/h); range 300 miles (480km); vertical obstacle 2ft 10in (0.85m); trench 9ft 2in (2.80m); gradient 60 per cent
History: Entered production in 1971 and subsequently built in large numbers for both home and export markets. In service with Algeria, Bulgaria, Cuba, Czechoslovakia (local manufacture), Finland, East Germany, Hungary (licensed production), Iraq, Libya, Poland (licensed production), Romania, Syria, USSR and Yugoslavia (licensed production).

Background: The T-72 MBT entered production some years after the T-64 but incorporated many features of the earlier vehicle, especially the main armament and fire control system. Like its predecessor, the T-72 has a 125mm smooth-bore gun fed by an automatic loader on the turret floor that holds 24 rounds of separate-loading ammunition. A 7.62mm machine gun is mounted coaxially with the main armament and there is a 12.7mm machine gun on the commander's cupola. Like the T-62 and other Soviet tanks, the T-72 can lay its own smoke screen by injecting diesel fuel into the exhaust outlet on the left side of the hull. It is fitted with an NBC system and night vision equipment and can be fitted with a snorkel for deep fording; and to extend its operational range supplementary fuel tanks can be mounted at the rear. Recent versions of the T-72 have a laser rangefinder to increase first round hit probability, smoke dischargers either side of the main armament and cladding on the turret roof which is believed to give increased protection against either sub-munitions or neutron radiation. The T-72 has seen combat with the Iraqi and Syrian armies in the Middle East, where Israeli 105mm-armed Merkava tanks have experienced no difficulty in penetrating frontal armour with APFSDS rounds.

Right: The T-72 is in service with the Soviet Army on a large scale and has also been exported. It has a three man crew and an automatic loader, its ammunition being of the separate loading type consisting of the charge (1) and projectile. Rounds available include the AT-8 Songster missile (artist's impression 2), APFSDS projectile without sabot (3) and with sabot (4) HEAT-FS (5) and HE-FRAG (FS) (6). It also carries smoke grenades (7), plus 12.7mm (8) and 7.62mm (9) machine gun ammunition in ready-use belts

AMX-30, AMX 10P and AMX10 RC

AMX-30

Origin: France
Crew: 4
Armament: One 105mm gun; one 12.7mm machine gun or one 20mm cannon coaxial with main armament; one 7.62mm anti-aircraft machine gun; two smoke dischargers each side of turret
Armour: Classified
Dimensions: Length including main armament 31ft 1in (9.48m); hull length 21ft 7in (6.59m); width 10ft 2in (3.10m); height 9ft 5in (2.86m)
Combat weight: 79,366lb (36,000kg)
Engine: Hispano-Suiza HS 110 12-cylinder water-cooled supercharged multi-fuel developing 720hp (537kW) at 2,000rpm
Ground pressure: 10.95lb/sq in (0.77kg/cm²)
Performance: Road speed 40mph (65km/h); range 310-372 miles (500; 600km); vertical obstacle 3ft 1in (0.93m); trench 9ft 6in (2.9m); gradient 60 per cent
History: Developed at the same time as Leopard I with first prototypes being completed 1960 and first production vehicles delivered by the Atelier de Construction Roanne in 1966. Current production model is AMX-30 B2. In service with Chile, France, Greece, Iraq (variants only), Qatar, Saudi Arabia, Spain (was made under licence), United Arab Emirates and Venezuela
Background: In the immediate postwar period the French Army took delivery of a large number of M47 tanks from the United States and these formed the backbone of French medium tank battalions until the introduction of the AMX-30 in the late 1960s. Although some 2,000 AMX-30 series MBTs have been built for the home and export

markets, the vehicle is not liked by all operators as it has no stabilisation system for the main armament and the powerpack has been a constant source of trouble.
Main armament comprises a 105mm gun with a 12.7mm machine gun or 20mm cannon mounted coaxially to the left, the latter being unusual in that independent elevation allows it to engage slow flying helicopters.

Above: The AMX-10PAC 90 Marine was developed by GIAT specifically for the export market and is essentially an AMX-10 IFV fitted with the GIAT TS-90 90mm turret.

Above: The smoke grenades (1 and 2) are fired by the launchers at rear of the hull. Types of ammunition fired by 90mm gun include HE(3) and APFSDS (4) and their respective training rounds (5 and 6). In addition canisters, HEAT, smoke and long range HE are available, all of which have fixed brass cartridge cases.

Right: The AMX-30 and AMX-30 B2 MBTs fire the same 105mm fixed ammunition which includes (above) APFSDS (1), HEAT (2), HE (3), Smoke (4) and illuminating (5) rounds. In addition there are 80mm smoke grenades (6) 20mm ammunition for the coaxial cannon (7) and 7.62mm MG ammunition in belts (8).

A 7.62mm machine gun mounted on the commander's cupola can be aimed and fired from within the vehicle. A total of 47 rounds of 105mm ammunition can be carried, including the recently developed APFSDS, as well as 480 rounds of 20mm and 2,070 rounds of 7.62mm. French Army AMX-30s are being upgraded to the AMX-30 B2 standard, which includes a fire control system with a laser rangefinder and an LLLTV system for commander and gunner. In the future additional armour protection will probably be fitted to the turret as the basic AMX-30 has very thin steel armour. The chassis of the AMX-30 is used for a wide range of specialised vehicles including a bridgelayer, GCT 155mm self-propelled gun (also used by Iraq and Saudi Arabia), Roland surface-to-air missile system, AMX-30D armoured recovery vehicle, EBG combat engineer vehicle, twin 30mm selfpropelled anti-aircraft gun system (for Saudi Arabia) and the Shahine

surface-to-air missile system (also for Saudi Arabia). The AMX-30 and AMX-30 B2 will start to be replaced in French Army service from the early 1990s by the new Leclerc MBT, which has a three man crew and is fitted with a 120mm gun fed by an automatic loader.

AMX-10RC

Origin: France
Crew: 4
Armament: One 105mm gun; one 7.62mm machine gun coaxial with main armament; two smoke dischargers each side of turret
Armour: Classified
Dimensions: Length including main armament 30ft 0in (9.15m); hull length 20ft 10in (6.357m); width 9ft 8in (2.95m); height 8ft 9in (2.68m)
Combat weight: 35,000lb (15,880kg)
Ground pressure: Not available
Engine: Hispano-Suiza HS-115 supercharged water-cooled 8 cylinder diesel developing 260hp (194kW) at 3,000rpm
Performance: Road speed 52.8mph (85km/h); range 621 miles (1,000km); vertical obstacle 2ft 4in (0.7m); trench 3ft 9in (1.15m); gradient 60 per cent
History: Developed by Atelier de Construction d'Issy-les-Moulineaux to meet requirements of French

Army; first prototype completed 1971; first production vehicles completed by the Atelier de Construction Roanne in 1978; in service with France and Morocco
Background: From 1950 the Panhard EBR 75 (8 x 8) vehicle was the standard long range armoured car of the French Army but by the late 1960s it was apparent that a new design would be needed for the 1970s and after studying designs from GIAT and Panhard the former's was selected. The resulting AMX-10RC (6 x 6) reconnaissance vehicle has a number of unique features of which its suspension is probably the most interesting. All six wheels are powered and the suspension is of the hydropneumatic type which allows the driver to adjust the ground clearance to suit the terrain being crossed; for example when travelling across rough country the suspension is lowered to give maximum possible ground clearance. The driver can also raise or lower the suspension on just one side or the front or rear. Most wheeled vehicles have conventional steering on the front wheels but the AMX-10RC has

skid steering. Many of the automotive components of the AMX-10RC are also used in the full tracked AMX-10P. The 105mm gun fires HEAT, HE or APFSDS rounds and a total of 38 are carried.
A 7.62mm machine gun is mounted coaxially with the main armament and 4,000 rounds are carried for it. The computerised fire control system includes a laser rangefinder and LLLTV system with displays for both commander and gunner, and the vehicle is fitted with night vision equipment and an NBC system. It is fully amphibious, being propelled in the water by two waterjets, mounted one either side at the hull rear, at a maximum speed of 4.47mph (7.2km/h). The AMX-10RC is normally deployed at Corps level with each Corps having one regiment of 36 vehicles; the French Force d'Action Rapide (FAR) also has two regiments each with 36 vehicles and some of the latter were deployed recently to Chad. The French Army did intend to purchase 525 vehicles but procurement was subsequently reduced to around 300 for financial reasons and Panhard ERC 90 F4 Sagaie (6 x 6) armoured cars were ordered instead.

Right: By 1986 the GIAT AMX-10RC (6x6) heavy armoured car had replaced the old Panhard EBR 75 (8x8) armoured car in the French Army and a quantity has also been sold to Morocco.

LAV-25 and M2/M3 Bradley

LAV-25

Origin: Canada
Crew: 3 + 6
Armament: One 25mm cannon; one 7.62mm machine gun coaxial with main armament; one 7.62mm or 12.7mm anti-aircraft machine gun (optional); four smoke dischargers each side of turret
Combat weight: 28,400lb (12,882kg) **Engine:** General Motors Detroit Diesel Model 6V-53T 6-cylinder diesel developing 275hp (205kW) at 2,800rpm
Performance: Road speed 62mph (l00km/h); range 415 miles (668km); vertical obstacle 1ft 8in (0.5m); trench 6ft 9in (2.057m); gradient 60 per cent
History: To meet the requirements of the US Army and Marine Corps for a new Light Armored Vehicle (LAV) that could be rapidly transported by air, prototypes were submitted by Alvis of the UK, Cadillac Gage of the USA and General Motors of Canada, the last being based on the 8 x 8 version of the MOWAG Piranha built under licence in Canada. In the end the MOWAG Piranha was accepted with the intention that 680 would be procured for the US Army and 289 for the Marine Corps. In the event the US Army pulled out and the Marine Corps purchased a total of 758 vehicles, all of which were delivered by late 1987. The Marine Corps has six versions of the LAV in service: the LAV-25 with 25mm cannon; LAV logistics with crane; LAV mortar carrier with 81mm mortar; LAV anti-tank with twin launcher for Hughes Tow missiles; LAV maintenance and recovery;

and command and control vehicle. Other variants under development or expected to be procured in the future include anti-aircraft, assault gun and mobile electronic warfare vehicle. The basic LAV 25 has a three-man crew (commander, gunner and driver) and carries six Marines in the rear, three each side facing outward, each of whom has a firing port with associated periscope. The two-man power-operated turret is armed with the same 25mm cannon as that installed in the M2 Bradley, with a 7.62mm machine gun mounted coaxially, and either a similar weapon or a 12.7mm machine gun can be mounted on the roof for anti-aircraft defence. A total of 210 rounds of 25mm and 420 rounds of 7.62mm ammunition are carried. The LAV is fully amphibious, being propelled in the water by two propellers mounted at the rear; steering is power-assisted on the front four wheels; and a full range of night vision equipment is fitted as standard. The main advantage of the LAV-25 over the M2 Bradley IFV is that the former is not only much cheaper to procure, operate and maintain but being a wheeled vehicle it also has greater mobility on roads and can therefore be deployed from one part of the country to another faster than a tracked vehicle. The US Air Force is expected

to procure a large number of LAVs in the 8 x 8 configuration under the designation of the Mobile Armored Reconnaissance Vehicle/ Standoff Munition Device (MARV/ SMUD) which will be used in the EOD (Explosive Ordnance Disposal) role on airfields; following air attacks.

M2/M3 BRADLEY

Origin: USA
Crew: 3 + 7
Armament: One 25mm cannon; one 7.62mm machine gun coaxial with main armament; twin launcher for Tow anti-tank missiles; four smoke dischargers each side of turret
Armour: Classified
Dimensions: Length 21ft 2in (6.45m); width 10ft 6in (3.2m); height 9ft 9in (2.97m)
Combat weight: 49,802lb (22,590kg) **Ground pressure:** 7.53lb/sq in (0.53kg/cm^2)
Engine: Cummins VTA-903T turbocharged 8-cylinder diesel developing 500hp (372k) at 2,600rpm
Performance: Road speed 41mph (66km/h); range 300 miles (483km); vertical obstacle 3ft 0in (0.914m); trench 8ft 4in (2.54m); gradient 60 per cent
History: Developed by FMC Corporation to meet requirements of US Army with first production

vehicles completed in 1981 and first unit equipped in 1983. A total of 6,882 M2 IFV and M3 CFV vehicles will be procured by the US Army by the early 1990s
Background: The US Army has had a requirement for an IFV since the early 1960s but for a variety of reasons development was protracted and in the end one vehicle was designed for the infantry - the XM2 IFV - while the very similar XM3 Cavalry Fighting Vehicle was designed for the cavalry. These were accepted for service late in 1979 and type-classified as the M2 and M3. Production of both vehicles is undertaken by FMC Corporation at San Jose in California, and although the vehicle has been demonstrated to a number of potential customers, so far no firm export order has been placed. The M2 is supplementing the M113 in the US Army, providing improved armour, mobility and firepower. The basic hull and turret is aluminium armour with an additional layer of spaced laminate armour for increased protection. The two-man power-operated turret is mounted in the centre of the hull and is armed with a stabilised 25mm cannon with a 7.62mm machine gun mounted coaxially to the right and a twin launcher for the Hughes Tow anti-tank missile on the left. A total

Below: The LAV-25 is one of a complete family of 8x8 light armoured vehicles now in service with the United States Marine Corps. The LAV-25 has a three-man crew and can carry six fully equipped Marines, but there are also specialised versions ranging from mortar carriers to anti-tank vehicles with long-range Tow missiles.

Right: US infantry dismount from an M2 Bradley IFV. They are provided with special versions of the M16 rifle called the M231 for use from the firing ports.

of 900 rounds of 25mm and 1,340 rounds of 7.62mm ammunition are carried, along with seven Tow missiles. The infantry enter and leave the vehicle via a large power operated ramp in the rear and each man is provided with a firing port and associated periscope to enable him to use a special version of the M16 series 5.56mm rifle called the M231. The 25mm cannon is used to engage light armoured vehicles with APDS-T rounds and other targets with HEI-T, tanks being engaged with the Tow missiles. The M2 Bradley has a full range of night vision devices and an NBC system and is fully amphibious with its flotation screen erected. The Fighting Vehicle Systems Carrier chassis uses many components of the Bradley, with the first application being the Multiple Launch Rocket System (MLRS) which has been adopted by five European countries. In the future additional improvements will be incorporated into the Bradley, and reactive armour has already been added, as there has been considerable debate in the US about the vulnerability of the Bradley to many battlefield threats, especially missiles with their HEAT warheads.

Above: The FMC Corporation has built more than 3,000 M2 Bradley Infantry Fighting Vehicles for the US Army. The two-man power operated turret is armed with a 25mm cannon, 7.62mm coaxial MG and a twin Tow ATGW launcher on the left side: (1 and 3) 25mm ammunition; (2) smoke grenades; (4) LAW rocket; (5) LAW launcher; (6) Tow ATGW; (7) Tow launcher tube. The Bradley is fully amphibious .

M113

Origin: USA
Crew: 2 + 11
Armament: One 12.7mm machine gun
Armour: 0.47-1.49in (12-38mm)
Dimensions: Length 16ft 0in (4.863m); width 8ft 10in (2.686m); height 8ft 2in (2.50m)
Combat weight: 24,595lb (11,156kg)
Ground pressure: 7.82lb/sq in (0.55kg/cm^2)
Engine: General Motors Detroit Diesel Model 6V-53 6-cylinder water-cooled diesel developing 215bhp (160kW) at 2,800rpm
Performance: Road speed 42mph (67.59km/h); range 300 miles (483km); vertical obstacle 2ft 0in (0.61m); trench 5ft 6in (1.618m); gradient 60 per cent
History: Developed in late 1950s with first production M113 being completed by FMC Corporation in 1960; Current production model is M113A2. In service with Argentina, Australia, Belgium, Bolivia, Brazil, Canada, Chile, Costa Rica, Denmark, Ecuador, Egypt, El Salvador, Ethiopia, West Germany, Greece, Guatemala, Haiti, Iran, Israel, Italy, Jordan, Kampuchea, Libya, Morocco, Netherlands, New Zealand, Norway, Pakistan, Peru, Philippines, Portugal, Saudi Arabia, Singapore, Somalia, Spain, Sudan, Switzerland, Taiwan, Thailand, Turkey, USA, Uruguay, Vietnam, North Yemen and Zaire—a total of 45 nations.

Background: In the mid-1950s the development of a new fully tracked armoured personnel carrier began with prototypes being built in both steel and aluminium. The latter was eventually accepted for service with the US Army as the M113 and first production vehicles were completed by the FMC Corporation in 1960. Since then the vehicle has been continuously modified and improved and by 1987 more than 73,000 had been built for the home and export markets, including some 4,500 built under licence in Italy by OTO Melara. The M113 has the distinction of being the most widely used armoured vehicle in the world and has formed the basis for the world's largest family of armoured vehicles, with new variants being added yearly. The hull of the M113 is of all-welded aluminium armour to save weight and provides the crew with protection from small arms fire and shell splinters. The driver is seated front left with the engine compartment to his right and the whole of the rear being kept clear for the troop compartment. The troops are seated on bench seats that run down either side of the hull and enter and leave via a large power operated ramp in the rear. There is also a roof hatch above the troop compartment and a cupola with an externally mounted 0.5in M2 HB machine gun which can be used for local and anti-aircraft defence, though no protection whatsoever is provided for the gunner. The original M113 was powered by a Chrysler petrol engine, but this model was replaced on the production lines in late 1964 by the diesel-engined M113A1, which has a much larger radius of action as the engine is more fuel-efficient; there is also a reduced risk of fire. The M113A1 was replaced in turn by the M113A2, whose many improvements include a tougher suspension. To meet different user requirements many kits have been developed for the M113 series including an NBC system, smoke dischargers, additional armour protection, night vision equipment, a dozer blade, self-recovery gear and so on, while many countries have modified the vehicle to meet their own specific requirements. For example, many Swiss vehicles have been fitted with a Swedish Hägglund and Söner turret armed with a 20mm cannon, while many Israeli Army vehicles have additional armour protection to their fronts and sides to give protection against RPG-7 anti-tank grenades with their HEAT warheads. The basic M113 is fully amphibious, being propelled in the water by its tracks; all that is required in the way of preparation is to switch on the bilge pumps and erect the trim vane at the front of the hull. It should be stressed that the M113 is amphibious only under almost ideal conditions and cannot swim in the open sea. The vehicle has seen combat in many parts of the world including the Middle East—with both Israel; and Lebanese forces—and in South-East Asia, especially Vietnam, where it was the workhorse in the ground war. In the latter campaign it proved very vulnerable to mines and many troops preferred to take the chances on top of the vehicle rather than inside. Although the M2 Bradley Infantry Fighting Vehicle is entering US Army service in increasing numbers, the M113 will remain in US service for many years to come, as the Bradley is not replacing the M113 on a one-for-one basis. The M113 has proved to be reliable and easy to maintain and has been produced in such large numbers that by today's standards it is cheap. There are literally hundreds of variants, but the more common ones are: M125 81mm and M106 107mm mortar carriers—in both cases the mortars can also be dismounted for use in the ground role; M163 20mm Vulcan clear-weather air defence system; the M577 command post vehicle, which has a higher roof and is fitted with extensive communications equipment; recovery vehicles; the M901 Improved Tow Vehicle, which has

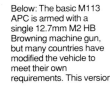

Below: The basic M113 APC is armed with a single 12.7mm M2 HB Browning machine gun, but many countries have modified the vehicle to meet their own requirements. This version has extensive external stowage, fuel tanks repositioned on each side of the rear ramp and an additional pair of 7.62mm machine guns mounted on the hull roof. Many Israeli M113s now have additional armour protection on hull front, sides and rear. The ammunition (1) and (2) for the 12.7mm and 7.62mm machine guns is carried in the familiar belts which are stowed in boxes.

an elevating arm with two Tow anti-tank missiles in the ready-to-launch position; and the M981 Fire Support Team vehicle, which designates targets for the field artillery. Another derivative, the M548 unarmoured tracked cargo carrier, itself has formed the basis for another complete family of vehicles. These include the launchers and loaders for the Lance surface- to-surface missile system; the Chaparral surface-to-air missile system; the British Army's Tracked Rapier air defence system; various electronic warfare systems carriers; ammunition resupply vehicles for self-propelled artillery such as the M107, M109 and M110; and a mine-carrying vehicle. Further development of the M113 series by the FMC Corporation resulted in the Armoured Infantry Fighting Vehicle, which is much cheaper than the M2 Infantry Fighting Vehicle and is armed with a turret-mounted 25mm cannon and has firing ports for the infantry but retains its amphibious capability. The AIFV is in service with Belgium, the Netherlands and the Philippines and has itself spawned a large family of vehicles. The M113 family is often seen as the Army equivalent of the Douglas DC-3 Dakota: many countries have tried to design a replacement, but it was still in production 30 years after the first ones came off the line in 1960.

Above: Over 73,000 M113 series vehicles have been built and examples are in use all over the world. The M2 Bradley is now replacing the M113 in US Army service.

Below: The M901 ITV (Improved Tow Vehicle) is one of the latest members of the M113 family of vehicles and more than 2,500 have already been built for the home and export markets. The M901 has an elevating arm carrying long-range Tow launchers which are aimed and fired from within the vehicle. The missile is shown in its launch tube (1) and in post-launch configuration (2) along with smoke grenades (3) and 7.62mm ammunition (4).

1

2   3   4

Scorpion and Warrior

SCORPION

Origin: United Kingdom
Armament: One 76mm gun; one 7.62mm machine-gun coaxial with main armament; four smoke dischargers on each side of turret
Armour: Classified
Dimensions: Length 15ft 9in (4.794m); width 7ft 4in (2.235m); height 6ft 11in (2.102m)
Combat weight: 17,797lb(8,073kg)
Ground pressure: 5.12lb/sq in (0.36kg/cm²)
Engine: Jaguar J60 petrol developing 190hp (142kW) at 4,750rpm
Performance: Road speed 50mph (80.5km/h); range 400 miles (644km); vertical obstacle 1ft 8in (0.5m); trench 6ft 9in (2.057m); gradient 60 per cent
History: First production vehicles completed in 1972; now in service with Belgium, Brunei, Honduras, Iran, Ireland, Kuwait, Malaysia, New Zealand, Nigeria, Oman, Spain, Tanzania, Thailand, Togo, Philippines, United Arab Emirates and the United Kingdom (Army and Air Force)
Background: The Alvis Scorpion Combat Vehicle Reconnaissance (Tracked) was developed as the replacement for the Alvis Saladin 6 x 6 armoured car with the requirement being for a smaller and lighter vehicle

Left: A standard Scorpion on exercise. Low ground pressure, high speed, reasonable protection and firepower make this an effective reconnaissance vehicle.

Right: Warrior has no firing ports, the British prefer their infantry to fight outside the vehicle. The 30mm cannon provides effective fire support, although an ATGW would have been useful.

but with a similar armament and greater cross-country mobility. To save weight the hull and turret of the Scorpion are of all welded aluminium with the wide tracks giving a low ground pressure to enable it to operate in soft terrain such as that encountered in the Falklands; it is equally at home in sandy desert conditions.
Main armament of the basic Scorpion is a 76mm gun, a further development of that installed in the Saladin, which fires canister, HESH, HE, smoke and illuminating projectiles, with 40 rounds of 76mm ammunition being carried. A 7.62mm machine gun is mounted coaxially with the main armament, and 3,000 rounds are carried for this. A full range of night vision equipment is installed, as is an NBC system, and with the aid of a flotation screen the Scorpion is fully amphibious. To meet different user requirements a wide range of options are available, including a diesel engine 90mm gun. So far some 3,500 Scorpions have been built for the home and export markets and the basic chassis has been developed into a complete family of vehicles, including the Striker anti-tank vehicle with Swingfire missiles, Spartan APC, Samaritan ambulance, Sultan command post vehicle, Samson amoured recovery vehicle, Scimitar reconnaissance vehicle and Streaker high-mobility load-carrier. Further development has resulted in the Stormer APC which has recently been adopted by the British Army to mount the Shorts Starstreak High Velocity Missile (HVM) system.

Below: By mid-1987 over 3,500 members of the Scorpion family had been built for home and export markets. 7.62mm ammunition for the coaxial MG is in belts (1), while the 76mm gun fires fixed canister (2), smoke\(3), HESH (4), high explosive (5) and practice rounds (6 and 7). Mounted on each side of the turret is a bank of four electrically operated smoke grenade launchers which fire smoke grenades (8 and 9). When fitted with a flotation screen the Scorpion is fully amphibious.

Operations to meet requirements of British Army; first production vehicle completed in December 1986
Background: The British Army started to study its requirements for a mechanised combat vehicle while the FV432 was still in production but for a variety of reasons progress was slow and it was not until the late 1970s that the first prototype was built. At one time serious consideration was being given by the British MoD to manufacturing the US FMC M2 Bradley Infantry Fighting Vehicle under licence but in the end it was decided to continue with the MCV-80. Following extensive trials with prototypes the MCV-80 was accepted for service with the British Army in 1984 and named Warrior. A total of 1,048 Warriors are to be built for the British Army at a rate of about 130 vehicles a year. The infantry carried in the Warrior would normally dismount and fight on foot as there is no provision for them to use their rifles from inside the vehicle, whereas the M2 and Soviet BMP-1/BMP-2 are provided with firing ports and vision devices. The armament of the Warrior

is the Royal Ordnance 30mm RARDEN already installed in the Scimitar and Fox reconnaissance vehicles. This highly accurate weapon fires APSE-T, HEI-T and the new APDS round which will penetrate 1.57in (40mm) of armour. A McDonnell Douglas Helicopters 7.62mm Chain Gun, manufactured under licence by Royal Ordnance, is mounted coaxially with the 30mm cannon. Warrior represents a substantial improvement in armour, mobility and firepower compared with the FV432 and gives the British infantry a capability it has never before possessed. Variants of the Warrior under development for the British Army include command post vehicle, mechanised repair and recovery vehicle, mortar carrier, engineer vehicle and artillery observation vehicle. The vehicle has already been demonstrated in Kuwait, Saudi Arabia and Turkey and GKN Defence Operations is proposing a wide range of variants, including a light tank armed with 105mm gun and antitank and anti-aircraft missile carriers, for the export market.

WARRIOR

Origin: United Kingdom
Crew: 3 + 7
Armament: One 30mm RARDEN cannon; one 7.62mm machine gun coaxial with main armament; four smoke dischargers each side of turret
Armour: Classified
Dimensions: Length 20ft 10in (6.34m); width 9ft 11in (3.03m); height 9ft 0in (2.73m)

Combat weight: 49,603lb (22,500kg)
Ground pressure: 9.24lb/sq in (0.65kg/cm²)
Engine: Rolls-Royce CV8 TCA V-8 diesel developing 550hp (410kw) at 2,300rpm
Performance: Road speed 46.6mph (75km/h); range 310 miles (500km); vertical obstacle 2ft 6in (0.75m); trench 8ft 2in (2.5m); gradient 60 per cent
History: Developed by GKN Defence

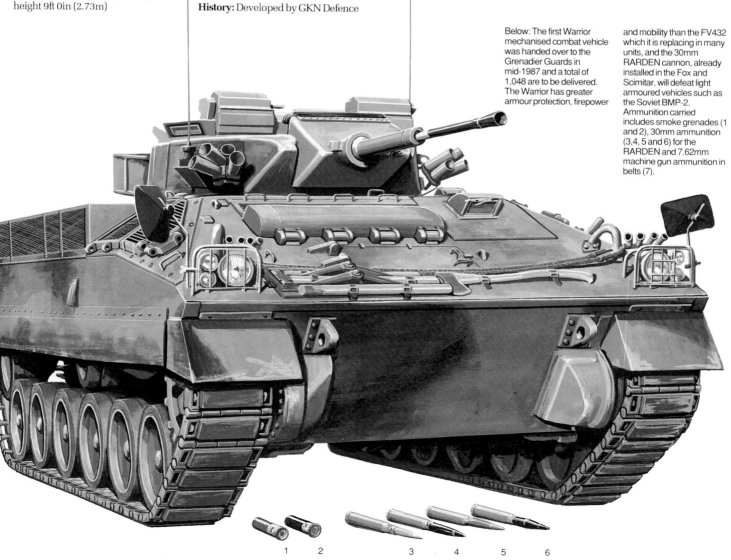

Below: The first Warrior mechanised combat vehicle was handed over to the Grenadier Guards in mid-1987 and a total of 1,048 are to be delivered. The Warrior has greater armour protection, firepower and mobility than the FV432 which it is replacing in many units, and the 30mm RARDEN cannon, already installed in the Fox and Scimitar, will defeat light armoured vehicles such as the Soviet BMP-2. Ammunition carried includes smoke grenades (1 and 2), 30mm ammunition (3,4, 5 and 6) for the RARDEN and 7.62mm machine gun ammunition in belts (7).

BMP-1 and BMP-2

BMP-1

Origin: USSR
Crew: 3 + 8
Armament: One 73mm gun; one 7.62mm machine gun coaxial with main armament; one launcher over 73mm gun for AT-3 Sagger anti-tank missile
Armour: 1.29in (33mm) max
Dimensions: Length 22ft 2in (6.74m); width 9ft 8in (2.94m); height 7ft 1in (2.15m)
Combat weight: 29,762lb (13,500kg) Ground pressure: 8.3lb/sq in (0.60kg/cm^2)
Engine: Type 5D20 6-cylinder inline water-cooled diesel developing 300hp (224kW) at 2,000rpm
Performance: Road speed 50mph (80km/h); range 310 miles (500km); vertical obstacle 2ft 8in (0.80m); trench 7ft 3in (2.2m); gradient 60 per cent
History: Developed in the early 1960s and first seen in public in 1967. In service with Afghanistan, Algeria. Bulgaria, Cuba, Czechoslovakia, Egypt, Ethiopia, Finland, East Germany, Hungary, India, Iraq, Iran, North Korea, Libya, Mongolia, Poland, Syria, USSR, North Yemen and Yugoslavia. Also built in China as the Type WZ 501
Background: Until the introduction of the BMP-1 in the mid-1960s Soviet infantry were transported as near as possible to their objective before dismounting and attacking the objective on foot. This meant that the whole momentum of the battle was slowed down. The

Right: Being the first infantry fighting vehicle to enter service with any Army, the BMP-1 had a number of shortcomings, such as the position of the commander.

Right: The introduction of the BMP-1 brought a new level of firepower to infantry vehicles. Its power operated turret is armed with a 73mm gun, 7.62mm coaxial machine gun and an AT-3 Sagger ATGW over the main armament, and it is fully amphibious and equipped with an NBC system.

introduction of the BMP, however, allowed the infantry to fight from within the vehicle, since each of the eight men carried is provided with a firing port for his rifle or machine gun and an observation periscope, and the vehicle was fitted with a more powerful armament system. (Early Soviet APCs such as the BTR-50P and BTR-152 had open tops, so the infantry were not protected from the elements, overhead shell splinters or NBC attack, and armament normally comprised one or two

7.62mm machine guns in unprotected mounts.) The BMP-1 has the driver seated front left, with the vehicle commander to his rear and the engine compartment to his right. In the centre of the vehicle is a large one man power-operated turret armed with a 73mm gun fed by an automatic loader and firing HEAT or HE-FRAG rounds; a total of 40 rounds of 73mm ammunition is carried. A 7.62mm machine gun is mounted coaxially with the main armament and 2,000 rounds are

carried for this weapon. Over the 73mm gun is a launcher for the AT-3 Sagger wire guided anti-tank missile, and in addition to the single round in the ready-to-launch position a further four missiles are carried in reserve. The eight infantry are seated in the rear, four on each side facing outward, and enter via two doors in the hull rear. The BMP-1 is fully amphibious, being propelled in the water by its tracks, and is fitted with an NBC system and a full range of night

vision equipment for commander, gunner and driver. Specialised versions of the BMP-1 include a command post vehicle, a mobile training centre, the BMP-R reconnaissance vehicle and the BRM-1, which is fitted with a Small Fred radar.

BMP-2

Origin: USSR
Crew: 3 + 7
Armament: One 30mm cannon; one 7.62mm machine gun coaxial with main armament; one launcher for AT-5 Spandrel anti-tank missiles; smoke dischargers on turret.
Armour: 1.29in (33mm) max
Dimensions: Length 22ft 0in (6.71m); width 10ft 2in (3.09m); height 6ft 9in (2.06m)
Combat weight: 32,187lb (14,600kg)
Ground pressure: 9.1lb/sq in (0.64kg/cm²)
Engine: 6-cylinder super charged diesel developing 400hp (298kW)
Performance: Road speed 40mph (65km/h); range 372 miles (600km); vertical obstacle 2ft 3in (0.7m); trench 8ft 2in (2.5m); gradient 60 per cent
History: Developed in the late 1970s and first seen in public in 1982. Still in production and in service with Czechoslovakia, East Germany, and the USSR
Background: While the BMP-1 was a giant step forward the vehicle did have two main disadvantages: the commander, being seated to the rear of the driver, had restricted vision, and the 73mm gun was inaccurate. The BMP-2 is designed to remedy these deficiencies. Slightly larger than BMP-1, it seats the driver front left with one infantrman to his rear

and the engine compartment to his right. In the centre is a two-man (commander and gunner) powered turret; armed with a 30mm cannon that fires AP-T or HE-T rounds and a coaxial 7.62mm machine gun. Mounted on the turret roof is a launcher for the AT-5 Spandrel anti-tank missile; additional missiles are carried inside for manual reloading, and some vehicles have been observed fitted with the shorter range AT-4 Spigot. Both the AT-5 and the AT-4 are second- generation

missiles and all the gunner has to do to ensure a hit is to keep his cross hairs on the turret. Mounted on each side of the turret there is a bank of three electrically operated smoke dischargers, though both the BMP-1 and the BMP-2 can also lay their own smoke screens by injecting diesel fuel into the exhaust outlet on the left side of the hull. As the turret of BMP-2 is much bigger than that of the BMP-1 there is only space for six infantrymen at the rear; these are seated three on each side facing out-

ward. There are four firing ports in the left side of hull, three in the right side and one in the left rear door, which also contains some diesel fuel. Like the BMP-1, the BMP-2 is fully amphibious and has a full range of night vision equipment and an NBC system. While there is much debate on the role of the IFV on the high-intensity battlefield it is interesting to note that the USSR was the first country to field a vehicle of this type: the US Army did not field the M2 Bradley until 1983.

Above: Three BMP-1s in Soviet service advance past a FROG missile TEL. The BMP was designed to operate in a nuclear environment and was the first Infantry Fighting Vehicle in service. The main design requirements were high mobility, good anti-tank and fire support armament, and the ability of the infantry passengers to fight from within the vehicle.

Left: The BMP-2 is the replacement for the BMP-1 and has a new two-man power operated turret armed with a 30mm cannon, 7.62mm coaxial machine gun and an AT-5 Spandrel ATGW launcher on the turret roof. The 30mm cannon can also be used against low flying helicopters.

BTR-70, BRDM-2 and MT-LB

BTR-70

Origin: USSR
Crew: 2 + 9
Armament: One 14.5mm machine gun; one 7.62mm machine gun coaxial with main armament
Armour: 0.35in (9mm) max
Dimensions: Length 24ft 9in; (7.54m) width 9ft 2in (2.80m); height 7ft 7in (2.32m)
Combat weight: 25,353lb (11,500kg)
Engines: 2 x ZMZ-4905 6-cylinder petrol developing 115hp (86kW) each
Performance: Road speed 49.7mph (80km/h); range 372 miles (600km); vertical obstacle 1ft 8in (0.5m); trench 6ft 7in (2.0m); gradient 60 per cent
History: Developed in late 1970s and first seen in 1980; used by Soviet client states.
Background: The BTR-70 is a further development of the BTR-60 (8 x 8) armoured personnel carrier which first entered service with the Soviet Army in 1960. Main improvements of the BTR-70 over the BTR-60PB include better protection over the frontal arc, more powerful engines for an improved power-to-weight ratio and a small entry hatch between the second and third road wheels. The manual turret of the BTR-70 is identical to that installed on the BTR60PB and has 14.5mm and 7.62mm machine guns which can be elevated from–5° to +30°; turret traverse is a full 360°.

A total of 500 rounds of 14.5mm and 2,000 rounds of 7.62mm ammunition are carried. The BTR-70 is fully amphibious, being propelled in the water by a single water jet at the rear, and is fitted with an NBC system and night Vision equipment. An unusual feature of the BTR-60, BTR-70 and later BTR-80 is that they are powered by two engines at the back, one of which drives four wheels on one side of the vehicle. The latest 8 x 8 APC, the BTR-80, which has already seen combat in Afghanistan, has a single 260hp (193kW) diesel, six smoke dischargers on the turret rear, guns that can be elevated to + 60° and improved means of entry and exit for the troops.

MT-LB

Origin: USSR
Crew: 2 + 11
Armament: One 7.62mm machine gun
Armour: 0.27-0.55in (7-14mm)
Dimensions: Length 21ft 2in (6.45m); width 9ft 4in (2.85m); height 6ft 1in (1.86m)
Combat weight: 26,234lb (11,900kg)
Ground pressure: 6.54lb/sq in (0.46kg/cm²)
Engine: YaMZ 238 V V-8 diesel developing 240hp (179kW) at 2,100rpm
Performance: Road speed 38mph (61.5km/h); range 310 miles (500km); vertical obstacle 2ft 4in (0.7m); trench 8ft 10in (2.7m);

gradient 60 per cent
History: The MT-LB multi-purpose armoured vehicle was developed to meet a wide range of roles within the Soviet Army, including towing anti-tank guns, carrying specialised communications equipment and acting as an armoured personnel carrier, especially in snow and swamp-covered terrain where its low ground pressure gives it a number of advantages over the more heavily armed and armoured BMP-1 and BMP-2. In service with Bulgaria, Czechoslovakia, Finland, East Germany, Hungary, Poland, the USSR and others.
Background: The MT-LB is one of the most versatile vehicles in service with the Soviet Army, although its original role was to replace the old

Below: The MT-LB is used for a wide variety of roles on the battlefield ranging from towing anti-tank guns, carring radars and specialised electronic equipment to use as an APC in marginal terrain.

Below: The BTR-70 8x8 APC is a further development of the older BTR-60 vehicle and has the same turret as the BTR-60BP. It is used in large numbers by the Soviet motorised rifle divisions and has seen extensive use in Afghanistan. Like all Soviet wheeled AFVs it is fitted with a central tyre pressure regulation system for rough terrain conditions.

Above: The BRDM-2, which has replaced the older BRDM-1 in Soviet service, is fitted with a one-man turret armed with a 14.5mm KPVT and a 7.62mm PKT coaxial machine gun, each of which is belt-fed (1 and 2).

AT-P armoured tracked artillery tractor. For example, infantry units on the Norwegian border use the MT-LB in place of other vehicles since it has a very low ground pressure and can be fitted with special wide tracks for use in snow conditions. The vehicle is armoured only against small arms fire and shell splinters, and armament is limited to a manually operated turret with a 7.62mm machine gun mounted on the forward right side of the hull roof. Troops enter and leave via two doors in the hull rear. The MT-LB is fully amphibious, being propelled by its tracks at a speed of 3.1-3.7mph (5-6km/h) and is fitted with night vision equipment and an NBC system. Specialised versions include the MT-LBU command vehicle, MTP-LB repair vehicle, ambulance, engineer vehicle, radar carrier with both Pork Trough and Big Fred radars, and it forms a basis for the SA-13 Gopher SAM system.

BRDM-2

Origin: USSR
Crew: 4
Armour: 0.55in (14mm)
Dimensions: Length 18ft 10in (5.75m); width 7ft 9in (2.35m); height 7ft 7in (2.31m)
Power-to-weight ratio: 20 hp/tonne (14.91kW/tonne)
Engine: GAZ-41 V-8 water-cooled petrol developing 140hp (104kw) at 3,400rpm
Performance: Road speed 62mph (100km/h); range 466 miles (750km); vertical obstacle 1ft 4in (0.4m); trench 4ft 1in (1.25m); gradient 60 per cent
History: Developed in early 1960s and first seen in public in 1966. Currently used by Algeria, Angola, Benin, Botswana, Bulgaria, Cape Verde Islands, Central African Republic, Chad, Congo, Cuba, Djibouti, Equatorial Guinea, Ethiopia, East Germany, Guinea, Guinea-Bissau, Hungary, India, Iraq, Israel, Libya, Madagascar, Malawi, Mali, Mauritania, Mongolia, Morocco, Mozambique, Nicaragua, Peru, Poland, Romania, São-Tomé Principe, Seychelles, Somalia, Sudan, Syria, Tanzania, USSR, Vietnam, North and South Yemen, Yugoslavia, Zambia and Zimbabwe
Background: In the 1950s the Soviet Union introduced the BRDM-1 4 x 4 amphibious scout car as the replacement for the BA-64 used during World War II. Although the BRDM-1 was a significant improvement, it still had a number of drawbacks, and in the early 1960s a new vehicle was developed. Subsequently called the BRDM-2, this had many improvements including a one-man turret armed with 14.5mm and 7.62mm machine guns and a more powerful rear mounted engine which gave improved land and water speeds. The BRDM-2 is fully amphibious, being propelled in the water by a single water jet mounted at the rear of the hull, and to improve its cross-country mobility a pair of belly wheels can be lowered either side between the front and rear wheels. Standard equipment includes infra-red night vision devices, a central tyre pressure regulation system and an NBC system. The BRDM-2 is widely used by the Warsaw Pact and has been exported in considerable numbers all over the world. The basic chassis has also been adopted to meet a large number of other roles, including command vehicle, chemical reconnaissance vehicle with lane-marking equipment installed at the rear, and both air defence and anti-tank carrier. The air defence variant is known as the SA-9 Gaskin and carries four missiles in the ready-to-launch position, while the latest of at least three anti-tank versions is the BRDM-3, whose Spandrel anti-tank guided missile system comprises five missiles carried in the ready-to-launch position with additional missiles carried inside ready for manual loading. Although the BRDM-2 has limited capabilities on the Central European Front its simple controls and ease of handling make it popular in the Third World a fact evidenced by the long list of customers—currently standing at a total of 35 nations— which have taken delivery of this efficient vehicle.

M109 and M110A2

M109

Origin: USA
Crew: 6 on weapon
Armament: One 155mm howitzer; one 12.7mm M2 HB anti-aircraft machine gun
Armour: Classified
Dimensions: Length including main armament 29ft 11in (9.12m); hull length 20ft 4in (6.19m); width 10ft 2in (3.1m); height 10ft 9in (3.28m)
Combat weight: 55,000lb (24,948kg)
Engine: General Motors Detroit Diesel Model 8V-71T turbo-charged diesel developing 405bhp (303kW) 2,300rpm
Performance: Road speed 35mph 56.3km/h); range 217 miles (3,49km); vertical obstacle 1ft 9in (0.53m); trench 6ft 0in (1.83m); gradient 60 per cent
History: Developed to meet the requirements of the US Army in the mid-1950s with first production vehicles completed in 1963; current production model is M109A2. In service with Austria, Belgium Canada, Denmark, Egypt, Ethiopia, West Germany, Greece, Iran, Iraq, Italy, Jordan, South Korea, Kuwait Libya, Morocco, the Netherlands, Norway, Pakistan, Peru, Portugal, Saudi Arabia, Spain, Switzerland, Taiwan, Tunisia, the United Kingdom and the United States Army and Marines.
Background: During the early 1950s the standard 155mm self-propelled howitzer of the US Army was the M4. This suffered from several major disadvantages, including a very short operational range, since it was powered by a petrol engine, and the fact that the 155mm weapon was installed in an open topped crew compartment at the rear with a traverse of 60° left and right. Originally it was intended to

develop a new self-propelled howitzer with the ordnance mounted in a turret that could be traversed through a full 360°: the M44 was to be replaced by a version with a 156mm howitzer while the M52 105mm self propelled

howitzer was to be replaced by a version with 110mm ordnance. In the end it was decided to remain with the existing 155mm and 105mm calibres as the ammunition was in such widespread use. Prototypes of the new 105mm howitzer were designated T195 while the 155mm version was the T196, both of which were powered by petrol engines, but further development resulted in the T195E1 and the T196E1 with more fuel efficient diesel engines. In the end the T195E1 was type classified as the M108 and the T196E1 as the M109. The M108 only served with the US Army for a few years as it was decided to concentrate on the M109; most of the M108s were supplied to other countries and even in 1987 these remained in service with several armies. Since production started in 1962 the M109 series of 155mm self propelled howitzers has become the most widely used weapon of its type in the world and is being constantly modified to meet the changing operational requirements

of the artillery. The original M109 was manufactured at the Cleveland Army Tank Plant in Ohio, a facility owned by the Army but run by private contractors—originally the Cadillac Division of the General Motors Corporation, which was followed by the Chrysler Corporation and finally the Allison Division of General Motors Corporation; the last orders were placed in fiscal year 1969. The M109 has a hull and turret of welded aluminium armour construction that provides the crew with protection from small arms fire and shell splinters; the driver is seated front left, with the engine compartment to his right and the turret at the rear. The 155mm howitzer has a very short barrel with a large fume extractor and muzzle brake and fires a wide range of separate-loading ammunition, including high explosive, smoke, tactical nuclear,chemical, rocket assisted high explosive and illuminating. The standard HE M107 round has a maximum range of 15,966 yards (14,600m). The M109A1 is basically an M109 with a new and longer ordnance (or barrel) and other modifications which allow the HE M107 projectile to be fired to a range of 19,794 yards (18,100m). All M109A1s were conversions of original M109s, while the M109A1B produced by BMY for the export market from the early 1970s was essentially an

Above and right: The M109 is the most widely used 155mm self-propelled howitzer in the world, well over 3,000 having been built so far. Since it was first introduced into service in 1963 it has been

constantly improved and the Howitzer Improvement Programme (HIP) is expected to become operational later this decade in both the United States and Israeli Armies. Recently the US Army Artillery arm

fielded the M992 Field Artillery Ammunition Support Vehicle (FMSV) which feeds fuzed projectiles and charges through its rear door and into the gun compartment of the M109 so enabling it to maintain a full supply of

on-board ammunition. The ammunition used by the M109 is of the separate loading type consisting of charge (2) and projectiles, the charge being set off by an igniter (1). Rounds available on the M109 include laser

guided Copperhead (3), M483A1 improved conventional munition, shown with fusible lifting lug (4), M109 HE (5), ADAM area denial artillery munition (6), RAAMS remote anti-armor minw system (7), NC (8), M485

illuminating (9), M825 smoke, white phosphorus, with fusible lifting lug (10), M110 Agent H/HD (11) and rocket-assisted HE (12). Ammunition for the 12.7mm M2 HB machine gun is in belts (13).

M109 incorporating all the modifications and improvements of the M109A1. The M109A2 was placed in production by BMY in 1978 both for the US Army and for overseas sales and is essentially the M109A1 with additional improvements in reliability, availability, maintainability and durability plus some key safety improvements. The US Army's M109A3 is the M109A1 with the same improvements of the M109A2, these modifications being carried out by the Army itself at its own depots. Using the chassis of the M109 BMY has designed and built the Field Artillery Ammunition Support Vehicle (FAASV), which is designed to carry nearly 100 155mm projectiles and charges and feed them to the M109 when the latter is in the firing position. The FAASV was developed as a private venture but was subsequently adopted by the US Army as the M992 and is also in service with several other countries, including Egypt, which has a command post vehicle based on a similar chassis.

M110A2

Origin: USA
Crew: 5 on weapon
Armament: One 203mm howitzer
Armour: Classified
Dimensions: Length including main armament 35ft 2.4in (10.73m); hull length 18ft 9in (5.72m); width 10ft 4in (3.15m); height to top of barrel when travelling 10ft 3in (3.14m)
Combat weight: 62,500lb (28,350kg)
Engine: Detroit Diesel Model 8V-71T turbo-charged diesel developing 405hp (303kW) at 2300rpm.
Performance: Road speed 34mph (55km/h); range 325 miles (523km); vertical obstacle 3ft 4in (1.016m); trench 6ft 3in (1.905m); gradient 60 percent.

History: Developed to meet a US Army requirement in the late 1950s, in service 1963. Current production model is M110A2. In service with Belgium, Germany, Greece, Iran, Israel, Italy, Japan, Jordan, Netherlands, Pakistan, South Korea, Spain, Taiwan, Turkey, UK and USA.
Development: This weapon originated in 1956 with a demand by the US Army for a heavy self-propelled artillery piece capable of being carried in transport aircraft. The chassis was to carry the 8 inch (203mm) howitzer, the 175mm gun or the 155mm gun interchangeably. The first production was ordered in 1961 from the Pacific Car & Foundry Company and the first M110 battalion was formed in 1963. The

Left: The A2 version of the M-110 is fitted with a longer-barrelled ordnance and muzzle brake. There is no protection for the crew and no ammo storage on the gun.

M107 175mm gun version appeared at the same time, and both equipments were subsequently used in Vietnam. The M110 howitzer tube was actually that of the M2 8 inch howitzer of World War Two and it used the same ammunition, giving a maximum range of 18,379yds (16,800m) with a 204lb (92.5kg) shell. The propelling charge was a seven-zone bag system. In 1969 development of a more powerful version began, which was to have a longer range and fire a new family of improved ammunition. This was standardised in 1976 as the M110A1 and had a new and much longer barrel which improved the range to 25,050ft (22,900m) using the same ammunition as before. However, a new propelling charge had been designed which required further modification; a double-baffle muzzle brake was fitted to the barrel, making the equipment into the M110A2, and this permitted the full new charge to be used, raising the maximum range to 32,800yds (30,000m) with rocket-assisted projectile. Other ammunition available for the M110A2 includes Improved Conventional Munitions carrying anti-tank or anti-personnel mines, chemical agent projectiles and nuclear projectiles. The British Army did not, at first, adopt the 203mm M110; instead it took the M107 175mm gun. This, however, was a less versatile weapon with a limited range of ammunition, and, in common with other users, the British weapons had their 175mm barrels removed and were re-barreled to become M110A2s.

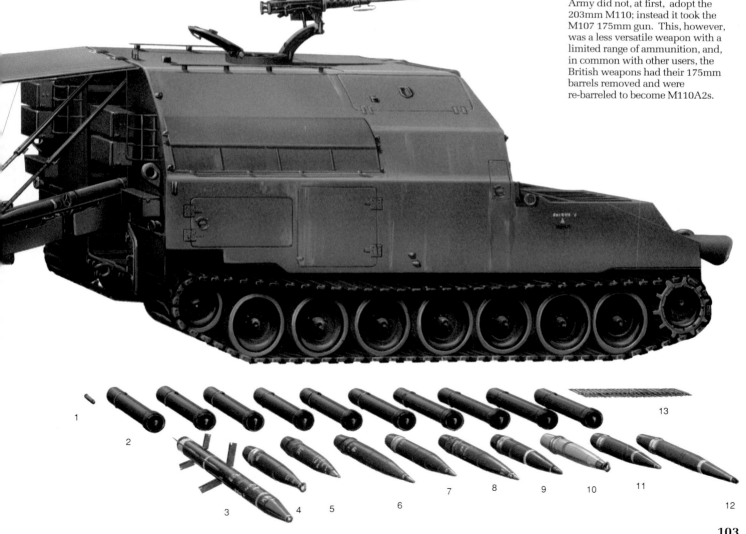

1
2
3
4
5
6
7
8
9
10
11
12
13

M198 and Light Gun

M198

Origin: USA
Calibre: 155mm (6.1in)
Length of barrel: 240in (609.6cm)
Weight in action: 15,791lb (7,163kg)
Muzzle velocity: 1,850ft/sec (564m/sec)
Rate of fire: Maximum 4rds/min; sustained 2rds/min
Maximum range: HE 19,850 yd (18,150m); RAP 32,808 yd (30,000m)
Shell weight: HE 94.6lb (42.91kg)
History: Development started in 1968 and first prototypes were ready in 1972. Standardised as the M198 in mid-1978, first examples were issued later the same year. Now in service with the US Army and Marine Corps and with several other nations including Saudi Arabia, Pakistan, Tunisia, Australia and Thailand
Background: The M198 was developed by several government and civilian agencies and production has been carried out by Watervliet Arsenal, Rock Island Arsenal and ConDiesel Mobile Equipment, among others. Although categorised by the Americans as a lightweight weapon—it can be air lifted under a CH-47D helicopter—it is really a hefty load and it lacks the auxiliary power unit and hydraulic actuating circuits featured on most comparable towed 155mm howitzers. The M198 requires at least a 6 x 6 truck to tow it over rough ground and manhandling the howitzer into a firing position is a considerable task requiring a gun crew of at least 11 men . However, it is a reliable and accurate weapon that has given good service so far and has been exported to several customers. It is still in production for overseas customers.

The design of the M198 is orthodox. For firing the split trail bottom carriage wheels are raised off the

Above: US Marine Corps M198 system in firing position. Unlike most other 155mm systems the M198 does not have an auxiliary

power unit, which makes it difficult to move across beaches. The crew have to rely on their strength to bring it into action.

ground using a hand-operated hydraulic pump, and the howitzer then rests on a firing base under the front axle and on the trail axle spades. This improves firing stability at all elevation angles as the carriage wheels have a rather narrow track. For normal towing the barrel points forward but it can be reversed over the trails for storage purposes. The barrel—the Cannon Assembly M199–can be elevated by hand to an angle of 72° for firing to close ranges but on-carriage traverse is limited to a total of 45°. The fire control system has direct-fire sights to deal with targets such as armoured vehicles at short ranges. One of the main strengths of the M198 is its ability to use virtually the entire range of American 155mm ammunition. This large family extends from the usual high explosive, smoke and similar orthodox projectiles to such things as tactical CS shells, cargo rounds containing scatterable land

mines or radio communication jammers, binary chemical agent shells and the laser-guided Copperhead anti armour munition, and includes tactical nuclear projectiles. All are fired using a variable charge system and to achieve the maximum range of 32,808 yd (30,000m) a rocket assisted projectile is used, a rocket motor in the shell base firing just as the projectile reaches the limit of its initial firing velocity. However, accuracy is poor at extreme ranges. The US Army has now called for a new version of the M198 light enough to be lifted under a Black Hawk helicopter but still using the basic ordnance of the M198 and having a similar overall ballistic performance. BMY is currently designing a suitable light carriage using various advanced techniques and modern light materials but no hardware had appeared by mid-1987.

Light Gun

Origin: United Kingdom
Calibre: 105mm (4.14in)
Length of barrel: 124.8in (317cm)
Weight in action: 4,100lb (1,860kg)
Muzzle velocity: 2,323ft/sec (708m/sec) max
Rate of fire: 8rds/min for 1 min; 6rds/min for 3 min; 3rds/min sustained
Maximum range: 18,810 yd (17,200m)
Shell weight: HE 35.49lb (16.1kg)
History; Developed to replace the 105mm Pack Howitzer used by the Royal Artillery. First production examples issued late 1974. Now in widespread use following active service in the 1982 Falklands campaign, and ordered by the US Army with a new barrel under the designation M119.
Background: The Light Gun was designed at the Royal Armament and Research Establishment at Fort

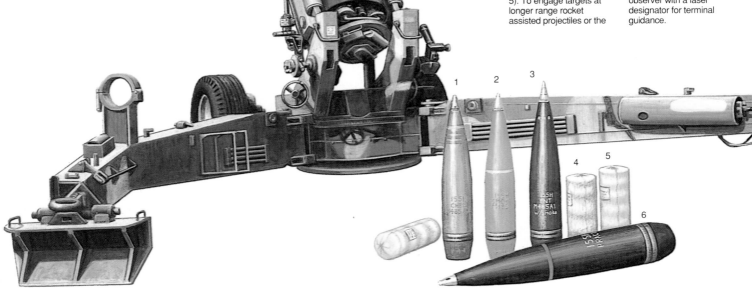

Below: The M198 fires a wide range of separate loading ammunition including chemical (1), smoke (2), anti-personnel (3) and practice (6) rounds with their associated propelling charges (4 and 5). To engage targets at longer range rocket assisted projectiles or the

more accurate base bleed rounds can be fired. The M198 can also fire the Cannon Launched Guided Projectile to engage enemy tanks with the actual target being illuminated by a forward observer with a laser designator for terminal guidance.

Right: The 105mm light gun provides artillery support to light mobile forces. While 105mm is not as destructive as 155mm, the light gun will provide effective support where no other gun can. It can be towed by a small vehicle or transported by a medium helicopter.

be rapidly traversed through 360° to engage any target that may appear from any direction, a useful facility in mobile warfare. For towing, the weapon's barrel is traversed to the rear over the trails, which allows the centre of gravity to be kept low for towing but means that the barrel has to be swung forward again when coming into action. This entails removing and replacing one of the carriage wheels, but the procedure takes only a few seconds using a racing hub on the wheel concerned. On several occasions during the Falklands campaign the Light Gun proved itself capable of firing for long periods without problems. The L118 version has a maximum range well in excess of any comparable gun but the ordnance can be changed in order to fire the American M1 family of 105mm ammunition. This conversion, the L119, is the one selected by the US Army. The ammunition fired by the L118 Light Gun is special to it, though it is a also fired by the Abbot self-propelled gun. Rounds include high explosive, smoke, marker smoke of various colours, several types of practice shell, illuminating and anti-armour HESH. The Americans are developing a rocket-assisted shell for their guns to improve the maximum range of their shorter-ranged M1 ammunition. The British Light Guns use a five-charge propellent system with an extra super charge to achieve maximum range. Minimum range is 2,734 yd (2,500m) and is achieved by using high angles of barrel elevation and fitting spoiler vanes on the shell nose to degrade its ballistic performance.The Light Gun requires only a light truck for towing, and British Army units use over-snow vehicles and mount the gun on skis in Arctic regions. The US Army will use a version of its Hummer as the tractor for its M119 Light Guns.

Halstead in Kent. After a period of development the first production examples were ready in 1974 and since then the Light Gun has been used by the British Army and adopted by many others. It has been ordered by the US Army for their new light divisions as the M119. The Light Gun makes extensive use of light alloys to keep down overall weight, the carriage uses a bowed tubular steel trail, and it is possible to carry a Light Gun slung under a Puma helicopter. In action the carriage wheels rest on a circular firing platform that allows the gun to

Left: The Royal Ordnance 105mm Light gun fires the same wide range of ammunition used by the Abbot self-propelled gun including HE (1), smoke (2), marker (3) and illumination (4), as well as US HESH (5) and HE (6) rounds, all of which are of the separate loading type using brass normal (7) or extended-range super (8) cartridge cases.

MLRS

Origin: USA

Dimensions: Length of rocket 12ft 11in (3.94m); diameter 8.66in (227mm)

Weight: Phase I rocket 675.4lb (307kg) Phase II rocket 566.5lb (257.5kg) Phase III rocket about 550lb (250kg)

Range: Phase I rocket 20 miles (32km) Phase II rocket 25 miles (40km) Phase III rocket 28.125 miles (45km)

Warhead weight: Phase I (bomblet carrier) 333.8lb (154kg); Phase II (anti-tank mine carrier) 235.4lb (107kg); Phase III (terminally guided submunition) about 231lb (105kg)

Background: The concept phase for a new multiple rocket launcher system for the US Army began in 1976 and by 1980 Vought had a contract to develop its system. In production and in service with the USA and ordered by France, Italy, the Netherlands, West Germany and the United Kingdom.

The MLRS is based on the three-man M987 Fighting Vehicle System Carrier; weighing 55,420.2lb (25,191kg) fully loaded, it is fitted with a lightly armoured cab with its own NBC defence system and the launcher fire control unit and computer. The vehicle is based on the M2 Bradley IFV chassis and carries a Launcher/Loader Module (LLM) which has a twin-boom crane unit for the self-loading and unloading of the two 4,994lb (2,770kg) fully loaded six-round Launch Pod Containers (LPCs). Ripples of up to twelve rockets can be fired at any one time, though re-aiming has to be automatically performed between each launch by the onboard fire control system as a result of the displacement of the vehicle by the launch forces released. The launcher, or Self-Propelled Launcher Loader (SPLL) as it is formally known, is in service with the US Army in West Germany and South Korea as well as in the continental United States, and well over half the 300 plus SPLLs planned for the 41 batteries had been delivered by mid-1987. By 1980 the US Army had already made the MLRS programme a multinational one, and a second production line was

Above: Each Vought Multiple Launch Rocket System has 12 rockets in the ready to launch position; once expended these are replaced by fresh pods, each holding six rockets. The US Army has already fielded over half its intended 41 MLRS batteries and each US division—except airborne, light and air assault divisions—has one combined M110A2/MLRS battalion.

Above and right: The Vought Multiple Launch Rocket System (MLRS) is already operational with the US Army in the continental United States, Europe and South Korea. The Netherlands has ordered the system direct from the United States while France, West Germany, Italy and the United Kingdom have formed a consortium to make the complete system and its rockets in Europe. The basic MLRS rocket (1) has a warhead (2) that carries 644 M42(3) submunitions with HEAT warheads for top attack of armoured vehicles. For the longer term the US Army has started to develop the long-range TACMS (4), which is designed to have a conventional warhead. The West German Army will use MLRS to deliver AT-2 anti-tank mines: each MLRS rocket would have 28 mines (5) in seven units of four (6); the warhead (7) is similar to that of the standard MLRS submunition. In the future a new warhead with terminally guided submunitions (8) is being developed by a consortium drawing on the expertise of both European and US companies.

set up in Europe. Apart from a few initial systems bought from Vought the European nations involved in the work will receive, from 1991 onward, the United Kingdom 67 (out of 71 total) SPLLs, West Germany 200 (202), France 55 (56) and Italy 20 (20). In addition, the Netherlands has ordered 30 SPLLs from the American production line. In practically every case the army involved will use the MLRS to replace elderly tube artillery, a doctrine which is diametrically opposite to all that the Soviets have done since they introduced MRLs during World War II. There are three types of warhead. The basic Phase I type, which is already in service and will be the standard type for all MLRS users, carries a total of 644 0.5lb (0.23kg) ribbon-stabilised M77 dual-purpose shaped-charge fragmentation bomblets, derived from the M42 type used in the conventional warhead variant of the Lance SSM and capable of penetrating light armour plate. The targets assigned to Phase I rockets are artillery and missile batteries,

airfields, the assembly areas of mechanised infantry units, radar sites and choke points such as road and rail junctions or river crossing points. The Phase II warhead, which was developed by West Germany and has entered production for its army and, eventually, Italy, is designed specifically to engage armour concentrations. It consists of 28 Dynamit Nobel AT-2 anti-tank mines in seven submunition carriers that are ejected at a pre-determined height of around 3,940ft (1,200m) above the target area; individual mines are then released from the carriers some seven seconds later and are slowed down by parachutes so that they land with the correct orientation on the ground.

On impact the parachute is released and the mine's trigger wires armed, and if not exploded by an armoured vehicle the mine will automatically detonate after one of six available pre-set intervals has elapsed.

A single SPLL can lay 336 mines into an area 1,100 yd by 5,500 yd (1,000m by 5,000m) within a minute of the firing sequence starting at a

range up to 25 miles (40km) from its launch position. The AT-2 is designed to penetrate up to 5.5in (140mm) of armour plate. The final warhead, the Phase III type, had only just entered its full-scale evelopment stage by mid 1987 as a joint project between US, German, French and British companies, and initial deployment with MLRS users is not due until 1992. The payload will be three millimetre-wave active radar terminally guided submunitions. Over the general target area a time fuze will release the weapons, which then begin individual glide manoeuvres to allow their radars to acquire a target. Once a valid one is detected the submunition initiates a terminal top-attack dive onto the target, where its contact fuze detonates the shaped charge warhead.

Other warheads known to be under examination by the Americans include a binary chemical type which has a payload of 91.9lb (41.8kg) of chemicals which form a semi-persistent nerve gas agent when mixed, and the

MLRS-SADARM, which has similar characteristics to the Phase II head but carries six sense and destroy armour (SADARM) submunitions. Vought was selected to develop the Army Tactical Missile System (TACMS) as the non-nuclear armed successor to the Lance tactical battlefield support missile. TACMS is designed to be carried and fired by the M987 MLRS SPLL with a single missile in its container-launcher replacing an LPC, and the weapon carries a payload of scatterable or terminally guided submunitions to attack enemy second-echelon forces. Details of TACMS are a length of 13ft (3.96m) and a diameter of 2ft (0.61m), and an advanced single-stage solid propellant rocket motor gives a maximum range of 150 miles (240km). Further warheads will include types designed to attack hard targets, SAM sites and airfields. The first TACMS missile was fired in the Gulf War, and only software changes in the MLRS fire control computer were required to integrate it into the overall fire support system.

D-30 and Giat GCT

D-30

Origin: USSR
Calibre: 121.92mm (4.8in)
Length of barrel: 191.9in (487.5cm)
Weight in action: 6,944lb (3,150kg)
Muzzle velocity: 2,428ft/sec (740m/sec)
Rate of fire: 7-8rds/min
Maximum range: HE 16,842 yd (1 5,400m); RAP 23,950 yd (21,900m)
Shell weight: FRAG-HE 47.97lb (21.76kg)
History: Designed as the replacement for the old M-30 howitzer, the D-30 has been exported widely and may be encountered in many parts of the world
Background: Although categorised as a howitzer the D-30 is really a gun-howitzer judged by its barrel length and the use of variable-charge ammunition, and is a simple weapon that is made to appear complicated by the employment of an unusual carriage system that has three trail legs. In action the three legs are separated and spread so that the entire weight of the weapon rests on them as the wheels are raised off the ground; there is also a centrally located firing jack that is lowered to the ground as the wheels are raised. To improve stability when firing the ends of the trail legs are secured by stakes that are hammered into the ground. It does not take long to emplace the weapon as a trained crew can get the D-30 into action in about one and a half minutes; however, getting it out of action again takes longer as the stakes have to be removed first. The emplaced trail arrangement provides a full 360° top carriage traverse and makes the D-30 a useful anti-armour weapon; it is provided with special HEAT projectiles for this role, and a hit from one of these projectiles would disable most tanks. A weight-saving feature of the D-30 is that it is towed by the muzzle, which has a folding towing eye under the multi-baffle muzzle brake for the purpose. This towing method lowers the centre of gravity of the towed load and also reduces the length of the tractor-weapon combination. The normal D-30 tractor is a light or medium 6 x 6 truck and the usual crew is seven. In order to reduce ammunition logistic supply requirements the D-30 can fire many of the projectiles used by the old M-30 howitzer, which dates from 1938; these include high explosive shells and smoke and illuminating rounds. It can also fire a high-explosive rocket assisted projectile to increase the maximum range. The weapon has few frills and the small shield is provided only to protect the gun mechanism, not the gun crew. The recoil mechanism is unusual among Soviet artillery weapons in being located over the barrel instead of underneath, the latter being the usual location. The D-30 is a very simple weapon to operate and relatively cheap to produce so it is widely used as a training gun, and each Soviet Army tank division had two

Above: The D-30 is a light, mobile and effective artillery piece used all over the world. It retains a secondary anti-tank capability.

battalions of 18 guns; more were used by the motorised rifle divisions. The D-30 has been sold or donated to many countries, as well as some African and Far Eastern freedom fighter organisations, and is produced in China- and exported –by NORINCO as the Type D30. The Egyptian Army has so many D-30s that is has investigated the use of the weapon on a locally produced self-propelled platform, while Syria has mounted D-30s on obsolete T-34/ 85 tank chassis and at one time the Egyptians did the same. The Soviet 122mm 2S1 (M1974 or S0-122) self propelled howitzer has a barrel very similar to that of the D-30, which it is replacing in Soviet service, and fires the same ammunition.

GCT

Origin: France
Crew: 4
Armament: One 155mm gun; one 7.62mm or 12.7mm anti-aircraft machine gun; two smoke dischargers each side of turret
Armour: 3.14in (80mm) max
Dimensions: Length including main armament 33ft 8in (10.25m); hull length 22ft 0in (6.7m); width 10ft 4in (3.1 5m); height 10ft 8in (3.25m)
Combat weight: 92,593lb (42,000kg)
Ground pressure: Not available
Engine: Hispano-Suiza HS 11012 cylinder water-cooled supercharged multi-fuel developing 720hp (537kW) at 2,000rpm
Performance: Road speed 37mph (60km/h); range 280 miles (450km); vertical obstacle 3ft 0in (0.93m); trench 6ft 3in (1.9m); gradient 60 per cent
History: Developed to meet the requirements of the French Army under the name GCT (Grande Cadence de Tir) with first prototype being completed in 1972 and first production vehicles in 1977. In service with France, Iraq and Saudi Arabia

Left and below: For many years the 122mm D-30 field gun has been the backbone of Soviet artillery regiments, but it is now being replaced by the self-propelled 2S1 weapon. When deployed in the firing position the wheels are raised clear of the ground, enabling the weapon to be traversed rapidly through 360° for laying on a new target. The D-30 is normally towed by a 6 x 6 tnuck or MT-LB which also carries the crew and ammunition. The latter is of the separate loading type and consists of brass cartridge case (1) and propelling charges (8 and 9), plus projectiles. Shown here are HE fragmentation (2), HE full (3) HE reduced (4), HEAT (5), APFSDS (6) and Smoke 7) rounds for the D-30.

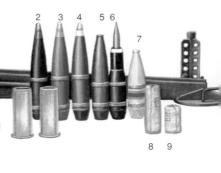

Above: By mid-1989 GIAT had built about 300 GCI self-propelled artillery systems for the French, Iraqi and Saudi Arabian armies. In the French Army each GCI regiment has four batteries of five GCI weapons with each battery tied into the ATILA artillery fire control system.

Background: Whereas West Germany, Italy and the United Kingdom developed the 155mm FH-70 towed howitzer first and then the self-propelled SP-70, France developed the self-propelled gun first following up much later with the towed TR. The GCT is essentially a slightly modified

AMX-30 MBT chassis fitted with a new fully enclosed power-operated turret mounting a 155mm gun with a double baffle muzzle brake. Turret traverse is a full 360° and the ordnance can be elevated from 1° to +66°, and a very high rate of fire can be achieved with the help of the automatic loader in the turret rear which contains 42 projectiles and charges. A typical ammunition load would consist of 36 high explosive and six smoke or 30 high explosive, six illuminating and six smoke. The wide range of projectiles that can be fired by the weapon includes Type 56/59 HE, smoke phosphorus, training and illuminating shells, a projectile carrying six anti-tank mines (under development), and rocket-assisted and base bleed rounds for extended range performance, the last having a maximum range of 31,676 yards (28,500m). Mounted on the turret roof is a 7.62mm machine gun, for

which a total of 2,050 rounds are carried, or a 12.7mm M2 HB with 800 rounds. The GCT can be brought into action in under two minutes and takes one minute to come out of action. The maximum rate of fire with the automatic loader is 8 rds/min; in the event of failure the weapon can be loaded manually at two or three rounds a minute, and the turret can be reloaded in 15 minutes.The ability to fire a large number of rounds is of crucial importance as modern target location systems can detect where the rounds are being fired from; this information can be passed to friendly artillery units and counter battery fire started within seconds. The actual gun is, however, only one part of an overall artillery system, which also includes target acquisition systems, artillery fire control and command and control systems and ammunition resupply vehicles and equipment.

Below: Propellant for GCT rounds is in combustible cartridge cases (1) and projectiles that can be fired include Copperhead (2), HE Type 56/59 (3), Smoke F1A (4), Training (5), HE Type F1 (6), Smoke (7), Training FI (8), Illuminating FI (9), mine dispensing (10), GIAT HE Base Bleed (11), HE Rocket Assist (12), Luchaire HE Base Bleed (13) and ERBER HE (14). In addition, the GCT carries percussion detonators (15). The GCT uses 76mm (16) or 80mm (17) smoke grenades;

12.7mm machine gun ammunition (18) is in belts.

SS-1 Scud B and BM-21 MLRS

SS-1 Scud

Origin: USSR

Dimensions: (Scud B) length 37ft 4³⁄₄in (11.4m); diameter 2ft 9in (0.84m)

Launch weight: 14,043lb (6,370kg)

Performance: Range 50-112 miles (80-180km) with nuclear warhead; 50-174 miles (80-280km) with conventional warhead; CEP 1,017-1,640 yd (930-1,500m) depending on range

Warhead: Weight 1,892lb (860kg); types HE, chemical, training, 40kT or 100kT tactical nuclear

Background: Classed as an operational tactical missile system by the Soviets, the NATO-designated SS-1 Scud B (Soviet designation R17E) entered service in the mid-1960s as a product improved version of the earlier SS1A Scud A (Soviet designation R-7) and SS-1B Scud B (Soviet designation R-17). Early Scuds were mounted on an obsolete tank chassis but current models are carried by and launched from an 8 x 8 chassis with good cross-country mobility. Deployed by the Soviets at army and front levels in brigades of three TELs and three reload vehicles, Scud is being replaced by the SS-23 Spider. However, it is still in service with all the Warsaw Pact nations and has been exported to Egypt, Iraq, Iran, Libya, North Korea, South Yemen and Syria. In 1987 Iraq developed an improved Scud named the "Al Hussein", which is believed to have improved the maximum range to 600km by reducing the warhead size, lengthening the missile by one metre and increasing the size of the fuel tanks. Some 135 of these were fired against Iran. In 1988 a further improvement, the "Al Abbas", was developed. This had another fuel tank extension and the warhead reduced to 300kg, which resulted in a range of 900km.

The "Al Hussein" was used against Israel and Saudi Arabia, and some reports say at least one "Al Abbas" was launched. Neither variants have improved on the poor accuracy of the basic Scud.

Above: The two Iraqi variants of Scud, seen at a Baghdad arms fair a few years before the war. The Al-Hussain is on the left, with the Al-Abbas alongside.

BM-21

Origin: USSR
Dimensions: Length (standard rocket) 10ft 7in (3.23m); length (short rocket) 6ft 3in (1.9m); diameter 4.8in (122mm)
Weights: Standard rocket 169.8lb (77kg); short rocket 101lb (45.8kg)
Range: Standard rocket 12.7 miles (20.4km); short rocket 6.83 miles (11km)
Warhead: 42.8lb (19.4kg) types HE fragmentation, incendiary, smoke, chemical and submunition
History: The concept of the Multiple Rocket Launcher, or Katyusha, was first introduced by the Soviets during World War II. Today the 40 round 122mm (4.8in) and its derivatives are standard Warsaw Pact MRL systems. Known users of the BM-21 include Afghanistan, Algeria, Angola, Bulgaria, Chad, China, Cuba, Egypt, Ethiopia, East Germany, Hungary, India, Iran, Iraq, Israel, North Korea, Libya, Morocco, Mozambique, Nicaragua, Pakistan, Poland, Syria, Tanzania, USSR, Vietnam, North and South Yemen and Zambia
Background: The BM-21 system, which first entered service in the early 1960s, is mounted on a URAL 375 (6 x 6) cross-country truck chassis which is fitted with a central tyre pressure regulation system to allow the driver to adjust the tyre pressure to suit the type of ground being crossed. As such the 40-tube 4.8in (122mm) BM-21 is cheap and easy to produce and is

deployed en masse either as an offensive salvo fire weapon against area targets such as troop and/or vehicle concentrations or as a defence suppression weapon against artillery and mortar battery positions. The Soviets view their MRL as a supplement rather than a replacement for the tube artillery. Versions of the BM-21 have been manufactured in China (40-round truck-mounted Type 81, 40-round tank chassis-mounted Type 81 and 24-round truck-mounted Type 83 systems); Egypt (40-round reverse engineered copy, 21- and 30-round modifications and the locally produced Sakr-18 and Sakr-30 systems); India (40-round LRAR systems); North Korea (30-round local model designated BM-11); and Romania (21-round version on a

Above: A row of Soviet BM-21s on exercise. The Soviets believe that these weapons have their maximum effect when fired in Battalion salvos of up to 320 rockets.

Bucegi SR-114 truck chassis). There is also a 36-round Soviet variant mounted on a ZIL-131 truck chassis known by the NATO designation M1976 and a special airborne 12 round launcher on a GAZ-66 (4 x 4) vehicle which is known as the M1975. The BM-21 is normally found in the Soviet Army in single battalions of 18 launchers integrated into the divisional artillery regiments of both tank and motorised rifle divisions. Most models have seen combat action throughout the world in conflicts in Africa, the Middle East, the Far East

and Central America, and Israel has captured a number of BM-21s and has used the system against its former Arab owners on a number of occasions. Two types of rocket can be fired, the only difference between the long and short rounds being in the size of solid propellant rocket motor fitted. It is the sight and sound of the rockets exploding which causes the greatest shock, and when used against low technology armies, especially in Africa, a salvo of BM-21 rockets has often caused considerable panic and confusion, allowing the attacking forces to win the battle easily. Against more sophisticated forces, however, a barrage will often bring retaliation in the form of an air strike or counter-barrage by similar MRLs or tube artillery. In Western Europe the Soviets would use their MRL battalions as primary delivery platforms for chemical agents, especially substances like hydrogen cyanide gas, which cause degradation of NBC filters and enable follow-up attacks by other agents to penetrate defensive clothing and vehicle protection systems and kill the personnel. In order to reduce the 10 minute manual reloading time of the BM-21 the Czechoslovakians took the 40 round BM-21 launcher and mounted it on their cross-country capable 8 x 8 TATRA 813 truck chassis with a reload pack of 40 rockets between it and he vehicle's armoured cab to produce the RM-70, an effective variant of the BM-21.

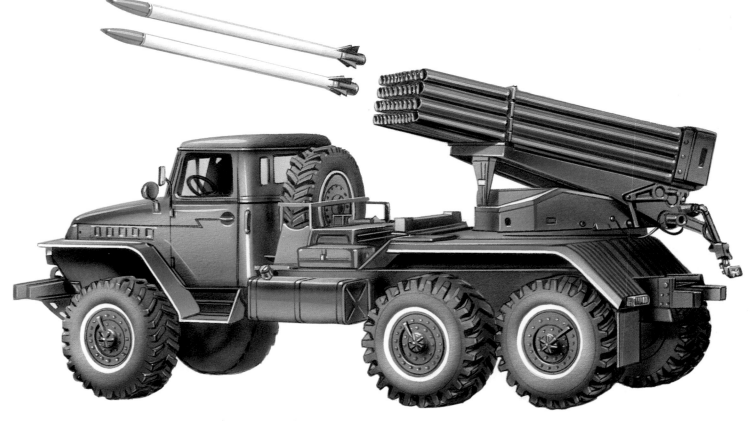

Left: Although the Scud B is now being replaced by the longer-range SS-23 system, it remains in service with several countries and has recently been used by both Iraq and Iran in Middle East conflicts. So far only high explosive warheads have been used in combat and delivery of these has proved to be inaccurate.

Above: The BM-21 122mm (4.8in) has been the standard multiple rocket system of the Soviet Army for many years, but it is now being supplemented by more modern systems. It is mounted on a 6 x 6 cross-country chassis to allow for rapid deployment. Many other countries have built copies of the BM-21 on various other chassis, and the system is in widespread service. Although less accurate than artillery the BM-21 can deliver a massive amount of firepower in a rapid salvo.

M163 Vulcan and Patriot

M163 VULCAN

Origin: USA
Crew: 4
Armament: One six-barrel 20mm cannon in power-operated turret with traverse of 360° and elevation from -5° to +80°
Armour: 0.47-1.49in (12-38mm)
Dimensions: Length 15ft 11in (4.86m); width 9ft 4in (2.85m); height including turret 9ft 0in (2.74m)
Combat weight: 27,082lb (13,310kg)
Ground Pressure: 9.52lb/sq in (0.61kg/cm²)
Engine: Detroit Diesel Model 6V-53 6-cylinder water cooled diesel developing 215hp (160kW)
Performance: Road speed 42.25mph (67.6km/h); range 302 miles (483km); vertical obstacle 2ft 0in (0.61m); trench 5ft 6in (1.68m);
gradient 60 per cent
History: Developed in the mid 1960s, the M163 Vulcan entered US Army service in 1968 and was subsequently exported to Ecuador, Israel, South Korea, Morocco, the Philippines, Sudan, Thailand, Tunisia and North Yemen. A similar system mounted on the Commando 4 x 4 APC chassis is in service with Saudi Arabian National Guard
Background: The M163 basically consists of an M113 APC fitted with a one-man power-operated turret which has an M61A1 Vulcan six-barrel cannon, gyro lead computing sight and a range-only VPS-2 radar mounted on the right-hand side. The chassis is designated M741 and differs only in minor details from the M113A1, while the cannon, a development of the standard USAF Vulcan aircraft gun, has two rates of fire, 1,000 and 3,000 rounds per minute; the former is used in the direct-fire ground role while the latter is used for air defence. The gunner can select bursts of 10,30,60 or 100 rounds and the maximum effective anti-aircraft range is 1,750 yd (1,600m) and maximum ground range 3,280 yd (3,000m) using M53 AP-T, M54 HPT, M56A3 HEI or HEIT combat rounds. From June 1984 the US Army fielded the Product Improved Vulcan Air Defence System (PIVADS), which has an improved fire-control system and the ability to fire the new Mk 149 APDS round, which increases the effective engagement range to 2,843 yd (2,600m) against aircraft. The M163 saw combat use in the ground role in Vietnam as a convoy escort vehicle, proving particularly useful in breaking up ambushes because of its very high rate of fire with the 1,100 ready-to-fire rounds available and the 1,000 reserve rounds inside the hull. The Israelis also used it during their 1982 Peace for Galilee invasion of South Lebanon, when several Syrian aircraft were engaged and destroyed during air attacks on Israeli armoured columns. The 20mm Vulcan's main drawback is its lack of all-weather capability. It was to have been replaced by the Sgt York DIVAD system, but that has now been cancelled, so the Vulcan will soldier on for some years yet.

PATRIOT

Origin: USA
Dimensions: Length 17ft 5in (5.31m); diameter 16in (406mm); wingspan 3ft (0.92m)

Left: A US Army gunner mans his 20mm M163 Vulcan self-propelled anti-aircraft gun system, with range only radar to the right of the mount. When engaging aircraft targets cyclic rate of fire is 3,000 rds/min, while 1,000 rds/min are fired against ground targets.

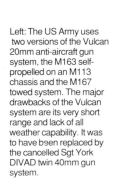

Left: The US Army uses two versions of the Vulcan 20mm anti-aircraft gun system, the M163 self-propelled on an M113 chassis and the M167 towed system. The major drawbacks of the Vulcan system are its very short range and lack of all weather capability. It was to have been replaced by the cancelled Sgt York DIVAD twin 40mm gun system.

Launch weight: 2,195lb (998kg)
Performance: Effective range 31.25-42.8 miles (65-68.5km); altitude limits 328-78,740ft (100-24,000m); speed Mach 3.0
Warhead: 221lb (100kg) HE-fragmentation with proximity fuze
History: Originally known as SAM-D. The development period extended from 1965, when the requirement was first specified, to 1980 due to the complexity of the system. Since then the weapon has entered service with the US Army and has been ordered by the Netherlands, West Germany and Japan as their replacement for the MIM-14 Nike Hercules. Total procurement for the US Army is 103 fire units and 6,200 missiles, of which 14 fire units and 840 missiles were to be loaned to the West Germans in addition to their own

14 fire units and 779 missiles purchased under a NATO air base defence agreement.
Background: The Patriot fire unit contains all the elements necessary to engage a target: the MPQ-53 phased-array radar set performs all the surveillance, IFF interrogation, acquisition, target tracking and guidance functions which in previous systems, such as Nike

Hercules and Hawk, required up to nine separate radars; the manned MSQ-104 engagement control station houses the weapon system's fire and operational status control computer; the MJQ-24 electric power plant; and eight four-tube launchers with Patriot rounds in their ready-to-fire canisters.
A Patriot battalion consists of six of these firing units. The single-stage

phased array command guided and semi-active homing solid-propellent missile carries an HE-fragmentation warhead and is capable of TVM (track via missile) radar guidance.
In the summer of 1986 a Patriot fire unit equipped with modified software for the anti-tactical missile role successfully intercepted a Lance surface-to-surface missile in flight. A development programme to provide for modifications to existing US Army and NATO SAM systems was initiated as part of the US Army's Tactical Missile Defence (TMD) plan, the need being for the SAMs to be able to intercept the increasingly accurate Soviet tactical missiles. This upgrade has proven its usefulness in intercepting Iraqi SCUDS over Israel and Saudi Arabia.

Left: The Patriot SAM system has been developed to replace the Nike Hercules and supplement the Hawk SAMs. Patriot is now operational in West Germany and the United States and has also been selected by West Germany, Japan and the Netherlands. Compared with Nike Hercules it is much more mobile and can engage more targets. With additional development it will be able to engage tactical battlefield missiles such as the Soviet SS-21 and SS-23.

Rapier

Origin: United Kingdom
Dimensions: Length 7ft 4in (2.23m); diameter 5.2in (133mm); wingspan 1ft 3in (0.38m)
Launch weight: 93.7lb(42.6kg)
Performance: Effective range Towed Rapier 875-7,500 yd (800-6,858m); Tracked Rapier 432.5-7,500 yd (400-6,858m); altitude limits 150-10,974ft (50-3,658m); speed Mach 2.0
Warhead: 3.1lb (1.4kg) HE semi-armour piercing with contact fuze
History: Development of Rapier began in the early 1960s with the first production rounds being issued to RAF Regiment and British Army in 1971. Since then it has been sold to Australia, Brunei, Indonesia, Iran (Army and Air Force), Oman, Qatar, Singapore, Switzerland, Turkey, the United Arab Emirates, the United States Air Force and Zambia. Well over 23,000 rounds have been produced and more than 10,000 have been launched during trials, training and in combat by the British and Iranian armed forces during the Falklands and Gulf wars.
Background: In its basic form the Towed Rapier system consists of the fire unit with an on-board surveillance radar, an optical tracker, a secondary sight, a generator and a

tactical control unit, all of which are connected by cable and towed by two lightweight 3/4- or 1-ton vehicles which carry a total of 13 rounds in sealed containers. The system can only engage targets in daylight conditions, and to meet the threat of day/night and all-weather attack a third vehicle is added which tows a DN181 Blindfire radar tracker unit with its own generator. This frequency-agile monopulse radar produces a very narrow beam which is used to track both target and missile in order to achieve a very high single- shot kill probability. The number of rounds carried by the unit is also increased to 17, and the Blindfire radar can be added to an optical Towed Rapier system as required, so that the British Army has only a 33 per cent Blindfire capability for its Towed Rapiers whereas the RAF Regiment, protecting valuable airfield targets, has a 100 per cent capability. In 1974 a tracked version of Rapier began development to meet the requirements of the Shah of Iran's armed forces. This was subsequently cancelled in 1979 by the new Iranian government after the-Shah was deposed but the system was subsequently adopted by the

British Army, the first order being placed in 1981 for for 50 units. In 1983 a further 20 were ordered so as to equip three Light Air Defence Regiments with four batteries each, two with 12 Towed systems apiece and two with 12 Tracked systems each. The tracked system, based on an M548 chassis designated RCM748, has a crew of three and is fitted with a Darkfire thermal imaging system for day/night capability; an all-weather Blindfire radar can be added as needed. The Tracked Rapier vehicle carries eight rounds in the ready-to fire position compared with the Towed Rapier's four, and each launcher also has a resupply M548 which carries a further 20 rounds in their sealed containers. To maintain and support the vehicle in the field a two-man Forward Area Support Team (FAST) M548 variant is deployed with each battery. For the mid-1990s and beyond Rapier manufacturer British Aerospace is developing the Rapier 2000 system, which will equip two Army Air Defence regiments and three RAF Regiment squadrons; this introduces an eight-round towed launcher, a steerable infrared optronic tracker inplace of the current

on-launcher surveillance radar, a new trailer-mounted 3D surveillance radar with built-in IFF and an updated Blindfire tracking radar. The system will also fire the new Mk 2A Rapier missile with a smart proximity-fuzed fragmentation warhead for use against RPVs, ARMs and cruise missiles and the Mk 2B with contactfuzed hollow-charge warhead for use against aircraft and helicopters. The range is increased to 8,750 yd (8,000m) and each system is able to fire and guide two-round salvoes whereas the current system is able to guide only one. The Mk 2 round is also compatible with existing launchers. It is also hoped to upgrade the current Towed Rapier launcher during the late 1980s with the Darkfire tracker system, a new surveillance radar with a 50 per cent increase in range, a console tactical control unit and a six-round launcher. BAe has also developed privately the Laserfire system, which offers 85 per cent of the performance of the towed system at a much lower cost using a millimetre-wave surveillance radar, an automatic laser tracker and four ready-to-fire Rapier Mk 1 missiles on a two-man

The British Aerospace Rapier is produced in two basic versions, towed (below) and tracked (right). The latter is only in service with the British Army. The basic Rapier is a clear weather system, but with the addition of a Marconi Blindfire radar it has an all-weather capability. So far more than 600 towed Rapiers have been built and the weapon is in service with more than a dozen countries as well as the British Army and Royal Air Force. Towed Rapier has seen combat in the Middle East and with the British Army in the 1982 Falklands campaign and the Gulf War.

self-contained fire unit which can be mounted either on a vehicle such as a medium sized Bedford truck or on the ground.

Right: A well camouflaged Tracked Rapier in British Army service, with launcher traversed right and operator using sight in cab roof. This version of Rapier, with eight missiles ready to launch, is unique to the British Army.

SA-4, SA-6, SA-8, SA-9 and SA-13

SA-4 GANEF

Dimensions: Length (SA-4a) 28ft 11in (8.8m), (SA-4b) 27ft 2½in (8.3m); diameter 35.4in (0.9m), max span 102in (2.6m)
Launch weight: 5,500lb (2,500kg)
Performance: Effective range (SA4a) 5.8-45 miles (9.3-72km), (SA-4b) 0.7-31.25 miles (1.1-50km); max altitude limit (SA-4a) 88,583ft (27,000m), (SA-4b) 78,740ft (24,000m); speed Mach 4.0
Warhead: 297lb (135kg) proximity fuzed HE fragmentation
Background: First displayed in the Red Square Parade on May Day, 1964, the ZRK-SO Krug (NATO code name SA-4 Ganef) medium- to highaltitude SAM system was not fully deployed until 1969 in brigades as the air defence element for Front (two brigades), Tank and Combined Arms Armies (one brigade each). The missile has four solid-fuel booster motors which fall away when the kerosene-fuelled ramjet sustainer motor's ignition speed is reached. Initial target detection is achieved by the Long Track radar, which passes the hostile track to the continuous-wave fire control and command guidance Pat Hand radar of a battery for engagement. A single missile is launched and guided to the target by the radar guidance beam with the terminal phase being handled by the round's own semi-active seeker head.

SA-6 GAINFUL

Dimensions: SA-6a length 19ft (5.8m); diameter 13.2in (0.335m); wingspan 49in (1.245m).
Launch weight: 1,276lb (580kg)
Performance: Effective range 2.3-15 miles (3.7-24km); effective altitude limits 262.5-47,244ft (80-12,000m); speed Mach 2.5
Warhead: 176lb (80kg) contact- and radar proximity-fuzed HE frag.
Background: First seen in the November 7,1967, Red Square Parade, RK-SD Kub (NATO designation SA-6 Gainful) is a mobile, air-portable and amphibious low-to- medium-altitude SAM system mounted on a modified ZSU23-4 self-propelled anti-aircraft gun chassis. In Soviet service the SA-6 is now found at divisional level in the anti-aircraft regiment. The latter has a Regimental HQ with one Thin Skin-B and two Long Track radars and five SA-6 batteries, each with an SSNR Straight Flush G/H/I-band fire control radar vehicle and four SPU launcher vehicles with three ready to-fire missiles apiece; in wartime two additional SPUs would be added. In 1979 the SA-6b variant entered service on a new SPU which carries its own guidance radar. Initially deployed on the basis of one SPU per SA-6a battery, the system effectively doubled the number of targets the battery could engage at one time.

Both systems are being complemented in Soviet service by the new SA-11 Gadfly.

SA-8 GECKO

Dimensions: Length 10ft 2½in (3.1m); diameter 8¼in (0.21m); wingspan 23.6in (0.6m)
Launch weight: 374lb (170kg)
Performance: Effective range (SA-8a) 1-7.5 miles (1.6-12km), (SA-8b) 1-9.4 miles (1.6-15km); effective altitude limits 32.8-42,651ft (10-13,000m); speed Mach 2.0
Warhead: 88lb (40kg) proximity and contact-fuzed fragmentation
Background: The ZRK-SD Romb (NATO designation SA-8 Gecko) low-altitude SAM system entered Soviet service in 1974 and was first seen in public during the November 1975 Red Square Parade. The SA-8 has replaced towed AA guns in a number of divisonal anti-aircraft regiments because of its greater mobility, each regiment hav-

ing 20 fire units. Known by the NATO code name Land Roll, the radar complex has a rotating H-band early warning and search radar, a pulsed J-band target tracking radar below that and two small I-band dish antennas to transmit guidance command signals to the missiles. Each SPU can engage a single target with a two missile salvo operating on different frequencies to overcome ECM.

SA-9 GASKIN

Dimensions: Length 5ft 11in (1.8m); diameter 4.72in (0.12m); wingspan 15in (0.38m)
Launch weight: 66lb (30kg)
Performance: Effective range 0.5-4.1 miles (0.8-6.5km); effective altitude limits 44.9-5,906ft (13.7-1,800m); speed Mach 15
Warhead: 5.7lb (2.6kg) proximity and contact-fuzed HE fragmentation
Background: The ZRK-BD Strela 1 (NATO designation SA-9 Gaskin)

Right: The SA-6 Gainful SAM system (second right) proved to be highly effective in the 1973 Middle East conflict as it forced Israeli aircraft to fly low within the range of the ZSU-23-4 self-propelled anti-aircraft guns system and SA-7 Grail SAMs.

Below: The SA-13 Gopher SAM system, replacement for the SA-9 Gaskin. The latter was based on the BRDM-2 (4 x 4) chassis, but the SA-13 is based on the MT-LB multi-purpose armoured vehicle and has four missiles in the ready to launch position, though only one can be fired at a time.

Below: The SA-4 Ganef is a medium-to high-level SAM system which is deployed by Bulgaria, Czechoslovakia, East Germany, Hungary, Libya, Poland and the USSR. There are also reports of SA-4 in Iraqi service. Each battery has one Pat Hand radar system and three launchers, each with two Ganef missiles. If the Pat Hand continuous wave radar system is knocked out missiles cannot be launched

low-altitude SAM system was developed in parallel with the ZSU-23-4 self-propelled anti-aircraft gun and entered service in 1968. It is issued to the anti-aircraft batteries of Warsaw Pact motorised rifle and tank regiments on the basis of four SPUs and four ZSUs to give a total of 16 SPUs and 16 ZSUs per division. The SPU is based on the BRDM-2 scout car chassis with the chain-driven belly wheels removed and the turret replaced by one with four ready-to-launch infra-red guided SA-9s in container-launcher boxes; four reloads are carried. The original SA-9a used an uncooled seeker but the latest SA-9b has a cryogenically cooled seeker to provide greater lock-on capability.

SA-13 GOPHER

Dimensions: Length 7ft 2in (2.2m); diameter 5in (0.127m); wingspan 15.75in (0.4m)
Launch weight: 121lb (55kg)
Performance: Effective range 0.3-6.1 miles (0.5-9.7km); effective altitude limits 32.8-10,499ft (10-3,200m); speed Mach 1.5
Warhead: 8.8lb (4kg) contact- and proximity-fuzed HE fragmentation
Background: First deployed in the mid-1970s, the ZRK-BD Strela 10 (NATO code name SA-13 Gopher) low-altitude SAM system is replacing the less capable SA-9 Gaskin on a one-for-one basis in motorised rifle and tank regiment anti-aircraft batteries. The amphibious tracked SPU is based on the MT-LB chassis and can also use either the SA-9 or a mixture of SA-9 and SA-13 container- launcher boxes on the four launcher rails. A simple range-only radar is fitted to prevent missile wastage on targets outside engagement range. The SA-13 uses a cryogenically cooled all-aspect IR-seeker which operates in two frequency bands to give high discrimination against defensive flares and decoy pods.

Below: The SA-8 Gecko replaced the 57mm towed anti-aircraft gun and is in service in two versions, the SA-8a shown here, with missiles on open launchers, and the SA-8b, which has the missiles in long boxes for both transport and launch. Iraq uses both SA-8a and SA-8b.

ZSU-23-4 Shilka and ZSU-57-2

ZSU-23-4 SHILKA

Origin: USSR
Crew: 4
Armament: 4 x 23mm cannon in power operated turret with traverse of 360° and elevation from -4° to + 85°
Armour: 0.35-0.59in (9.2-15mm)
Dimensions: Length 21ft 6in (6.54m); width 9ft 8in (2.95m); height without radar 7ft 5in (2.25m); height with radar up to 12ft 6in (3.8m)
Combat weight: 45,194lb (20,500kg)
Ground pressure: 9.81lb/sq in (0.69kg/cm²)
Engine: Model V-6R 6-cylinder inline diesel developing 280hp (208kW)
Performance: Road speed 27.3mph (44km/h); range 280 miles (450km); vertical obstacle 3ft 7in (1.1m); trench 9ft 2in (2.8m); gradient 60 per cent
History: Developed in the early 1960s and entered service in 1966. In service with Afghanistan, Algeria, Angola, Bulgaria, Cuba, Czechoslovakia, Egypt, Ethiopia, East Germany, Hungary, India, Iran, Iraq, Jordan, Kampuchea, North Korea, Libya, Mozambique, Nigeria, Peru, Poland, Somalia, Syria, USSR, Vietnam, North and South Yemen and Yugoslavia

Left: The ZSU-23-4, developed as the replacement for the clear weather ZSU-57-2 system, is used in large numbers by the Warsaw Pact and many other countries that have received Soviet aid. It has an all-weather fire control system and is armed with four 23mm water-cooled cannon in a power operated turret. It is now being supplemented by the 2S-6 system armed with twin 30mm cannon.

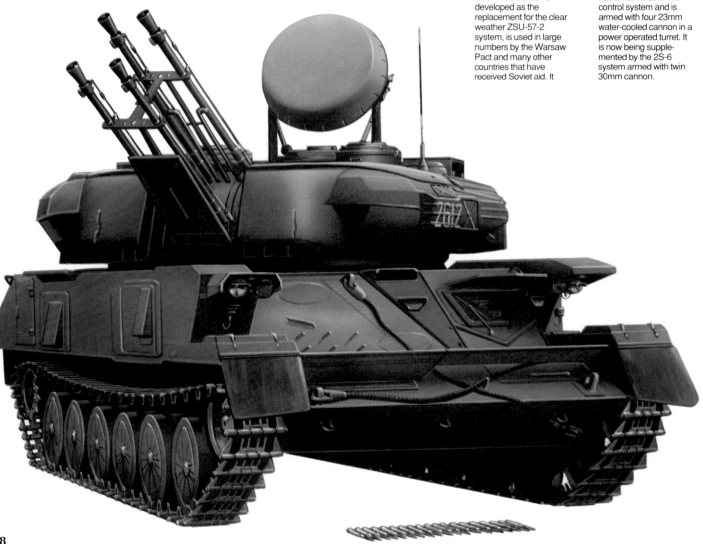

The crew of an East German ZSU-23-4 carrying out routine maintenance work in the field. The weapon was used successfully in the 1973 Middle East conflict to engage Israeli aircraft forced low by Egyptian SAMs.

Background: Until the introduction of the ZSU-23-4 the standard self-propelled anti-aircraft gun system of the Soviet Army, apart from the twin 14.5mm KPV machine guns installed on modified BTR-152 (6 x 6) and BTR-40 (4 x 4) chassis, was the ZSU-57-2 twin 57mm gun developed from the towed 57mm S-60. The main disadvantages of the ZSU-57-2 were its low rate of fire and lack of an on-board fire control system. The ZSU-23-4 has a chassis similar to that of the SA-6 Gainful surface-to air missile system and is armed with four 23mm AZP-23 cannon which are almost identical to those used on the ZU-23 twin 23mm towed system. In the ZSU-23-4 application the barrels are water-cooled and have a cyclic rate of fire of 800-1,000rds/ min, but in practice bursts of a maximum of 30 rounds are fired; a total of 2,000 rounds are carried. The 23mm cannon can be used in both anti-aircraft and ground roles and have a maximum effective range of about 1,750 yd (2,500 m). Mounted on the turret roof at the rear is a Gun Dish radar which carries out search, detection, automatic tracking and other fire control functions; targets can be acquired on the move but the vehicle normally comes to a halt before opening fire. The ZSU-23-4 has seen extensive combat service in the Middle East and was one of the most effective systems of the 1973 Middle East war when used in combination with other air defence weapons including SAMs. The latter would force Israeli aircraft to fly very low, whereupon they would encounter the ZSU-23-4s and man-portable SA-7 SAMs. The ZSU-23-4 is being replaced by a new self-propelled air defence system based on a T-72 MBT chassis called the 2S-6 by NATO. This is very similar in appearance to the West German Gepard used by the Belgian, West German and Netherlands armies and is armed with twin 30mm cannon and IR homing missiles and fitted with both tracking and surveillance radars.

ZSU-57-2

Origin: USSR
Crew: 6
Armament: Two 57mm S-68 guns
Armour: 0.59in (15mm) maximum
Dimensions: Length with guns forward 27ft 10in (8.48m); hull length 20ft 5in (6.22m); width 10ft 9in (3.27m); height 9ft (2.75m)
Combat weight: 61,949lbs (28,100kg)
Ground pressure: 8.96lb/in² (0.63kg/cm²)
Engine: Model V-54 12-cylinder water-cooled diesel developing 520hp at 2,000rpm
Performance: Road speed 30mph (48km/h); range 249 miles (400km); vertical obstacle 2ft 8in (0.8m); trench 8ft 10in (2.7m); gradient 60 per cent
History: Entered service with Soviet Army in 1955. In service with Warsaw Pact countries, Egypt, Finland, Iran, Iraq, North Korea, Romania, Syria Vietnam, Yugoslavia.
Background: The ZSU-57-2 was introduced in the mid-1950s to provide mobile anti-aircraft defence to Soviet armoured forces. Based on a modified T-54 chassis, it is lighter and slightly shorter, with one less road wheel. Armament consists of two 57mm guns in an open-topped turret with 360° traverse. The guns are an adaption of the S-60 towed gun with an effective range of 4,300yds

Above: The ZSU-57-2 relies totally on optical sights and has no night or poor weather capability.

(4,000m) and a rate of fire of 70 rounds per minute from each barrel. The ZSU-57-2 has no radar, relying totally on radio warning from other sensors and simple optical sights. The open turret gives little protection against shell or cluster bomb fragments and none whatsoever against NBC attack. The effectiveness of this system against today's low-flying battlefield threats must be marginal and the ZSU-23-4 has replaced it in most Soviet units.

Right: The large open-topped turret holds a crew of five; commander, gunner, fuze setter and two loaders. The driver is in the front of the hull. There is no weather or NBC protection.

Stinger, Blowpipe, Javelin and SA-7

STINGER

Origin: USA
Dimensions: Length 5ft 0in (1.52m); diameter 2.76in (70mm); wingspan 5.5in (140mm)
Launch weight: 34.76lb (15.8kg)
Performance: Effective range 220-5,500 yd (200-5,000m); altitude limits 11-5,250 yd (10-4,800m)
Warhead: 6.6lb (3kg) HE-fragmentation with automatic proximity fuze.
History: Stinger, a man-portable infra-red guided shoulder-launched SAM which is designed to engage low-altitude high-speed jet, propeller-driven or helicopter targets, is in service with Chad, Denmark, West Germany, Italy, Japan, South Korea, Netherlands, Saudi Arabia, Turkey and United Kingdom and the United States.
Background: Developed in the 1970s, the FIM-92a Stinger has replaced the earlier tail-chase IR-guided FIM-43A Redeye in the US Army, US Marine Corps, US Navy and US Air Force light air defence and special forces units.

Above: The Shorts Javelin, now replacing the earlier Blowpipe SAM, has a number of advantages including more powerful warhead and extended range.

Stinger proved to be highly effective in the hands of Afghan guerilla forces, who downed over 100 Soviet aircraft and helicopters. Further development of the FIM-92A's all-aspect IR seeker resulted in the later FIM-92B production variant which is also known as Stinger Post (Passive Optical Scanning Technique) with enhanced capabilities.

BLOWPIPE

Origin: United Kingdom
Dimensions: Length 4ft 7in (1.39m); diameter 3in (76mm), span (wings) 10.6in (270mm)
Launch weight: 24.2lb (11kg)
Performance: Effective range 760-3,937 yd (700-3,600 m); altitude limits 33-2,190 yd (30-2,000m); speed Mach 1.6
Warhead: 4.84lb (2.2kg) HE fragmentation with contact fuze.

Right: The Shorts Blowpipe was the first man-portable SAM to enter service with the British Army and has been exported to a number of countries. Some have also found their way to Afghanistan, where local guerillas found them difficult to operate without prior training in the system's launch procedure.

Right: The Stinger was developed as the replacement for the older Redeye SAM and large numbers of Stingers were supplied to Afghan guerilla units, where they forced Soviet aircraft and helicopters to fly much higher. The Stinger is an extremely effective man-portable system but it does need comprehensive training to ensure the selected target is shot down.

Above: The SA-7 (Grail) is probably the most widely used shoulder-launched SAM in the world, although in the Soviet Army has been replaced by the SA-14 Gremlin. The SA-7 has been supplied to many guerilla units which have used it to shoot down numerous aircraft, the targets often being civilian-operated.

History: Blowpipe was developed in the 1960s by Short Brothers Missile Systems Division to meet the requirements of British Army. In service with 10 other countries including Argentina, Canada, Chile, Ecuador, Malawi, Nigeria, Oman, Portugal and Thailand. Some have also found their way to Afghanistan

Background: The Blowpipe system is entirely self-contained, with no external power requirements, and consists of two main components, the aiming unit and the missile within its launcher container. Reloading, which takes only seconds, involves clipping the arming unit onto a new missile/canister combination; the aimer then lifts the complete system to his shoulder and acquires the target in his monocular sight, fires the missile and flies it into the target using his thumb controller, a task which requires some dexterity The missile is fitted with flares which in the early stages of flight are automatically detected by a sensor in the arming unit in order to gather the missile to the centre of the aimer's field of view. A contact fuze

detonates within the target.

JAVELIN

Origin: United Kingdom
Dimensions: Similar to Blowpipe
Launch weight: 26.4lb (12kg) approx
Performance: Effective range 328-4,920 yd (300-4,500m); altitude limits 11-3,280 yd (10-3,000m); speed Mach 1.8
Warhead: 6.05lb (2.75kg) HE-fragmentation with proximity fuze
History: Javelin has largely replaced Blowpipe in the British Army and Royal Marines and has been exported to at least one country
Background: Javelin evolved from the earlier Blowpipe SAM but has a semi-automatic line-of-sight command (SACLOS) guidance system coupled with a new higher-impulse two-stage solid-propellent rocket motor to increase the engagement envelope, a larger warhead and a new fuzing system that can be deactivated by the operator to enable him to steer the missile away from friendly aircraft or an incorrectly engaged target. During an engagement all the

operator has to do is keep the target centred in his sight and the command guidance signals are automatically generated and sent to the missile's control surfaces via a radio link. To engage future low-level aircraft and attack helicopter threats the British Army is taking delivery in the early 1990s of Shorts' Starstreak high-velocity SAM systems on Stormer APCs. Each Starstreak missile contains three highly accurate manoeuvrable darts.

SA-7 GRAIL

Origin: USSR
Dimensions: Length 4ft 3in (1.29m); diameter 3.94in (100mm)
Launch weight: 20.24lb (9.2kg)
Performance: Effective range (SA-7a) 49.2-3,830 yd (45-3,500m); (SA7-b) 49.2-6,125 yd (45-5,600m); altitude limits (SA-7a) 164-1,640 yd (150-1,500m); (SA-7b) 27.3-4,700 yd (25-4,300m); speed (SA-7a) Mach 1.5; (SA-7b) Mach 1.95
Warhead: (SA-7a) 3.96lb (1.8kg); (SA-7b) 5.5lb (2.5kg) HE- frag
History: Designed as a platoon self-defence weapon, the two-stage solid

propellent NATO-designated SA-7a Grail (Soviet name Strela-2; designation 9M32) entered service in 1966 with the enhanced capability SA-7b version (Soviet designation 9M32M) following in 1972. Since its introduction it has been supplied to practically all the Soviet-supplied client states and every Warsaw Pact army and has found its way to a number of terrorist and guerilla groups around the world.

Background: The SA-7 uses a simple optical sighting and tracking device with the operator activating the IR seeker when he has acquired a target; an indicator light denotes seeker lock-on and he then fires the missile, which adopts a tail-chase flight profile. Improved versions of the SA-7 are being manufactured by Egypt as the Sakr Eye and by China as the HN-5 series. Since the early 1980s the SA-7 has undergone replacement by the SA-14 Gremlin system, and in 1987 a further portable SAM, the SA-16, was revealed to be in service with Soviet Army; the last is believed to be laser-guided.

Above: The Shorts Javelin man-portable SAM has now started to replace the older Blowpipe in the British Army and a version with four missiles in the ready to launch position on a Spartan tracked APC is in service, giving the system greater mobility. Javelin is also carried on Royal Navy ships for extra self-defence.

TOW, MILAN and RPG-7

TOW

Origin: USA

Dimensions: Length (BGM-71A/B) 3ft 10in (1.174m); BGM-71C 5ft 1in (1.55m); BGM-71D 5ft 8in (1.714m); diameter 6in (152mm); wingspan 13.5in (343mm)

Weight: Basic launcher 172.7lb (78.5kg); BGM-71D launcher 204.6lb (93kg); BGM-71A/B missiles 49.6lb (22.5kg); BGM-71C missile 56.65lb (25.7kg); BGM-71D missile 61.95lb (28.1kg)

Range: BGM-71A 70-3,280 yd (65-3,000m); BGM-71B/C/D 70-4,100 yd (65-3,750m)

Warhead: BGM-71A/B/C 7.7lb (3.5kg) HEAT; BGM-7 1D1 3lb (5.9kg) HEAT

Armour penetration: BGM-71A/B 23.6in (600mm); BGM-71C 27.6in (700mm); BGM-71D 31.5in (800mm) plus

History: The Hughes BGM-71A Tube-launched, optically-tracked wire command-link guided (Tow) heavy anti-tank weapon system entered the design stage in 1962 and reached operational service in 1970. Since then it has been adopted by more than 36 countries and seen combat service in the Middle East and Far East in both air - and ground-launched modes

Background: Tow is a semi-automatic command-to-line-of-sight system, which means that all the operator has to do is keep the crosshairs of his sight on the target and flight control commands are automatically transmitted via the wire-guidance link. The basic BGM-71A, the first model produced, was superseded in 1976 by the extended range BGM-71B. In order to meet the threat of new Soviet armour the weapon had to under go a two-stage upgrade programme. The first part resulted in the new BGM-71C Improved Tow with a new 5in (127mm) diameter warhead fitted with a telescopic nose fuze that pops out after launch to give an optimum stand-off armour penetration capability. I-Tow was followed by the BGM-71D Tow-2 missile which has a 6in (152mm) diameter warhead with a large telescopic nose fuze probe, improved guidance features and an updated propulsion system.

MILAN

Origin: France/West Germany

Dimensions: Length 2ft 6in (0.769m); diameter 3.54in (90mm); wingspan 10.4in (265mm)

Weight: Complete system 60.9lb (27.7kg); missile 14.7lb (6.65kg)

Performance: Range 27-2,190 yd (25-2,000m)

Warhead: Milan 1 2.64lb (1.2kg) HEAT; Milan 2 3.96lb (1.8kg) HEAT

Armour penetration: Milan 1 25.6in (650mm); Milan 2 41.7in (1,060mm)

History: Entered production in mid 1970s and now in service with 36 countries. Produced under licence in India, Italy and UK

Background: The Euromissile Milan is an advanced second-generation man-portable spin-stabilised anti tank guided weapon designed for use mainly from defensive positions. It is a SACLOS wire-controlled missile using infra-red tracking to allow a computer to generate the control signals. The weapon has seen combat service in Chad, the Falklands, Iran and Iraq, and the MIRA thermal imaging sight has been developed for use by the French, West German and British armies. The missile is self-contained in its own tube which is automatically discarded following a launch; once the engagement is over a new tube is fitted to the launcher/ guidance unit. To meet new Soviet armour developments Euromissile started production in 1984 of the Milan 2 with a warhead of greater diameter. Further developments to defeat reactive armour are planned.

RPG-7

Origin: USSR

Dimensions: Length 3ft 3in (1.0m); calibre 1.57in (40mm)

Launcher weight: 15.43lb (7kg)

Performance: Range 330 yd (300m) against moving target, 545 yd (500m) against stationary target; muzzle velocity 393.7ft/sec (120m/sec)

Projectile: Weight 4.96lb (2.25kg); types PG-7 HEAT, PG-7M HEAT, OG-7 HE anti-personnel; armour penetration (PG-7) 12.6in (320mm), (PG-7M) 15.75in (400mm)

History: Similar to the earlier RPG-2 in having a calibre of 1.57in (40mm), the RPG-7V was introduced into service as an anti-tank rocket with a diameter of 3.35in (85mm). The system is widely deployed all over the world especially by guerrilla forces and terrorist groups

Background: The RPG-7 operator screws the cylinder containing rocket propellant into the warhead section, loads the complete round into the muzzle of the launcher unit, then uncovers the nosecap of the warhead and extracts the safety pin. A pull on the trigger fires the round, which is fairly accurate when no crosswinds are present. In 1968 a folding version, the RPG-7D, was introduced into service for use by the Soviet Airborne troops. By the late 1970s the RPG-7 was being replaced in Soviet and Warsaw Pact service by the RPG-16, which is 3ft 7in (1 .1m) long, of 2.3in (0.58mm) calibre and fires a 6.6lb (3kg) one piece 3.15in (80mm) diameter rocket capable of piercing over 14.8in (375mm) of armour plate at ranges up to 875 yd (800m). This weapon was supplemented in service by the single-shot throw-away RPG18 and RPG-22 light anti-armour weapons, which are tele-scoped open and used to engage tar-gets out to a range of approximately 275 yd (250m). A number of countries have built their own versions and others have begun manufacture of ammunition for this popular and widespread weapon.

Right: The Hughes Tow heavy anti-tank missile has been built in larger numbers than any other missile in the West. It is also launched from armoured vehicles and helicopters. Three types of Tow missile have been produced: Tow-2 (1), Improved Tow (2) and the original Tow (3). A new warhead is under development to counter new Soviet reactive armour developments

Below: US troopers at the sights of a TOW launcher in desert conditions. This large system can destroy any tank at ranges of up to 4,000yds.

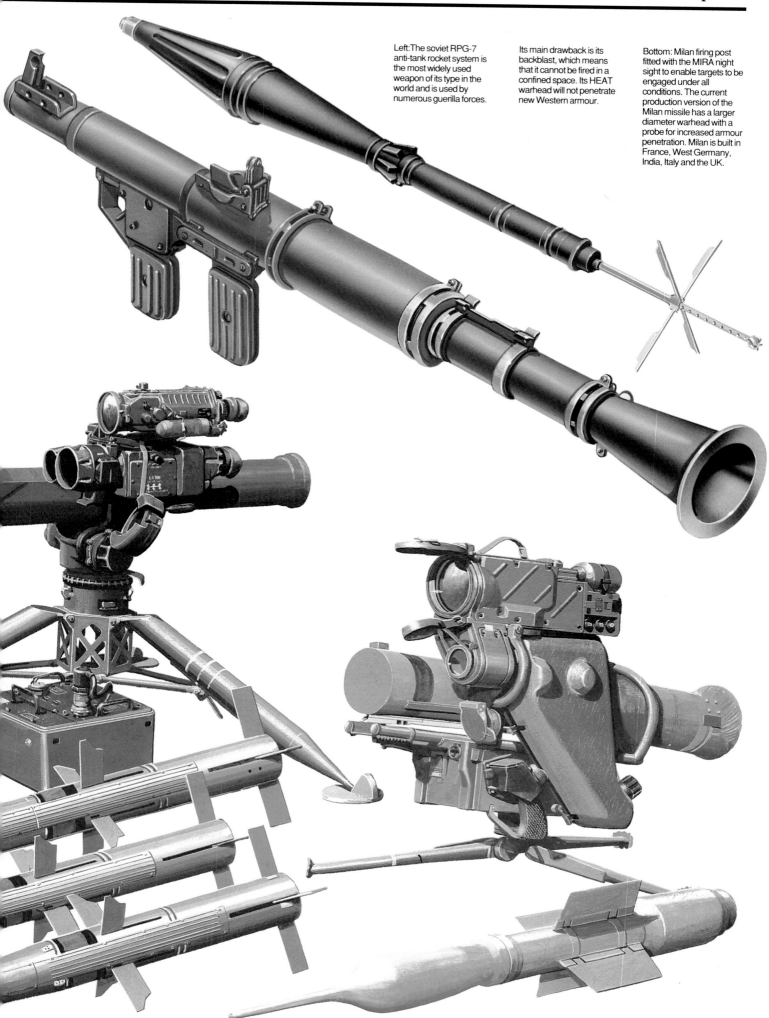

Left: The soviet RPG-7 anti-tank rocket system is the most widely used weapon of its type in the world and is used by numerous guerilla forces.

Its main drawback is its backblast, which means that it cannot be fired in a confined space. Its HEAT warhead will not penetrate new Western armour.

Bottom: Milan firing post fitted with the MIRA night sight to enable targets to be engaged under all conditions. The current production version of the Milan missile has a larger diameter warhead with a probe for increased armour penetration. Milan is built in France, West Germany, India, Italy and the UK.

SA-80, M16 and AK-74

SA-80

Origin: United Kingdom
Calibre: 5.56mm (0.223in)
Length: IW overall 30.9in (70.5cm);
IW barrel 20.4in (51.8cm); LSW
overall 35.43in (90cm); LSW barrel
25.43in (64.6cm)
Weight loaded: IW 10.98lb (4.98kg);
LSW 14.5lb (6.5kg)
Type of feed: 30-round box magazine
Muzzle velocity: IW 3,084ft/sec
(940m/sec)
Rate of fire: IW 650-800rds/min;
LSW 700-850rds/min
Effective range: IW up to 437 yd
(400m); LSW up to 1,094 yd (1,000m)
History: Originally developed from a
family of 4.85mm (0.191in) weapons
and intended to replace existing rifles and sub-machine guns in the
British armed forces. The first
5.56mm full production examples
were issued during 1987
Background: The SA 80 is also
known as the Enfield Weapon
System and comprises two main
weapons, the L85A1 Individual
Weapon (IW), or Endeavour, and the
larger L86A1 Light Support Weapon
(LSW), or Engager. The IW is a combat rifle of the bullpup type with the
magazine located behind the trigger
group to make it short, compact and
handy. The LSW may be termed a
light machine gun but can be
regarded as a machine rifle; it is
intended to provide longer range
support fire for infantry sections and
can fire from an open or closed bolt

whereas the IW fires from a closed
bolt only. Both weapons share
many common components and the
same general bullpup layout but the
LSW has a longer barrel and a light
folding bipod. Both use an optical
sight but non-infantry versions of
the IW have orthodox metal sights
with the rearsight incorporated into
a carrying handle over the receiver.
The IW and LSW both use an all-

inline layout and have very similar
gas-operated mechanisms. They are
produced by Royal Ordnance Guns
and Vehicles Division, Nottingham.

M16

Origin: USA
Calibre: 5.56mm (0.223in)
Length: Overall 38.97in (99cm);
barrel 20in (50.8cm)
Weight: 7lb (3.18kg)

**Above: British infantry advance
with Royal Ordnance Individual
Weapons; the man standing is also
carrying a Royal Ordnance 51 mm
mortar which is already in service
with the British Army. The
Individual Weapon, which has a
day optical sight and can also be
fitted with a night sight and has a
30-round magazine which is also
used by the Light Support Weapon.**

Below: When fitted with
the M203 grenade
launcher attachment (3)
under the barrel, the M16
can fire a wide range of
40mm grenades (1 and
2), such as smoke, high
explosive and even
armour piercing. The
latest version is the
M16A2 which has a
number of improvements

and can fire the new
SS109 round. It was first
issued to the US Marine
Corps, with the Army
receiving its first weapons
early in 1987.

Type of feed: 20- or 30-round box
magazine
Muzzle velocity: 3,280ft/sec
(1,00m/sec)
Rate of fire: 700-950rds/min cyclic
rate
Effective range: 437 yd (400m)
History: The original Armalite AR15
was designed by Eugene Stoner in
the early 1960s; adopted by the US
Army in 1967 as the M16, later to become the M16A1. The latest model is
the M16A2. and the main producer
has been the Colt Industries factory.
Background: The Armalite AR-15
was designed to make use of the new
5.56mm (0.223in) cartridge that became the M193. This enabled the
weapon to fire on full automatic
without the recoil forces making the
fire inaccurate . The US Army and
Air Force adopted the AR-15 as the
M16 but combat experience in Vietnam showed the need for a bolt return plunger to ensure the bolt was
closed if the rifle jammed after foul-
ing produced by prolonged firing.
The M16A1, the main production

Below: The EWS (Enfield
Weapon System), or
SA80, comprises two
weapons, the Individual
Weapon (IW) shown here
and the Light Support
Weapon (LSW). The
former is now replacing the
7.62mm rifle in the British
Army and fires standard
5.56mm ammunition (1)
and can be fined with a
bayonet (2), the scabbard
of which (3) can be used
as a wire cutter.

model to date, uses a 20- or 30-round
box magazine with the 30-round
version being the most favoured.
The M1 6A2 fires the new NATO
standard 5.56mm (0.223in) SS109
round and has a heavier barrel. It
also has a revised flash hider at the
muzzle The ammunition fired by the
M16A1 was designed to have an effective combat range of some 437
yards (400m), the maximum expected to be effective in combat.
Several attempts have been made to
produce a light machine gun version
but none has been adopted in any
numbers, though carbine and
sub-machine gun versions have been
produced for use by Special Forces.
There is also a special version
intended to be fired from the firing
ports of the M2 Bradley IFV; this has
a telescopic wire butt and is known
as the M231. It is in the vehicle when
the crew de-bus.

AK-74

Origin: USSR
Calibre: 5.45mm (0.2145in)
Length: AK-74 overall 36.6in

(93cm); AKS-74 butt folded 27.16in
(69cm); barrel 15.75in (40cm)
Weight: 7.93lb (3.6kg) unloaded
Type of feed: 30-round box
magazine
Muzzle velocity: 2,953ft/sec
(900m/ sec)
Rate of fire: 650rds/min cyclic
Effective range: 328-437 yd
(300400m)
History: Small-calibre development
of the 7.62mm (0.3in) AK-47 and
AKM series that first appeared in
1959; now widely used by the
Soviet armed forces and some other
Warsaw Pact nations
Background: Taking the basic form
of the classic 7.62mm AK-47 and
AKM rifles as a starting point, the
decision was taken to adopt a new
Soviet 5.45mm cartridge and the
AK-47 design was scaled down to
fire it. Consequently the AK-74
closely resembles the AK-47 and
AKM rifles but is slightly smaller
and lighter overall. The AK-74
differs in detail from the earlier
weapons but uses the same basic
gas-operated mechanism.

It has a revised and very efficient
muzzle brake to reduce recoil forces
and the magazine is manufactured
from a distinctive light tan-coloured
plastic. It also has a solid wooden
butt but a variant, known as the
AKS-74 intended for use by airborne
and other special forces has a
tubular skeleton butt that folds along
the left-hand side of the weapon.
There is also a light machine gun
version known as the RPK-74 which
has a longer barrel, a 40-round
magazine and a light bipod. A much
shortened submachine gun version
known as the AKR has been
encountered in Afghanistan. The
bullet fired by the AK-74 is unusual
in having a steel core that is so
arranged that the bullet nose will
bend even if it strikes a soft target.
This will enable the bullet to tumble
and so inflict wounds much larger
than the small calibre could
otherwise inflict. The AK-74 and
AKS-74 are now the standard
assault rifles for the Soviet armed
forces and some other Warsaw Pact
armies.

Left: The AKS-74 is the
latest in the long line of
famous AK-47 rifles which
have been produced in
larger numbers than any
other rifle since World
War II. It fires a new
5.45mm cartridge that has a
steel core. The LMG
version is called the
RPK-74 and has a bipod
and 40-round magazine.

M249, RPK, and M60

M249

Origin: Belgium
Calibre: 5.56mm (0.233in)
Length: Overall 40.94in (1,040mm); barrel 18.35in (466mm)
Weight loaded: 22lb (10kg)
Type of feed: 200-round belt or 30-round M16A1 box magazine
Muzzle velocity: 3,000ft/sec (915m/sec)
Rate of fire: 750-1,000 rds/min cyclic
Effective range: 875 yd (800m)
History: Originally the FN Minimi and adopted by the US armed forces as their M249 Squad Automatic Weapon (SAW)
Background: The M249, which only entered service with the US Army and Marine Corps in 1987, is based on the FN Minimi, which uses the basic gas-operated mechanism of the Belgian FNC assault rifle allied to a new light machine gun form. The M249 differs only in detail from the original and uses the optional feed system that accepts either 200-round belts or a 30-round M16A1 box magazine, the belts being carried in plastic boxes clipped under the weapon. It fires the new NATO SS109 ammunition, but earlier versions fire the M193 round. Although the M249 is fitted with a bipod it can be fired from a tripod. If the barrel becomes hot from firing it can be rapidly changed; a handle is provided for barrel changing and carrying, and the butt stock may be

Above: The M-60 is typical of all general purpose machine guns - too heavy for the LMG role, too light to put down massive sustained firepower. This US paratrooper is on an exercise in Egypt, although his colleague is carrying less offensive equipment!

gas-operated mechanism from the AK-47 allied to an AKM receiver with a longer and heavier barrel plus a bipod. The trigger mechanism has been revised and a large wooden butt shaped for a comfortable left-hand grip when firing bursts is provided, and although the barrel is fixed, so that automatic firing has to be carried out in short bursts to prevent overheating of the barrel, this hardly restricts the use of the weapon as it is normally employed as a light section fire support weapon. Although the RPK is sighted up to 1,094 yd (1,000m) it is normally used at much shorter combat ranges and some examples have been seen equipped with infra-red night sights. The RPK can use the normal 30- round box magazine of the AK-47 and AKM or a larger 40-round box. It can also be used with a special 75- round drum magazine that fits into the usual magazine slot. A version with a folding butt stock, known as the RPKS, is used by airborne troops and other special forces requiring such compactness and lightness.

M60

Origin: USA
Calibre: 7.62mm (0.3in)
Length: Overall 43.5in (1,105mm); barrel 22in (560mm)
Weight: 23.17lb (10.51kg)

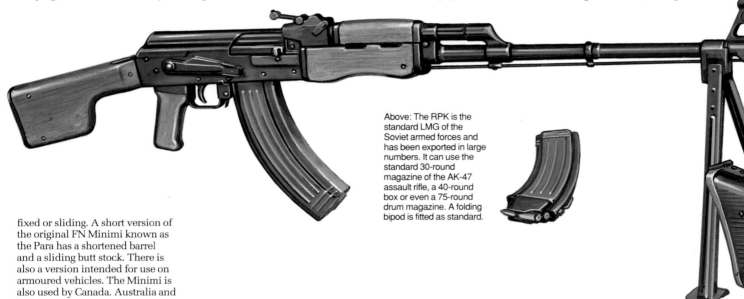

Above: The RPK is the standard LMG of the Soviet armed forces and has been exported in large numbers. It can use the standard 30-round magazine of the AK-47 assault rifle, a 40-round box or even a 75-round drum magazine. A folding bipod is fitted as standard.

fixed or sliding. A short version of the original FN Minimi known as the Para has a shortened barrel and a sliding butt stock. There is also a version intended for use on armoured vehicles. The Minimi is also used by Canada. Australia and Indonesia.

RPK

Origin: USSR
Calibre: 7.62mm (0.3in)
Length: Overall 40.75in (1,035mm); barrel 23.27in (591mm)
Weight loaded: 15.65lb (7.1kg)
Type of feed: 30- or 40-round box magazine or 75-round drum
Muzzle velocity: 2,402ft/sec (732m/sec)
Rate of fire: 660rds/min cyclic
Effective range: 875 yd (800m)
History: Based on the AKM assault rifle. Entered service during the early 1960s and now in widespread use by various Warsaw Pact nations
Background: The Soviet RPK light machine gun may be regarded as an enlarged AKM assault rifle, using the

Above: A US soldier using his 7.62mm M60 machine gun with empty cartridge cases being ejected to the right of the weapon. When not required the bipod folds up under the barrel to save space. A carrying handle is provided on top of the weapon.

Type of feed: Variable-length belts
Muzzle velocity: 2,805ft/sec (855m/sec)
Rate of fire: 550rds/min cyclic
Effective range: As LMG 1094 yd (1,000m); as HMG 1,969 yd (1,800m)
History: The M60 is a composite design that entered service with the US armed forces during the late 1950s and is still in production
Background: The M60 was a design amalgamation of several types of machine gun into a new weapon. It uses an all-in-line layout and on the early production versions the barrel and bipod were connected and had to be changed together when the barrel got hot, a drawback which was later removed. Other drawbacks were a poor sighting system and long ammunition feed belts which were a disadvantage in the light machine gun role; the carrying handle also proved to be too flimsy for hard use. Overall, the M60 has proved to be too heavy as a light machine gun while the barrel is too light to deliver sustained fire for long periods when used as a heavy tripod-mounted weapon. Gradual design changes have removed most of the worst features of the M60 and it is still widely used in several forms, including a tank coaxial weapon and as a helicopter weapon on pintles or in pods. The M60 was widely employed during the Vietnam conflict and has been adopted by Australia, Taiwan, South Korea and several other nations. Saco Defense Industries have produced a lightened model known as the M60E3 for use as a light machine gun, but this has not been adopted.

Right: the M249 Squad Automatic Weapon (SAW) is the US version of the Belgian FN Minimi and is currently being produced in the United States. In addition to using the standard 30-round M16 magazine it can also accept a 200-round box as shown here. A bipod is also provided.

Above: The 7.62mm M60 is the standard machine gun of the United States armed forces although when first introduced it did have a number of shortcomings, The weapon is air-cooled, belt-fed and fitted with a bipod. There are also versions for mounting on armoured fighting vehicles and in helicopters doors.

Left: The RPK is a modified and beefed-up AK-47, and shares its reputation for reliability and ease of use. It is an uncompromised section-level light machine gun.

AH-64 Apache

Origin: U.SA
Engines: Two 1,696shp General Electric T700-701 turboshafts. All Apaches being retrofitted with 1,857shp T700-701C engines.
Dimensions: Main rotor diameter 48ft 0in (14.63m); length over tail rotor ignoring main rotor 48ft 2in (14.68m); height overall to tip of airdata sensor 16ft 9.5in (5.12m)
Weights: Empty 10,760lb (4,881kg); primary mission weight 14,445lb (6,552kg); maximum loaded 21,000lb (9,525kg).
Performance: Maximum level speed 186mph (300km/h); max cruise 182mph (293km/h); max sea level vertical rate of climb 2,500ft (762m)/min; OGE hover ceiling 10,200ft (3,109m); max range on internal fuel 428 miles (689km)
Background: The US Army recognised the potential and the need for a dedicated armed helicopter in the early 1960s, but it was not until 1976 that the Hughes YAH-64 was selected for production ahead of the rival Bell YAH-63.
Subsequent development was protracted, hundreds of small and large changes being introduced before production was authorised in March 1982. Apart from the rotors, most of each Apache is made by Teledyne Ryan, and Hughes—since 1984 a subsidiary of McDonnell Douglas—assembles the helicopters at a new plant at Mesa, Arizona. Compared with the prototype AH-56 Cheyenne of 20 years earlier, the Apache is roughly the same size, rather less powerful (though it has two engines instead of one) and somewhat slower. Avionics are in many ways similar, and in fact in some respects the earlier machine was more versatile. The biggest advances are in survivability, the Apache having IR-suppressed engines, comprehensive electronic warfare installations and, above all, an airframe and systems designed to survive strikes from fire of up to 12.7 and 23mm calibre.
In general the whole helicopter is conventional, with an all-metal semi-monocoque fuselage and stainless- steel/glassfibre rotor blades. Main blades are attached by multi-laminate straps with quickly removed pins for folding. The hub is articulated, with offset flapping hinges and elastomeric lead/lag dampers. As in the AH-1 Cobra the pilot sits above and behind the copilot/gunner and non-retracting tailwheel gear with long-stroke main units are designed to cushion crash descents. The tailplane is a powered control surface. The Apache's eyes are its TADS/ PNVS (target acquisition/ designation sight and pilot's night vision sensor). Though independent the two systems are physically linked and work in parallel. TADS comprises direct-view optics with wide-field 18° and magnified 4° fields of view, a TV camera (0.9° and 4° FOVs), a laser spot tracker and an International Laser Systems

laser rangefinder/ designator. These are all mounted in a turret able to rotate ±120° in azimuth, +30° up and -60° down and there are extensive fuselage boxes, as well as a primary display for the copilot/ gunner. The TADS can also be switched to provide the back-up night vision to the pilot in the event of PNVS failure. The PNVS is simply a FLIR, gyrostabilised and mounted in its own turret above the nose (±90° in azimuth, +20°/−45° vertically). The FLIR has narrow, medium and wide FOV, respectively 3.1°,10.1° and 50.0°. The FLIR information is normally presented on a monocular IHADSS (integrated helmet and display sighting system) on which is superimposed key flight data such as airspeed, radar altitude and heading. In emergency either crew-member can receive video from either the TADS or the PNVS, and both wear IHADSS. Weapons comprise a remotely aimed gun and stores carried under fixed wings. The gun, contracted for along with the helicopter, is the Hughes 30mm M230A1 Chain Gun, a unique single-barrel weapon with external power and a rotating bolt driven by a chain which permits a simplified cycle. In the Apache it is normally controlled to 625rds/min, the magazine capacity being 1,200 rounds. Lear Siegler provide the electronic control system, with aiming possible anywhere in the area covered by the sighting systems. In a crash the complete gun mount collapses upwards between the cockpits. The weapon wings, of 17ft 2in (5.23m) span, can carry four pylons each supporting either a quadruple group of Hellfire anti-tank missiles (maximum 16) or a 19-tube 2.75in rocket launcher (maximum 76 rockets); or up to four 192 gal (871 lit) external fuel tanks. The accompanying illustration also shows the armament proposed for the stillborn naval version.
The Advanced Apache and a multistaged improvement version were also allowed to lapse, and

(apart from exports) the programme will be completed in 1993 at 807 machines. Of these 227 are being upgraded to Longbow standard, the main upgrade being a millimetric-waveband radar plus an RF seeker, which can track small moving targets through rain, fog and smoke. It also allows Hellfires to lock-on at shorter ranges or to accept target co-ordinates from which it can lock-on after launch at longer ranges. Other upgrades may include Stinger self-defence missiles, digital avionics and GPS precision navigation.

Left: An AH-64 Apache fires a salvo of Hydra 70 rockets at the US Army's Yuma proving ground. The rockets are launched from 7-round or 19-round pods, are provided with a comprehensive range of warheads and have a maximum range of 9,600 yards (8,800m).

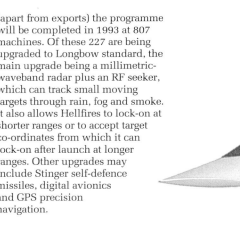

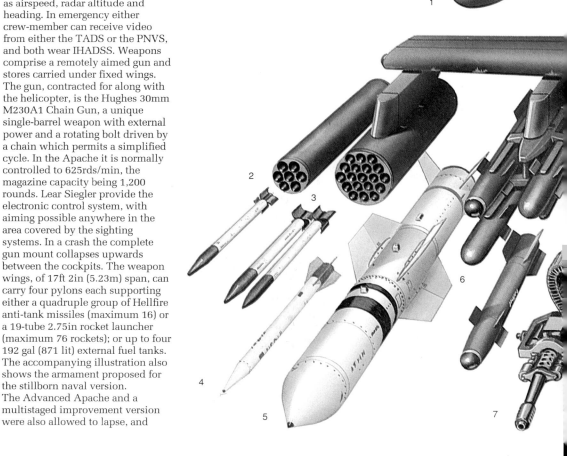

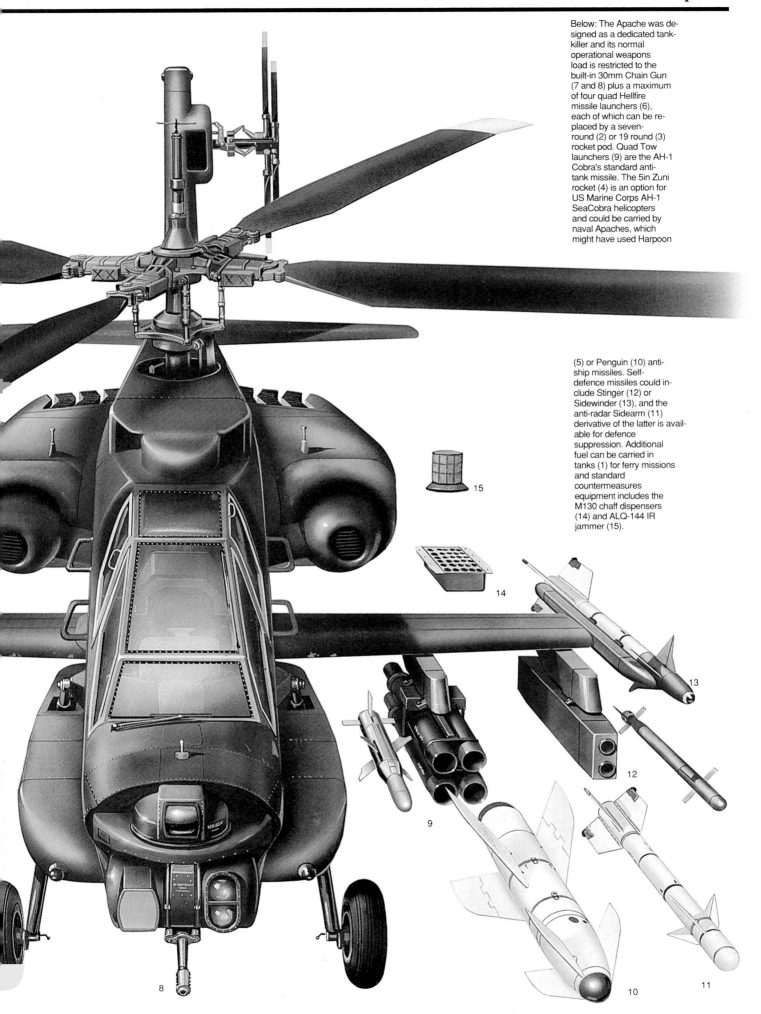

Below: The Apache was designed as a dedicated tank-killer and its normal operational weapons load is restricted to the built-in 30mm Chain Gun (7 and 8) plus a maximum of four quad Hellfire missile launchers (6), each of which can be replaced by a seven-round (2) or 19 round (3) rocket pod. Quad Tow launchers (9) are the AH-1 Cobra's standard anti-tank missile. The 5in Zuni rocket (4) is an option for US Marine Corps AH-1 SeaCobra helicopters and could be carried by naval Apaches, which might have used Harpoon

(5) or Penguin (10) anti-ship missiles. Self-defence missiles could include Stinger (12) or Sidewinder (13), and the anti-radar Sidearm (11) derivative of the latter is available for defence suppression. Additional fuel can be carried in tanks (1) for ferry missions and standard countermeasures equipment includes the M130 chaff dispensers (14) and ALQ-144 IR jammer (15).

Bell AH-1

Origin: USA, first flight 7 September 1965
Type: Armed attack and anti-armour helicopter.
Engine(s): (AH-1G) one 1,400shp Avco Lycoming T53-13 turboshaft, (J) one 1,800shp Pratt & Whitney Canada T400-400 turboshaft with twin coupled power sections, (S) one 1,800shp T53-703 turboshaft, (T) 1,970shp T400-402 with coupled power sections, (T/700 and W) two 1,625shp General Electric T700-401 turboshaft engines.
Dimensions: Diameter of two-blade main rotor (G, J, S) 44ft 0in (13.4m), (T,W) 48ft 0in (14.63m); length (rotors turning) (G) 52ft 11.4in (16.14m), (J) 53ft 4in (16.26m), (S) 53ft 1in (16.18m), (T,W) 58ft 0in (17.68m); (ignoring rotors) (G, J, S) 44ft 7in (13.59m), (T) 48ft 2in (14.68m); height overall (main blades at rest) (G, S) 13ft 6in (4.11m), (J) 13ft 8in (4.16m), (T) 14ft 2in (4.32m).
Weights: Empty (including crew and fluids other than fuel) (G) 6,073lb (2755kg), (J) 7,261lb (3294kg), (S) 6,479lb (2939kg), (T) 8,030lb (3642kg), maximum loaded (G) 9,500lb (4309kg), (J, S) 10,000lb (4536kg), (T) 14,000lb (6350kg).
Performance: Maximum level speed at SL (G,T) 172mph (277km/h), (J) 207mph (333km/h), (S, with TOWs) 141mph (227km/h); maximum rate of climb (G) 1,230ft (375m)/min, (J) 1,090ft (332m)/min, (S) 1,620 (494m)/min, (T) 1,785ft (544m)/min; hovering ceiling OGE (T) 1,200ft (366m); range (SL, max fuel, 8 per cent reserve) (G) 357 miles (574km), (S) 315 miles (507km), (T) 261 miles (420km).
Background: Bell studied armed helicopter possibilities in the 1950s, and in 1963 flew the company-funded Model 207 Sioux Scout. This was a greatly modified OH-13G Sioux (Model 47) with a streamlined nose housing a pilot and gunner in tandem, and with weapon wings and a chin turret. It was clear that a true armed helicopter needed much more power and using the familiar UH1-B/C Huey as a basis the company funded Model 209 HueyCobra appeared in late 1965 just as the US Army was recognising an urgent need for armed helicopters in Vietnam. It bought 110 Cobras as early as April 1966, as an interim machine pending development of the bigger and very complex Lockheed

AH-56A Cheyenne. In the event the latter was cancelled in 1972 while the Cobra was bought in ever-greater numbers. The US Army took 1,075 AH-1Gs, others going to Israel and (in the anti-ship role) to Spain. The twin engined AH-1J SeaCobra was developed for the US Marine Corps (with TOW, Iran) and has been upgraded to the AH-1T Improved SeaCobra. US Army production after 1978 comprised 100 AH1P, 98 AH-lE and 149 AH-1F, as well as 378 AH-1Gs brought up to full -1F standard (including 41 TAH-1F trainers). All incorporate comprehensive avionics upgrades.
Design: The original AH-1G retained most dynamic parts of the UH-1B/C but introduced a new narrow fuselage with stub wings to carry weapons and also help unload the rotor in cruising flight. All models seat the pilot above and behind the co-pilot/gunner who manages the nose sight system and fires the chin turret. The pilot normally fires the wing stores and can also fire the turret when it is in its stowed (fore/aft) position, which it assumes whenever the co-pilot/gunner lets go of the slewing switch. In emergency the co-pilot/gunner can fly the helicopter and fire the wing stores. Current 1S versions have a low-glint flat-plate canopy.
Avionics: Most versions have FM and UHF com, and a single-channel secure voice link, HSI/ VSI, gyrosyn, DF, radar altimeter, IFF, radar beacon and (1S) doppler. Early G and T models had a simple pantograph optical sight slaved to the turret, but all TOW Cobras (S, T and Iranian J) have a TOW M65 system telescopic sight unit in the nose. The current 1S has the FACTS (FLIR-augmented Cobra TOW sight) or LAAT (laser-augmented airborne TOW) sight both giving a stabilized magnified target picture with (FACTS) vision through darkness and smoke or (LAAT) precise ranging. Other-1S updates include the APR-39 RWR IR suppressor and ALQ-144 IR jammer, and a digital fire-control computer and pilot HUD sight.
Armament: Initial 1Gs had the Emerson TAT-102A (Minigun) turret, later replaced by the M28

Below: All US Army Cobras are various forms of AH-1S, with single T53 engine and, in current models, the flat-plate canopy.

with one or two Miniguns and/or one or two M129 40mm grenade launchers. The 1J introduced the GE turret with M197 gun, but the 1S now has a Universal Turret whose M197 can be replaced by other 20mm or 30mm weapons. Normally the M197 has a 750-round magazine which represents a 60sec supply, but in practice the ammunition lasts much longer because a 16-round burst limiter is included in the firing circuit. The long barrels could obstruct wing store firing

when slewed (limit, 110° each side) so the turret is centred before firing wing weapons. The wealth of stores combinations is obvious. Modification programmes will improve night capability, air-to-air self defence capability (Stinger missiles) and life-extension modifications. An update package may be launched to enable worldwide operators to fit the 2,000shp T53-70X engine, Bell 412 rotor with composite hub, longer tailboom and many other changes.

Key to stores:
1 Mk82 GP bomb (Mk81, Mk 115 and CBU 55 fuel air explosive other options).
2 M20/19 rocket launcher with 2.75in rocket.
3 M157 launcher with 2.75in rocket.
4 M16 Minigun pod (GE 7 62mm gun).
5 XM260 launcher with 2.75in rocket (LAU-68 similar).
6 Quad Hellfires (one missile shown detached).
7 M28 Minigun 7.62mm.
8 TAT turret, two M28 Miniguns, or two 40mm grenade launchers or one of each.
9 M129 40mm grenade launcher.
10 M197 three-barrel 20mm cannon.
11 FACTS (FLIR-augmented Cobra TOW sight).
12 GE GAU-12/U 25mm gun.
13 M230 30mm Chain Gun.
14 Complete M197 installation.
15 Emerson FTS (Flexible Turret System) with M28 Minigun.
16 M35 system with 20mm gun.
17 Quad TOW launcher, with missile in front.
18 Dispenser, eg M130 or ALE-39 chaff or SU-44 flares.
19 Self-defence Sidewinder (AIM-9L shown; AN/AGM-122A Sidearm antiradiation

missile is another option).
20 Twin Stinger launcher with one missile.
21 IRCM jammer.
22 Laser sight unit.

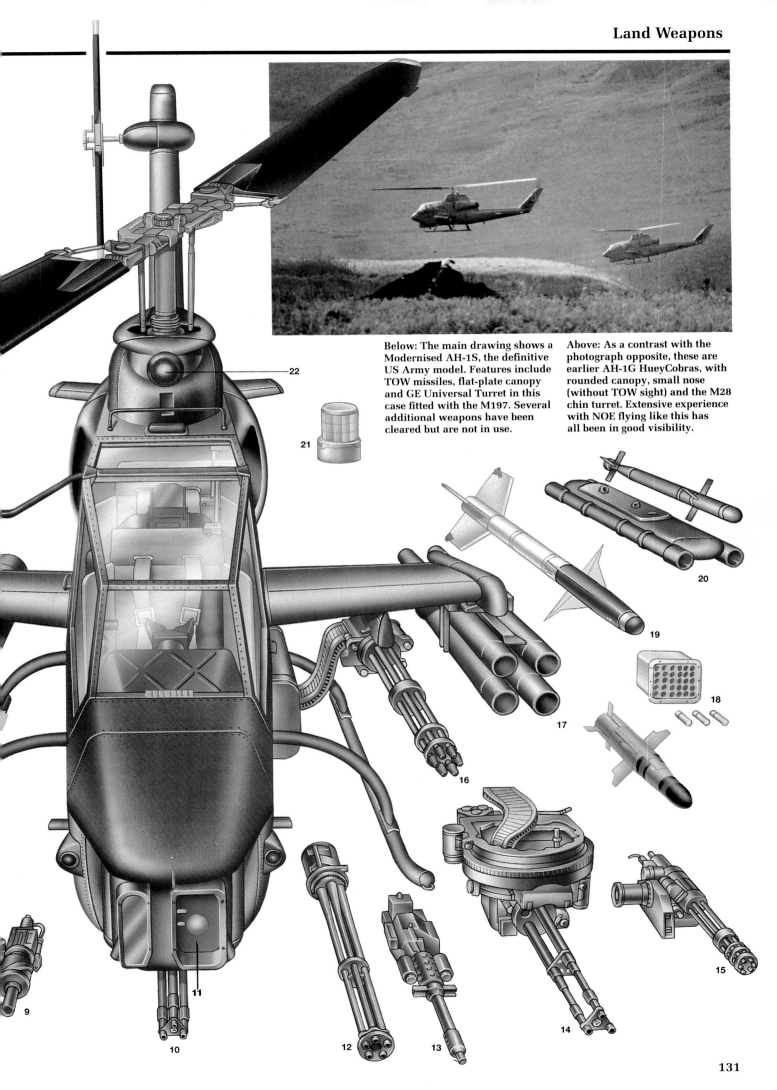

Below: The main drawing shows a Modernised AH-1S, the definitive US Army model. Features include TOW missiles, flat-plate canopy and GE Universal Turret in this case fitted with the M197. Several additional weapons have been cleared but are not in use.

Above: As a contrast with the photograph opposite, these are earlier AH-1G HueyCobras, with rounded canopy, small nose (without TOW sight) and the M28 chin turret. Extensive experience with NOE flying like this has all been in good visibility.

Lynx (Army)

Origin: Great Britain

Engines: Two Rolls-Royce Gem turboshafts; (most) 900shp Gem 2, (AH.5,7) 1,120shp Gem 41-1;.

Dimensions: Diameter of four-blade main rotor 42ft 0in (12.8m); length, rotors turning (most) 49ft 9in (15.16m), (-3) 50ft 9in (15.47m); length, main blades folded (most) 43ft 2.3in (13.16m), (-3) 45ft 3in (13.79m); height over rotors (most) 12ft 0in (3.66m).

Weights: Empty (AH.1) 5.683lb (2.578kg), maximum takeoff (1) 10,000lb (4,536kg), (AH.7) 10,750lb (4,876kg), (AH.9) 11,300lb (5,125kg).

Performance: (maximum weight) maximum speed at sea level 190mph (306km/h); cruising speed (1) 161mph (259km/h); maximum rate of climb (1) 2,480ft (756m)/min; hovering ceiling OGE (1) 10,600ft (3,231m); typical range with troops, 20min reserve (1) 336 miles (541km).

Background: Originally designated WG.13, the Lynx is the only helicopter to have been designed by Westland; it was also the first metric British design. Planned as a multirole military, naval and civil machine in the 4.5-ton class, it quickly proved outstanding in such matters as flight performance, agility (including aerobatics) and mission versatility, and in the Falklands it's toughness was also apparent (in contrast to some other helicopters).

As part of the Anglo-French Helicopter Agreement of 1967 Aerospatiale were awarded 30 per cent of the manufacturing task, this being the intended French proportion of purchases. In fact France has so far bought 12 per cent, and competed with the Lynx wherever possible: nevertheless, the British machine has sold to 11 air forces and navies. First generation Lynx are all broadly similar, being divided into skid-equipped army versions and wheel-equipped naval models, each group having appropriate avionics and weapons. Like all parts of the Lynx, the engines, gearboxes and rotors were designed to incorporate state-of-the-art late-1960s technology. The compact three-shaft engines have electrically de-iced inlets and are fed from bag tanks with a fuel capacity of 1,616lb (733kg) with every conceivable arrangement for front-line fuelling/defuelling. The main gearbox has conformal gears and set new standards in compact design with few parts, while the main rotor hub is machined from a single titanium forging and its four extension arms are attached direct to tubular ties whose end-fittings are bolted to the blade root. Each rotor blade has a stainless steel two-spar box to which is bonded a Nomex-filled glassfibre rear section. The AH.9 blades are entirely of filament-wound composite construction with advanced BERP (British Experimental Rotor Programme) tips. The tail rotor has a light-alloy spar (all-composite in the Lynx AH. 7 and AH.9, with rotation reversed to reduce noise). Current Lynx have a fixed half-tailplane at the top on the right side of the swept fin, the AH.9 has a large symmetric tailplane of inverted aerofoil profile at the bottom of the tailboom, the army variant also having end-plate fins; all these tail surfaces are fixed.The fuselage is a streamlined pod-and-boom, mainly light alloy but with much glassfibre. The two hinged cockpit doors and large sliding cabin doors are all jettisonable. Behind the pilots' seats the minimum cabin length is 81in (2.06m), width 70in (1.78m) and height 56in (1.42m);. Normal loads in the Lynx AH.1 include 10 armed troops, three stretchers and attendant or a cargo load of 2,000lb (907kg) internal of 3,000lb (1,361kg) external. Westland offer a tremendous variety of customer options, but standard kit includes a GEC Avionics autopilot-autostabilisation system. Missile-armed versions have various targeting system options, but the British Army AH.1 and 7 have the Hughes Tow sight (made by BAe) on the cockpit roof. In 1986 BAe received a £60m contract to add a full night-vision capability. Standard ECM dispenser is ALE-39. The AH.9 can have TADS/PNVS or other sensors in the nose, on the roof or in an MMS, and an IRCM jammer will be carried. All data will be digital, via 1553B bus.The anti-tank AH.1s of the British Army each carry eight Tow anti-tank missiles plus eight reloads in the cabin, or a team of three gunners with their own launcher and missiles; in addition, all the weapons depicted in the accompanying illustration have been cleared for use. Development proceeded from the AH.1, 113 of which were delivered, through the similar AH.5 to the AH.7 with improved systems, reversed-direction composite tail rotor, box-type exhaust diffusers and increased weight. AH.1s are being converted to Mk 7 standard. The AH.9 has the new BERP main rotor, wheel landing gear and further increased weight. At present AH.9s are rapid-intervention transports without missiles. In 1991 Westland flew a Lynx with LHTEC T800 engines, each rated at 1,200 shp.

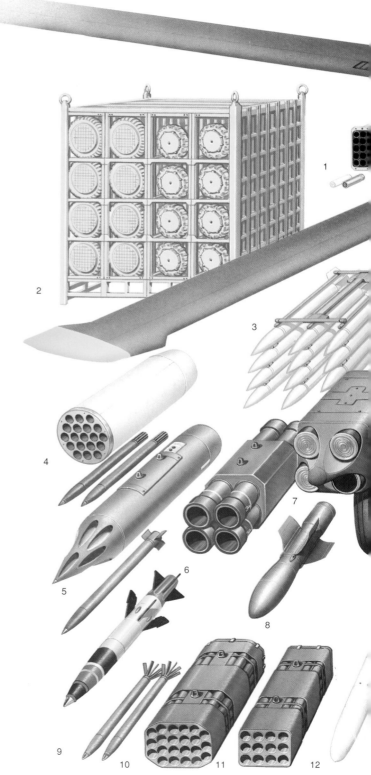

Above: An Army Lynx equipped for the anti-armour mission, with roof-mounted sight and quad Tow missile launchers. The cabin can accommodate eight reloads for the missile launchers or an anti-tank team of three gunners with their own missiles and launchers.

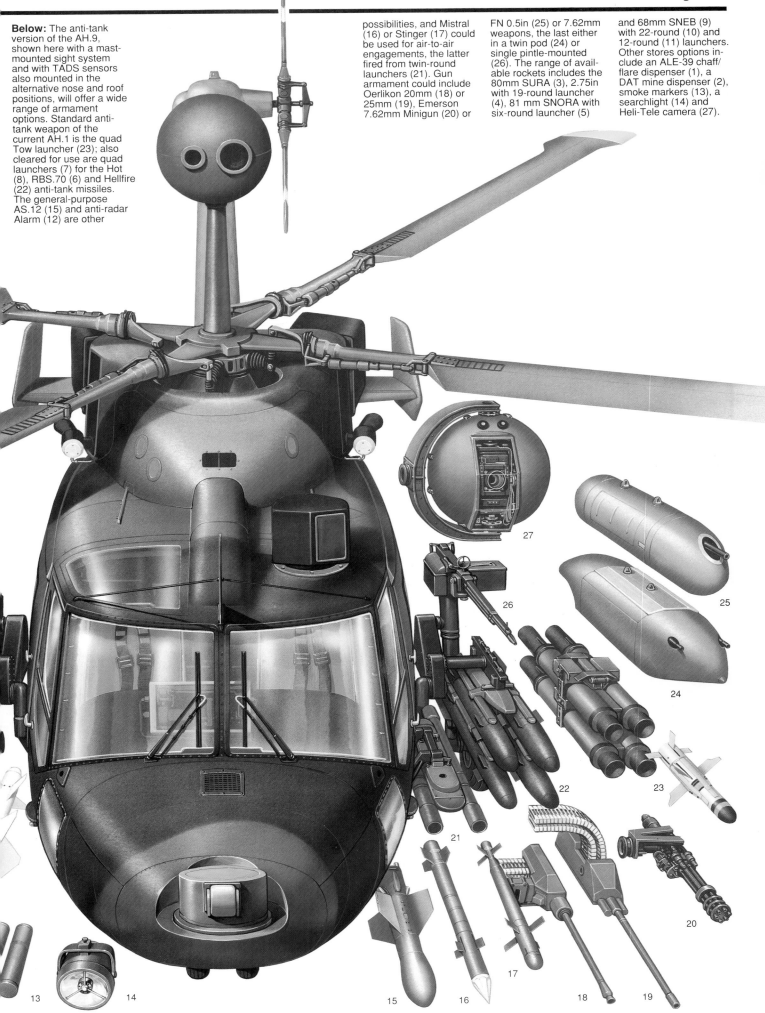

Below: The anti-tank version of the AH.9, shown here with a mast-mounted sight system and with TADS sensors also mounted in the alternative nose and roof positions, will offer a wide range of armament options. Standard anti-tank weapon of the current AH.1 is the quad Tow launcher (23); also cleared for use are quad launchers (7) for the Hot (8), RBS.70 (6) and Hellfire (22) anti-tank missiles. The general-purpose AS.12 (15) and anti-radar Alarm (12) are other

possibilities, and Mistral (16) or Stinger (17) could be used for air-to-air engagements, the latter fired from twin-round launchers (21). Gun armament could include Oerlikon 20mm (18) or 25mm (19), Emerson 7.62mm Minigun (20) or

FN 0.5in (25) or 7.62mm weapons, the last either in a twin pod (24) or single pintle-mounted (26). The range of available rockets includes the 80mm SURA (3), 2.75in with 19-round launcher (4), 81 mm SNORA with six-round launcher (5)

and 68mm SNEB (9) with 22-round (10) and 12-round (11) launchers. Other stores options include an ALE-39 chaff/flare dispenser (1), a DAT mine dispenser (2), smoke markers (13), a searchlight (14) and Heli-Tele camera (27).

Mi-24, 25 and 35 Hind

Origin: Soviet Union
Engines: Two 2,200shp Isotov TV-3117 turboshafts
Dimensions: Diameter of five-blade main rotor 56ft 9in (17.3m); length overall (rotors turning) 70ft 7in (21.5m); height over tail rotor 21ft 4in (6.5m).
Weights: (Mi-24P) Empty 18,078lb (8,200kg); maximum external stores 5,290lb (2.4t); normal loaded 26,455lb (12t).
Performance: Maximum level speed in service about 199mph (320km/h), but A-10 (the Mil design bureau designation) helicopters of the Hind C- type, without modification, have set speed records at up to 228.9mph (368.4km/h); cruising speed (full weapon load) 183mph (295km/h); maximum rate of climb 2,953ft (900m)/min; hovering ceiling OGE 7,218ft (2,200m); combat radius 99 miles (160km), but an A-10 prototype has set a record at full throttle round a 621-mile (1,000km) course.

Background: The Soviet Union has always shown itself willing to finance totally new weapons to meet specific requirements, even when it would be simpler and cheaper to modify an existing design. This family of helicopters was regarded as so important that it is based on a completely new design, despite the fact that it bears a very close resemblance to the Mi-8. Compared with the earlier model the Mi-24 is slightly smaller, and has a much smaller main rotor and it was originally sized to carry a unique mixture of eight troops in a cabin as well as heavy loads of attack weapons, including missiles. New versions introduced greater power, new rotors and a new tandem-seat forward fuselage. For ten years production at two plants, at Arsenyev and Rostov, has exceeded 15 per month, and more than 300 have been exported outside the Warsaw Pact. No other helicopter combines the weapons, sensors, armour and flight performance of this family, to say nothing of adding a cabin for eight troops, or four stretcher casualties, or urgent front-line cargo, including reloads for the helicopter's own weapon launchers. The main rotor has a fully articulated hub of machined steel, with the usual hydraulic lead/lag dampers, and retains the blades by unusually short coupling links. These are bolted to the extruded multiple spars of titanium alloy, around which are bonded the honeycomb-fllled glass-fibre skins. The leading edge of each blade has an anti-erosion strip and electrothermal de-icing, and a balance tab is fitted to the outer trailing edge. The tail rotor has three alumunium-alloy blades and except for the first Mi-24 version is on the left of the fin, a modification which substantially reduced rotor 'slap' and tail-rotor noise. The metal fuselage is not of the pod-and-boom form but is quite streamlined, and the tricycle landing gears are fully retractable. The main gears fold straight back, up and in to stow the wheels transversely, while the twin-wheel nose unit is longer in current versions to provide ground clearance for the chin-mounted sensors. The large wings, which are always fitted, are set at a high angle of incidence and provide about a quarter of the lift in cruising flight, thereby unloading the rotor and increasing attainable speeds. They also have pronounced anhedral, which enables rockets and missiles to be loaded easily from ground level. The engines are close together ahead of the gearbox, and usually have hemispherical inlet protectors to deflect ice and other matter. Above and between the engines is the oil cooler, and aft of the rotor is an APU mounted transversely. The first Mi-24 production versions, had a large four-seat cockpit (pilot, copilot, navigator/gunner and forward observer) with access via the two giant left-side windows, the forward one hinging up and the bulged rear one sliding aft. The main cabin has a large door on each side which opens above and below, the lower section having integral steps. Current versions have a flight crew of only two, the weapon operator in front having a canopy hinged to the right and the pilot, above and behind, having a door on the right. All versions have extensive armour. All versions also have extremely comprehensive electronic flight control and engine-management systems, communications and all weather navaids including a projected map display. The long nose probe is a sensitive low-airspeed system. Most versions have an electro-optical (LLTV) sensor on the tip of the left wing and radar and LLTV and, since 1982, a FLIR. All feed the integrated front cockpit sight system. Outstandingly comprehensive electronic and infra-red warning and jamming systems are installed. The Mi-24 carried a manually aimed 0.5in (12.7mm) nose gun and six pylons, usually loaded with four UV-16-57s and two pairs of AT-2- Swatters. Many other stores can be carried, including GSh-23 gun pods, together with a very comprehensive range of sensors. The basic Mi-24P illustrated seats the flight crew in tandem as noted above, plus a flight mechanic in the cabin. Export models of the 24P are designated as subtypes of Mi-25. The Mi-24W has modified wingtip launchers and four underwing pylons for a total of 12 Spiral missiles and R-60 AAMs. It has an enlarged undernose missile guidance pod, a searchlight and a pilot Hud. Export versions are designated as subtypes of Mi-35. The Mi-24P replaces the chin turret by the powerful GSh-30-2 gun fixed to fire ahead.
Above and ahead of the sensors the

Right: Missing its wingtip AT-2 Swatter anti-tank missiles but mounting the standard rocket pods, an example of the Mi-24 Hind-A, which paved the way for the much more heavily armed Hind-D and Hind-E gunship variants.

nose is streamlined. Export versions are designated Mi-35P. Total production by 1991 exceeded 2,450.

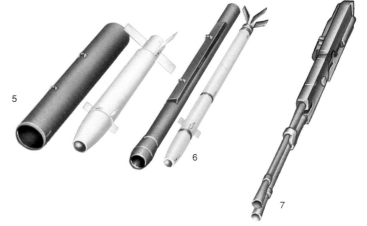

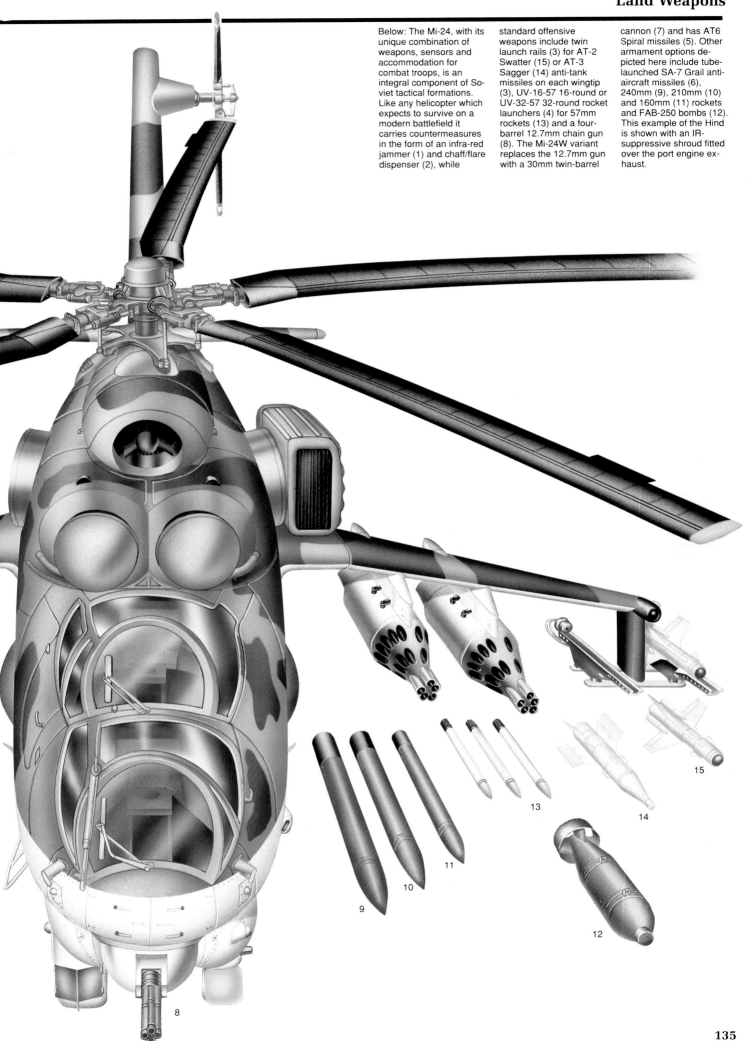

Below: The Mi-24, with its unique combination of weapons, sensors and accommodation for combat troops, is an integral component of Soviet tactical formations. Like any helicopter which expects to survive on a modern battlefield it carries countermeasures in the form of an infra-red jammer (1) and chaff/flare dispenser (2), while standard offensive weapons include twin launch rails (3) for AT-2 Swatter (15) or AT-3 Sagger (14) anti-tank missiles on each wingtip (3), UV-16-57 16-round or UV-32-57 32-round rocket launchers (4) for 57mm rockets (13) and a four-barrel 12.7mm chain gun (8). The Mi-24W variant replaces the 12.7mm gun with a 30mm twin-barrel cannon (7) and has AT6 Spiral missiles (5). Other armament options depicted here include tube-launched SA-7 Grail anti-aircraft missiles (6), 240mm (9), 210mm (10) and 160mm (11) rockets and FAB-250 bombs (12). This example of the Hind is shown with an IR-suppressive shroud fitted over the port engine exhaust.

Sikorsky UH-60 Black Hawk

Origin: USA, first flight 17 October 1974.

Type: (UH) multirole utility transport, (EH) Comint and jamming, (HH) combat SAR.

Engines: Two General Electric T700 turboshafts, (UH) 1,560shp T700-700, (UH-60L) 1,857shp T700-701C, (export option) 2,312shp RRTI RTM322.

Dimensions: Diameter of four-blade main rotor 53ft 8in (16.36m); length (rotors turning) 64ft 10in (19.76m), (rotors and tail folded) 41ft 4in (12.6m); height (overtail rotor) 16ft 10in (5.13m), (to top of main rotor head) 12ft 4in (3.76m).

Weights: Empty 11,284lb (5,118kg), mission takeoff 16,994lb (7,708kg), maximum 22,000lb (9,979kg).

Performance: (at mission TO weight) Maximum speed at SL (UH) 184mph (296km/h), (HH) 167mph (269km/h); maximum cruising speed (UH) 167mph (269km/h), (HH) 147mph (237km/h); hovering ceiling OGE (UH) 10,400ft (3170m); range (UH, max internal fuel) 373 miles (600km); endurance (UH) 2h 18min, (HH) 4h 51min.

Background: In the late 1960s the US Army received approval for an UTTAS (utility tactical transport aircraft system) to replace the UH-1H "in the late 1970s". Today the UH-1Hs are being refurbished for service beyond year 2000, but UTTAS not only exists, as the UH-60A, but is a giant programme which has enabled Sikorsky to develop a whole family of military, naval and commercial helicopters in the 10-ton class. Three prototypes were built, and the UH-60A was declared winner of a contest against a Boeing Vertol rival in December 1976. At the time of writing in 1986 Sikorsky had delivered 760 to the US Army and 11 to the USAF as SAR machines.

Design: The S-70 was a judicious blend of proven and new technology, with major constraints on overall dimensions imposed by the requirement that the helicopter should fit inside a C-130. For this purpose Sikorsky not only made the design compact and able to fold but also developed special air-transportability kits. As finally cleared for production, the main rotor has a hub machined from a single titanium forging, with elastomeric bearings and bifilar self-tuning vibration dampers. The blades have a titanium oval tubular spar, Nomex-filled graphite rear section with glassfibre/epoxy skin, glass-fibre leading-edge counterweight, titanium leading edge sheath and backswept Kevlar tip. Sikorsky BIM pressurization crack-detection is used, but amazingly there is no brake. The tail rotor comprises two crossed two-blade units entirely of composite materials and without hub bearings, tilted over to the left at 20°. The tail includes a large electrically driven tailplane whose angle is determined by airspeed, collective demand, pitch rate and lateral acceleration. The tail permits roll-on landings to be made following loss of the tail rotor, and the entire unit folds to the right. The fuselage, which only in plan has a pod/boom configuration, is mainly light alloy but incorporates various composites in the cockpit, floors and cowls. It is designed to withstand severe crashes from any direction. The cabin is typically 12ft 7in (3.84m) long and 92in (2.34m) wide but only 54in (1.37m) high, and has an aft-sliding door on each side. Loads include 11 equipped troops (14 high-density), six stretchers or four stretchers and three seats. The external slungload hook is rated at 8,000lb (3629kg), and an option is a 600lb (272kg) rescue hoist. The tailwheel-type landing gear is fixed. Main tanks are behind the cabin; auxiliary fuel can be carried on the ESSS. The planned EH-60A Night Hawk was cancelled, but other versions include the Enhanced Black Hawk, JUH-60A, GUH-60A, HH-60D, MH-60A (Special Operations), VH-60A (VIP), MH-60G Pave Hawk (rescue and recovery), MH-60K (Special Operations), a wide range of S-70A export versions (including the specially equipped Saudi Desert Hawk) and eight variants based on the naval S-70B (SH-60B Seahawk, SH-60F Ocean Hawk and various HH-60 search/rescue models).

Avionics: Basic UH equipment includes doppler, ADF, VOR/marker/glideslope, radar altimeter, secure voice radio, RWR and the ALQ-144 IRCM. The HH-60A has a 1553B data bus, cockpit MFDs, new doppler, INS, GPS, special ADF for locating survivors, FLIR, NVGs, APR-39 RWR, chaff/flare dispenser and auto approach/hover coupler.

Armament: One 7.62mm M60 machine-gun can be aimed from each forward cabin window, one by crew chief (third member of flight crew) and the other by one of the troops. The General Electric Black Hawk Weapon System provides either two 7.62mm Miniguns or two GECAL .50 Gatling guns which are pintlemounted. An option (not used by the US Army) adds the ESSS (external stores support system), anhedralled wings attached above the cabin with four pylons plumbed for tanks giving range of 1,380 miles (2221km) for staged deployment to Europe. The ESSS can carry 16 Hellfires, M56 mine dispensers, gun or rocket pods, self-defence Stingers, ECM or even motorcycles. The EH is unarmed but the HH has provision for the side-firing M60s. By 1991 deliveries of all Hawk variants had passed the 1,300 mark. The standard utility model is the UH-60L, with uprated engines, and both A and L versions are being progressively upgraded to Enhanced standard with Omega navigation, satellite communications, two threat-warning systems and, in a separate programme, IR jetpipe suppressors for hovering flight.

M134 Miniguns are replacing M60s. Additions being tested include night capability (with goggles), an automatic target handoff system, and the Honeywell Volcano mine dispenser system.

Above: A standard US Army UH-60A seen about to uplift a light utility carrier. Note the large angle of incidence of the horizontal stabilizer (tailplane).

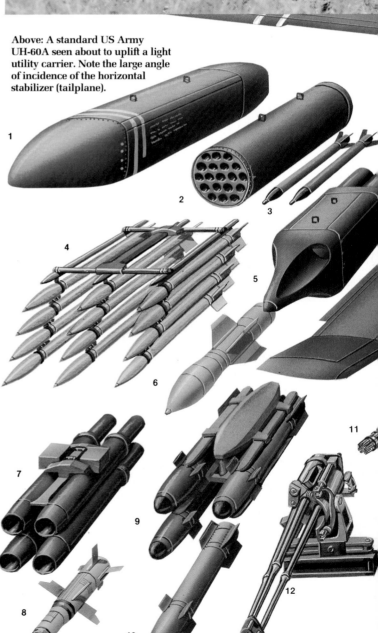

Key to stores:
1. Mk 56 mine dispenser (ESSS only).
2 19x70mm FFAR (Hughes M-261 or similar).
3 70mm (2.75in) FFAR rockets.
4 RAK 052 Oerlikon/SURA 81mm rocket installation.
5 Quadruple HOT or HOT 2 launcher
6 HOT 2 missile.
7 Quadruple TOW launch installation.
8 TOW missile (wings/fins deployed).
9 Quadruple Hellfire launcher

10 AGM-114A Hellfire missile.
11 7.62mm Minigun on pintle door mount.
12 GECAL 50 0.5in HMG on pintle mount.
13 Handrail/aerial array.
14 M60 7.62mm machine gun (pintle mount not shown).
15 SUU-25 flare launcher and flare.
16 450 US gal (1703lit) fuel tank.
17 230 US gal (871lit) fuel tank.
18 External Stores Support System (ESSS) wing.
19 FN ETNA HMP/MRL70 (combined 0.5in M3P gun and four 70mm rockets).
20 Stinger self-defence missile.
21 Twin Stinger launcher.
22 ALE-39 chaff/flare cartridge dispenser.
23 ALQ-144 IRCM pulsed beacon jammer.

Below: The standard US Army UH-60A which is the subject of the main drawing is shown surrounded by numerous weapon and stores fits, some of which are cleared for use by export customers only.

Sikorsky CH/HH-53 Super Stallion

Origin: USA, first flight 14 October 1964.

Type: Assault transport helicopter with MCM and SAR versions.

Engines: Two General Electric T64 turboshafts, (A) 2,850shp T64-6, (B) 3,080shp T64-3, (C, D, G) 3,925shp T64-7 or -413, (CH/MH-53E) three 4,380shp T64-416.

Dimensions: (early) six-blade main rotor of 72ft 3in (22.02m) diameter; length (rotors turning) 88ft 3in (26.9m); height over tail rotor 24ft 11in; (E versions) seven-blade main rotor of 79ft 0in (24.08m) diameter; length (rotors turning) 99ft 1in (30.19m); height over tail rotor 29ft 5in (8.97m).

Weights: Empty (D) 23,485lb (10,653kg), (E) 33,228lb (15,072kg), (MH) 36,336lb (16,482kg); maximum (D) 42,000lb (19,05lkg), (E) 73,500lb (33,340kg).

Performance: Maximum speed at SL 196mph (315km/h); cruising speed 173mph (278km/h); maximum rate of climb 2,180ft (664m)/min; hovering ceiling OGE 6,500ft (1981m); range (no external fuel, 10 per cent reserve) 257 miles (414km).

Background: The existence of this extremely important family of transport helicopters is owed to the US Marine Corps, which was pushing for such a helicopter when the S-61 first flew in 1959. The requirement included the ability to fly day or night in adverse (not blind) weather and load vehicles and other bulky loads through a rear ramp door. Another requirement was a sealed fuselage for water landings. Development was speeded by using the rotors and transmission already developed for the US Army CH-54 Tarhe (S-64) crane helicopter.

Design: Using an existing rotor was no problem, though the main gearbox was driven by different engines and the main hub was redesigned to be made partly in titanium and to have power-folding blades. The blades were identical to those of the Tarhe, being traditional aluminium alloy throughout. Likewise the fuselage and tail were conventional riveted light alloy, and Sikorsky did extensive tunnel testing to try to combine a streamlined shape with the inevitable pod-and-boom arrangement necessitated by the rear cargo door. Steel and titanium are used in certain areas of high stress or (cargo floor) subject to impact loads. The cockpit in the bluff nose seats pilot (on the right) and copilot in armoured seats, with a folding seat for the Flight Leader or other supernumerary behind. The main cabin is some 30ft (9.14m) long, and has a maximum cross section of 90in (2.29m) wide by 78in (1.98m) high. The normal load is 37 armed troops on fold-down wall seats, or 24 stretcher casualties and four attendants or 8,000lb (3629kg) of cargo. When operating at maximum weight much greater loads are possible, and in 1968 an uprated CH-53A flew a payload/ fuel mass of 28,500lb (12928kg). The rear door is a single-piece ramp, and when a water dam is fitted it can be opened when afloat. Water stability is provided by two large sponsons, the forward part of which houses the fuel (525gal, 2384lit) and the rear section the retracted twin-wheel main landing gears, which pivot forwards. The castoring twin-wheel nose gear retracts rearwards. The tail, which folds downwards to the right for shipboard stowage, has a tall fixed fin, four-blade rotor on the left and fixed horizontal stabilizer on the right. Apart from the power of the engines most of this first generation of Sea Stallion helicopters were generally similar. The most modified machines were a succession of HH-53 special armed SAR helicopters for the USAF Aerospace Rescue and Recovery Service, which had a rescue hoist, flight-refuelling probe, armour, various complex defensive armament schemes, jettisonable long-range tanks on sponson extensions, and a wealth of mission avionics which in Pave Low 3 aircraft included INS, doppler, FLIR and TFR. Some CH-53Ds were modified for minesweeping, leading to the purpose-built RH-53D (later MH-53E) with greater power and special MCM gear.

Avionics: All versions have communications, navaids, lighting and advanced flight-control systems to fly the mission in day or night visual conditions. The specially equipped Pave Low 3 (HH-53H) is no longer in service. The special MCM versions have equipment for indicating tow-cable yaw angle an tension, and for automatically linking yaw angle to the desired heading and aircraft attitude. The towboom is rated at 40,000lb (18,144kg). compared with 36,000lb (1,330kg) for the normal vertical cargo sling, and can handle the Mk 103 mechanical mine-sweeping gear, Mk 104 acoustic, Mk 105 magnetic and Mk 106 combined magnetic/ acoustic. Little has been published on defensive electronics fits but it is clear that most CH-53s now carry passive receivers, one type being the APR-39(V). Sea Stallions of the US Marine Corps, and probably of other operators, can also protect themselves with chaff/flare dispensers.

Among upgrades the most important is the MH-53J Pave Low III Enhanced, 33 of which are being produced (as rebuilds of older models) for Special Operations Forces. These have every conceivable avionic aid for independent missions by night or in adverse weather through hostile territory, including terrain-avoidance radar and guns fired through side windows or the rear ramp.

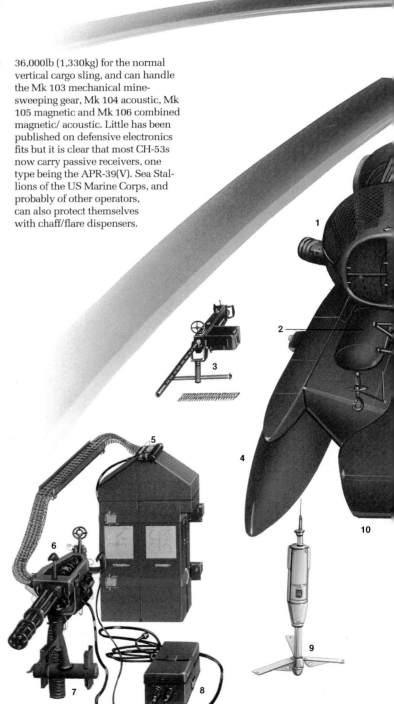

Below: The US Navy's RH-53D Sea Stallion is the specialized MCM (mine countermeasures) version. This example from squadron HM-14 has the MCM gear deployed, the sled being towed through the water astern. The crew watch via rear-view mirrors.

Right: The HH-53H (Pave Low 3) was a very special USAF version, eight of which were packed with sensors for night rescue missions. Equipment included extra navigation aids, AAQ-10 FLIR, APQ-158 terrain-following radar and a flight-refuelling probe.

Key to stores:
1 Inlet particle separators.
2 Rescue hoist.
3 Browning MG3 0.5in heavy machine gun.
4 1703lit (450 US gal) auxiliary fuel tanks.
5 Booster unit at top of four-can ammunition storage.
6 M134 (GAU-28/A) 7.62mm Minigun, with MAU-56A delinking feed and electric drive.
7 Pintle mount with case/link disposal.
8 Control box, 600 to 6,000spm.
9 Jungle Penetrator with three fold-down seats for jungle rescue.
10 Fuel-filled sponsons.
11 Retractable inflight refuelling probe.
12 AAQ-10 FLIR installation.
13 7.62mm Browning or FN GPMG on side-door pintle.
14 Westinghouse AQS-14 towed minehunting sonar vehicle.
15 Chaff/flare cartridge dispenser (ALE-39, M130 or similar).
16 Xerox/Loral ALQ-157 IRCM jammer.

Above: The main drawing shows an HH-53E Super Stallion of USAF No 601 TASS, from Sembach AB.

Naval Weapons

For at least 2,000 years navies have had a role to play in land warfare in protecting sea lanes and in intercepting and capturing or sinking vessels of the enemy. Somewhat later shore bombardment became important, at first with cannon with a range of 650 ft (200m) or less, and from 1806 with rockets. By World War 1 the monitor was a recognised class of warship, with shallow draught to enable it to come close inshore and bombard enemy fortifications with the same guns as fitted to contemporary battleships (at the time, of 13.5 or 15in calibre). In World War 2 all kinds of surface warships bombarded enemy land positions with guns, while there was also a large-scale return to the rocket. The latter were fired thousands at a time, though they were even less accurate than guns.

Remarkably, it was not until the 1970s that moves began in the United States to develop a class of weapon that had been deployed in large numbers in World War 2 – the cruise missile – to ship and submarine launch platforms. Key elements in the new breed of cruise missile were compact overall design, folding wings and tail (and engine inlet, if necessary), launch by rocket boost from a tube, air-breathing cruise propulsion, very low radar signature, and the ability to be preprogrammed to fly difficult manoeuvres to render interception almost impossible. Such vehicles could be made very compact, loaded into their launch tube and thereafter treated as just another round of ammunition, yet able to convey a wide range of warheads up to distances of 60 miles (100km) or even 1,550 miles (2,500km), with almost 100 per cent reliability. Over such long distances the guidance system becomes all-important. It was clear that both the warhead and the guidance method could be tailored to the type of target. Attacks on land targets needed somewhat different warheads, and utterly different guidance systems, from those used to destroy or disable surface ships.

Among sea-to-land missiles for conventional warfare the most important is Tomahawk, described later. This enables surface ships and submarines to make attacks of exceedingly high precision on any type of land target from a great distance offshore. The long range means that in most war situations the launching platform need not be close to the enemy shore, where any surface vessel would present a prominent target. On the other hand, a launch platform of the calibre of a Battleship is very difficult to destroy or even disable by today's relatively puny anti-ship weapons, which without exception were designed to counter vessels of destroyer or frigate size and hardness.

Of course, naval forces can play other roles in land battles besides direct sea/land firepower. Naval aircraft based on giant carriers can do almost anything land-based airpower can do. STOVL (Harrier type) aircraft can operate from any small helicopter platform or even the top of a commercial cargo container. Not least, Marine units can make direct sea/land assaults over beaches, supported by airpower, whenever the enemy has a coastline. A third, more indirect, role of a navy is to enforce a blockade of maritime trade.

LAND TARGETS

Aircraft
In general the naval attack aircraft types and capabilities are similar to those used by land-based air forces. Of course, naval forces would have immediate realtime access to all

Right: Expensive to run maybe, but the heavy guns and cruise missiles of the Iowa class battleships give the US Navy a fearsome shore bombardment capability.

Below: An A-6 Intruder fires two AGM-123A Skipper IR guided stand-off missiles on a pre-war test. The rocket motor was taken from the obsolete Shrike missile.

reconnaissance, ELINT, COMINT and other intelligence information gathered by friendly air and satellite platforms. It would be up to the overall theatre commander to decide when to call upon naval aircraft to attack surface targets. In an evenly balanced war, in which the enemy retains powerful retaliatory forces, it is a moot point whether a giant carrier standing off at a considerable distance might be more or less vulnerable than an airfield. (Of course, in such a conflict, STOVL aircraft would almost certainly be the only ones to continue operating, from a sequence of sites unknown to the enemy.)

As noted earlier, the US Navy and Marine Corps use a stand-off version of the Paveway III smart bombs known as AGM-123A Skipper II. This is a very close naval equivalent of the USAF AGM-130A, though as the basic bomb is the Mk 83, of the 1,000lb (500kg) size, Skipper has a generally shorter range and less-powerful effect. The Mk 78 rocket motor is described as smokeless, but certainly leaves a highly visible trail during the first few seconds. It gives the 1,283lb (582kg) smart weapon a speed slightly in excess of Mach 1, but the guidance system limits range to 10.25 miles (16.5km).

Another Navy weapon in this category is the SLAM, described below.

Ships
As noted, SLAM is a powerful missile whose acronym signifies Standoff Land Attack Missile. It is a variant of the Harpoon, and uses essentially the same airframe and propulsion system. The main differences are that, instead of having active radar homing guidance, which would probably fail to lock on to the desired land target, SLAM has the Maverick AGM-65D IIR (imaging IR) seeker and the data-link from the obsolescent Walleye TV-guided glide bomb. The warhead is also redesigned for use against buildings and fortifications rather than metal-skinned ships. These changes considerably increase the missile's length and launch weight, but range is not greatly altered (see Harpoon under air weapons). SLAM was first fired from a ship launch tube in July 1990, and is also dropped by A-6E Intruder aircraft. Surface warships have a choice of

Above: Air power at sea. Four EA-6B Prowler EW aircraft fly over the nuclear-powered *USS Eisenhower* and its air wing of up to 86 aircraft and helicopters.

Right: Sophisticated sensors and command and control systems are essential in naval warfare. This is the Sperry Mk92 fire control system on an FFG-7 class frigate.

many species of tactical land-attack missile, though these are small weapons unable to penetrate inland. At the other extreme is the powerful American BGM-109 Tomahawk. This extremely potent and versatile weapon entered FSD (full-scale development) in 1981. Several versions were planned, including an air-launched AGM-109 and the GLCM (Ground-Launched Cruise Missile). The model currently in service with the US Navy is BGM-109 SLCM (Sea-Launched Cruise Missile). It can be fired from platforms as diverse as the battleships *Missouri* and *Wisconsin* and submerged submarines.

Tomahawk attack profile

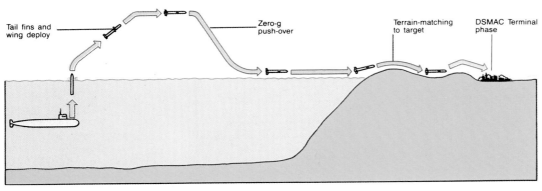

Tail fins and wing deploy — Zero-g push-over — Terrain-matching to target — DSMAC Terminal phase

Dimensionally it is not much larger than Harpoon, with a length of 21 ft (6.4m) and body diameter of 20.9 in (0.53m). Launch weight varies with sub-type; the BGM-109C, for use against tactical land targets, weighs 3,450lb (1,565kg). It is fired from a tube with the 7,000lb (3,175kg) thrust of a tandem rocket boost motor. During the boost phase wings, tail surfaces and an air inlet are unfolded, and the 600lb (272kg) thrust Williams F107 turbofan sustainer engine is started and run up to speed. The booster then burns out and falls away. Tomahawk can cruise at 550 mph (885 km/h) for up to 808 miles (1,300 km); indeed the nuclear version with similar fuel capacity has the potential of hitting targets 1,550 miles (2,500 km) distant. The tactical 109C version flies on INS guidance, at a height that will take it well above any cliffs, until it crosses the coast.

Above: Tomahawk can be launched from a surface ship, or as seen here, from a submarine. A boost motor propels the missile up to the surface, where the fins and wings deploy and the cruise engine starts. After a zero-G push-over, it heads for the coast on inertial guidance. When over land, the TERCOM system compares the terrain with a digital map to refine its position. Near the target, a TV camera compares the view ahead with stored data to steer within feet of the desired impact point.

Naval gunfire support

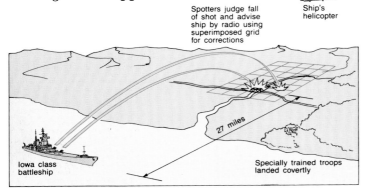

Spotters judge fall of shot and advise ship by radio using superimposed grid for corrections

Ship's helicopter

Iowa class battleship

27 miles

Specially trained troops landed covertly

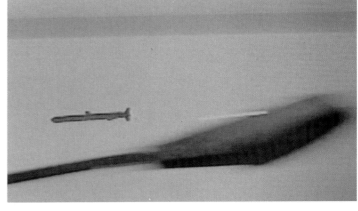

Above: Ships capable of firing inland are ideal for the support of ground forces. Often unable to see the target, the ship requires guidance from a spotter either on the ground or in the air. Corrections are måde by reference to a superimposed map grid.

Below: *USS Wisconsin* and *Missouri* led the way in the initial attacks on Iraqi strategic installations. Waves of cruise missiles were fired from the box launchers amidships, each Tomahawk programmed with the exact location of a key target.

Above: This startling picture, taken by a western journalist in Baghdad, shows a cruise missile streaking past his hotel window, using a major road as terrain reference. Tomahawk enabled key targets to be destroyed with unbelievable accuracy.

Right: The heavy 16in (406mm) guns of the US battleships are an awe-inspiring sight when they salvo their 863kg (1,903lb) shells towards targets up to 24 miles (38km) away. *USS Missouri* and *Wisconsin* were used in this role in the Gulf conflict.

Then it follows the preprogrammed flight path (which need not be straight) on inertial guidance, but periodically using TERCOM (terrain contour matching) to refine the accuracy. TERCOM compares the undulations of the terrain over which it is flying with those of the desired course stored in the guidance library. Nearing the target the terminal guidance is switched on. This DSMAC (digital scene-matching area correlation) is one of the most precise guidance methods known. The missile studies the actual scene ahead, in selected square blocks of terrain, with digital pictures in its library. This enables the missile to be aimed at any chosen window of a building, for example. The warhead is conventional, weighing 264 lb (120 kg). The 109D version dispenses submunitions.

Tomahawk Block III incorporates further improvements. One is the addition of GPS satellite navigation, which gives extremely accurate en route navigation that is particularly useful in extremely flat country, or in any other situation where TERCOM runs into difficulties, such as among tall trees whose radar signature varies with the seasons. Extra computer power refines the DSMAC-IIA terminal guidance to give absolutely bull's-eye accuracy. A new warhead and fuze gives increased lethality, and allows fuel capacity to be increased which, together with the more powerful and more economical F107-402 engine, gives appreciably greater range. Addition of TOA (time of arrival) control allows the US Navy to control the land-attack conventional missile so that it arrives at the target precisely to the second. This enables the missiles to be exactly co-ordinated with air strikes.

Guns

Naval guns have several important advantages over other weapons, out to the limit of their range. They deliver projectiles which, with most calibres, are selectable by type according to the nature of the target. A few modern SAM systems, notably the British Sea Wolf, have demonstrated their ability to intercept even quite small shells, but for all practical purposes gun-fired projectiles are uninterceptible. Fire can be sustained as long as there are rounds in the ship's magazine. The system is unaffected by day, night or adverse weather. At relatively close ranges the gun can be used 'with open sights'; the gun points almost directly at the target and the shell arrives almost horizontally. This method, direct fire, is especially effective against hardened targets such as fortifications. At greater distances the gun has to be elevated to an angle depending on the range; in a few large guns range can also be adjusted by selecting different numbers of bagged charges of propellant. Thus the projectiles arrive at an oblique angle which can even approach the vertical, and this plunging fire can with some targets be much more effective than a horizontal arrival.

One obvious drawback is lack of accuracy. Except in rare cases where the ship has a clear view of the target it is almost essential for the fall of shot to be reported by an aerial or land-based observer. Even after such an observer has reported "On target", motion of the ship, caused by recoil, rolling, wind and other factors, requires continued direction from the observer. Bombardment of land targets is the one duty where guns may be required to maintain a high rate of fire over a long period. This is extremely demanding on the barrel, and eats into barrel life much more rapidly than training or even a ship-to-ship engagement. The 16in (406 mm) Mk 7 gun is the largest in service anywhere. Triple turrets are fitted to the four US Navy battleships, which for the second time are expected to be mothballed from 1992. Each turret weighs about 1,527 tons (1,551 tonnes) and a single gun weighs 239,220lb (108,510 kg). It fires several types of ammunition, all comprising a projectile driven out of the gun by bagged full charges or reduced charges of propellant. Each ship has a magazine capacity of 1,220 projectiles, and the hoist/loading system can sustain a rate of fire of 2 rds/min per gun. The two standard types of ammunition, of which large stocks were held, are generally highly effective against any kind of battlefield target worthy of such attention. Examples include major choke points, bridges, infrastructure (such as fuel depots) and all forms of hardening such as aircraft shelters and fortifications. Guns of this size are not cost/effective against infantry or armour, but in 1986 development began on two

Below: The Pioneer Remote Piloted Vehicle (RPV) carries a stabilised TV camera to observe the fall of shot for US warships when bombarding shore targets.

Above: Used in the Falklands war and during the Iran-Iraq war, Exocet is a sea-skimming missile effective against most naval targets. It is in service with many navies around the world.

Left: Using a lightweight launcher and with a 60nm (42km) range, Harpoon is carried by most US Navy warships. After launch, Harpoon travels under inertial guidance until close enough to switch on its own homing radar.

Right: The positioning of the air defence ships within a task force will be determined by the range of their missile systems. Here the main body is a carrier with an escorting cruiser which would use its point defence systems - guns, short range missiles and CIWS - to supplement those of the carrier. Further out, beyond the screen of ASW escorts are air defence ships with area defence systems to provide defence in depth against aircraft and missiles.

new types of ammunition specifically designed for use against such targets. The ERAP (Extended-Range Anti-Personnel) round has a calibre of 13in (330mm), and is fired at very high velocity by a discarding sabot (see Weapons for Land Warfare). Range is almost doubled, to about 43 miles (70km), and the projectile splits open near the target to dispense over 600 submunitions. The second new round was based on the Sadarm (Sense And Destroy ARMor) programme, in which the main projectile dispenses a cloud of muni-

tions each with active dual-wavelength guidance which select an individual tank and destroy it with an SFF (Self-Forging Fragment) warhead fired downwards. Other ammunition could convey chaff, smoke and other payloads.

Smaller guns
Secondary armament, and the main gun armament of destroyers and frigates, all have calibres from 4 to 5in (100 to 127mm). Modern guns of these calibres use fixed ammunition, the projectile and propellant

case being joined into a single unit. Thus ammunition can be fed automatically, almost in the manner of a machine gun, with a minimum of manual labour. Rate of fire is typically 20 rds/min for the US 5in, 25 for the British 4.5in, 45 for the Italian 127mm (5in) and 80 for the French 100mm (3.94in). Maximum range varies from 9 nautical miles (17 km) for the smaller calibres up to 13 nm (24 km) for the 4.5 and 5in. Such guns can be of interest where the enemy offers targets along a shoreline, and can be cost/effective

against armies moving inland. They are dual-purpose weapons, used against surface targets and aircraft.

Rockets
Unguided but spin-stabilized rockets have been used for offshore bombardment of land targets in the past, but today are relatively rare. They would normally be used as a prelude to, and during, a seaborne assault landing. During the Second World War, rocket-firing barges were used to pound the D-Day beaches.

Below: Corvettes of the Saudi Navy on patrol. Each carries eight Harpoon and a single 76mm Mk 75 DP gun, together with torpedoes and light anti-aircraft guns.

Right: Light guns such as this Bofors 40mm are still used extensively by most navies, although their effectiveness is questionable in modern warfare.

Air defence of a task force

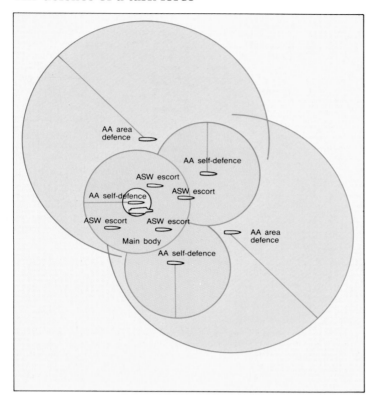

AA area defence

AA self-defence

ASW escort

ASW escort

AA self-defence

ASW escort

ASW escort

ASW escort

AA area defence

Main body

AA self-defence

SEA TARGETS

Guns

All the aforementioned guns can be used against surface vessels. Where these are warships, AP ammunition would be used. In addition, many kinds of smaller weapon can be effective against light craft using calibres from rifle calibre (typically 7.62mm) up through 0.5in (12.7mm) to 20mm, 25mm, 30mm, 35mm and 57mm. All these are fast-firing automatic weapons, equally suitable for use against aircraft.

Missiles

A complete range of dedicated anti-ship missiles has been developed, as described under Weapons for Air Warfare. Most are sea-skimmers with active radar homing. Navies also use several other types of missile designed specifically for ship launch. By far the longest-established is the Soviet P-15 (NATO SS-N-2 Styx), which cruises at high-subsonic speed over ranges up to 50 miles (80km) with a 1,000lb (450kg) warhead. Exocet, Sea Skua and Sea Eagle exist in ship-

launched forms, and a similar weapon is the Franco-Italian Otomat, which has a 'fire and update' guidance, using active radar homing, which is effective up to about 100 miles (160km).

Mines

Purely for use against naval forces, mines are normally laid fairly densely in distinct areas of sea, the extent of the field being supposedly unknown to the enemy. With round-the-clock satellite and aircraft surveillance the only way a mine-field could be laid undetected would be by submarine, and these have limited capacity. Most mines have an explosive charge from 200 to 1,100lb (100 - 500kg), the larger sizes being sufficient to disable (possibly even to sink) a destroyer or frigate. They can be laid to float on the surface, become stabilized moored to the bottom at a depth less than typical ship draught, or be laid on the bottom. They can be triggered by any combination of the following methods: magnetic, sensing the change in the terrestrial field caused by the target's passage; seismic, sensing gross water disturbance; acoustic, sensing the target's noise (especially its propellers); and pressure, sensing the reduction in pres-

sure caused by the close passage of the target.

AIR TARGETS

Almost all naval surface vessels have weapons and sensors intended to give protection again attack by aircraft. A much smaller number have sensors and weapons giving at least some protection again anti-ship missiles. Any major surface combatant has weapons graded according to effective range, SAMs (surface/air missiles) being used to kill oncoming targets at a distance greater than several kilometres or miles, a mid-range system, and then a last-ditch close-range system normally of gun type and envisaged chiefly for use against missiles (which might fail to be detected by the ship's radar until quite close). All are major elements in a navy's AAW (anti-air warfare) potential. Some navies either could not afford such a comprehensive protection system, while others simply failed to address the problems (the most glaring example being the

Below: The BAe Buccaneer was deployed to the Gulf, mainly to mark targets for RAF Tornados, but also to carry Sea Eagle anti-ship missiles as seen here.

Task force air defence zones

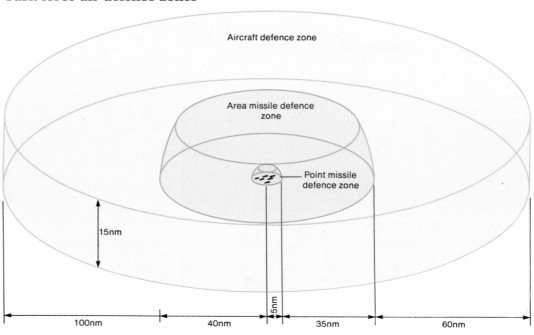

Aircraft defence zone

Area missile defence zone

Point missile defence zone

15nm

5nm

100nm | 40nm | 35nm | 60nm

Above: Air defence in depth is essential for a task force at sea, where the aim must be to destroy the enemy at as great a distance as possible from the main body of ships before a missile attack can be launched. A carrier group would therefore move with an air-craft defence zone some 100nm deep, with the area and point defence missile zones ensuring terminal protection from missiles.

Royal Navy in the Falklands war, where long-range defence was easily swamped and close-range defence non-existent, except for infantry machine guns bolted on to various bits of the structure).

SAMs

By far the largest, most capable and most costly of all ship AAW systems is the US Navy's Aegis, which is intended to offer wide-area defence against all aerial targets. It has to be designed from the start into a ship of cruiser size, and comprises an exceptionally large computer-controlled multi-function phased-array radar, a fire-control system, SAMs, magazines, automatic loading systems and launchers. This system initially used the Mk 26 twin launcher, but experience of the Royal Navy in the Falklands war showed how easily even a power-loaded twin launcher can become saturated. Accordingly, almost all future AAW systems, including Aegis, use VLS (vertical launch systems) in which large numbers of missiles are stored in vertical boxes, with lids flush with the deck, from which they can be fired by tandem boost motors in rapid succession. After launch each missile quickly tilts over on to the target heading. This method, first deployed by the Soviet Union, is a vast improvement over the traditional types of missile launcher. There are two principal advantages. One is that reaction time is reduced; typically the time elapsed between sending the signal to the launcher and getting the first missile to a distance or 330ft (100m) is reduce from 4.2 sec to 1.1 sec. Perhaps even more important, the number of rounds at instant readiness is increased from 2 to (in the case of US Navy CG-47 class ships) 122. Thus, the system cannot be overwhelmed by any likely mass attack of aircraft or missiles.

It is probably fair to claim that no navy has a perfect AAW defence. Even the US Navy, whose task forces and battle groups are far bet-

ter protected than those of any other Western nation, has identified a problem area between the inner limit of effective range of the Aegis system and the outer limit of effectiveness of CIWS (close-in weapon systems). The advent of new anti-ship missiles which are smaller (and increasingly incorporate stealth design features), faster and more manoeuvrable is seen as posing a severe threat. Cancellation of the RIM-116A Rolling Airframe Missile and NATO AAWS (Anti-Air Warfare System) is considered to have left a gap in local-area air defence. The long-established British Sea Wolf would fill the bill perfectly, but because of its 'foreign' design this battle-proven weapon has no chance of being accepted by the Americans.

The chief area-defence naval SAMs are the US Navy SM-2ER (Standard Missile type 2, Extended-Range) and the Royal Navy Sea Dart. Despite having all-rocket propulsion the former is claimed to be able to engage targets out to a radius of 75nm (137km) at Mach 2.5, with a mixture of command and inertial guidance to give optimum trajectory to the target. (Of course, this presupposes a high-flying target; one skimming the waves could not be engaged until it was very much closer.) Sea Dart, despite having much more efficient air-breathing ramjet cruise propulsion, is not credited with a range greater than 21nm (40km), which is most surprising. It does have the ability to engage ships or sea-skimming missiles and demonstrated this by downing an Iraqi Silkworm missile aimed at the *USS Wisconsin*.

Among closer-range weapons the most important are the Sea Sparrow, Sea Wolf and Crotale. The US Navy's Sea Sparrow has been widely adopted by friendly navies, even though it is only an adaptation of the small and inherently limited Sparrow AAM. Normally fired from octuple box launchers, Sea Sparrow has semi-active homing out to a claimed range of 8 nm (14.6 km). Sea Wolf was specifically developed for ship AAW defence, and is the only missile in the world to have repeatedly demonstrated the ability of killing aircraft, sea-skimming

Below: These screens of the Aegis air defence system give some idea of the complexity needed to manage the speed and confusion of a modern naval and air battle.

Above: Aegis air defence cruisers use the Standard SM-2 MR missile, firing them from either two Mk 26 twin launchers or, as seen here, two vertical launch arrays.

Below: The Royal Navy's Sea Dart is a relatively elderly missile, although upgrades after the 1982 Falklands war have kept it an effective area air defence system.

Sea Wolf operations

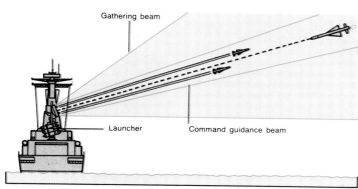

Above: The principal elements of the Sea Wolf system, which is equally effective against missiles diving onto the ship and surface sea-skimmers, are shown here. Sea Wolf uses command-to-line-of-sight guidance with radar

missiles, small agile targets and even shells fired from naval guns.

It has radio/TV command and differential radar tracking out to 2.7nm (5km). It is normally fired from a six-box launcher or, with a tandem boost motor, from a 32-box vertical launcher. Naval Crotale is the ship version of a land SAM; fired from an octuple box launcher it has command guidance and IR homing out to 7nm (13km). Many ships in the Gulf, especially support and amphibious warfare vessels, sprouted hand-held missiles for extra close-in defence. The US Stinger is probably the most effective of these; its IR homing head enables it to engage targets at 5,500yds (5,000m) range. Combat proven in Afghanistan, Stinger is a fire-and-forget weapon, highly resistant to any countermeasures. British vessels often carried Javelin which uses a semi-automatic command line-of-sight (SACLOS) system. Javelin relies on the operator continuously tracking the target after launch; although it can engage from any angle.

Guns
Guns are the obvious last-ditch weapon for use against incoming missiles, though France has developed two alternatives, one based on the short-range Mistral IR homing missile and the other on firing a

differential or TV tracking and radio command. Error signals proportional to the missile deviation from the datum are processed, and correction signals are sent to the missile to return it to the correct flightpath.

cloud of very small armour-piercing rockets. Most ships have various single-barrel installations, as noted previously, 20mm being a common calibre. This is also the calibre of the widely used American Phalanx, a self-contained installation incorporating a radar, fire-control link and a navalised version of the M61Al Vulcan six-barrel aircraft gun. This normally fires at 3,000 rds/min, out to an effective range of from 4,900 to 6,600ft (1.5 to 2km). An alternative lightweight installation uses the M197 gun, which has three barrels instead of six, but can still fire at up to 3,000 rds/min. A much more powerful weapon is the Dutch-developed

Right: The Goalkeeper Close-in Weapons System (CIWS) uses a multi-barrelled 30mm cannon based on that in the A-10 Thunderbolt II close-air support aircraft.

Right: The Phalanx CIWS is used by most major warships in the US Navy and some in the British Royal Navy. Once the system is switched on, target detection, tracking and engagement are fully automatic.

Below: Hand-held missiles, such as this Stinger, are useful to quickly give ships extra anti-aircraft protection. Note the Phalanx in the background.

Goalkeeper. Self-contained like Phalanx, this uses more capable surveillance and tracking radars linked to the 30mm GAU-8/A anti-tank gun used in the A-10A aircraft, firing 4,200 exceedingly powerful rounds per minute. Goalkeeper includes an automatic kill-assessment subsystem to optimise its effectiveness in the case of multiple attacks.

The last line of defence for a warship is anti-missile countermeasures. Very little is revealed in the open press, but most major navies equip their units with electronic countermeasures and jamming equipment to foil enemy radars, especially those associated with missile systems. Alongside onboard jamming, ships often launch chaff, IR emmitters and floating radar-reflecting decoys to spoof missiles in the terminal phase.

A typical system is the US Mk36 SRBOC (Super Rapid-Blooming

Overboard Chaff launcher), which uses two or four six-tubed mortars. They fire the Mk182 cartridge which forms clouds of chaff away from the ship. A radar homing missile such as Harpoon or Exocet will see this as a large target and hopefully head for the chaff rather than the ship. SRBOC also fires the "Torch" IR decoy.

Should a warship be hit, effective damage control can mean a damaged but repairable vessel rather than a catastrophic loss. Most navies have learned from the experiences of the Royal Navy during the Falklands war, especially about the use of flammable materials on warships. Crew casualties can be reduced by the use of anti-flash hoods, and by not using synthetic materials in uniforms. Extensive damage control training is essential, as quick action can often save a ship from disaster.

Broadsword (Type 22) class

Origin: United Kingdom
Type: Frigate (FF)
Built: 1975
Class: 14 in service;
Displacement: (Batch 1) 3,500 tons standard; 4,200 tons full load (Batch 2) 4,100 tons standard; 4,800 tons full load (Batch 3) 4,200 tons standard; 4,900 tons full load
Dimensions: (1) Length 430ft (131.2m) oa; beam 48.5ft (14.8m); draught 19.9ft (6m) (2 and 3) Length 471ft (143.6m) oa; beam 48.5ft (14.8m); draught 21ft (6.4m)
Propulsion: (All Batch 1 and Batch 2 *Boxer, Beaver*) 2-shaft COGOG (2 Rolls-Royce Olympus TM3B/2 Rolls-Royce Tyne RM1C gas turbines), 50,000/9,700shp (Batch 2 *Brave*) 2-shaft COGOG (2 Rolls-Royce Spey SM1A/2 Rolls-Royce Tyne RM1C gas turbines), 37.540/9.700shp (Batch 2 *London, Sheffield, Coventry* and all Batch 3) 2-shaft COGAG (2 Rolls-Royce Spey SM1A/2 Rolls-Royce Tyne RM1C gas turbines), 37,540/9,750shp
Performance: Speed 30-32 knots max: 18 knots on Tynes
Weapons: Missiles: 4 Exocet (Batch 1 and 2); 8 Harpoon (Batch 3); 2 6-cell Sea Wolf launchers Guns: 1 4.5in/55 Mk 8 (3); 2 single 40mm (1 and 2); 2 single 20mm GAM-BO1 (on deployment); 1 30mm Goalkeeper (3) Torpedo tubes: 2 x 3 STWS for Mk 46 or Stingray torpedoes (except *Broadsword* and *Battleaxe*)
Aircraft: 2 Westland Lynx Mk 2 (only 1 normally carried; *Brave* and subsequent ships can operate Westland Sea King)
Sensors: Radar: Type 967 (967M from *Brave* on) and Type 968 surveillance: 2 Type 910 (Marconi 805 from *Brave* onwards) SAM control; Type 1006 navigation Sonar: Type 2050; Type 2008; Type 2031 towed array (2 and 3)
Complement: Batch 1 224; Batches 2 and 3 273

Background: The United Kingdom has an outstanding success with the Leander class anti-submarine frigates, which have had an excellent record of service in the Royal Navy and have also sold well overseas. After an unsuccessful attempt to agree a standard design with the Netherlands, the Type 22 frigate was designed as the Leanders' successor; the first of the class—HMS Broadsword— was laid down on February 7,1975, and commissioned on May 3, 1979, and another three Batch 1 vessels were commissioned at yearly intervals thereafter. Changes in the requirement led to the lengthened Batch 2, launched between 1981 and 1985, and Batch 3, which utilize the lengthened hull of Batch 2, but with armament revised to incorporate the lessons of the 1982 South Atlantic war. In the process the Type 22 has changed from a specialized ASW frigate to a multi-role destroyer, and the latest ships of the class are, in fact, virtually equal in dimensions and displacement to the Soviet Kynda class cruisers and larger than the British Type 42 destroyer. The Batch 1 ships, designed for the ASW mission, carry two triple Mk 32 torpedo tubes for Mk 46 and Stingray torpedoes and two Lynx helicopters. They also have an excellent anti-missile and anti-aircraft capability in their two six-cell Sea Wolf launchers, and anti-ship weapons in the form of two single MM39 Exocet launchers on the forecastle. It was then decided to fit so many additional facilities

Below: *HMS Battleaxe* (F 89), second of the Royal Navy's Type 22 frigates, as completed in 1980. All the later Type 22's have the smaller, more streamlined funnel apparent in the main illustration, while all but the first four (Batch 1) ships of the class have the lengthened hull evident in the line profiles opposite.

that the hull had to be lengthened by some 41 ft (12.9m), resulting in a 600-ton increase in displacement. This group, designated Batch 2 and sometimes referred to as the Boxer class, differ from the Batch 1 ships principally in having enlarged Action Information Organization (AIO) facilities to handle data from the new Type 2031 towed array sonar. Two very useful by-products of the stretching are an increase in range from 4,500nm to 7,000nm and an increase in maximum speed of about 2 knots. In addition, water displacement fuel tanks have been fitted to enable virtually all their fuel to be used without compromising stability, although no captain would allow his fuel stocks to run so low if he could avoid it. The first two ships of Batch 2 are otherwise identical to Batch 1, but the third (HMS Brave) has Rolls-Royce Speys in place of the Olympus in a COGOG arrange-

ment, while the fourth and fifth ships have Speys and Tynes in a COGAG arrangement. Batch 3 ships have the lengthened hull, towed array and larger AIO facilities of the Batch 2 and the Spey/Tyne CO-GAG arrangement of the later Batch 2s. Following the 1982 South Atlantic war, however, the decision was made to fit a Vickers 4.5in gun, to replace the Exocet SSMs by Harpoons, and to fit the Dutch Goalkeeper CIWS.

It is already planned to update the earlier units of the class by fitting new weapons and sensors wherever possible. This may include the replacement of Exocet by Harpoon, Sea Eagle or Otomat, and the fitting of the Type 2031 towed array in the Batch 1 ships. Vertical launch tubes for Seawolf will also be fitted, as will facilities to operate the much heavier Sea King or Merlin ASW helicopter.

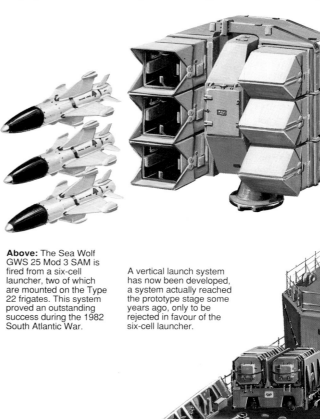

Above: The Sea Wolf GWS 25 Mod 3 SAM is fired from a six-cell launcher, two of which are mounted on the Type 22 frigates. This system proved an outstanding success during the 1982 South Atlantic War.

A vertical launch system has now been developed, a system actually reached the prototype stage some years ago, only to be rejected in favour of the six-cell launcher.

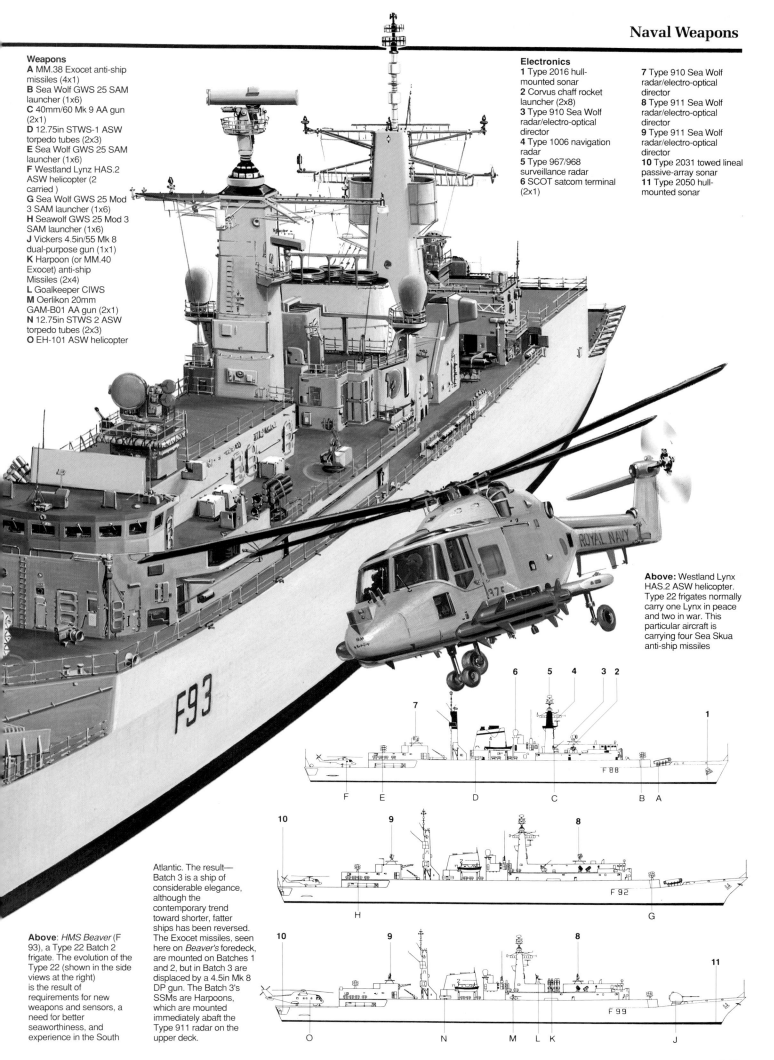

Weapons
A MM.38 Exocet anti-ship missiles (4x1)
B Sea Wolf GWS 25 SAM launcher (1x6)
C 40mm/60 Mk 9 AA gun (2x1)
D 12.75in STWS-1 ASW torpedo tubes (2x3)
E Sea Wolf GWS 25 SAM launcher (1x6)
F Westland Lynx HAS.2 ASW helicopter (2 carried)
G Sea Wolf GWS 25 Mod 3 SAM launcher (1x6)
H Seawolf GWS 25 Mod 3 SAM launcher (1x6)
J Vickers 4.5in/55 Mk 8 dual-purpose gun (1x1)
K Harpoon (or MM.40 Exocet) anti-ship Missiles (2x4)
L Goalkeeper CIWS
M Oerlikon 20mm GAM-B01 AA gun (2x1)
N 12.75in STWS 2 ASW torpedo tubes (2x3)
O EH-101 ASW helicopter

Electronics
1 Type 2016 hull-mounted sonar
2 Corvus chaff rocket launcher (2x8)
3 Type 910 Sea Wolf radar/electro-optical director
4 Type 1006 navigation radar
5 Type 967/968 surveillance radar
6 SCOT satcom terminal (2x1)
7 Type 910 Sea Wolf radar/electro-optical director
8 Type 911 Sea Wolf radar/electro-optical director
9 Type 911 Sea Wolf radar/electro-optical director
10 Type 2031 towed lineal passive-array sonar
11 Type 2050 hull-mounted sonar

Above: Westland Lynx HAS.2 ASW helicopter. Type 22 frigates normally carry one Lynx in peace and two in war. This particular aircraft is carrying four Sea Skua anti-ship missiles

Above: *HMS Beaver* (F 93), a Type 22 Batch 2 frigate. The evolution of the Type 22 (shown in the side views at the right) is the result of requirements for new weapons and sensors, a need for better seaworthiness, and experience in the South Atlantic. The result— Batch 3 is a ship of considerable elegance, although the contemporary trend toward shorter, fatter ships has been reversed. The Exocet missiles, seen here on *Beaver's* foredeck, are mounted on Batches 1 and 2, but in Batch 3 are displaced by a 4.5in Mk 8 DP gun. The Batch 3's SSMs are Harpoons, which are mounted immediately abaft the Type 911 radar on the upper deck.

149

Iowa (BB 61) class

Origin: USA
Type: Battleship (BB)
Built: 1940-1944
Class: 4 in service
Displacement: 45,000 tons standard; 58,000 tons full load
Dimensions: Length 887.2ft (270.4m) oa; beam 108.2ft (33m); draught 38ft (11.6m)
Propulsion: 4-shaft geared turbines. 212,000shp
Performance: Speed 30 knots; range 5,000nm at 30 knots, 15,000nm at 17 knots
Weapons: SSM: 8 quad Mk 43 launchers for Tomahawk; 4 quad launchers for Harpoon Guns: 9 16in/50 (3 x 3);12 5in/38 (Iowa and New Jersey); 20 5in/38 (Missouri, Wisconsin); 4 20mm Mk 15 Phalanx CIWS (New Jersey. Iowa, Missouri)
Aircraft: 4 LAMPS II or III helicopters
Sensors: Surface search radar: SPS-67(V) Air search radar: SPS-49(V) Navigation radar: LN-66
Complement: 1,606
Background: In 1938 the US Navy started design work on a new class of fast battleship to succeed the South Dakota class then building. Armed with nine 16in/50 guns in three triple turrets and 20 5in/38 DP guns, these ships had very powerful engines giving them a maximum speed of 33 knots and making them the fastest battleships ever built. They were also exceptionally well armoured, with a 12.1in (30.7cm) main belt designed to survive direct engagement by the 18in guns of the rumoured Japanese battleships. Commissioned in 1943-44, all four ships fought in the Pacific campaign; they were then placed in reserve in the late 1940s, when the era of the battleship was almost universally considered to be over. Reactivated during the Korean War (1950-53) for use in the shore bombardment role. they were then mothballed again, only for *New Jersey* to be reactivated once more in 1967 for use in the Vietnam War before

decommissioning for the third time in 1969. The appearance of the Soviet Navy's Kirov class battlecruisers resulted in yet another reappraisal of these elderly ships, and it was decided to reactivate them with the task of providing "a valuable supplement to the carrier force in performing presence and strike missions, while substantially increasing our ability to provide naval gunfire support for power projection and amphibious assault missions" (Caspar Weinberger, US DoD Annual Report to the Congress, FY1985). On December 28,1982, *USS New Jersey* joined the Pacific Fleet: starting her first operational deployment on June 9, 1983, she served first off Central America and later off Lebanon, before returning to the USA on May 5, 1984 after one of the US Navy's longest peacetime deployments. In 322 days at sea she covered a distance of some 76,000 miles (122,307km). *Iowa* was recommissioned in April 1984, to be followed by *Missouri* in July 1986 and *Wisconsin* in January 1988. The reactivation programme involves the modernization of all electronic and communications equipment, renovation of all accommodation and domestic utilities to meet contemporary standards, conversion to US Navy distillate fuel, the reshaping of the afterdeck to accommodate four LAMPS helicopters and the removal of extraneous equipment such as the aircraft crane. It was planned at one time to remove the rear turret and to install a proper aircraft hangar and a flight-deck, but this idea was dropped. The main armament remains the massive 16in guns firing armourpiercing projectiles weighing up to 2,700lb (1,225kg) to a maximum range of 23 miles (39km) at a theoretical rate of two rounds per gun per minute. Both barrels and ammunition are long out of production, but no fewer than 34 spare barrels remain in

storage, together with over 20,000 shells and charges. The secondary armament comprises 5in guns, but four of the original ten turrets have been removed to make way for eight quadruple Mk 143 Tomahawk SLCM launchers. Two quadruple Harpoon SSM launchers have been fitted either side of the after funnel, while four Phalanx CIWS mounts are also fitted, two just forward of the foremast and two forward of the after funnel. The reactivation of these ships is a triumph, achieved at a cost per ship less than that of a new Oliver Hazard Perry class frigate, and the US Navy owes a large debt of gratitude to the man who decided to preserve these fine ships instead of scrapping them, the fate of battleships in every other navy. Two, *Wisconsin* and *Missouri* played a major role in the Gulf War. By late 1991, these ships were to be returned to "mothball" status.

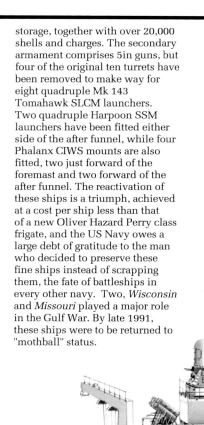

Left. *USS New Jersey* (BB 62) following her refurbishment and return to active duty. A far-sighted naval administrator ensured years ago that, instead of being scrapped like the battleships of other nations, these ships were preserved against some possible future requirement. His perspicacity served the US Navy well and, refitted and partially modernized at a cost less than that of one new Oliver Hazard Perry class frigate, these four ships are an important addition to the US Navy's global capability. Prominent in this view are the four Vulcan/Phalanx CIWS and the port Tomahawk SSM launchers between the funnels.

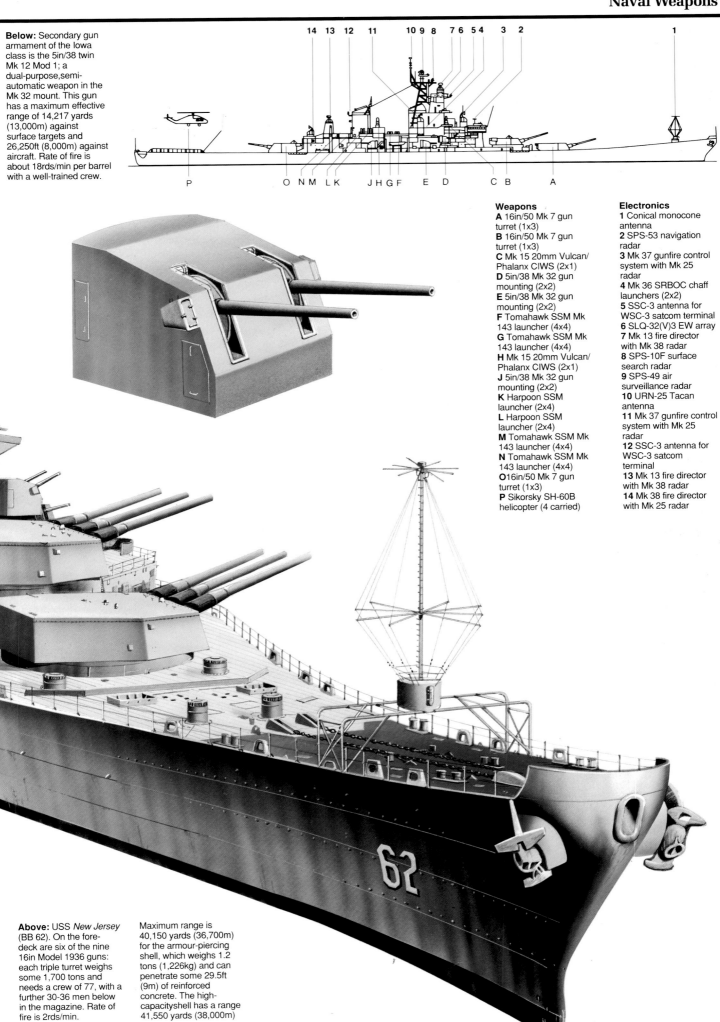

Below: Secondary gun armament of the Iowa class is the 5in/38 twin Mk 12 Mod 1; a dual-purpose,semi-automatic weapon in the Mk 32 mount. This gun has a maximum effective range of 14,217 yards (13,000m) against surface targets and 26,250ft (8,000m) against aircraft. Rate of fire is about 18rds/min per barrel with a well-trained crew.

Weapons
A 16in/50 Mk 7 gun turret (1x3)
B 16in/50 Mk 7 gun turret (1x3)
C Mk 15 20mm Vulcan/ Phalanx CIWS (2x1)
D 5in/38 Mk 32 gun mounting (2x2)
E 5in/38 Mk 32 gun mounting (2x2)
F Tomahawk SSM Mk 143 launcher (4x4)
G Tomahawk SSM Mk 143 launcher (4x4)
H Mk 15 20mm Vulcan/ Phalanx CIWS (2x1)
J 5in/38 Mk 32 gun mounting (2x2)
K Harpoon SSM launcher (2x4)
L Harpoon SSM launcher (2x4)
M Tomahawk SSM Mk 143 launcher (4x4)
N Tomahawk SSM Mk 143 launcher (4x4)
O 16in/50 Mk 7 gun turret (1x3)
P Sikorsky SH-60B helicopter (4 carried)

Electronics
1 Conical monocone antenna
2 SPS-53 navigation radar
3 Mk 37 gunfire control system with Mk 25 radar
4 Mk 36 SRBOC chaff launchers (2x2)
5 SSC-3 antenna for WSC-3 satcom terminal
6 SLQ-32(V)3 EW array
7 Mk 13 fire director with Mk 38 radar
8 SPS-10F surface search radar
9 SPS-49 air surveillance radar
10 URN-25 Tacan antenna
11 Mk 37 gunfire control system with Mk 25 radar
12 SSC-3 antenna for WSC-3 satcom terminal
13 Mk 13 fire director with Mk 38 radar
14 Mk 38 fire director with Mk 25 radar

Above: USS *New Jersey* (BB 62). On the fore-deck are six of the nine 16in Model 1936 guns: each triple turret weighs some 1,700 tons and needs a crew of 77, with a further 30-36 men below in the magazine. Rate of fire is 2rds/min.

Maximum range is 40,150 yards (36,700m) for the armour-piercing shell, which weighs 1.2 tons (1,226kg) and can penetrate some 29.5ft (9m) of reinforced concrete. The high-capacityshell has a range 41,550 yards (38,000m)

Kitty Hawk (CV 63) class

Origin: USA
Type: Multi-purpose aircraft carriers (CV)
Built: 1956-1968
Class: 4 in service
Displacement: 60,100-61,000 tons standard; 79,724-81,773 tons full load
Dimensions: Length 1,046-1,052ft (318.8-320.7m) oa; beam 130ft (39.6m); draught 37ft (11.3m)
Propulsion: 4-shaft (4 Westinghouse geared turbines), 280,000shp
Performance: 30 knots
Weapons: SAM: 3 Mk 29 launchers for NATO Sea Sparrow Guns: 3 20mm Phalanx Mk 15 CIWS.

Aircraft: 24 F-4 Phantom or F-14 Tomcat; 24 A-7 Corsair II or F/A-18 Hornet; 10 A-6 Intruder; 10 S-3 Viking; 6 SH-3 Sea King; 4 EA-6B Prowler; 4 KA-6 Intruder; 4 E-2 Hawkeye; 1 C-2A Greyhound
Sensors: Air search radar: (CV 63, 66) SPS-49(V) and SPS-48 (3D); (CV 64) SPS-37A, SPS-48C (3D); (CV 67) SPS-65(V), SPS-48C (3D). Surface search radar: SPS-10 series Fire control: Mk 91 MFCS for Sea Sparrow
Complement: 3,000, plus 2,480 air wing
Background: There are major differences between the first pair of aircraft carriers completed, *Kitty Hawk* (CV 63) and

Constellation (CV 64), and the second two, *America* (CV 66) and *John F Kennedy* (CV 67). These four ships are, however, generally grouped together because of their common propulsion systems and flight-deck layout. *Kitty Hawk* and *Constellation* were ordered as improved versions of the Forrestal class, incorporating a number of important modifications. The flight-deck was increased slightly in area, and the layout of the lifts revised to enhance aircraft-handling arrangements. On the Forrestals the port side lift is located at the forward end of the angled deck, making it unusable during landing operations, so the

lift was repositioned at the after end of the overhang on the Kitty Hawks, where it no longer interferes with flying operations. In addition, the centre lift on the starboard side has been repositioned to be ahead of the island structure, enabling two lifts to be used to serve the forward catapults. A further improved feature of the lifts themselves is that an angled section at the forward end enables longer aircraft to be accommodated. This arrangement is so successful that it has been copied in all subsequent US carriers. The third ship of the class, *America* (CV 66), was laid down four years

Above: *USS America* (CV 66) under way in the Indian Ocean, with F-14 Tomcats, A-6 Intruders, S-3 Vikings, E-2 Hawkeyes and other aircraft on the flight deck—the air wing is some 90 aircraft strong. One of three Mk 29 launchers for

the Mk 57 NATO Sea Sparrow surface-to-air missile system can be seen on the forward starboard sponson and the unique white radome of a Mk 15 Vucan Phalanx CIWS is just visible on the forward port sponson.

Below: USS *Constellation* (CV 64), second of this class to be completed. The huge extent of the flight deck makes an interesting comparison with carriers of earlier design. The three lifts are sited well clear of flying operations: the port side lift is at the after end of the overhang, while the two starboard lifts, serving the forward catapults, are sited ahead of the island. The relatively small landing area leaves a lot of deck space clear for launching and aircraft marshalling.

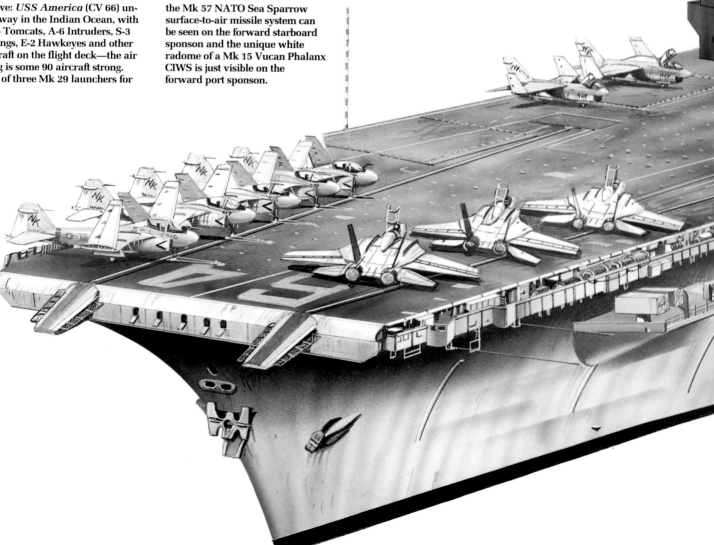

after *Constellation* and incorporates a number of further modifications. She has a narrower smokestack and is fitted with a bow anchor, in anticipation of the fitting of an SQS-23 sonar. It was decided in 1963 that the fourth carrier due to be laid down in FY1984 should be nuclear powered, but Congress flatly refused to fund it and the ship was finally built to a modified *Kitty Hawk* design as a conventionally-powered carrier. The major visible

differences are that the *John F Kennedy* has a canted stack– designed to keep the flight-deck clear of corrosive exhaust gases– and a flight deck of differently shaped forward end. The Terrier missile system, which consumed valuable space on the flight-deck and, in any case, duplicated similar area defence systems aboard the carrier escorts, was dropped in favour of the Mk 57 NATO Sea Sparrow Missile System and has subsequently been deleted from the previous three ships. These four ships are very powerful fighting units, second only to the US Navy's nuclear powered aircraft carriers in combat

capability. However, all recent US Congresses have set their faces against anything but nuclear power for ships of this size, rejecting proposals for a CVV in 1979 and for a modified *John F Kennedy* in 1980, finally forcing the President to order a fourth Nimitz class CVN in the FY80 programme. It would, therefore, seem that these four ships could be the last conventionally powered aircraft carriers to be build for the US Navy. All four of these carriers were to be modernized under the US Navy's Service Life Extension Programme (SLEP). *Kitty Hawk* was the first (July 21, 1987 to November 29,

1989) at a cost of $717 million, to be followed by Constellation (October 1989 to February 1992), America (April 1994 to August 1996) and finally Kennedy (July 1996 to November 1998). These 28-month refits will extend each ship's life by some 10-15 years. The work programme includes fitting new and more powerful catapults, updating the aircraft facilities, modernizing all electronics and extensive refurbish- ment of the hull, propulsion systems and electrics. The *Kitty Hawk's* condition is so good that a less extensive and much cheaper SLEP than anticipated was required.

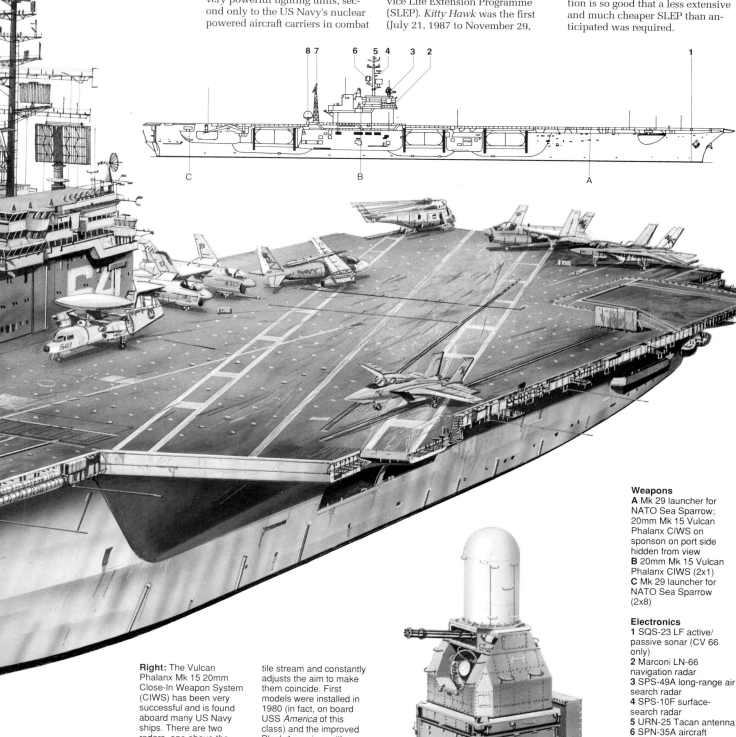

Right: The Vulcan Phalanx Mk 15 20mm Close-In Weapon System (CIWS) has been very successful and is found aboard many US Navy ships. There are two radars, one above the gun which tracks the target and a second below the gun which tracks the projectiles: an on-board computer correlates the target track and projec- tile stream and constantly adjusts the aim to make them coincide. First models were installed in 1980 (in fact, on board USS *America* of this class) and the improved Block 1 version, with more rounds and a higher rate of fire, entered service in 1983. The Block 1 also introduced the Mk 149 depleted uranium round.

Weapons
A Mk 29 launcher for NATO Sea Sparrow; 20mm Mk 15 Vulcan Phalanx CIWS on sponson on port side hidden from view
B 20mm Mk 15 Vulcan Phalanx CIWS (2x1)
C Mk 29 launcher for NATO Sea Sparrow (2x8)

Electronics
1 SQS-23 LF active/ passive sonar (CV 66 only)
2 Marconi LN-66 navigation radar
3 SPS-49A long-range air search radar
4 SPS-10F surface-search radar
5 URN-25 Tacan antenna
6 SPN-35A aircraft approach control radar
7 SPS-48C FRESCAN 3D air surveillance radar
8 OE-82 satellite communications antenna
9 Mk 91 Mod 1 director for NATO Sea Sparrow

Los Angeles (SSN 688) class

Origin: USA
Type: Nuclear-powered attack submarine (SSN)
Built: 1972
Class: 53 in service;
3 building;
Displacement: 6,000 tons standard; 6,900 tons submerged
Dimensions: Length 360ft (109.7m) oa; beam 33ft (10.1m); draught 32.3ft (9.9m)
Propulsion: l-shaft nuclear (1 S6G pressurized-water-cooled nuclear reactor; 2 geared turbines), 35.000shp
Performance: 30+ knots dived
Weapons: Torpedo tubes: 4x 21in (533mm) for conventional torpedoes, Subroc and Mk 48 A/S torpedoes; tube-launched Tomahawk SLCM in SSN 688-720 Vertical launch tubes: 15 for Tomahawk SLCM from SSN 721 onwards
Sensors: Sonar: BQQ-5 long-range; BQS-15 short-range; BQR-15 towed array Radar: BPS 15
Complement: 133
Background: In the late 1960s the US Navy was considering two separate classes of SSN: a highspeed attack and ASW submarine, and a very quiet type

intended for barrier operations. The latter requirement led to the *USS Glenard P Lipscomb* (SSN 685), the outcome of a development programme for a quiet submarine stretching back to *USS Tullibee* (SSN 597) of the early 1960s. The *Lipscomb*, which was launched in 1973, has many interesting features aimed at achieving silent running, a number of which have been incorporated into the Los Angeles class. Like *Tullibee*, *Lipscomb* is powered by a pressurized-water-cooled reactor driving a turbo-electric plant. This removes the requirement for gearing, which is one of the prime sources of noise in nuclear submarines. It was decided, however, that rather than go in for the considerable extra expense of two separate classes, the Los Angeles could perform both roles, and, although *Lipscomb* remains in front-line service, the turbo-electric drive system was not repeated in the Los Angeles class. The *USS Los Angeles* (SSN 688) entered service in 1976, and by the end of 1991 there were 53 in service. They are much larger than any previous US SSN and the hull is

optimised for high submerged speed, with a very small sail. One unfortunate consequence is that the sail-mounted planes cannot be rotated to the vertical so the Los Angeles class boats cannot break through ice. It has been reported that later boats will have their planes moved back to the more traditional bow position to restore the under-ice capability. The comprehensive sensor fit includes the BQQ-5 sonar system in the bows and a passive tactical towed sonar array. The cable and winch for the latter are mounted in the ballast tanks, but the array itself is housed in a prominent fairing running almost the entire length of the hull. The most remarkable feature of the class, however, is its armament. These powerful submarines are armed with Subroc and Sub-Harpoon, as well as conventional and wire-guided torpedoes. SSN 703, 704, 712 and 713 are already fitted to fire tube-launched Tomahawk and eventually all boats from SSN 688-720 will be able to carry up to 12 Tomahawk as part of their torpedo loads. From SSN 721 onward, however, 15 vertical

launch tubes for Tomahawk are fitted in the space in the bow between the inner and outer hulls, thus restoring the torpedo capacity. So, although their primary mission is still to hunt other submarines and to protect SSBNs, they can also be used without modification to sink surface ships at long range with Sub-Harpoon while Tomahawk enables them to operate against strategic targets well inland, as demonstrated in Iraq.

Right: The Los Angeles (SSN 688) class has proved to be one of the US Navy's great successes, with 35 in service, six building and a further seven on order. At a cost in 1981 dollars of some 495.8 million each, they represent one of the most costly military programmes in history. These are the most sophisticated attack submarines in any navy: their ASW armament comprises torpedoes (including the Mk 48) and Subroc, while Tomahawk cruise missiles provide a tactical and strategic capability against surface

targets. SSN 688-720 use the tube-launched version of Tomahawk, but SSN 721 onward have 15 Tomahawks in vertical launch tubes, thus restoring the full torpedo load. The hull design is exceptionally clean, with very few protuberances, though the mounting of the forward hydroplanes on the fin has led to criticism, especially of their inability to surface through ice, and it has recently been announced that in future designs the planes will be mounted in the traditional bow position. An improvement programme for the Los

Angeles class includes relocating the torpedo tubes in the bow, an increase in the number of tubes from six to eight, and enhancements to the command and control facilities. It is also likely that to achieve yet further sound reduction the hull will be coated with anechoic tiles, the first time this will have been done in the US, although it has been the practice of the British and Soviet navies for some time. The hull form, and especially the bow shape, makes an interesting contrast with that of the Soviet Oscar and Sierra classes.

From 1985 the Los Angeles class was given a mine-laying capability. The Los Angeles class is very sophisticated: each boat is an extremely potent fighting machine, and with a production run of at least 56 it must be considered a very successful design. However, these boats are becoming very expensive: the first cost $221.25 million, while the boat bought in 1979 cost 325.6 million, and the two in 1981 $495.8 million each. It would seem that not even the USA can

afford to go on spending money at that rate indefinitely. The Reagan Administration ordered a speeding-up of the Los Angeles building programme: two were built in 1982 and by 1986 the rate was three per year. The Tomahawk missile programme was also been accelerated, with these new missiles being fitted in SSN 719 onward. The new SSN 21 class of submarine, currently under development, in which the key design objective will be sound-quieting, will carry even more

weapons, have improved sensors and be able to operate under the ice more effectively. The new class is scheduled to enter service from 1995. There has been much criticism of the complexity and cost of the Los Angeles design, and it is alleged that too many sacrifices were made to achieve the very high speed. A design for a cheaper and smaller SSN, under consideration in 1980 as a result of Congressional pressure, was later shelved, but may well reappear, especially if the

proposed new class should turn out to be even more expensive than the Los Angeles, which is entirely possible. Meanwhile, there are plans to improve the Los Angeles boats, especially their sensors, weapon systems and control equipment. Such-improvements will include moving the torpedo tubes back to the bow and increasing their number to eight. The Los Angeles boats will also probably be the first US submarines to be given anechoic tile coatings.

Left: *USS Salt Lake City* **(SSN 716) on trials prior to commissioning. The long fairing running down the starboard side of the boat houses the BQR-15 towed array. SSN 716 is one of the earlier units of the class with tube-launched Tomahawk; the vertical-launch version is fitted in SSN 721 onward.**

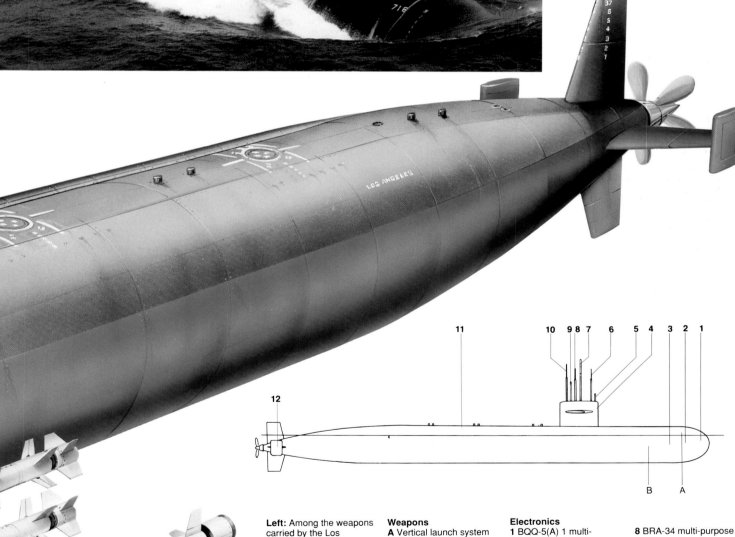

Left: Among the weapons carried by the Los Angeles class SSNs are UUM-44A-2 SUBROC (far left), UGM-84 Sub-Harpoon (centre) and BGM-109 submarine launched Tomahawk (right). In addition, any of the current range of US Navy torpedoes can be carried. These are the most heavily armed submarines ever deployed.

Weapons
A Vertical launch system (VLS) for Tomahawk anti-ship missiles (from SSN 721)
B 21 in torpedo tubes (2x2) for Harpoon SSM (4 carried); Tomahawk SSM (8 carried SSN 703/704/712/713); Subrock ASW missiles (to be superseded by Sea Lance ASW/SOW) Mk 48 ASW torpedoes; total 25 weapons

Electronics
1 BQQ-5(A) 1 multi-purpose spherical sonar array
2 Hydrophone array
3 BQR-21 DIMUS (Digital MUltibeam Steering) sonar conformal array
4 BQS-15 short-range sonar array
5 BPS-15 surface detection radar
6 BRA-34 multi-purpose antenna group
7

8 BRA-34 multi-purpose antenna group
9 General-purpose periscope Type 15B Mod 1
10 BRD-7 radio directionfinding antenna
11 BRQ-15 towed array fairing
12 Hydrophone array

Nimitz (CVN 68) class

Origin: USA
Type: Nuclear-powered aircraft carrier (CVN)
Built: 1968-1991
Class: 6 in service
Displacement: (Nimitz) 72,798 tons light; 90,944 tons full load; (Others) 72,916 tons light; 91,487 tons full load
Dimensions: Length 1,092ft (332.9m) oa; beam 134ft (40.8m); draught 37ft (11.3m)
Propulsion: 4-shaft nuclear (2 A4W/A1G pressurized-water-cooled nuclear reactors; 4 geared teamn turbines). 260,000shp
Performance: 30 + knots
Weapons: Guns: 3 20mm Phalanx CIWS (Nimitz, Eisenhower); 4 20mm Phalanx CIWS (remainder) SAM: 3 Basic Point Defence Missile System (BPDMS) launchers for Sea Sparrow
Aircraft: 24 F-14A or F-14D Tomcat; 24 F/A-18 Hornet: 10 A-6E Intruder; 4 KA-6D Intruder; 5 E-2C Hawkeye; 5 EA-6B Prowler; 10 S-3B Viking; 6 SH-3H Sea King
Sensors: Radar: SPS-48 3D air search; SPS-43A air search (Nimitz, Eisenhower) SPS-49(V) air search (others); SPS-10F surface search (Nimitz, Eisenhower, Vinson); SPS-67(V), SPS-64 surface search (others); LN-66 navigation
Complement: 3,300, plus 2,800 air wing
Background: The Nimitz class aircraft carriers are the mightiest and most powerful warships in history. Each ship normally carries some 90 aircraft whose capabilities range from nuclear strike, through interception and ground-attack to close-in anti-submarine protection —a more powerful and better balanced tactical air force than many national air forces. Each carrier is manned by a crew of 3,300 with an air wing of a further 2,800. And their nuclear reactors have cores which enable them to operate for thirteen years at a stretch, equivalent to steaming up to one million miles. Such extraordinary statistics will only be challenged when the Soviet Navy's nuclear-powered supercarriers enter service in the late1990s, and it is, in fact, the perceived threat from the Nimitz class that has caused such massive development in the Soviet Navy over the past 15 years. The original nuclear-powered carrier, *USS Enterprise* (CVN 65), commissioned in 1961, was built in the remarkably short time of 45 months and was so successful that, when the time came to plan a replacement for the Midway class, nuclear power was the preferred means of propulsion. The advances that had been made meant that the eight A2W reactors used in *Enterprise* (each producing 35,000shp) could be replaced by just two A4W reactors, each producing approximately 130,000shp. In addition, the uranium cores need to be replaced much less frequently than those originally used in *Enterprise*. This

Right: *USS Carl Vinson* (CVN 70) approaching Pearl Harbor, with virtually her entire air wing and most of her crew on deck for the entry into the naval base.

reduction in the number of reactors also permitted major improvements in the internal arrangements below hangar deck level. In *Enterprise* the entire centre section of the ship is occupied by machinery rooms, with the aviation fuel compartments and the missile magazines pushed out towards the end of the ship, but in *Nimitz* the propulsion machinery is divided into two separate units with the magazines between and forward of them. The improved layout has resulted in an increase of 20 per cent in aviation fuel capacity and a similar increase in the volume available for munitions and stores. The flight-deck layout for the Nimitz class is almost identical to that of the *John F Kennedy* (CV 67) of the Kitty Hawk class. The provision of defensive weapons and sensors on the first two—*Nimitz* (CVN 68) and *Eisenhower* (CVN 69)—was initially on a par with that on the *John F Kennedy* (CV 67), although the third ship, *Carl Vinson* (CVN 70), has NATO Sea Sparrow and

Phalanx in place of the BPDMS launchers on earlier ships, which will be similarly fitted in the near future. This parallels the increase in defensive armament taking place on the carriers of other navies. *Vinson* is also fitted with an ASW control centre and specialized maintenance facilities for the S-3 Viking; these will also be installed in *Nimitz* and *Eisenhower* at future refits. Delays in construction caused by shipyard problems resulted in rocketing costs and in the late 1970s the Carter Administration attempted unsuccessfully to block authorization funds for the construction of a fourth carrier in favour of a smaller (50,000 ton), conventionally-powered design,

known as the CVV. However, the CVV was never popular with the US Navy, and the Reagan Administration committed itself to the continuation of the CVN programme. Current deployment has *Eisenhower* and *Roosevelt* in the Atlantic and *Nimitz* and *Vinson* in the Pacific.

Right: Raytheon RIM-7H Sea Sparrow missile being launched from a Mk 29 lightweight launcher; Mk 25 launchers are installed on *Eisenhower* (CVN 69). The Basic Point Defence Missile System (BPDMS) Sea Sparrow system used Asroc launchers and RIM-7E versions of the AIM-7E Sparrow missile.

Below: The sheer size of these nuclear carriers can be gauged from the way the aircraft are dwarfed by the flight deck. The Carrier Air Wing carried by each of the CVNs is larger and better balanced than most national air forces. The CAW usually comprises 24 F-14 Tomcats, 24 F/A-18 Hornets, 10 A-6E Intruders, four KA-6D Intruder tankers, five E-2C Hawkeye AEW aircraft, 10 S-3B Viking ASW aircraft, and six SH-3H Sea King ASW helicopters plus transports.

Weapons
A Mk 29 launcher for NATO Sea Sparrow SAM (1x8)
B Mk 15 20mm Vulcan Phalanx CIWS (2x1)
C Mk 29 launcher for NATO Sea Sparrow SAM (2x8)
D Mk 15 20mm Vulcan Phalanx CIWS (2x1)

Electronics
1 LN-66 navigation radar
2 SPS-48B 3D long-range air surveillance radar
3 SPS-10F surface search radar
4 URN-20 Tacan antenna
5 SPS-49 2D air search radar
6 SPS-43A long-range air search radar

Oliver Hazard Perry (FFG 7) class

Origin: USA
Type: Frigate (FFG)
Built: 1975
Class: (US Navy) 51 in service: (Royal Australian Navy) 5 in service: 1 building (Royal Spanish Navy) 4 in service:
Displacement: 2,750 tons light; 3,605 tons full load
Dimensions: Length 445ft (135.6m) oa; beam 45ft (13.7m); draught 14.8ft (4.5m) keel, 24.5ft (7.5m) sonar
Propulsion: l-shaft gas turbine (2 General Electric LM2500), 40,000shp
Performance: Speed 29 knots; range 4,500nm at 20 knots
Weapons: Missiles: 1 Mk 13 launcher for Harpoon SSM (4 carried) and Standard SAM (36 carried)
Guns: 1 3in Mk 75;1 20mm Phalanx CIWS Torpedo tubes: 2 x 3 Mk 32
Aircraft: 2 LAMPS helicopters
Sensors: Radar: SPS-49 long-range search: SPS-55 search and navigation; STIR (modified SPG-60) weapon control
Sonar: SQS-56 hull mounted; SQR19 TACTAS towed array (US Navy FFG 36-43, 45-60).
Complement: 185
Background: The Oliver Hazard Perry (FFG 7) class originated in the Patrol Frigate programme, which was to constitute the cheaper component of a high/low technology mix, providing large numbers of escorts with reduced capabilities and correspondingly reduced price. These were intended to balance the very expensive specialized ASW and AAW ships, whose primary mission was to protect carriers, and strict limitations were placed on cost, displacement and manpower.

The FFG 7s have been built in small yards utilizing simple construction techniques, making maximum use of flat panels and bulkheads and ensuring that internal passageways are kept as straight as possible. In addition, the hull structure is prefabricated in modules of varying size (35,100,200 or 400 tons) to permit shipyards to select the most convenient size for their capabilities. As with the US Navy's previous frigate classes, the Perrys have only one screw, but the use of gas turbines means that engine-room layout is much more compact. The gas turbines are of the same model used in the Spruance class, and are located side by side in a single engine room. An unusual feature is that two small retractable propulsion pods are fitted just aft of the sonar dome to provide emergency power and to give assistance in docking; each has a 325hp engine, and the two in combination can propel the ship at a speed of some 10 knots. The armament is air-defence orientated, including a Mk 13 launcher forward for Standard (MR) SAMs and Harpoon ASMs.

and an OTO-Melara 76mm (US Navy Mk 75) gun on top of the superstructure. Asroc is not fitted, but there is a large hangar aft for the two LAMPS helicopters. Starting with *USS Underwood* (FFG 36), the Rapid Haul Down and Traversing System (RAST) was installed, necessitating an 8ft (2.4m) increase in overall length. This is achieved by angling out the ship's transom to approximately 45°, and without increasing the waterline length. RAST, TACTAS and LAMPS III support facilities were installed in all new-build ships from FFG 36 onward. RAST and LAMPS III support facilities will not, at least for the time being, be retrofitted into the earlier ships (FFG 7, 9-16 and 19-34), which will continue to operate LAMPS I (FFG 8 was used as the prototype for the LAMPS III conversion). The SQS-56 sonar, hull-mounted inside a rubber dome, is a new type, much less sophisticated than the SQS-26. It was planned, however, that the FFG 7 class frigates would operate in company with other frigates equipped with the SQS-26 and would receive target information from sensors on board those ships via data links. The success of the design can be gauged from the large numbers built for the US Navy and the fact that it was also ordered by the Royal Australian and Royal Spanish Navies. The former took delivery of four built in the USA, with another two ordered for construction in Australia, while the latter took delivery of its first two FFG 7 frigates in 1986, when it had a further three on order. The FFG 7 has been tailored to accommodate only those systems envisaged currently or in the near future, including the SH-60 LAMPS III, SQR-19 towed tactical array, fin stablizers, Link 11 data transfer system and Phalanx CIWS. Once these have been installed, however, there remains only a further 50-ton margin for additional equipment.

Fifty-one of the class are currently in service with the US Navy. The Royal Australian Navy ordered two to be built to a slightly modified design in Australia (in addition to four built in the US); these were completed in 1991 and 1993. Five were built at Ferrol by Bazan for the Royal Spanish Navy. The first was commissioned in 1986 and the remainder joined the fleet between late 1986 and 1990.

Below: *USS Robert E Bradley* (FFG 49) showing her flight deck, large hangars, Vulcan/Phalanx CIWS and SPG-60 STIR search and tracking radar. These ships have good protection against fragmentation and splinter damage, including 3/4in (1.9cm) Kevlar over vital compartments.

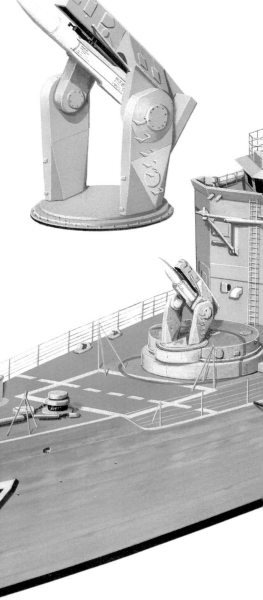

Right: The RIM-66B Standard SM-1 (MR) missile has a range of 25nm (46.3km) and uses semi-active homing. The FFG 7 frigates now carry SM-1 (MR) Block 6 missiles with a digital computer and monpulse radar, and 36 are stored in a below-deck magazine. The SM-1 (MR) is fired from a single-arm Mk 13 launcher, which is also capable of firing Harpoon anti-ship missiles four are carried in the same magazine). The Mk 92 Mod 4 system controls the fire of both the SAMs and the 76mm Mk 75 dual-purpose gun, using a STIR antenna and a US built HSA WM-28 radar.

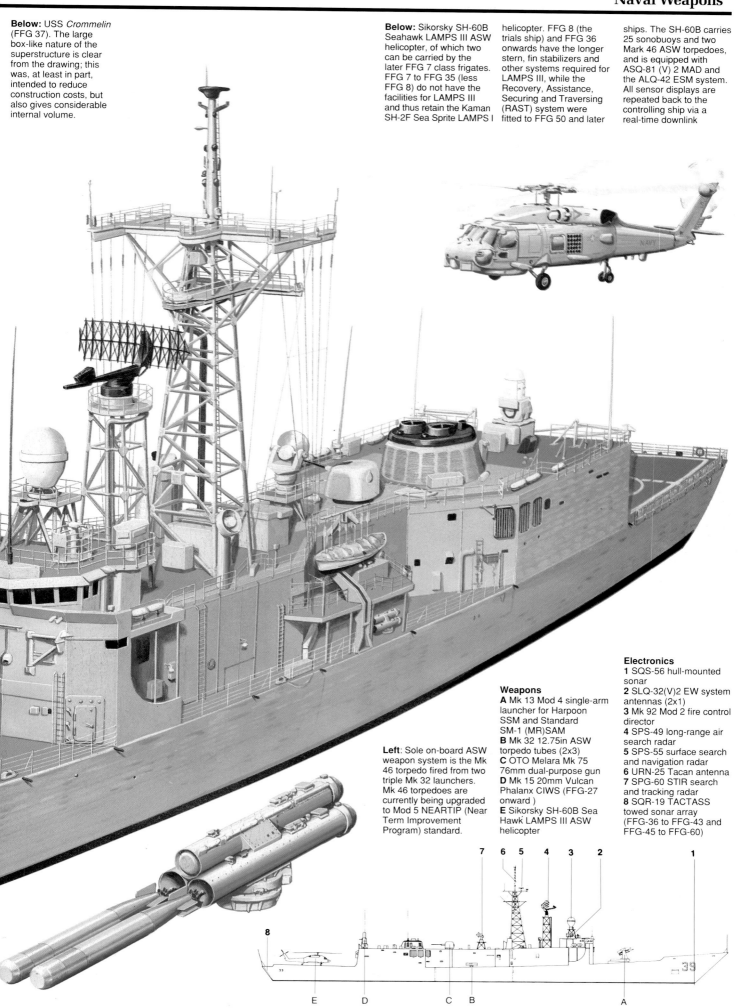

Below: USS *Crommelin* (FFG 37). The large box-like nature of the superstructure is clear from the drawing; this was, at least in part, intended to reduce construction costs, but also gives considerable internal volume.

Below: Sikorsky SH-60B Seahawk LAMPS III ASW helicopter, of which two can be carried by the later FFG 7 class frigates. FFG 7 to FFG 35 (less FFG 8) do not have the facilities for LAMPS III and thus retain the Kaman SH-2F Sea Sprite LAMPS I helicopter. FFG 8 (the trials ship) and FFG 36 onwards have the longer stern, fin stabilizers and other systems required for LAMPS III, while the Recovery, Assistance, Securing and Traversing (RAST) system were fitted to FFG 50 and later ships. The SH-60B carries 25 sonobuoys and two Mark 46 ASW torpedoes, and is equipped with ASQ-81 (V) 2 MAD and the ALQ-42 ESM system. All sensor displays are repeated back to the controlling ship via a real-time downlink

Left: Sole on-board ASW weapon system is the Mk 46 torpedo fired from two triple Mk 32 launchers. Mk 46 torpedoes are currently being upgraded to Mod 5 NEARTIP (Near Term Improvement Program) standard.

Weapons
A Mk 13 Mod 4 single-arm launcher for Harpoon SSM and Standard SM-1 (MR)SAM
B Mk 32 12.75in ASW torpedo tubes (2x3)
C OTO Melara Mk 75 76mm dual-purpose gun
D Mk 15 20mm Vulcan Phalanx CIWS (FFG-27 onward)
E Sikorsky SH-60B Sea Hawk LAMPS III ASW helicopter

Electronics
1 SQS-56 hull-mounted sonar
2 SLQ-32(V)2 EW system antennas (2x1)
3 Mk 92 Mod 2 fire control director
4 SPS-49 long-range air search radar
5 SPS-55 surface search and navigation radar
6 URN-25 Tacan antenna
7 SPG-60 STIR search and tracking radar
8 SQR-19 TACTASS towed sonar array (FFG-36 to FFG-43 and FFG-45 to FFG-60)

Sheffield (Type 42) class

Origin: United Kingdom
Type: Destroyer (DDG)
Built: 1972-1985
Class: (Batch 1) 4 in service (Batch 2) 4 in service (Batch 3) 4 in service
Displacement: (1 and 2) 3,500 tons standard: 4,100 tons full load (3) 4,775 tons full load
Dimensions: (1 and 2) Length 412ft (125m) oa; beam 47ft (14.3m); draught 19ft (5.8m) (3) Length 462ft (141.1m) oa; beam 49ft (14.9m); draught 19ft (5.8m)
Propulsion: 2-shaft COGOG (2 Rolls-Royce Olympus TM3B and 2 Rolls-Royce Tyne RMIC gas turbines), 50,000/9,700shp
Performance: Speed 29 knots (30 knots 3); range 4,000nm at 18 knots **Armament:** SAM: 1 x 2 Sea Dart launcher (22 missiles)
Guns: 1 x 4.5in/55 Mk 8; 2 20mm Oerlikon (GAM-B01)
Aircraft: 1 Lynx Mk 2 helicopter
Sensors: Radar: Type 1022 search; Type 992Q/R surveillance and target indication; 2 Type 909 Sea Dart fire control; Type 1006 navigation
Sonar: Type 184M (Type 2016 in later ships) hull mounted
Complement: (1 and 2) 253; (3) 301
Background: Area air defence for Royal Navy carrier-based task forces was provided in the 1960s and 1970s by the County class destroyers armed with the Sea Slug SAM and these were to have been followed by the Bristol class (Type 82) guided-missile destroyers. These three-funnel warships of 7,100 tons full load displacement were designed around the smaller, more capable Sea Dart SAM with a single 4.5in Mk 8 mount and an Ikara ASM launcher forward. Their great cost (over £30 million at 1970 prices), coupled with the cancellation of the aircraft carrier CVA-01, led to the cancellation of the class as a whole, although one Type 82—*HMS Bristol* (D 23)—was actually completed. The Type 42 class was designed as a cheaper, smaller and less sophisticated version of *Bristol*, although the vessels are still complex and highly automated vessels, and the latest of the class cost some £78.5-85 million each at 1979 prices. They have the Rolls-Royce Olympus/Type COGOG machinery combination, which is virtually standard for this generation of surface warships in the Royal Navy, and a hangar and flight deck aft for a Lynx ASW helicopter. The Sea Dart SAM has a limited SSM capability and the single launcher is fitted forward between the gun mount and the bridge. The unsightly and extremely unpopular exhausts fitted to Sheffield's funnel to overcome efflux problems were removed and have not featured on any other ships of the class. Two ships of this class were lost during the 1982 South Atlantic war. On May 4 *HMS Sheffield* sank after being hit by an air-launched Exocet several days earlier, while on May 25 *HMS Coventry* was hit by several bombs which exploded in or near her machinery spaces, and she capsized shortly afterwards with the loss of 19 lives. The third batch of ships of this class has been completed to a rather different design, with beam and length increased, in an operation similar to that performed on the Type 22 frigates, to improve speed and sea-keeping qualities and to provide more space for weapon systems, although it goes against the modern concept of shorter, beamier ships. These later ships also incorporate a number of improvements based on experiences with their sisters in the South Atlantic war.

A number of ships of this class took part in the 1982 South Atlantic war and two—Sheffield and Coventry—were lost in combat. This led to a reappraisal of the weapons fit and extra mountings can be embarked on all ships when required. These will normally comprise two BMARC twin 30mm and two extra single 20mm (GAM-B01) at either side of the forward end of the hangar. Consideration is also being given to fitting the vertical launch version of Sea Wolf. If this goes ahead *Birmingham* (Batch 1) will probably be the first to be so fitted. Perhaps the major area of controversy in future British surface warship design is that of the hull shape of destroyer/frigate sized ships. So involved and heated have the arguments been between the traditional 'long thin' and the innovatory 'short fat' schools become that an unofficial committee, chaired by former Chief of the Defence Staff Admiral of the Fleet Lord Hill-Norton, has examined the whole issue. It reported in June 1986 that an official enquiry, chaired by an independent expert, was needed to resolve the issues, having concluded that the shorter, beamier S90 frigate (designed by naval architects Thornycroft Giles and Associates) could be built for £73.8 million compared with £100 million for the new officially designed Type 23.

Right: The Westland Lynx HAS.2 has proved itself to be an excellent ASW weapons system. It carries two Mk 44 or Mk 46 ASW torpedoes or up to four Sea Skua air-to-surface missiles.

Right: Having followed the common trend and progressively reduced close-in anti-aircraft gun armament during the 1960s and 1970s, the Royal Navy found itself woefully short of such systems in the 1982 South Atlantic War. Various weapons were hastily procured, including the Vulcan/Phalanx CIWS (which were fitted to the carriers), Oerlikon single 20mm Type GAM-B01 and Oerlikon 30mm twin GCM-A02 (shown here). Eight GCM-A02 mounts were acquired, all of which were fitted to Type 42 destroyers. In the long term, however, the US Phalanx is being progressively fitted to this class.

Left: Type 42 Batch 1 guided-missile destroyer, *HMS Glasgow* (D 88), which suffered a fire during fitting-out; her completion was much delayed as a result. The 4.5in Mk 8 DP gun shares the foredeck with the Sea Dart GWS 30 Mod 2 guided missile system. Note the huge twin-stack Type 965M radar and the two radomes for the Type 909 fire control radar, which controls both the Sea Dart missiles and the 4.5in gun. Two of the class, *Sheffield* (D 80) and *Coventry* (D 118), were lost in the South Atlantic War, the first to an Exocet, the second to bombs.

Weapons
A Vickers 4.5in/55 Mk 8 dual-purpose automatic gun (1 x1)
B GWS 30 Mod 2 Sea Dart SAM launcher (1 x2)
C 20mm AA gun (2x1)
D 12.75in STWS-1 ASW torpedo tubes (2x3)
E Westland Lynx HAS.2 ASW helicopter
F 30mm Oerlikon GCM-A02 AA gun (2x1)
G 20mm Oerlikon GAM-B01 AA gun (2x1)

Electronics
1 Type 162M sonar
2 Type 184M sonar
3 Type 909 fire control radar for GWS 30 Sea Dart system and gunlaying
4 Type 965M long-range air search radar
5 SCOT satellite communications antenna
6 Type 1006 navigation radar
7 Type 992Q surface/air target information radar
8 Corvus chaff rocket launcher (2x8)
9 Type 909 fire control radar for GWS 30 Sea Dart system/gunlaying
10 Mk36 Super RBOC chaff rocket launcher (2x6)
11 Type 2016 sonar
12 Type 1002 air search radar

Type 42 Batch 1
Birmingham (D86)
as completed, 1976

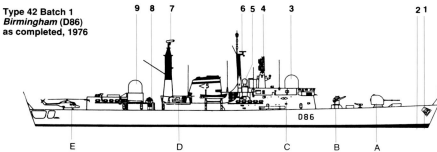

Type 42 Batch 1
Cardiff (D108)
post-Falklands, 1982

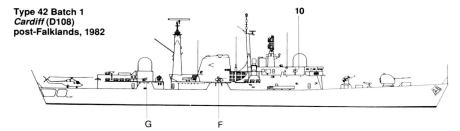

Type 42 Batch 3
Manchester

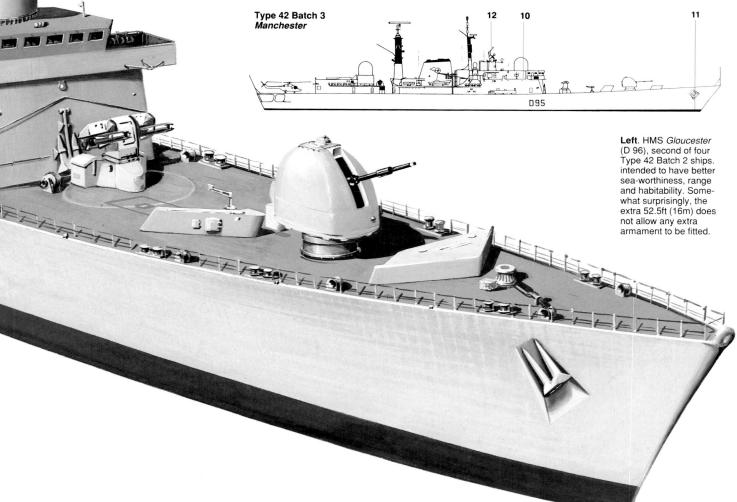

Left. HMS *Gloucester* (D 96), second of four Type 42 Batch 2 ships. intended to have better sea-worthiness, range and habitability. Somewhat surprisingly, the extra 52.5ft (16m) does not allow any extra armament to be fitted.

Spruance (DD 963) class

Origin: USA
Type: Destroyer (DDG)
Built: 1972-1983
Class: 31 Spruance plus 4 Kidd class in service
Displacement: 5,770 tons light; 7,810 tons full load
Dimensions: Length 563.2ft (171.7m) oa; beam 55.1ft (16.8m); draught 29ft (8.8m) sonar, 19ft (5.8m) keel
Propulsion: 2-shaft gas turbine (4 General Electric LM2500), 80,000shp
Performance: Speed 33 knots; range 6,000nm at 20 knots
Weapons: SSM: 2 x 4 Harpoon launchers SAM: 1 NATO Sea Sparrow Mk 29 launcher Guns: 2 x 1 5in/54 Mk 45; 2 20mm Phalanx Mk 15 CIWS ASW weapons: 1 8-tube Asroc launcher (24 rounds); 2 x 3 Mk 32 torpedo tubes (14 torpedoes)
Aircraft: 1 SH-3 Sea King or two SH-2D LAMPS II helicopters
Sensors: Radar: SPS-55 and SPS-40 search (SPS-49(V) in DD 997); SPG-60 and SPQ-9A fire control Sonar: SQS-53 or SQS 53C hull-mounted; SQR-19 TACTAS towed array
Complement: 296
Background: One of several postwar classes to arouse considerable controversy, especially in the US Congress, the Spruance class was designed to replace the war-built destroyers of the Gearing and Sumner classes, which, despite modernization programmes, were nearing the end of their useful lives by the early 1970s. The Spruances epitomize the US Navy's design philosophy of the 1970s, with their large hulls and block superstructures maximizing internal volume. They would be fitted with machinery that was easy to maintain or replace and equipped with high-technology weapon systems that could be added to or updated by modular replacement at a later date. The object was to minimize platform costs in favour of greater expenditure on the weapon systems payload in order to ensure that the ships would remain in the front-line throughout their 30-year life expectancy. In a further attempt to minimize platform costs the entire class was ordered from a single builder (Litton/Ingalls), which invested heavily in a major production facility at Pascagoula, using advanced modular construction techniques. The only visible weapon systems aboard the Spruances are two single 5in Mk 45 lightweight gun mountings and an Asroc box launcher forward of the bridge. In view of the size and cost of the ships this caused an immediate public outcry. The advanced ASW capabilities of the ships are, however, largely hidden within the hull and the bulky superstructure. The Asroc launcher, for example, has a magazine beneath it containing no fewer than 24 reloads, while the

accommodate two LAMPS II helicopters and two sliding doors on either side of the superstructure conceal triple Mk 32 torpedo tubes and torpedo handling rooms. Of even greater significance are the advanced submarine detection features of the class. The SQS-53C bow sonar can operate in a variety of active and passive modes, including direct path, bottom-bounce and convergence zone. This system has proved so successful that the SQS-35 VDS initially scheduled was never fitted. The all-gas turbine propulsion system, with paired General Electric LM2500 gas turbines en echelon, was selected primarily for its ease of maintenance and low manning requirements. Gas turbines also have significant advantages in reducing underwater noise emission and the Spruances are therefore capable of near-silent ASW operations. The Spruances are fitted with the latest computerized data systems in well designed Combat Information Centres. They also have the most up-to-date digital fire control systems in the Mk 86 Gun Fire Control System and the Mk 116 underwater system.
Besides the weapon systems fitted on completion, the ships of the Spruance class were designed to accept a variety of other systems then at the design stage. All ships have now received the Sea Sparrow Improved Point Defence System (IPDMS) and Harpoon anti-ship missiles (aft of the forward funnel), and three Whiskey-3 (WSC-3) satellite communications transceivers and SLQ-32(V)2 ECM systems have also been fitted. The inherent flexibility of the Spruance design is such that it has formed the basis for the new Ticonderoga class Aegis cruisers. The Kidd class also stemmed from the Spruance design: originally destined for the Imperial Iranian Navy, and optimized for the general warfare role rather than ASW, the four-ship order was cancelled following the Iranian revolution, and the ships were purchased by the US Navy and completed as designed, making them the most powerful destroyers in the fleet. The major difference from the Spruances is

Starting from the FY85 overhauls, major improvements were made to the Spruances to enable them to remain effective ASW units well into the next century. Improvements include the installation of the LAMPS III shipboard electronics and the Recovery Assist Secure and Traverse system (RAST) for helicopter handling. An improved version of the 5in/54 Mk 65 gun is

under consideration, and the Tomahawk system is being fitted in all ships of the class, as will the Mk 41 Vertical Launch System with a 61-round magazine in place of the Asroc.

Below: *USS Deyo (DD 989). Like many US ships, the Spruance class was subject to ill-informed criticism in their early days, but their merits are now appreciated.*

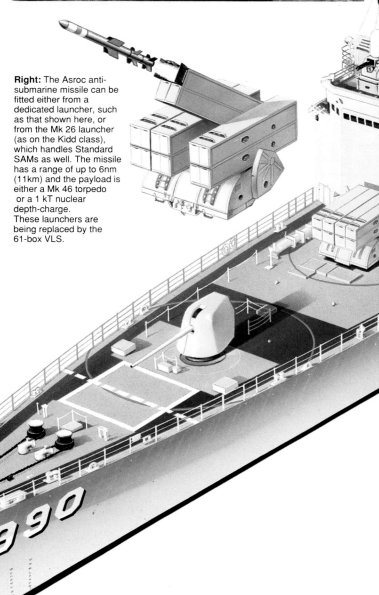

Right: The Asroc anti-submarine missile can be fitted either from a dedicated launcher, such as that shown here, or from the Mk 26 launcher (as on the Kidd class), which handles Standard SAMs as well. The missile has a range of up to 6nm (11km) and the payload is either a Mk 46 torpedo or a 1 kT nuclear depth-charge. These launchers are being replaced by the 61-box VLS.

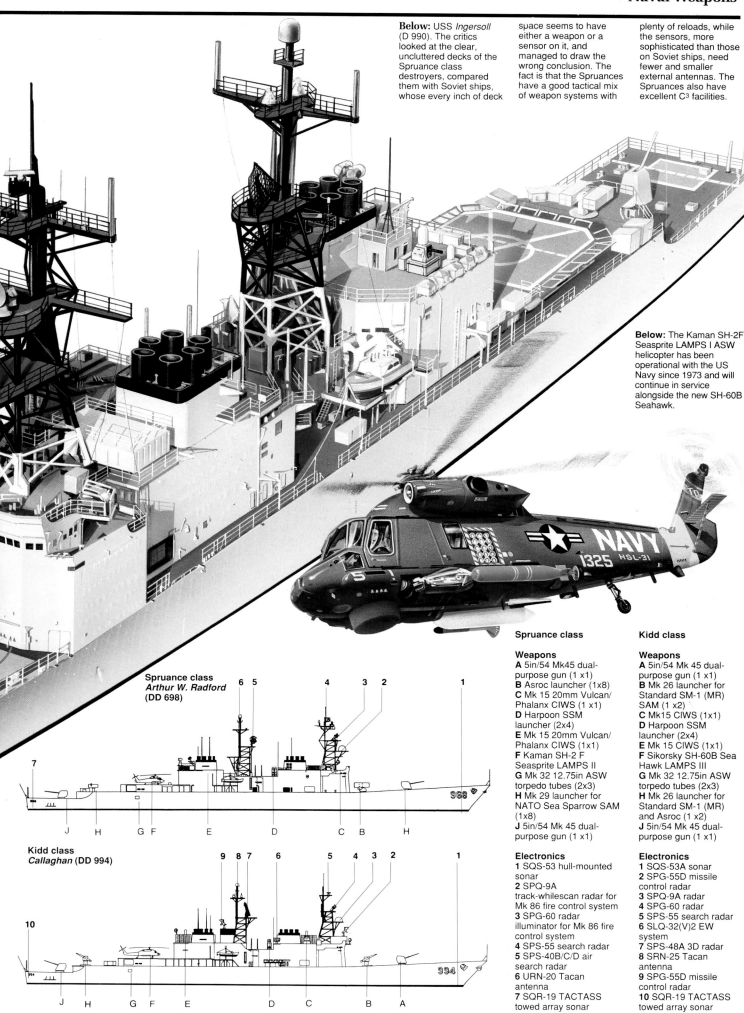

Below: USS *Ingersoll* (D 990). The critics looked at the clear, uncluttered decks of the Spruance class destroyers, compared them with Soviet ships, whose every inch of deck space seems to have either a weapon or a sensor on it, and managed to draw the wrong conclusion. The fact is that the Spruances have a good tactical mix of weapon systems with plenty of reloads, while the sensors, more sophisticated than those on Soviet ships, need fewer and smaller external antennas. The Spruances also have excellent C³ facilities.

Below: The Kaman SH-2F Seasprite LAMPS I ASW helicopter has been operational with the US Navy since 1973 and will continue in service alongside the new SH-60B Seahawk.

Spruance class
Arthur W. Radford
(DD 698)

Kidd class
Callaghan (DD 994)

Spruance class

Weapons
A 5in/54 Mk45 dual-purpose gun (1 x1)
B Asroc launcher (1x8)
C Mk 15 20mm Vulcan/Phalanx CIWS (1 x1)
D Harpoon SSM launcher (2x4)
E Mk 15 20mm Vulcan/Phalanx CIWS (1x1)
F Kaman SH-2 F Seasprite LAMPS II
G Mk 32 12.75in ASW torpedo tubes (2x3)
H Mk 29 launcher for NATO Sea Sparrow SAM (1x8)
J 5in/54 Mk 45 dual-purpose gun (1 x1)

Electronics
1 SQS-53 hull-mounted sonar
2 SPQ-9A track-whilescan radar for Mk 86 fire control system
3 SPG-60 radar illuminator for Mk 86 fire control system
4 SPS-55 search radar
5 SPS-40B/C/D air search radar
6 URN-20 Tacan antenna
7 SQR-19 TACTASS towed array sonar

Kidd class

Weapons
A 5in/54 Mk 45 dual-purpose gun (1 x1)
B Mk 26 launcher for Standard SM-1 (MR) SAM (1 x2)
C Mk15 CIWS (1x1)
D Harpoon SSM launcher (2x4)
E Mk 15 CIWS (1x1)
F Sikorsky SH-60B Sea Hawk LAMPS III
G Mk 32 12.75in ASW torpedo tubes (2x3)
H Mk 26 launcher for Standard SM-1 (MR) and Asroc (1 x2)
J 5in/54 Mk 45 dual-purpose gun (1 x1)

Electronics
1 SQS-53A sonar
2 SPG-55D missile control radar
3 SPQ-9A radar
4 SPG-60 radar
5 SPS-55 search radar
6 SLQ-32(V)2 EW system
7 SPS-48A 3D radar
8 SRN-25 Tacan antenna
9 SPG-55D missile control radar
10 SQR-19 TACTASS towed array sonar

Ticonderoga (CG 47) class

Origin: USA
Type: Guided-missile cruiser (CG)
Built: 1980
Class: 20 in service;
7 building;
Displacement: 9,600 tons full load
Dimensions: Length 566.8ft
(172.8m) oa; beam 55ft (16;.8m);
draught 31ft (9.5m)
Propulsion: 2-shaft gas turbine
(4 General Electric LM2500),
80,000shp
Performance: Speed 30 knots
Weapons: SSM: 8 Harpoon; 30
Tomahawk (CG 52 onward) SAM:
2 twin Mk 26 launchers with 68
Standard SM-2(ER)/Asroc (CG
47-51); 2 Mk 41 Vertical Launch
Systems for 122 Standard SM-2
(MR)/Asroc/Tomahawk (CG 52
onward)
Guns: 2 single 5in/54 Mk 45; 2
Phalanx 20mm/76 Mk 16 CIWS; 2
40mm (saluting) Torpedo tubes: 2 x
3 Mk 32 21in
Aircraft: 2 LAMPS I or
III helicopters
Sensors: Radar: SPY-1A 3D phased
arrays (CG 47-58); 2 SPY-1B (CG 59
onward); SPS-49(V) air search;
SPS-55 surface search; SPQ-9 fire
control; LN-66 navigation
(CG 47-53): SPS-64 navigation (CG
54 onward) Sonar: SQS-53A (CG
47-CG 53) bow-mounted; SQS-53B
(CG 54 onward); SQR-19 (TACTAS)
towed array (CG 54 onwards)
Complement: 358
Background: The US Navy is well
used to public criticism of its new
ships, especially from Congress and
the Spruance, Oliver Hazard Perry
and Virginia classes have all had
their fair share. Seldom, however,
has so much ill-informed and
hostile comment been directed at
any one class as that provoked by
the Ticonderogas. The ship and her
electronics systems have recently
vindicated themselves in a series of
rigorous tests, backed up by some
very successful operational
deployments, and they are now
among the most potent warships
afloat. The Aegis Combat System,
one of the most important
breakthroughs in naval technology
of recent years, was developed in
response to the threat of saturation
missile attacks that form the basis
of Soviet anti-carrier tactics during
the 1980s and beyond. To cope
with such tactics, sensors must be
able to react virtually
instantaneously and have a
virtually unlimited tracking
capability, but conventional
rotating radars are limited both in
data-processing capacity and in the
number of target tracks they can
handle; therefore a new system had
to be found. The solution adopted
with the Aegis system is to mount
four fixed planar arrays on the
super-structure of the ship, two on
each of the forward and after
deckhouses. Each array has 4,100
radiating elements and is controlled
by a UYK-1 digital computer to
produce and steer multiple beams
for target search, detection and
tracking. Targets are evaluated,
arranged in priority of threat and

Below: The McDonnell
Douglas Harpoon has
proved an outstanding
success, with well
over 2,000 on order for
the US and numerous
foreign navies. The
missile can be fired
from aircraft (AGM-84),
submarines (UGM-84)
and surface ships (RGM-
84A), and is propelled by
a turbojet, though the
surface and submarine
versions both have an
additional rocket booster;
cruise speed is Mach
0.85. Maximum range is
60nm (111km) in the
original version and 85nm
(157km) in the improved
Block 1 missiles, but
external targeting sys-
tems such as helicopters
are required to achieve
over-the-horizon ranges.
The shipborne version is
usually launched from a
simple canister. Despite
its ruggedness, the
mounting on the
Ticonderogas is in an
exposed position and
must suffer in a seaway.

Right: *USS Vincennes* (CG 49), her
massive superstructure and its
two SPY-1A arrays clearly visible.
Note also the two Mk 80 il-
luminator- directors above the
bridge with the ball-shaped cover
for the SPQ-9
fire control radar antenna above
them. The hull of the Ticonderoga
class cruisers is identical with that
of the Spruance class destroyers, a
fact which has produced
considerable savings.

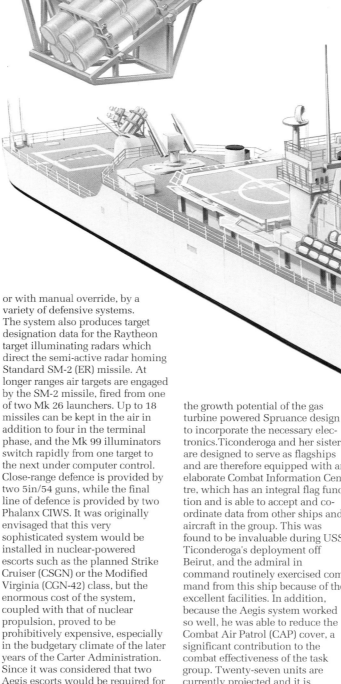

or with manual override, by a
variety of defensive systems.
The system also produces target
designation data for the Raytheon
target illuminating radars which
direct the semi-active radar homing
Standard SM-2 (ER) missile. At
longer ranges air targets are engaged
by the SM-2 missile, fired from one
of two Mk 26 launchers. Up to 18
missiles can be kept in the air in
addition to four in the terminal
phase, and the Mk 99 illuminators
switch rapidly from one target to
the next under computer control.
Close-range defence is provided by
two 5in/54 guns, while the final
line of defence is provided by two
Phalanx CIWS. It was originally
envisaged that this very
sophisticated system would be
installed in nuclear-powered
escorts such as the planned Strike
Cruiser (CSGN) or the Modified
Virginia (CGN-42) class, but the
enormous cost of the system,
coupled with that of nuclear
propulsion, proved to be
prohibitively expensive, especially
in the budgetary climate of the later
years of the Carter Administration.
Since it was considered that two
Aegis escorts would be required for
each of the 12 carrier battle groups
and because not all of the carriers
concerned would be nuclear
powered, it was decided to utilize

the growth potential of the gas
turbine powered Spruance design
to incorporate the necessary elec-
tronics.Ticonderoga and her sisters
are designed to serve as flagships
and are therefore equipped with an
elaborate Combat Information Centre, which has an integral flag function and is able to accept and co-
ordinate data from other ships and
aircraft in the group. This was
found to be invaluable during USS
Ticonderoga's deployment off
Beirut, and the admiral in
command routinely exercised command from this ship because of the
excellent facilities. In addition,
because the Aegis system worked
so well, he was able to reduce the
Combat Air Patrol (CAP) cover, a
significant contribution to the
combat effectiveness of the task
group. Twenty-seven units are
currently projected and it is
envisaged that they will operate in
conjunction with specialized ASW
and AAW DDGs of the Spruance
and Arleigh Burke classes.

Weapons

A 5in/54 Mk 45 dual-purpose gun (1x1)
B Mk 26 Mod 1 missile launcher (1x2) for Standard SM-2(ER) SAM and Asroc ASW missiles
C 20mm/76 Mk 15 Vulcan/Phalanx CIWS (2x1)
D Sikorsky SH-60B Sea hawk LAMPS III ASW helicopter (2 carried)
E Mk 32 12.75in ASW torpedo tubes (2x3) for Mk 46 torpedoes
F Mk 26 Mod 1 missile launcher (1x2) for Standard SM-2(MR) SAM and Asroc ASW missiles
G 5in/54 Mk 45 dual-purpose gun (1x1)
H Mk 141 launchers for RGM-84A Harpoon SSM (2x4)

Electronics

1 SQS-53 bow-mounted sonar
2 SPY-1A phased array radar forward and star-board arrays (SPY-B from CG 59)
3 WSC-1V satellite communications antenna
4 Mk 80 illuminator-director (SPG-62 radar) (2x1)
5 SPQ-9 gun fire control radar
6 SPS-55 surface search radar
7 URD-1 direction-finding antenna
8 SLQ(V)3 jammer (2x1)
9 Communications antenna
10 UPX-29 IFF interrogator (circular array)
11 SPS-49(V)6 air search radar
12 Mk 80 illuminator-director (SPG-62 radar)
13 Mk 80 illuminator-director (SPG-62 radar)
14 SPY-1A phased array radar aft and port arrays (SPY-1 B from CG 59 onward)
15 SQR-19 variable depth sonar (to be installed in Cg 54 onward)

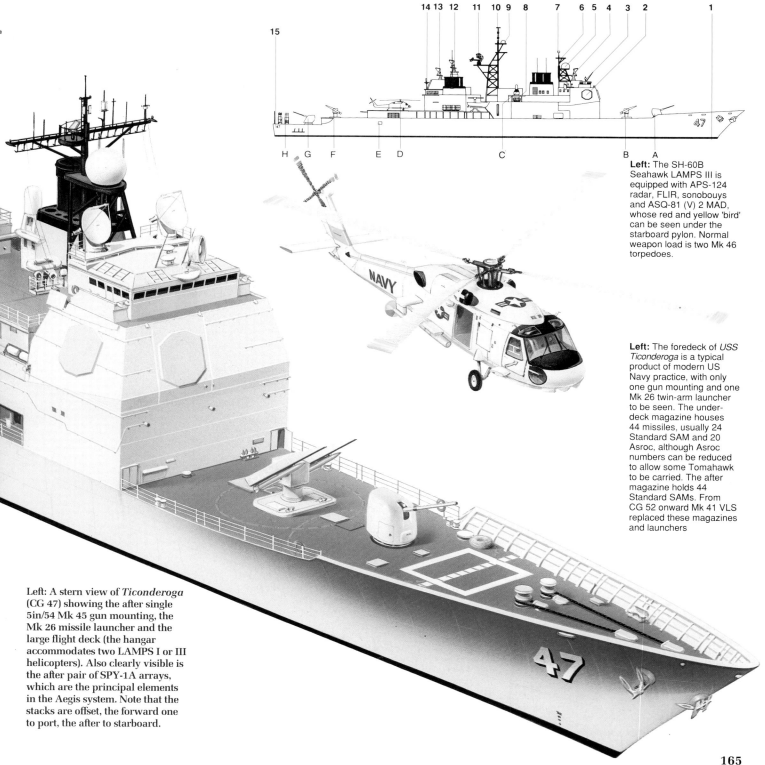

Left: The SH-60B Seahawk LAMPS III is equipped with APS-124 radar, FLIR, sonobouys and ASQ-81 (V) 2 MAD, whose red and yellow 'bird' can be seen under the starboard pylon. Normal weapon load is two Mk 46 torpedoes.

Left: The foredeck of USS Ticonderoga is a typical product of modern US Navy practice, with only one gun mounting and one Mk 26 twin-arm launcher to be seen. The under-deck magazine houses 44 missiles, usually 24 Standard SAM and 20 Asroc, although Asroc numbers can be reduced to allow some Tomahawk to be carried. The after magazine holds 44 Standard SAMs. From CG 52 onward Mk 41 VLS replaced these magazines and launchers

Left: A stern view of *Ticonderoga* (CG 47) showing the after single 5in/54 Mk 45 gun mounting, the Mk 26 missile launcher and the large flight deck (the hangar accommodates two LAMPS I or III helicopters). Also clearly visible is the after pair of SPY-1A arrays, which are the principal elements in the Aegis system. Note that the stacks are offset, the forward one to port, the after to starboard.

Trafalgar class

Origin: United Kingdom
Type: Nuclear powered attack submarine (SSN)
Built: 1978
Class: 7 in service; no more ordered
Displacement: 4,200 tons light; 5,208 tons submerged
Dimensions: Length 280.1ft (85.4m) oa; beam 32.1ft (9.8m); draught 26.9ft (8.2m)
Propulsion: l-shaft nuclear (1 pressurized-water-cooled nuclear reactor; two General Electric geared steam turbines), 15,000shp; 2 Paxman auxiliary diesels. 4,000shp
Performance: Speed 32 knots submerged
Weapons: Missiles; Sub-Harpoon (tube-launched) Torpedo tubes: 5 x 21in (533mm), 20 reloads; Spearfish or Tigerfish torpedoes mines, Sea Urchin or of Shellfish
Sensors: Sonar: Type 2007; Type 2020; Type 183; Type 2026 or 2046 towed array
Complement: 97.

Background: The British Royal Navy now has its fourth class of SSN in production and now has 18 boats in service, including two of the Valiant and three of the very similar Churchill classes, and one of the latter, *HMS Conqueror*, has the distinction of being the only nuclear-powered submarine to have sunk a surface warship in anger—the Argentinian cruiser *Belgrano*, on May 2,1982. The next class—the Swiftsures—entered production in 1969 and have a shorter, fuller hull form, together with a somewhat shorter sail, which reduces the periscope depth. The Swiftsures are coated with anechoic tiles which, together with other noise-reducing measures, makes them much quieter than any other contemporary class of SSN. The first of the Trafalgar class was launched on July 1, 1981, and commissioned on May 27,1983. By 1991 all seven boats were in Royal Navy service.

They are a logical development of the Swiftsure design with a very similar hull, except that the parallel section has been stretched by the inclusion of one more 6ft (2.5m) section; the diameter of the pressure hull remains unchanged, but there is an increase in submerged displacement over the Swiftsures' 4,500 tons to 5,208 tons. A new type of reactor core is used, and the machinery is mounted on rafts to insulate it from the hull and cut down radiated noise. HMS Trafalgar has a seven-bladed propeller, but later boats have a shrouded pump-jet. The cost of these boats is a good indicator of the problem facing the major navies. At 1976 prices the building costs of the Swiftsure class were: Swiftsure £37.1 million. Superb £41.3 million, Sceptre £58.9 million and Spartan £68.9 million, while the cost of the fourth Trafalgar, including weapon systems and equipment, was £175

million. The cost of the seventh, HMS Triumph, was £200 million, which is reported to be considerably less than that of the sixth. The Trafalgar class boats are claimed by the Royal Navy to be the quietest submarines in service. quieter even than the diesel-electric Oberon class. It is interesting to note, however, that despite its large and very successful SSN fleet the Royal Navy continues to commission conventional diesel electric submarines, and the first of the new Vickers Type 2400 Upholder class were recently ordered. In this respect the Royal Navy's attitude is similar to that of its Soviet equivalent, but contrary to that of the US Navy.

If past patterns are repeated a new class, again a logical development of the Trafalgar class, can be expected to appear in the later 1990s. The end of the Cold War puts further submarine projects in doubt.

Below: A Trafalgar class submarine. The hull is rather fatter than those of other SSNs, indicating plenty of interior space. This illustration shows the submarine with a conventional propeller, but there are a number of authoritative reports to the effect that this class may be fitted with a shrouded pump-jet, which would greatly reduce the noise signature, though possibly at the cost of a degree of propulsive efficiency. The hull is coated with anechoic tiles, and the machinery is mounted on rafts to insulate the hull from vibration to reduce the critical noise signature. The seven Trafalgars are complemented by Upholder class conventional boats.

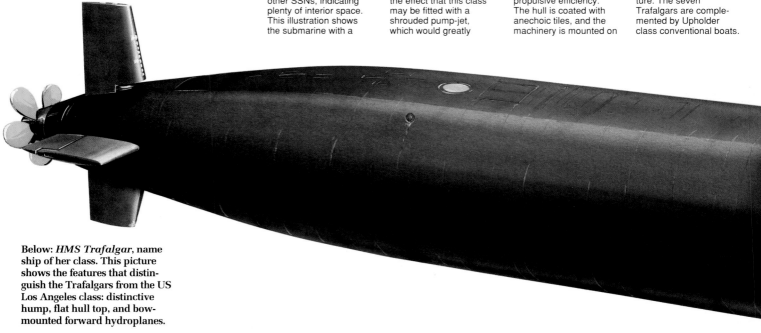

Below: *HMS Trafalgar*, name ship of her class. This picture shows the features that distinguish the Trafalgars from the US Los Angeles class: distinctive hump, flat hull top, and bow-mounted forward hydroplanes.

Right: Some of Trafalgar's weaponry. In the left-hand row, nearest the submarine hull, are three Tigerfish torpedoes, with outboard of them two Sub-Harpoon capsules and a Stonefish mine. In the right-hand row are a Sea Urchin mine and two Sub-Harpoon missiles. The Tigerfish wire-guided/acoustic homing submarine-launched ASW torpedo has an electric motor and twin contra-rotating propellers, giving it a speed of some 50 knots and a range of about 21km. Sub-Harpoon is a submarine-launched version of the successful US anti-ship missile. Sea Urchin and Stonefish are British-designed ground mines.

Right: *HMS Trafalgar* running on the surface. The Royal Navy has pursued a very successful policy of gradual improvements to its SSNs, starting with the Dreadnought, completed in 1963, and moving through the Churchills, Valiants and Swiftsures to the current Trafalgar class. It was one of the earlier SSNs, *HMS Conqueror* (S 48), which achieved the distinction of being the first SSN to sink a surface warship in anger, on May 2, 1982, when she sank the Argentinian cruiser *General Belgrano* in the South Atlantic.

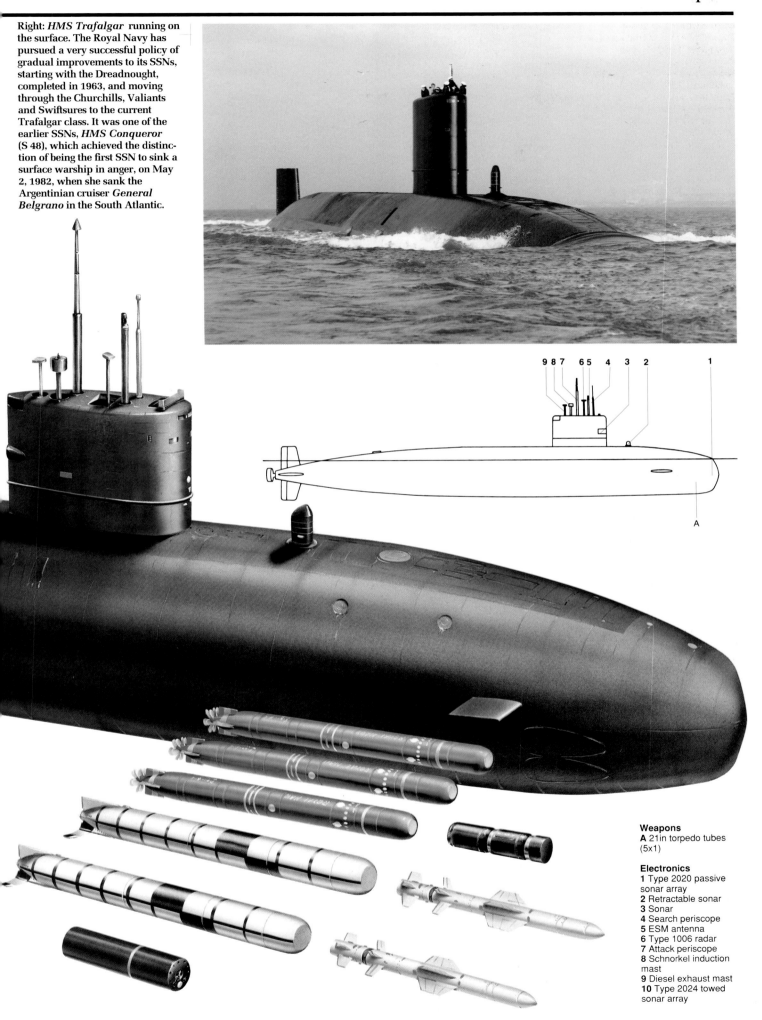

Weapons
A 21in torpedo tubes (5x1)

Electronics
1 Type 2020 passive sonar array
2 Retractable sonar
3 Sonar
4 Search periscope
5 ESM antenna
6 Type 1006 radar
7 Attack periscope
8 Schnorkel induction mast
9 Diesel exhaust mast
10 Type 2024 towed sonar array

Sikorsky S-70L (SH-60B and SH-60F Seahawk)

Origin: USA, first flight 12 December 1979.
Type: Multirole shipboard helicopter.
Engines: Two 1,900shp General Electric T700-401C turboshaft engines
Dimensions: Main-rotor diameter 53ft 8in (16.36m); length overall (rotors turning) 64ft 10in (19.76m), (main rotor and tail folded) 40ft 11in (12.47m); height (over tail rotor) 17ft 0in (5.18m).
Weights: Empty (ASW mission) 13,648lb (6191kg); gross (ASW mission) 20,244lb (9183kg), (max) 21,884lb (9927kg).
Performance: maximum speed (5,000ft/1524m, tropical) 145mph (233km/h); VROC (SL,32.2C) 700ft (213m)/min; hover IGE/OGE, range, not released.
Background: In 1970 the US Navy issued a requirement for a LAMPS (light airborne multi-purpose system) helicopter to operate from the platforms of major surface combatants in both the ASW (antisubmarine warfare) and ASST (anti-ship surveillance and targeting) missions. This was won by the Kaman SH-2 described elsewhere. Seeking to update the demand the LAMPS II was issued, but in 1974 this was supplanted by a LAMPS III, for which the prime contract was placed with IBM Federal Systems, as manager of the vital avionics systems. The helicopter thus became secondary; Boeing Vertol and Sikorsky each submitted developed versions of their existing UTTAS utility machines (YUH-61 and 60, respectively), the Sikorsky S-70L being selected after a 1977 fly-off.
Design: Though it uses an airframe basically similar to the Army UH-60A the SH-60B is a far more complicated helicopter. Compared with other machines in the same class, it is bigger and several times more expensive, and it is compatible with very few ships outside the US Navy. The rotors and transmission are as on the UH-60 except for the addition of a rotor brake and electric power folding of the main rotor. The tailplane is larger and rectangular. The landing gear differs in having a much shorter wheelbase to improve deck spotting, the new tail gear having twin wheels on a long- stroke extensible vertical leg which is raised for normal flight. The main gears are, surprisingly, designed to a lower energy requirement and so are simpler and have shorter stroke, but multi-disc brakes are added. The engines and all systems are marinized against salt-water operation, and other features include an inflight-refuelling probe (used with tankers or, hovering, in refuelling from ships), a Rast (recovery assist, secure and traversing) for safe recovery on deck in bad weather, buoyancy devices, rescue hoist and, of course, a totally redesigned fuselage packed with avionics and mission equipment. Almost the only parts simpler than the UH-60, apart from main legs, are the two unarmoured front cockpit seats.
Avionics: Largest of the sensors, the Texas Instruments APS-124 radar occupies almost the entire space under the forward fuselage, the large rectangular aerial (antenna) rotating inside a shallow circular radome. Fast scanning is claimed to give good detection of targets in high sea states, with a digital scan converter to give scanto-scan integration. The radar supplies an on-board MPD (multipurpose display) and also, via the ARQ-44 data link, displays on LAMPS-equipped ships. The US Navy has always regarded its seagoing helicopters as extensions of the ship, rather than as totally independent platforms like those of the Royal Navy. Texas Instruments also supply the MAD, with the ASQ-81 (V)2 towed "bird" carried on a winch-equipped pylon well aft on the right side. The section of cabin under the rotor is filled by a large rack with 25 sonobuoy launch tubes, arranged 5 x 5, each tube having five buoys fired pneumatically (a total of 125). The SO (sensor operator) station is on the left; he has to monitor the radar, MAD, acoustics (including control of active sonobuoys) and ESM systems. The ESM installation is the Raytheon ALQ142, with four square aerials facing to four diagonally opposite points of the compass, two on the nose and two on the tapered flanks of the fuselage. It provides identification and bearing of hostile surveillance radars, using sorting techniques to analyse the emissions. Though the belly contains attachments for the Rast hauldown and a 6,000lb (2722kg) cargo hook, there is no provision for dipping sonar. Other avionics include doppler, Tacan, UHF/DF, radar altimeter, various processors and comprehensive secure communications and IFF.
Armament: Normal armament comprises two Mk 46 torpedoes, though the later British Sting Ray is an alternative offering much higher lethality. In due course it is expected that the EX-50 ALWT (advanced lightweight torpedo) will become available. So far no attempt has been made to fit antiship weapons, but the US Navy is known to have studied plans to deploy the Kongsberg Penguin Mk 2 Mod 7 (AGM-119B).

The main new variant in production is the SH-60F, the "CV-helo" which is replacing the Sea King SH-3H in the dedicated ASW role operating from aircraft carriers. This is visibly different, with a simple nose resembling the UH-60, the radar, ESM, MAD, sonobuoy launcher, acoustic processor, data link and cargo hook all deleted. Instead it has the Bendix AQS-13F dipping sonar, the latest version of the long established AQS-13 family, on a hydraulically driven 1,500ft (457m) cable. On the left an extended folding sponson carries a 100gal (454lit) long-range tank inboard of the torpedo to give up to 4.25h mission endurance. Of course, the basic Seahawk is being continually updated, Lot 4 (Fiscal 1985) having an increased capacity main transmission rated at 3,400shp and later batches being planned eventually to have composite main-rotor blades to eliminate the current titanium spars .

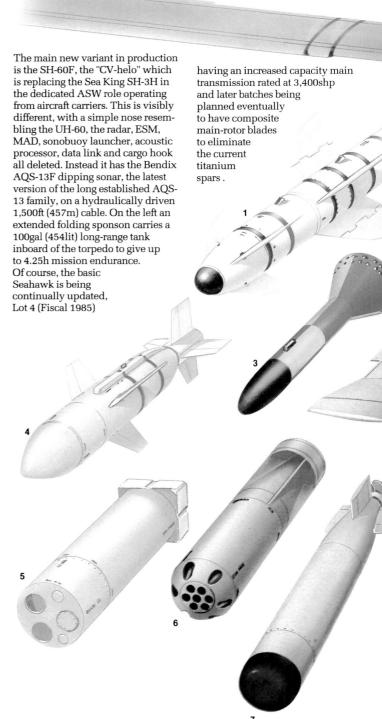

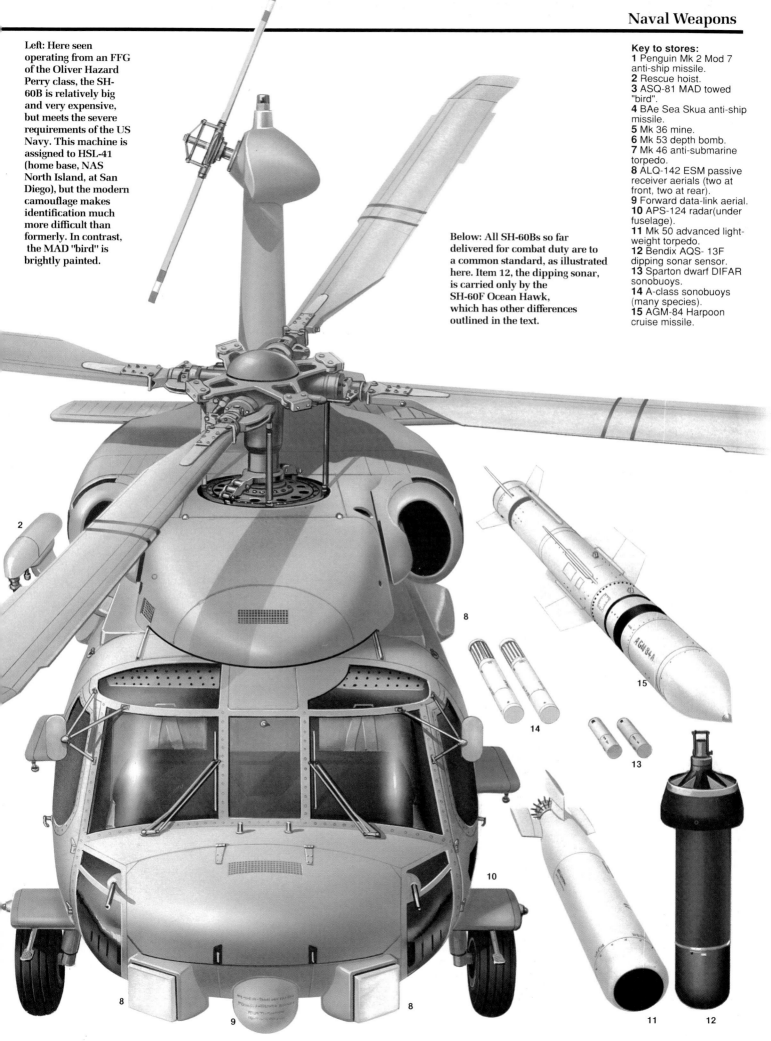

Left: Here seen operating from an FFG of the Oliver Hazard Perry class, the SH-60B is relatively big and very expensive, but meets the severe requirements of the US Navy. This machine is assigned to HSL-41 (home base, NAS North Island, at San Diego), but the modern camouflage makes identification much more difficult than formerly. In contrast, the MAD "bird" is brightly painted.

Below: All SH-60Bs so far delivered for combat duty are to a common standard, as illustrated here. Item 12, the dipping sonar, is carried only by the SH-60F Ocean Hawk, which has other differences outlined in the text.

Key to stores:
1 Penguin Mk 2 Mod 7 anti-ship missile.
2 Rescue hoist.
3 ASQ-81 MAD towed "bird".
4 BAe Sea Skua anti-ship missile.
5 Mk 36 mine.
6 Mk 53 depth bomb.
7 Mk 46 anti-submarine torpedo.
8 ALQ-142 ESM passive receiver aerials (two at front, two at rear).
9 Forward data-link aerial.
10 APS-124 radar(under fuselage).
11 Mk 50 advanced light-weight torpedo.
12 Bendix AQS- 13F dipping sonar sensor.
13 Sparton dwarf DIFAR sonobuoys.
14 A-class sonobuoys (many species).
15 AGM-84 Harpoon cruise missile.

Westland Lynx (navy)

Origin: Great Britain, first flight 25 May 1972.

Type: Multirole shipboard helicopter, for ASW, ASST, ASM attack, SAR, reconnaissance, vertrep transport etc.

Engines: Two Rolls-Royce Gem turboshafts, (2) 900shp Gem 2, (3, 4 and exports) 1,120shp Gem 41-1, (Lynx-3) 1,346shp Gem 60.

Dimensions: Diameter of four-blade main rotor 42ft 0in (12.8m), length (rotors turning) 49ft 9in (15.16m), (main rotor and tail folded) 34ft 10in (10.62m), (-3 figures respectively 50ft 9in, 15.47m, and 45ft 3in, 13.79m); height (rotors turning) 11ft 9.7in (3.6m), (-3) 12ft 5in (3.79m).

Weights: Empty (2,3) 6,040lb (2740kg), (-3) about 7,500lb (3400kg); maximum loaded (2) 10,000lb (4536kg), (3, 4 and exports) 10,500lb (4763kg), (-3) 11,300lb (5,125kg).

Performance: Maximum cruising speed 144mph (232km/h); (-3) 159mph (256km/h); cruising speed on one engine 140mph (225km/h); maximum rate of climb 2,170ft (661m)/min; hovering ceiling OGE (3, 4) 8,450ft (2575m); radius (SAR, max speed, three crew and seven rescuees, full allowances) 111 miles (179km); time on station (ASW, full sensors and weapons, max speed transits to station at 58 miles/93km radius) 2h 29min; range (normal fuel) 368 miles (592km), (-3) 426 miles (685km).

Background: At the start of the Lynx programme in 1967 it was agreed with France that one version of this versatile helicopter would be developed for naval roles. The first five development Lynx were of Army configuration, the first naval (HAS.2) prototype being the sixth. Subsequently the naval Lynx was produced not only for the two original customers but also for eight export customers, with progressive upgrading in power and equipment. A mock-up has been built of the new generation naval Lynx-3 but no order has yet been placed.

Design: The basic design of the Lynx has already been outlined in the Army Lynx entry. The existing naval versions are virtually identical in engine installation, rotors and dynamic parts, and in most parts of the airframe and onboard systems. The main differences are found in the landing gear, shipboard features, and in the cockpit, avionics and weapons. The original HAS.2 for the Royal Navy entered service at a weight of 9,500lb (4309kg) but was upgraded later to the figure given above. This introduced all the naval features, most prominent of which is the use of wheeled landing gear. The main gears have vertical shock struts mounted on short rear-fuselage sponsons. Each carries a single wheel toed out at 27° for deck operations. After landing these wheels are manually rotated fore/aft and locked in that position for movement into and out of the hangar. The nose gear has twin wheels and is hydraulically

steerable to 90° left/right. All four wheels have sprag (positive locking) brakes to prevent motion on deck in a heavy sea. The brakes engage automatically following hydraulic failure. Customer options include pop-out flotation bags and a hydraulically powered harpoon deck lock and haul-down system. For shipboard stowage the main rotor can be folded manually and the complete tail folds down to the right. Early HAS.2s had a slimmer tailboom than the main production, three windows in each of the large cabin sliding doors, a different nose profile and other changes. The main dropped stores are attached to pylons on the sides of the fuselage under the main doors. A third hydraulic system, at the same 2,050lb/sq in (144kg/cm²) as the others, is installed in naval Lynx to operate such mission equipment as dipping sonar, MAD, deck-lock harpoon and rescue winch (in most Lynx the winch is a clip-on electric installation). The 3,000lb (1361kg) external load cable normally has electric emergency release (not fitted on army Lynx). In the late 1970s the requirement of the Royal Netherlands Navy for an ASW helicopter led to an upgraded Lynx with Gem 41-1 engines driving through a new three-pinion gearbox, and this became standard on all later Lynx including the HAS.3 (RN) and Mk 4 (French Aeronavale).

Avionics: Naval Lynx have full night and (almost) all-weather capability. Navaids include VOR/DME, ILS, Tacan, ADF and I-band ship transponder. Mission equipment includes surveillance radar (Ferranti Seaspray or Héraclés ORB 31W), IFF and ESM, the latter usually being Racal Orange Crop (MIR-2). ASW gear includes Texas Instruments or Crouzet MAD, Bendix or Alcatel dipping sonar (not in the RN yet) and marine markers. For wire-guided missiles an AF.530 or APX.334 roof-mounted sight can be fitted.

Armament: Standard AS armament comprises two torpedoes, of the types depicted. Standard anti-ship missile is Sea Skua, four of which can be carried (in the South Atlantic war in 1982 the Lynx/Skua combination scored four out of four in blizzard conditions, the missile then not having been cleared for use). Sea Skua also performed well in the Gulf. Other compatible sensors and stores are shown in the main artwork. Royal Navy Lynx flights, currently numbering over 50, are being upgraded with Seaspray Mk 3, Gem 42 engines, Racal RAMS and new avionics. Westland hope that, despite part-ownership by competitor Sikorsky, it will also be possible to develop the Lynx-3 in its naval form (HAS.8 for the RN). This would have the BERP rotor (with negative-thrust capability for recovery on pitching decks), low tailplane without fins, nose-mounted 360° radar and FLIR, MAD, dipping sonar and active/passive sonobuoys.

Above: With MIR-2 Orange Crop on the nose, landing gear and rear fuselage, and four Sea Skuas, this Lynx HAS.2 has been fully updated. Home base is HMS *Osprey,* at Portland.

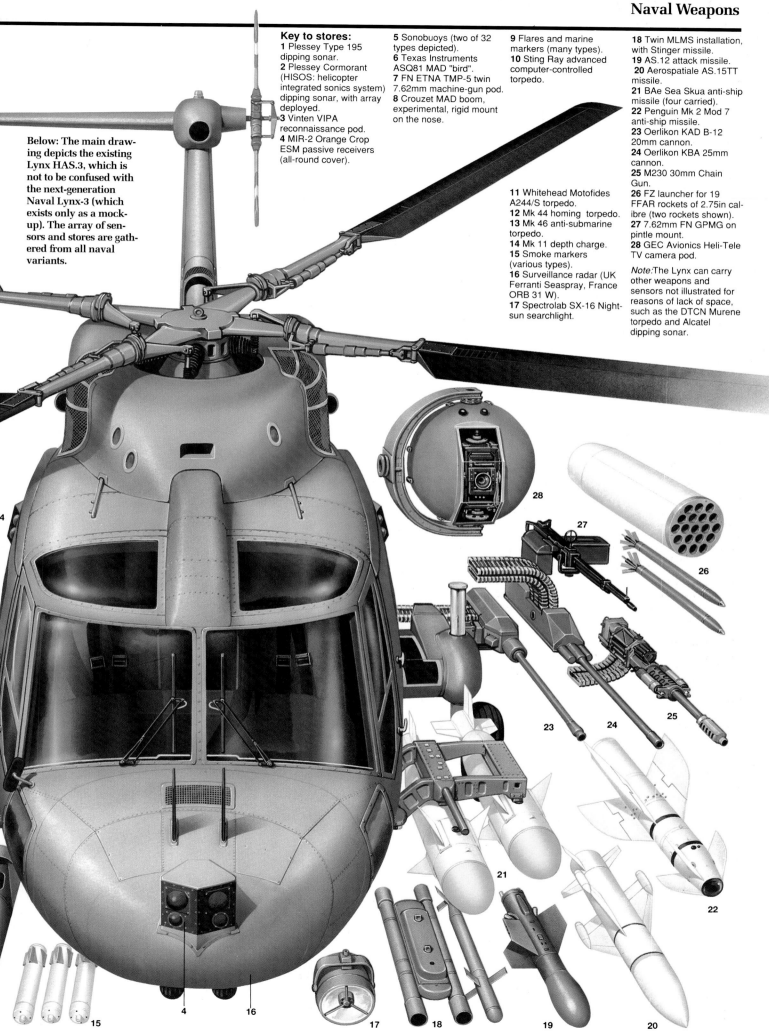

Key to stores:

1 Plessey Type 195 dipping sonar.
2 Plessey Cormorant (HISOS: helicopter integrated sonics system) dipping sonar, with array deployed.
3 Vinten VIPA reconnaissance pod.
4 MIR-2 Orange Crop ESM passive receivers (all-round cover).

5 Sonobuoys (two of 32 types depicted).
6 Texas Instruments ASQ81 MAD "bird".
7 FN ETNA TMP-5 twin 7.62mm machine-gun pod.
8 Crouzet MAD boom, experimental, rigid mount on the nose.

9 Flares and marine markers (many types).
10 Sting Ray advanced computer-controlled torpedo.

11 Whitehead Motofides A244/S torpedo.
12 Mk 44 homing torpedo.
13 Mk 46 anti-submarine torpedo.
14 Mk 11 depth charge.
15 Smoke markers (various types).
16 Surveillance radar (UK Ferranti Seaspray, France ORB 31 W).
17 Spectrolab SX-16 Nightsun searchlight.

18 Twin MLMS installation, with Stinger missile.
19 AS.12 attack missile.
20 Aerospatiale AS.15TT missile.
21 BAe Sea Skua anti-ship missile (four carried).
22 Penguin Mk 2 Mod 7 anti-ship missile.
23 Oerlikon KAD B-12 20mm cannon.
24 Oerlikon KBA 25mm cannon.
25 M230 30mm Chain Gun.
26 FZ launcher for 19 FFAR rockets of 2.75in calibre (two rockets shown).
27 7.62mm FN GPMG on pintle mount.
28 GEC Avionics Heli-Tele TV camera pod.

Note: The Lynx can carry other weapons and sensors not illustrated for reasons of lack of space, such as the DTCN Murene torpedo and Alcatel dipping sonar.

Below: The main drawing depicts the existing Lynx HAS.3, which is not to be confused with the next-generation Naval Lynx-3 (which exists only as a mock-up). The array of sensors and stores are gathered from all naval variants.

Sikorsky S-80 (CH-53E Super Stallion and MH-53E Sea Dragon)

Origin: USA, first flight 1 March 1974.

Type: (CH) Heavy transport, (MH) mine countermeasures helicopter. Data for CH-53E.

Engines: Three 4,380shp General Electric T64-416 turboshafts.

Dimensions: Diameter of seven-blade main rotor 79ft 0in (24.08m); length (rotors turning) 99ft 0.6in (30.19m), (ignoring rotors, FR probe and tail folded) 60ft 6in (18.44m); height (over tail rotor) 28ft 5in (8.66m), (rotor and tail folded) 18ft 7in (5.66m).

Weights: Empty (CH) 33,226lb (15071kg); maximum takeoff (internal payload) 69,750lb (31639kg),(external slung load) 73,500lb (33340kg).

Performance: (all at 56,000lb, 25401kg) Maximum level speed at SL 196mph (3l5km/h); cruising speed 173mph (278km/h); maximum rate of climb (payload of 25,000lb, 11340kg) 2,500ft (762m)/min; hovering ceiling OGE 9,500ft (2896m); self-ferry range at weight given above 1,290 miles (2076km).

Background: At first glance this appears to be just another version of the original CH-53A Sea Stallion. So it is, but the degree of transformation is shown by the fact that installed power has risen from 5,700 to 13,140shp and maximum payload from 8,000lb (3629kg) to 36,000lb (16330kg)! Development of a growth version of the Stallion series began in 1971 to meet an urgent need for increased assault transport and heavy-lift capability for the Vietnam war. That it took just ten more years to get the first CH-53E into the hands of the Marine Corps merely underlines how hard this outstanding helicopter had to fight for funding for every stage of development. As of spring 1986 107 had been delivered, and Navy/Marines requirements are expected to exceed 300 by year 2000.

Design: The main rotor blades are geometrically similar to those of the earlier CH-53s, though they are attached via extension straps which increase rotor diameter. Blade construction is of a type intended for use on earlier versions with a titanium spar and Nomex filled glassfibre/epoxy skin. With the added seventh blade this roughly doubles maximum lifting power. The hub had to be modified with a new steel and titanium structure and elastomeric bearings which need little maintenance. Sikorsky BIM (blade inspection method) is used, with a pressurized gas filling to warn of any cracks, and all blades fold hydraulically. The gearbox had to be upgraded to 13,500shp, and the third engine is mounted aft on the left side driving straight into the box, unlike the original engines which drive bevel boxes well forward near the cockpit from which.shafts run back diagonally across the fuselage. The third jetpipe faces left, the same position on the right side being occupied by the fan-assisted oil

cooler. Ahead of the totally redesigned upper fairing (which improves appearance) is a Solar turbine APU. This is started by an hydraulic accumulator, no batteries being carried, and it provides ground power and starts the main engines hydraulically. The fuselage is little altered, though the front end is now a separate glassfibre structure, but the tail is entirely new. The enlarged fin slopes 20° to the left, as does the much bigger aluminium tail rotor, while the fixed tailplane on the right has a gull-wing form to bring the main strut-braced section horizontal. The CH-53E has additional sponson tanks raising internal capacity to 1,017 US gal (3850lit), augmented by two 650 US gal (2460lit) optional drop tanks. The Navy MH-53 MCM (mine countermeasures) version has gigantic sponsons increasing internal fuel to 3,200 US gal (12113lit), giving an endurance on internal fuel of over 20hrs. Both versions can be refuelled by ship hose or via a retractable FR probe. The CH-53E carries 55 troops, or seven standard cargo pallets or a 36,000lb (16330kg) slung load. The MH-53E has uprated hydraulic and electrical systems, special navigational and minefield guidance systems and an even more advanced flight-control system with automatic tow couplers and automatic approach to hover at any desired height whilst towing any available MCM sweeping equipment. The MH weighs 36,336lb (16482kg) empty, has composite tail-rotor blades and various minor changes. The US Navy is receiving 75 from 1986.

Avionics: All versions have advanced Hamilton Standard digital flight controls, with two computers and a four-axis autopilot. Standard equipment includes VHF/UHF, Tacan, VOR and ILS.

Armament: No weapons are carried, though CH-53Es have

successfully fired self-defence AIM-9 Sidewinders (see below). Stinger is another self-defence option. Addition of self-defence AAMs is one of numerous planned upgrades. Others include: an all composite rotor hub with all composite blades (spar, carbon fibre) with swept anhedral tips, all composite tail rotor (as on MH-53E), electric blade folding, uprated T64-418 engines, Omega navigation, ground-proximity warning, full crew night-vision systems, exhaust IR suppression, missile alert system, chaff/flare dispensers, the ability to

top up the hydraulics from the cargo hold and improvements to the cargo-handling system. The improved rotor blades will increase useful load by at least 3,000lb (1361kg). The S-80E (cargo) and S-80M (MCM) are export versions.

Left: Few publicity pictures can equal this shot of a Marine Corps KC-130F refuelling two CH-53E Super Stallions which are each carrying an LAV-25 armoured vehicle.

Key to stores:
1. Engine inlet particle separators.
2 Mk 104 acoustic mine-sweeping gear.
3 Edo Mk 105 hydrofoil towed anti-magnetic mine vehicle.
4 Giant (3850lit, 1,017 US gal) sponson tank (MH53E).
5 Rescue hoist.
6 Minesweeping mirrors.
7 Air-data probe.

8 Browning MG3 0.5in HMG on pintle mount.
9 Twin MLMS Stinger box with missile.
10 Standard 1925lit (508.5 US gal) sponson tank (CH-53E).
11 2460lit (650 US gal) auxiliary tank.
12 AIM-9L self-defence Sidewinder.

13 Chaff/flare dispenser.
14 ALQ-157 IRCM jammer.

Above: Unquestionably the most impressive-looking helicopter in this book, the main artwork depicts a CH-53E Super Stallion, but fitted with the right-hand enlarged tank sponson of the Navy MH-53E Sea Dragon AMCM (airborne mine countermeasures) version. Most of the weapons shown are not standard at present.

Page numbers in **bold type** refer to subjects mentioned in captions to illustrations

Picture Credits

Endpaper: US DoD; Half-title: Associated Press; Title: Associated Press; pp4/5: US DoD; pp6/7: (Top left); Associated Press, (Centre left) Associated Press, (Bottom left) BAe, (Bottom Centre) Rex Features, (Rest) US DoD; pp8/9: (Top right) Chif Hires/Gamma, (Bottom centre) Associated Press, (Rest) US DoD; pp10/11: (Centre left) Associated Press, (Bottom centre) Rockwell, (Bottom right) Barry Iverson/KATZ, (Rest) US DoD; pp12/13: (Left, Top to Bottom) Rex/Kol-Al-Arab, Associated Press, Syndicat International, Katz; (Top centre) Associated Press, (Top Right) Associated Press, (Bottom left and centre) BAe, (Bottom right) Associated Press; p14/15: (Top left) McDD, (Top centre, left) Aerospatiale, (Top centre, right) Matra, (Top right) BAe, (Rest) US DoD; pp16/17: (Bottom left) Soldiere Magazine, (Top centre and Top right) US Army, (Rest) US DoD pp18/19: (Top left) Ian Black/Katz, (Right, centre bottom) BAe, (Bottom) Matra, (Rest) US DoD; pp20/21: (Top left) US Air Force; (Centre left) Grumman, (Top right) Hunting Engineering, (Bottom right) Cardoen, (Rest) US DoD; pp22/23: (Top, left and centre) Rockwell, (Bottom, left and centre) Matra, (Top right) Patrick Bunce/Salamander, (Right, centre and bottom) Hughes, (Rest) US DoD; pp24/25: (Bottom left) BAe, (Top centre) McDD, (Bottom centre and centre right) Aerospatiale, (Bottom right) McDD; pp26/27: (Top left) Tom Stoddard/Katz, (Bottom left) Patrick Bunce/Salamander, (Top right) Euromissile, (Centre right) Hughes, (Rest) US DoD; pp28/29: (Top left) Rex Features, (Centre Left) Ferranti, (Rest) US DoD; pp30/31: Dassault Breguet; pp32/33: Fairchild Republic; pp34/35: US DoD; pp36/37: Ford Aeronautronics, pp38/39: US Navy; pp40/41: US Navy; pp42/43: (Bottom left) US DoD, (Top right) Lockheed; pp44/45: (Top left) IAF, (Top right) US Navy pp46/47: McDD; pp48/49: McDD; pp50/51: US Air Force; pp52/53: Northrop; pp54/55: Salamander; pp56/67: (Top left) US DoD, (Bottom right) Peter Steinemann; pp58/59: US DoD; pp60/61:

BAe; pp62/63: BAe; pp64/65: Matra; pp66/67: US DoD; pp68/69: US DoD; pp74/75: (Top left) Associated Press, (Centre left) Hughes, (Bottom left) Associated Press, (Top right) GIAT, (bottom right) Associated Press, (Rest) US DoD; pp76/77: (Top left) Gilles Bassignac/Gamma, (Bottom left) Hughes, (Rest) US DoD; pp78/79: (Top, left and centre) US DoD, (Bottom, left and centre) Rex Features; pp80/81: (Top left) Gamma, (Top right) US DoD, (Centre right) Associated Press, (Bottom right) Rafael, (Bottom centre) FMC; pp82/83: (Centre left) Syndicat International, (Rest) US DoD; pp84/85: US DoD, pp86/87: UKLF; pp88/89: US Army; pp92/93: US DoD; pp94/95: US DoD; pp96/97: (Top left) USH, (Top right) GKN Defence; pp98/99: US DoD; pp102/103: US DoD; pp104/105: (Top left) US DoD, (Top right) Royal Ordnance; pp106/107: US DoD; pp108/109: (Top left) Salamander, (Top right) GIAT; pp110/111: (Left) US DoD, (Right) Salamander; pp112/113: US Army; pp114/115: UK MoD; pp118/119: Salamander; pp120/121: Shorts; pp122/123: US DoD; pp124/125: US DoD; pp126/127: Royal Ordnance; pp128/129: McDD; pp130/131: US DoD; pp132/133: UK MoD; pp134/135: UK MoD; pp136/137: Sikorsky; pp138/139: UK MoD; pp140/141: (Top centre) US Navy, (Bottom right) Sperry, (Rest) US DoD; pp142/143: (Centre left) Rex Features, (Bottom left) McDD, (Centre right) US DoD, (Bottom right) US Navy; pp144/145: (Top left) McDD, (Bottom left) Associated Press, (Top centre) Aerospatiale, (Bottom centre) Salamander, (Centre right) BAe; pp146/147: (Top left) Raytheon, (Bottom left) US DoD, (Bottom centre, left) BAe, (Bottom centre, right) Associated Press, (Bottom right) US DoD, (Centre right) HSA; pp148/149: Plessey Marine; pp150/151: US Navy; pp152/153: US Navy; pp154/155: US Navy; pp156/157: US Navy; pp158/159: US Navy; pp160/161: MoD; pp162/163: US Navy; pp164/165: US DoD; pp166/167: MoD; pp169/169: MoD; pp170/171: Sikorsky; pp172/173: USN.